D0453742

MOON HANDBOOKS®

ACADIA
NATIONAL PARK

triple-arched Stanley Brook Bridge, over the Seal Harbor access road to Acadia

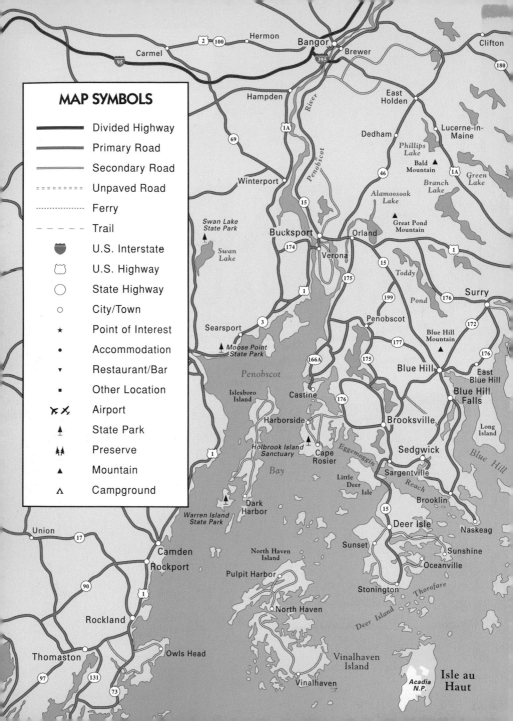

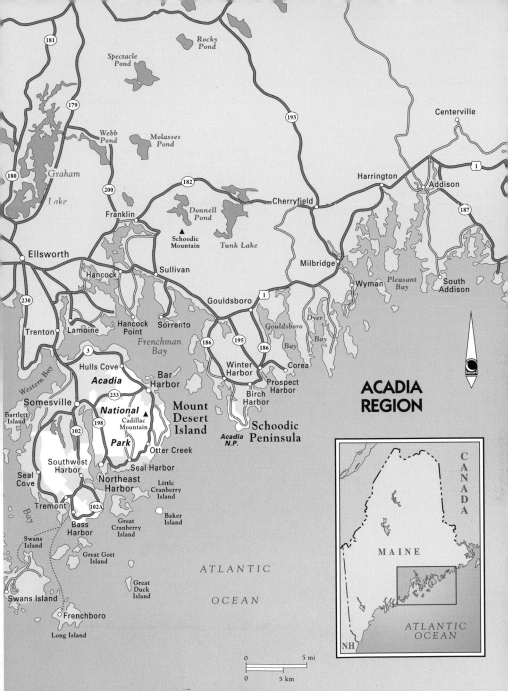

181

Rocky
Pond

Spectacle
Pond

179

Centerville

Webb
Pond

Molasses
Pond

193

180

Graham
Lake

200

182

Harrington

Addison

1

187

Franklin

Donnell
Pond

▲
Schoodic
Mountain

Cherryfield

Tunk Lake

Ellsworth

Hancock

Sullivan

Milbridge

Wyman

Pleasant
Bay

South
Addison

Gouldsboro

1

230

Trenton

Lamoine

Hancock
Point

Sorrento

Gouldsboro

Dyer

Frenchman
Bay

186

195

186

Bay

Bay

Western Bay

Hulls Cove

Acadia

3

Winter
Harbor

Corea

Bar
Harbor

Prospect
Harbor

Somesville

233

National

Mount
Desert
Island

Birch
Harbor

**ACADIA
REGION**

Bartlett
Island

198

▲
"
Cadillac
Mountain

Schoodic
Peninsula

*Acadia
N.P.*

102

Park

Seal
Cove

Otter Creek

Bay

Southwest
Harbor

Seal Harbor

Northeast
Harbor

Little
Cranberry
Island

CANADA

Tremont

102A

Baker
Island

Bass
Harbor

Great
Cranberry
Island

Swans
Island

MAINE

Great Gott
Island

ATLANTIC

Great
Duck
Island

OCEAN

Swans Island

Frenchboro

Long Island

0   5 mi

0   5 km

NH

ATLANTIC

OCEAN

© AVALON TRAVEL PUBLISHING, INC.

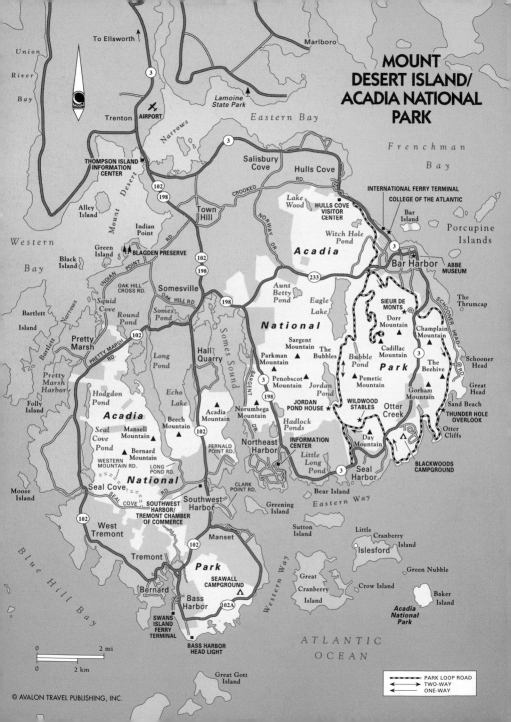

MOUNT DESERT ISLAND/ ACADIA NATIONAL PARK

To Ellsworth

Marlboro

Union

River

Bay

Trenton

AIRPORT

Lamoine State Park

Eastern Bay

Frenchman Bay

Narrows

THOMPSON ISLAND INFORMATION CENTER

Salisbury Cove

Hulls Cove

RD.

CROOKED

Lake Wood

HULLS COVE VISITOR CENTER

INTERNATIONAL FERRY TERMINAL

COLLEGE OF THE ATLANTIC

Town Hill

Witch Hole Pond

Bar Island

Porcupine Islands

Alley Island

Mount Desert

Acadia

NORWAY DR.

Bar Harbor

ABBE MUSEUM

Green Island

Indian Point

BLAGDEN PRESERVE

Western Bay

Black Island

OAK HILL CROSS RD.

Somesville

OAK HILL RD.

Aunt Betty Pond

Eagle Lake

SIEUR DE MONTS

The Thrumcap

233

Dorr Mountain

Champlain Mountain

SCHOONER HEAD

Bartlett Island

Squid Cove

Round Pond

Somes Pond

198

National

Sargent Mountain

The Bubbles

Cadillac Mountain

Schooner Head

Bartlett Narrows

102

Long Pond

Hall Quarry

Parkman Mountain

Bubble Pond

Park

The Beehive

Pretty Marsh

PRETTY MARSH RD.

Somes Sound

SARGENT DR.

Penobscot Mountain

Pemetic Mountain

Great Head

Pretty Marsh Harbor

Echo Lake

198

Jordan Pond

Gorham Mountain

Sand Beach

Folly Island

Hodgdon Pond

Beech Mountain

Acadia Mountain

Norumbega Mountain

JORDAN POND HOUSE

WILDWOOD STABLES

Otter Creek

THUNDER HOLE OVERLOOK

Otter Cliffs

Acadia

Seal Cove Pond

Mansell Mountain

102

FERNALD POINT RD.

Hadlock Ponds

Day Mountain

Moose Island

Bernard Mountain

WESTERN MOUNTAIN RD.

LONG POND RD.

National

Northeast Harbor

INFORMATION CENTER

Little Long Pond

BLACKWOODS CAMPGROUND

Seal Cove

SEAL COVE RD.

Southwest Harbor

Seal Harbor

CLARK POINT RD.

SOUTHWEST HARBOR/ TREMONT CHAMBER OF COMMERCE

Bear Island

Eastern Way

West Tremont

102

Manset

Greening Island

Sutton Island

Little Cranberry Island

Islesford

Green Nubble

Tremont

Park

102

SEAWALL CAMPGROUND

Western Way

Great Cranberry Island

Crow Island

Baker Island

Acadia National Park

Bernard

Bass Harbor

102A

SWANS ISLAND FERRY TERMINAL

BASS HARBOR HEAD LIGHT

ATLANTIC OCEAN

Blue Hill Bay

0   2 mi

0   2 km

Great Gott Island

Great Gott Island

© AVALON TRAVEL PUBLISHING, INC.

	PARK LOOP ROAD
	TWO-WAY
	ONE-WAY

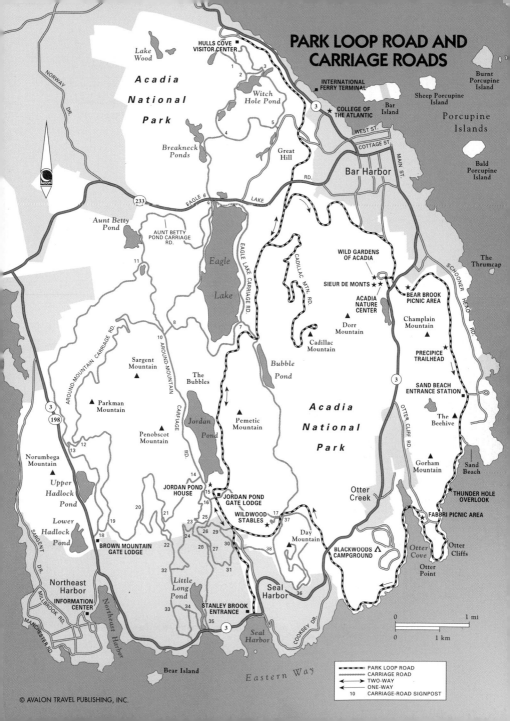

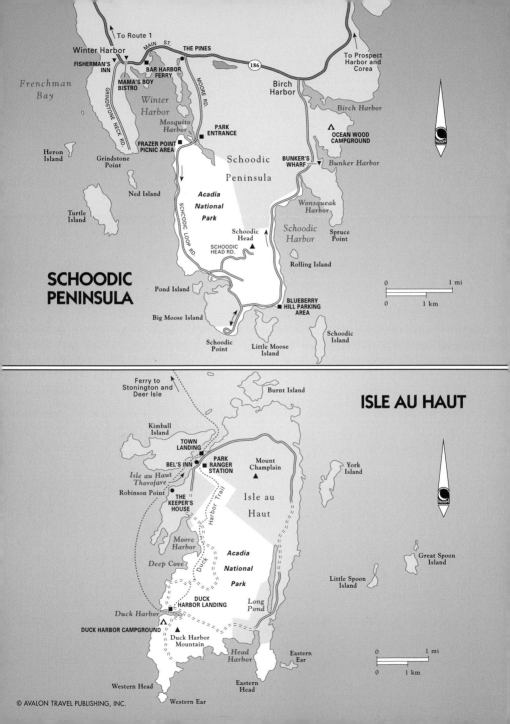

SCHOODIC PENINSULA

To Route 1

Winter Harbor

MAIN ST.

THE PINES

FISHERMAN'S INN

BAR HARBOR FERRY

MAMA'S BOY BISTRO

186

To Prospect Harbor and Corea

Birch Harbor

Frenchman Bay

MOORE RD.

Winter Harbor

Mosquito Harbor

Birch Harbor

GRINDSTONE NECK RD.

PARK ENTRANCE

OCEAN WOOD CAMPGROUND

FRAZER POINT PICNIC AREA

Heron Island

Grindstone Point

Schoodic Peninsula

BUNKER'S WHARF

Bunker Harbor

Ned Island

Acadia National Park

Wonsqueak Harbor

Turtle Island

SCHOODIC LOOP RD.

Schoodic Harbor

Spruce Point

Schoodic Head

SCHOODIC HEAD RD.

Rolling Island

Pond Island

BLUEBERRY HILL PARKING AREA

Schoodic Island

Big Moose Island

Schoodic Point

Little Moose Island

0   1 mi

0   1 km

ISLE AU HAUT

Ferry to Stonington and Deer Isle

Burnt Island

Kimball Island

TOWN LANDING

BEL'S INN

PARK RANGER STATION

Mount Champlain

York Island

Isle au Haut Thorofare

Robinson Point

THE KEEPER'S HOUSE

Harbor Trail

Isle au Haut

Moore Harbor

Duck

Deep Cove

Acadia National Park

Little Spoon Island

Great Spoon Island

DUCK HARBOR LANDING

Long Pond

Duck Harbor

DUCK HARBOR CAMPGROUND

Duck Harbor Mountain

Western Head

Head Harbor

Eastern Ear

Eastern Head

Western Ear

0   1 mi

0   1 km

DEER ISLE

To Blue Hill

15

Sargentville

Sedgwick

175

Billings Cove

DEER ISLE INFORMATION CENTER

Little

Deer

Isle

Stave Island

Benjamin R.

175

Haven

Blastow Cove

Eggemoggin

Carney Island

Pickering Island

REACH RD.

Reach

North   Deer

Isle

15

Conary Island

DOW RD.

Torrey Pond

Oak Point

Northwest Harbor

Pressey Cove

Lily Pond

Campbell Island

White Island

Deer Isle Village

Mill Pond

Greenlaw Cove

Stinson Neck

South

Sunset

Long Cove

SUNSHINE RD.

Mountainville

Sylvester Cove

Sheephead Island

Deer

ISLAND COUNTRY CLUB

SOUTH DEER ISLE CROSS RD.

Southeast Harbor

EDGAR M. TENNIS PRESERVE

Freese Island

Sunshine

15

Isle

Smalls Cove

GOOSE COVE RD.

15A

Crockett Cove

Oceanville

HAYSTACK MOUNTAIN SCHOOL OF CRAFTS

BARRED ISLAND PRESERVE

CROCKETT COVE WOODS PRESERVE

AIRPORT RD.

OCEANVILLE RD.

SETTLEMENT QUARRY

Sheep Island

Goose Cove

Burnt Cove

Webb Cove

Ames Pond

MAIN ST.

Stonington

Bold Island

Devil Island

Saddleback Island

Moose Island

Deer Island Thorofare

Camp Island

Millet Island

Crotch Island

Green Island

Bare Island

Spruce Island

Ferry to Isle au Haut

0   1 mi

0   1 km

© AVALON TRAVEL PUBLISHING, INC.

MOON

MOON HANDBOOKS®

ACADIA
NATIONAL PARK

FIRST EDITION

KATHLEEN M. BRANDES

**AVALON
TRAVEL**

Contents

Acadia on Mount Desert Island

Drink in the sunrise from the summit of Cadillac Mountain. Witness Thunder Hole's saltwater eruptions. Take afternoon tea at Jordan Pond House. But to truly know Acadia, you need to get lost— figuratively, not literally—wandering mile after mile of its coastal and mountain trails.

Sieur de Monts Spring; Sand Beach; Thunder Hole; Jordan Pond House; Cadillac Mountain; East-Side Trails; West-Side Trails

Mount Desert Island Communities

Fishing and lobstering are a way of life in these island communities, which eked out a living from the sea long before Acadia's first tourists arrived. Today that island lifestyle continues, but you're just as likely to meet day-trippers, writers, and artists as you are hardy fishermen and lobsterwomen.

Schoodic Peninsula

The eastern side of Frenchman Bay offers a different perspective—not just of Acadia's mountains silhouetted against the sunset, or the surf slamming onto Schoodic Point, but the peace of seaside villages where time seems to stand still.

Winter Harbor; Gouldsboro; Schoodic Point

Blue Hill Peninsula

Blue Hill exudes charm—from its handsome old homes to its waterfront setting and many shops, restaurants, and galleries. Nearby, quiet college town Castine belies its tumultuous Revolutionary past, while Brooklin and Brooksville are known as refuges for city sophisticates seeking the good life.

Deer Isle and Isle au Haut

Deer Isle has long been romancing authors and artisans, but it's unmistakably real to the generations of quarrymen and fishermen who've been here for centuries. Tiny Isle au Haut boasts a unique lighthouse inn and just 79 residents. Only 50 visitors are allowed a day, ensuring each will have a singular experience.

Resources

Maps

ABOUT THE AUTHOR
Kathleen M. Brandes

Anyone who makes her first plane trip at the age of eight months aboard a TWA DC-3 probably has travel in her blood. So it's been for Kathleen Brandes, who has spent quality time in most of the United States and in more than 50 other countries since that initial flight between New York and Chicago (never mind what year, but when's the last time you saw a DC-3?).

"Spending time" has meant month-long visits to India, Germany, New Zealand, Greece, Finland, and the United Kingdom; summers studying in France and digging in Jordan; a year at a Swiss university; seven winters in Turkey; and two years as a Peace Corps volunteer in the Liberian bush—teaching French and history by day to high schoolers, and English by night to three wives of a local taxi driver.

Along the way, Kathleen worked as a proofreader for the United Nations in New York—in an office conveniently close to the Delegates' Lounge—then crossed town to work for Time-Life Books for eight years as a researcher, writer, and editor.

In 1974, she and her husband abandoned Manhattan for a coastal Maine fishing village ("going from Saks to Sears," as one wag put it). She completed an eight-year stint as a marine-book editor before establishing Wordsworth Editorial Services, a one-woman freelance operation. For a decade, she was a contributing editor for *Down East*, the state's oldest lifestyle magazine (where she focused on Maine travel).

For 30 years, Kathleen has been gathering up houseguests and carting them off to Acadia National Park—to hike the trails, bike the carriage roads, drive the Park Loop Road, and appreciate the natural wonders. So *Moon Handbooks Acadia National Park* was the logical choice for Kathleen's third book. She likes to think that kismet has led to each of her travel guides, *Moon Handbooks Maine*, *Moon Handbooks Coastal Maine*, and now *Acadia*. But surely all this started with that flight in the DC-3. . . .

*Dedicated to the Acadia National Park staff
and the Friends of Acadia—for whom my admiration is limitless.*

Introduction

Acadia National Park, located about two-thirds of the way along the Maine coastline between New Hampshire and New Brunswick, is a miniature masterpiece, a gem of a natural and cultural resource that dangles like a pendant just south of the mainland. Some 30,000 Acadia acres (of its 46,000 or so) fit into a Maine island that's only 15 miles from north to south and 12 miles from west to east.

If stretched taut, Hancock County—with Acadia as its centerpiece—would have more than 1,000 miles of coastline. No saltwater locale on the entire eastern seaboard can compete with the variety of scenery on Mount Desert Island. The vistas from the park's 26 mostly open summits look out on ocean and lighthouses and boats and dozens of large and small islands near and far.

Within and beyond the park's boundaries, you can hike and bike, paddle and picnic, swim and stroll, camp and climb. With Acadia's 130 miles of hiking trails and 57 miles of car-free carriage roads (created between 1913 and 1940 by John D. Rockefeller, Jr.) you'll never run out of ways to play.

Fringing the island is the park's support network—the towns and villages where you'll find beds, bars, food, shops, boat cruises, and a handful of small museums. The contrast with Acadia's lakes and woodlands is astonishing, as the park struggles to maintain its image and character.

Bar Harbor, the largest and best-known of the island's communities, is the source of just about anything you could want (if not need)—from T-shirts to tacos, books to bike and kayak

sunrise, Eagle Lake

rentals. You can go lobster fishing, whale-watching, or sailing.

Elsewhere on the island are Southwest Harbor, Tremont (including Bass Harbor and Bernard), and the town of Mount Desert, encompassing the villages of Northeast Harbor, Seal Harbor, Otter Creek, Somesville, Pretty Marsh, Beech Hill, and Hall Quarry. From Bass, Northeast, and Southwest Harbors, private and state ferries shuttle bike and foot traffic to offshore Swans Island, Frenchboro (Long Island), and the Cranberry Isles, and cars to Swans Island.

Beyond Mount Desert, don't miss the park's splendid acreage on the mainland Schoodic Peninsula and offshore Isle au Haut. (Wend your way to Isle au Haut through the Blue Hill Peninsula and Deer Isle.)

In 1907, author Henry van Dyke wistfully described a late-19th-century Mount Desert holiday in his book *Days Off:* "It was really a good little summer resort where the boy and I were pegging away at our vacation. There were the mountains conveniently arranged, with pleas-

ant trails running up all of them, carefully marked with rustic but legible guide-posts; and there was the sea comfortably besprinkled with islands, among which one might sail around and about, day after day, not to go anywhere but just to enjoy the motion and the views; and there were cod and haddock swimming over the outer ledges in deep water, waiting to be fed with clams at any time, and on fortunate days ridiculously accommodating in letting themselves be pulled up at the end of a long, thick string with a pound of lead and two hooks tied to it. There were plenty of places considered proper for picnics, like Jordan's Pond and Great Cranberry Island, and the Russian Tea-house, and the Log Cabin Tea-house, where you would be sure to meet other people who also were bent on picnicking; and there were hotels and summer cottages . . ."

A much more recent quote put this area in its proper contemporary perspective: "Maine is so lovely," a British visitor to Acadia sighed nostalgically, "I do wish England had fought harder to keep it."

The Land

IN THE BEGINNING . . .

Maine is an outdoor classroom for Geology 101, a living lesson in what the glaciers did and how they did it. I've often told anyone who will listen that I plan to be a geologist in my next life— and the best place for the first course is Acadia National Park.

Geologically, Maine is something of a young-ster; the oldest rocks, found in the Chain of Ponds area in the western part of the state, are only 1.6 billion years old—more than two billion years younger than the world's oldest rocks.

But most significant is the great ice sheet that began to spread over Maine about 25,000 years ago, during the late Wisconsin Ice Age. As it moved southward from Canada, this continental glacier scraped, gouged, pulverized, and depressed the bedrock in its path. On it continued, charging up the north faces of mountains, clipping off their tops and moving southward, leaving

behind jagged cliffs on the mountains' southern faces and odd deposits of stone and clay. By about 21,000 years ago, glacial ice extended well over the Gulf of Maine, perhaps as far as the Georges Bank fishing grounds.

But all that began to change with meltdown, beginning about 18,000 years ago. As the glacier melted and receded, ocean water moved in, covering much of the coastal plain and working its way inland up the rivers. By 11,000 years ago, glaciers had pulled back from all but a few minor corners at the top of Maine, revealing the south coast's beaches and the intriguing geologic traits—eskers and erratics, kettleholes and moraines, even a fjord—that make Mount Desert Island and the rest of the state such a fascinating natural laboratory.

Mount Desert's Somes Sound (named after pioneer settler Abraham Somes)—the only fjord on the eastern seaboard—is just one distinctive feature on an island loaded with geologic won-

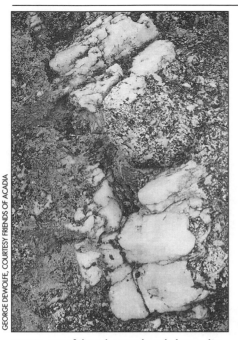

GEORGE DEWOLFE, COURTESY FRIENDS OF ACADIA

quartz, one of the primary minerals in granite

ders. There are pocket beaches, pink-granite ledges, sea caves, "pancake" rocks, wild headlands, volcanic "dikes," a handful of pristine ponds and lakes. And once you've glimpsed The Bubbles—two curvaceous, oversize mounds on the edge of Jordan Pond—you'll know exactly how they earned their name.

CLIMATE

Acadia National Park fits into the National Weather Service's **coastal** category, a 20-mile-wide swath that stretches from Kittery on the New Hampshire border to Eastport on the Canadian border. In the park (and its surrounding communities), the proximity of the Gulf of Maine moderates the climate, making coastal winters generally warmer and summers usually cooler than elsewhere in the state.

Average June temperatures in **Bar Harbor,** adjoining the park, range from 53 to 76°F; July

and August temperatures range from 60 to 82°. By December, the average range is 20–32°.

The Seasons

Maine has four distinct seasons: summer, fall, winter, and mud. Lovers of spring weather need to look elsewhere in March, the lowest month on the popularity scale, with mud-caked vehicles, soggy everything, irritable temperaments, tank-trap roads, and occasionally the worst snowstorm of the year.

Summer can be idyllic—with moderate temperatures, clear air, and wispy breezes—but it can also close in with fog, rain, and chills. Prevailing winds are from the southwest. Officially, summer runs from June 20 or 21 to September 20 or 21, but consider summer as June, July, and August. The typical growing season is 148 days long.

A poll of Mainers might well show autumn as the favorite season—days are still warmish, nights are cool, winds are optimum for sailors, and the foliage is brilliant—particularly throughout Acadia. Fall colors usually reach their peak in the park in early October, about a week before Columbus Day. Early autumn, however, is also the height of hurricane season, the only potential flaw this time of year.

Winter, officially December 20 or 21 to March 20 or 21, means an unpredictable potpourri of weather along the park's coastline. But when the cold and snow hit this region, it's time for cross-country skiing, snowshoeing, and ice-skating.

Spring, officially March 20 or 21 to June 20 or 21, is the frequent butt of jokes. It's an ill-defined season that arrives much too late and departs all too quickly. Spring planting can't occur until well into May; lilacs explode in late May and disappear by mid-June. And just when you finally can enjoy being outside, blackflies stretch their wings and satisfy their hunger pangs. Along the shore, fortunately, steady breezes often keep the pesky creatures to a minimum.

Northeasters and Hurricanes

A northeaster is a counterclockwise, swirling storm that brings wild winds out of—you guessed it—the northeast. These storms can occur any time of year, whenever the conditions brew them up. Depending on the season, the winds are accompanied by rain, sleet, snow, or all of them together.

Hurricane season officially runs from June through November, but it is most active in late August and September. Some years, Maine remains out of harm's way; other years, head-on hurricanes and even glancing blows have eroded beaches, flooded roads, splintered boats, downed trees, knocked out power, and inflicted major residential and commercial damage. Winds—the greatest culprit—average 74–90 mph. A hurricane watch is announced on radio and TV about 36 hours before the hurricane hits, followed by a hurricane warning that indicates that the storm is imminent. Find shelter away from plate-glass windows, and wait it out. If especially high winds are predicted, make every effort to secure yourself, your vehicle, and your possessions. Resist the urge to head for the shore to watch the show; rogue waves combined with ultrahigh tides have been known to sweep away unwary onlookers. Schoodic Point, the mainland section of Acadia, is a particularly perilous location in such conditions.

Sea Smoke and Fog

Sea smoke and fog, two atmospheric phenomena resulting from opposing conditions, are only distantly related. But both can radically affect visibility and therefore be hazardous. In winter, when the ocean is at least 40°F warmer than the air, billowy sea smoke rises from the water, creating great photo ops for camera buffs but seriously dangerous conditions for mariners.

In any season, when the ocean (or lake or land) is colder than the air, fog sets in, creating nasty conditions for drivers, mariners, and pilots. Romantics, however, see it otherwise, reveling in the womblike ambience and the muffled moans of foghorns.

Storm Warnings

The National Weather Service's official daytime signal system for wind velocity consists of a series of flags representing specific wind speeds and sea conditions. Beachgoers and anyone planning to venture out in a kayak, canoe, sailboat, or powerboat should heed these signals. The signal flags are posted on all public beaches, and warnings are announced on TV and radio weather broadcasts, as well as on cable TV's Weather Channel and the NOAA broadcast network.

Flora and Fauna

In the course of a single day at Acadia National Park—where more than two dozen mountains meet the sea—the casual visitor can pass through a landscape that lends itself to a surprising diversity of animal and plant life. On one outing, you can explore the shoreline—barnacles encrust the rocks and black crowberry, an arctic shrub that finds Maine's coastal climate agreeable, grows close to the ground alongside the trail. On the same outing, you can wander beneath the boughs of the leafy hardwood forest that favors more southern climes, as well as the spruce–fir forest of the north. A little farther up the trail are subalpine plants more typically associated with mountain environments, and neotropical songbirds providing background music.

Acadia's creatures and plants will endlessly intrigue any nature lover; the following is but a sampling of what you might encounter during a visit.

OFFSHORE

Acadia National Park is surrounded by the sea—from the rockbound Schoodic Peninsula jutting from the mainland Down East to the offshore island in Penobscot Bay that Samuel de Champlain named Isle au Haut. While the park's boundaries do not extend out to sea, the life that can be found there draws tourists and scientists alike.

The Maine coastline falls within the Gulf of Maine, a "sea within a sea" that extends from Nova Scotia to Cape Cod and out to the fishing

ACADIA FACTS

A cadia National Park was established by Congress in 1929, after previous incarnations as Lafayette National Park (1919) and Sieur de Monts National Monument (1916).

• Acadia covers more than 46,000 mainland and island acres, including more than 10,000 acres protected by conservation easements. Its permanent boundaries were established by Congress in 1986.

• Acadia has 26 mountains ranging in height from 284 feet (Flying Mountain) to 1,530 feet (Cadillac). Cadillac is the highest point on the eastern seaboard of the United States.

• Nine "great ponds" (covering more than 10 acres) lie within the park boundaries. Five others abut parkland. Depths of these lakes and ponds range between 7 feet (Aunt Betty Pond) and 150 feet (Jordan Pond). Mount Desert Island's lakes and ponds have restrictions on swimming and personal and motorized watercraft.

• Acadia has about 130 miles of hiking trails. At the height (so to speak) of trail construction, in the early 20th century, there were some 230 miles. Some of the discontinued trails are being rehabilitated via the Acadia Trails Forever program, a joint project of the park and Friends of Acadia.

• Acadia has close to three million visitors each year, most in the months of July, August, and September.

• The "creature counts" in Acadia, on Mount Desert Island, and in the surrounding waters include 273 species of birds, more than 6,500 insect species and subspecies, at least seven reptile species, 24 species of fish, at least 11 species of amphibians, and at least 40 mammal species.

• The Park Loop Road is 20 miles, with an additional seven miles for a round trip to the summit of Cadillac Mountain.

• The park has 45 miles of car-free, broken-stone carriage roads for walking, biking, and horseback riding, as well as cross-country skiing and snowshoeing in winter; 12 miles of privately owned carriage roads south of Jordan Pond are usable by walkers and horses but no bicycles.

• Acadia has three campgrounds—two on Mount Desert Island, one on Isle au Haut. Only one (Blackwoods) is open all year. Backcountry camping is not allowed in Acadia. (A dozen or so commercial campgrounds are located on Mount Desert Island beyond park boundaries.)

• The Schoodic Peninsula is the only park acreage that's on the mainland; all other park properties are on islands. A bridge connects Mount Desert Island to the mainland town of Trenton, but other parcels must be reached by boat.

grounds of Brown and Georges Banks. It is one of the most biologically rich environments in the world. Surface water, driven by currents off Nova Scotia, swirls in counterclockwise circles, delivering nutrients and food to the plants and animals that live there. Floating microplants, tiny shrimp-like creatures, and jellyfish benefit from those nutrients and once supported huge populations of groundfish, now depleted by overfishing.

These highly productive waters lure not only fishing vessels but also **sea mammals.** Whales may rarely swim into the inshore bays and inlets bounded by Acadia, but whale-watch cruises based on Mount Desert Island ferry passengers miles offshore to the locales where whales gather. Whales fall into two groups: toothed and baleen. Toothed whales hunt individual prey, such as

squid, fish, and the occasional seabird; they include porpoises and dolphins, killer whales, sperm whales, and pilot whales. Baleen whales have no teeth, so they must sift food through horny plates called baleen; they include finback whales, minke whales, humpback whales, and right whales. Any of these species may be observed in the Gulf of Maine.

Harbor porpoises, which grow to a length of six feet, can be spotted from a boat in the inshore waters around Mount Desert Island, traveling in pods as they hunt schools of herring and mackerel. The most you'll usually see of them are their gray backs and triangular dorsal fins as they perform their graceful ballet through the waves.

Of great delight to wildlife watchers is catching

INTRODUCTION

© KATHLEEN M. BRANDES

hanging out at the seal ledge

glimpses of **harbor seals.** While the shores of Mount Desert Island are too busy with human activity for seals to linger, they are usually spotted during nature cruises that head out to the well-known "seal ledges." Check the tide chart and book an excursion for low tide. Seals haul themselves out of the ocean at low tide to rest on the rocks and sunbathe. Naps are a necessity for harbor seals, which have less blubber and fur to insulate them from the frigid waters of the Gulf of Maine than other seal species. Hauling out preserves energy otherwise spent heating the body, and it replenishes their blood with oxygen.

At high tide, you might see individual "puppy dog" faces bobbing among the waves as the seals forage for food. Harbor seals, sometimes called "sea dogs," almost disappeared along the coast of Maine in the early 20th century. It was believed they competed with fishermen for the much-prized lobster and other valuable catches, and they were hunted nearly into oblivion. When it became obvious that the absence of seals did not improve fish stocks, the bounty placed on them was lifted. The Marine Mammal Protection Act of 1972 made it illegal to hunt or harm any marine mammal, except by permit—happily, populations of harbor seals now have rebounded all along the coast.

Every now and then, park rangers receive reports of "abandoned" seal pups along Acadia's shore. Usually it's not a stranded youngster, but rather a pup left to rest while its mother hunts for food. If you discover a seal pup on the shore, leave it undisturbed and report the sighting to rangers.

ALONG THE SHORE

Whether walking the shore or cruising on a boat, there is no symbol so closely associated with the coast as the ubiquitous **gull.** Several species of gulls frequent Acadia's skies, but none is more common than the herring gull. Easily dismissed as brassy sandwich thieves (which, of course, they are), herring gulls almost vanished in the 20th century as a result of hunting and egg collecting. Indeed, many seabird populations declined in the early 1900s due to the demand for feathers to adorn the hats of ladies. Conservation measures have helped some of these bird species recover, including the large, gray-backed herring gull, an elegant flyer that often lobs sea urchins onto the rocky shore from aloft to crack them open for the morsels within.

Common **eider-duck** females, a mottled brown, and the black-and-white males (nick-

ADOPT A FINBACK WHALE

Here's a trump card. When everyone else is flashing photos of kids or grandkids, you can whip out images of your very own adopted whale. And for that you can thank the **Adopt-a-Finback-Whale** program at the College of the Atlantic (COA) in Bar Harbor.

In 1972, COA established Allied Whale, a marine-mammal laboratory designed to collect, interpret, and use research on the world's largest mammal. Although Allied Whale's primary focus is the Gulf of Maine, its projects span the globe, involving international scientific collaboration. Since 1981, part of the research has involved assembling an enormous photo collection (more than 25,000 images) for identification of specific humpback and finback whales (with names such as Quartz and Elvis . . .) and tracking of their migration

routes. The photo catalog of finbacks already numbers more than 1,000.

And here's where the adoption program comes in—a way to support the important research being done by Allied Whale and its colleagues. If you sign up as an adoptive "parent" for a year, you'll receive a Certificate of Adoption, a large color photo and a biography of your whale, its sighting history, an informational booklet, and a subscription to Allied Whale's newsletter. It's a superb gift for budding scientists. The adoption fee is $30 for a single whale or $50 for a mother and calf.

For further information, obtain *The Finback Catalogue* from College of the Atlantic, 105 Eden Street, Bar Harbor 04609, 207/288-5644, fax 207/288-4126, www.coa.edu/alliedwhale/adopt.htm.

named "floating skunks"), congregate in large "rafts" on the icy ocean during the winter to mate. When spring arrives, males and females separate. While the males provide no help in raising the young, the females cooperate with one another, often gathering ducklings together to protect them from predators. Adult eiders may live and breed for 20 years or more, though the morality rate is high among the young. Present along Acadia's shore all year long, they feed on mussels, clams, and dog whelks, their powerful gizzards grinding down shells and all.

A smaller seabird regularly espied around Acadia is the **black guillemot,** also known as the "sea pigeon" and "underwater flyer" because it seems to fly through the water. Guillemots learn to swim before they learn to fly. Black-and-white with bright red feet, guillemots are cousins to puffins. They nest on rock ledges along the shore, laying pear-shaped eggs that won't roll over the edge and into the waves below.

Bald eagles and **ospreys** (also known as fish hawks) take advantage of the fishing available in Acadia's waters. Both of these majestic raptors suffered from the effects of the pesticide DDT, which washed down through waterways and into the ocean, becoming concentrated in the fish

the raptors consumed. As a result, they laid thin-shelled eggs that broke easily, preventing the development of young. The banning of DDT in the United States has resulted in a strong comeback for both species, and the removal of the bald eagle from the federal endangered species list. Along the coast of Maine, however, the bald eagle's return has been less triumphant than in other parts of the country. Biologists continue to seek explanations for the lag, and the bald eagle remains on state and federal lists as a threatened species.

Boat cruises (some with park rangers aboard) departing from several Mount Desert Island harbors offer good chances for sightings. They allow passengers to approach (but not too closely) nesting islands of eagles and ospreys. Both species create large nests of sticks, from which they can command a wide view of the surrounding area. Some osprey nests have been documented as being 100 years old, and researchers have found everything from fishing tackle to swim trunks entwined in the sticks of the nests.

Look also for eagles and ospreys flying above inland areas of the park. Ospreys hunt over fresh-water ponds and lakes, hovering till a fish is sighted, then plummeting from the sky into the

INTRODUCTION

water to grab the prey. For aerodynamic reasons, they carry the fish headfirst.

Acadia visitors often ask rangers if there are sea otters in the park. After all, there is an Otter Creek, which flows into Otter Cove, which is bounded by Otter Cliffs. At one time, Gorham Mountain was known as Peak of Otter! With all these place names devoted to the otter, it would be logical to assume that Mount Desert Island teems with them. In fact, though, there are no sea otters along the entire eastern seaboard of the United States—perhaps the earliest European settlers mistook sea minks (now extinct) for sea otters. River otters do reside in the park, though they are reclusive and spend most of their time in freshwater environments. You might observe one during the winter frolicking on a frozen pond.

> *Some of the most alien creatures on earth live where the ocean washes the rocky shoreline. The creatures of this intertidal zone are at once resilient and fragile, and always fascinating.*

INTERTIDAL ZONE

Some of the most alien creatures on earth live where the ocean washes the rocky shoreline. The creatures of this **intertidal zone** are at once resilient and fragile, and always fascinating. Some of the creatures and plants live best in the upper reaches of the intertidal zone, which is doused only by the spray of waves and the occasional extra-high tide. Others, which would not survive the upper regions, thrive in the lower portions of the intertidal zone, which is almost always submerged. The rest live in rocky pockets of water in between, and all are influenced by the ebb and flow of the tide. Temperature, salinity, and the strength of crashing waves all determine where a creature will live in the intertidal zone.

As you approach the ocean's edge, the first creatures likely to come underfoot are **barnacles**—vast stretches of rock can be encrusted with them. Step gently, for walking on barnacles crushes them. Their tiny, white, volcanoshaped shells remain closed when exposed to the air, but they open when submerged to feed.

Water movement encourages them to sweep the water with feathery "legs" to feed on microscopic plankton.

Despite the tough armor with which barnacles cover themselves, they are preyed upon by dog whelks (snails), which drill through the barnacle shells with their tongues to feed on the creature within. A **dog whelk** can be distinguished from the common periwinkle by the elliptical opening of its shell. Periwinkles have teardrop-shaped openings.

Sea stars find blue mussels yummy. Blue mussels siphon plankton from the water and anchor themselves in place with byssal threads. Sea stars creep up on the mussels, wrap their legs around them, and pry open their shells just enough to insert their stomachs and consume the animal inside. Look for sea stars and mussels in the lower regions of tide pools.

Related to sea stars are **sea urchins**—spiky green balls most often seen as empty, spineless husks littered along the shoreline. They are frequently preyed upon by gulls. If you come upon a live sea urchin, handle it with care. While their spikes are not poisonous, they *are* sharp. Gently roll a sea urchin over to see its mouth and the five white teeth with which it gnaws on seaweeds and animal remains. (While the green sea urchins found in Acadia do not possess poisonous spines, some of their counterparts in other regions do.)

Limpets, with cone-shaped shells, are snails that rely on seaweeds for food. They suction themselves to rocks, which prevents them from drying up when exposed at low tide. Do not tear limpets from rocks—doing so hurts the animal.

Many intertidal creatures depend on seaweed for protection and food. **Rockweeds** drape over rocks, floating with the waves, their long fronds buoyed by distinctive air bladders. **Dulse** (edible for people) is common along the shore, as is Irish moss, used as a thickener in ice cream, paint, and other products.

Tide Pool Tips

The best way to learn about the fascinating world that exists between the tides is to look for creatures in their own habitat, with a good field guide as a reference.

- Go at low tide—there are two low tides daily, 12 hours apart.
- Tread carefully. Shoreline rocks are slippery.
- Do not remove creatures from their habitats; doing so could harm them.
- Be aware of the ocean at all times. Sudden waves can wash the shore and sweep you to your death.
- Join a ranger-guided shoreline walk to learn more about this unique environment. Check the *Beaver Log,* Acadia's official park newspaper, for the schedule and details.

© KATHLEEN M. BRANDES

tide pools, Park Loop Road

FRESHWATER LAKES AND PONDS

Known best for its rocky shoreline and mountains, Acadia National Park cradles numerous glistening lakes and ponds in its glacially carved valleys. Several lakes serve as public water supplies for surrounding communities, and swimming is prohibited in most. Echo Lake and the north end of Long Pond are excellent designated swimming areas. Freshwater fishing requires a state license for adults. Please obey posted regulations.

The voice of the northern wilderness belongs to the **common loon,** whose roots are so ancient it is the oldest bird species found in North America. During the summer months, loons are garbed in striking white-and-black plumage, which fades to gray during the winter when loons migrate to the ocean's open waters. Graceful swimmers, loons are clumsy on land. Their webbed feet are set to the rear of their bodies, making them front-heavy. Land travel is a struggle. Consequently, they nest very close to the water's edge, which makes them vulnerable to such manmade hazards as the wakes of motorized watercraft.

The loon's mysterious ululating call can often be heard echoing across lakes on most any summer evening, an eerie sound not quickly forgotten.

Evening is actually an excellent time to observe wildlife. Creatures that seem shy and reclusive by day tend to be most active at dawn and dusk (crepuscular) or at night (nocturnal). Carriage roads along Eagle Lake, Bubble Pond, and Witch Hole Pond make nighttime walking easy. (Hint: Go at dusk so your eyes adjust with the darkening sky, and keep in mind that flashlight use abruptly ruins night vision.)

Frog choruses form the backdrop to the cries of loons. In Acadia, there are eight **frog and toad species,** which tend to be most vocal during the spring mating season. Close your eyes and listen to see if you can distinguish individual species, such as the "banjo-twanging" croak of the green frog and the "snore" of the leopard frog.

The onset of moonlight may reveal small winged creatures swooping, darting, and careening

TIDES

Nowhere is the adage "Time and tide wait for no man" more true than along the Maine coastline. The nation's most extreme tidal ranges occur in Maine, and they become even more dramatic as you head "Down East," toward the Canadian Maritime provinces. Every six hours or so, the tide begins either ebbing or flowing, so you'll have countless opportunities for observing tidal phenomena.

Tides govern coastal life, and everyone is a slave to the tide calendar or chart, which coastal community newspapers diligently publish in every issue. Each issue of the official park visitor guide, the *Beaver Log*, also contains a tide chart (as well as times of sunrise and sunset). In tidal regions, boats tie up with extra-long lines, clammers and worm-diggers schedule their days by the tides, hikers have to plan ahead for shoreline exploring, and kayakers need to plan their routes to avoid getting stuck in the muck.

Average tidal ranges (between low tide and high tide) in the area around Acadia National Park are 10 or 11 feet, and extremes are 12 or 13 feet. Visit www.harbortides.com—it's free to join. Plug in Bar Harbor (or the zip code—04609), then print out the tide chart for the time you'll be in Acadia. (Moon phases and times of sunrise and sunset are also included.)

Tides, as we all learned in elementary school, are lunar phenomena, created by the gravitational pull of the moon; the tidal range depends on the lunar phase. Tides are most extreme at new and full moons—when the sun, moon, and earth are all aligned. These are **spring tides,** supposedly because the water springs upward (the term has nothing to do with the season). And tides are smallest during the moon's first and third quarters—when the sun, earth, and moon have a right-angle configuration. These are **neap tides** ("neap" comes from an Old English word meaning "scanty"). Other lunar/solar phenomena, such as the equinoxes and solstices, can also affect tidal ranges.

The best time for shoreline exploration is on a new-moon or full-moon day, when low tide exposes mussels, sea urchins, sea cucumbers, sea stars, periwinkles, hermit crabs, rockweed, and assorted nonbiodegradable trash. Rubber boots or waterproof, treaded shoes are essential on the wet, slippery terrain.

Caution is also essential in tidal areas. Unless you've carefully plotted tide times and heights, don't park a car or bike or boat trailer on a beach; make sure your sea kayak is lashed securely to a tree or bollard; don't take a long nap on shoreline granite; and don't cross a low-tide land spit without an eye on your watch.

A perhaps apocryphal but almost believable story goes that one flatlander stormed up to a ranger at a Maine state park one bright summer morning and demanded indignantly to know why they had had the nerve to drain the water from her shorefront campsite during the night. When it comes to tides . . . you just have to go with the flow.

over lakes and ponds. Acadia is home to several species of **bats,** including the common little brown bat. Don't scream! Bats have no desire to get entangled in your hair. Their echolocation (radar) is so fine-tuned that it can detect a single strand of human hair. Bats are far more interested in the mosquitoes attracted to your body heat. True insect-munching machines, a single pinky-size little brown bat can eat hundreds, if not thousands, of insects in one evening.

Bandit-faced **raccoons** are also creatures of the night, and they sometimes can be found scampering alongside the shore. They are om-nivorous, dining on anything from grubs, frogs, and small mammals to fish, berries, and garbage. Rabies is present in Maine, and raccoons are common carriers of the disease. Do not approach sick-acting animals (seeing them during the daytime may indicate illness), and report any strange behavior to a park ranger. When camping or picnicking, stow food items in your vehicle and dispose of scraps properly. Raccoons are opportunistic thieves that have been known to claw their way into tents to find food.

And where are the moose? The question is asked often at Acadia's Visitor Center, and wildlife watchers are disappointed to learn that moose, the largest member of the deer family, are rarely sighted in the park. Moose are more frequently observed in western and northern Maine, in the Moosehead Lake and Baxter State Park regions. However, individuals are spotted from time to time on Mount Desert Island, and there may even be a small family group residing on the west side. Moose like to dine on aquatic vegetation, such as the tubers of cattails and lily pads, and they frequent marshes and lakes to escape biting flies. Bass Harbor Marsh is inviting habitat for moose, but good luck spotting one.

A prehistoric-looking creature sometimes encountered on carriage roads near ponds is the **snapping turtle.** An average adult may weigh 30 pounds or more. Keep well clear of the snapper's powerful beak, which is lightning-quick when grabbing prey; it can do real damage, such as biting off fingers. Adult snappers have no predators (except people), and they will dine on other turtles, frogs, ducklings, wading birds, and beaver kits.

By midsummer, many of Acadia's ponds are beautifully adorned with yellow water lilies and white pond lilies. Lily pads are a favorite food of beavers. **Beavers** emerge from their lodges—large piles of sticks and mud—at dusk and dawn to feed and make necessary repairs to their dams. Beavers create their own habitat by transforming streams into ponds. They move awkwardly on land, so they adjust the water level close to their source of building materials and other favored foods: aspen and birch trees. Doing so limits their exposure to dry land and predators.

Beavers are large rodents that were trapped excessively for centuries for the fur trade. They have since made a strong comeback in Acadia—to the point that their ponds now threaten roads, trails, and other park structures. Resource managers try to keep ahead of the beavers by inserting "beaver foolers" (PVC pipes) through dams that block road culverts. This moderates pond levels and prevents damage to roads by allowing water to drain through the culvert. Sometimes the beavers, however, get ahead of the resource managers. They have been known to plug the "beaver

foolers" with sticks and mud, or chew through them with their strong teeth.

Amazingly adapted for life in the water, beavers are fascinating to watch. A very accessible location along the Park Loop Road, just past Bear Brook Picnic Area, is Beaver Dam Pond, featuring a few lodges, a dam, and an active beaver population. The best viewing times are dawn and dusk. In the fall the beavers are busiest, preparing food stores for the winter to come. The park often presents a beaver-watch program at that time of year, which is a great way to learn more about the habits and adaptations of the beaver.

Beavers act as a catalyst for increasing natural diversity in an area. Their ponds attract ospreys, herons, and owls; salamanders, frogs, and turtles; insects and aquatic plants; foxes, deer, muskrats, and river otters. Their ponds help maintain the water table, enrich soils, and prevent flooding.

While beavers may bring diversity to a wetland, an invader has been endangering Acadia's ponds and lakes. **Purple loosestrife,** a showy stalked purple flower nonnative to North America, was introduced into gardens as an ornamental. Highly reproductive and adaptive and with no natural predators, purple loosestrife escaped the confines of gardens and has literally choked out the life of some wetlands by crowding out native plants on which many creatures depend and creating a monoculture. Few native species find purple loosestrife useful.

Purple loosestrife has been contained at Acadia, but it's an ongoing process. Uprooting it seems to encourage more to grow, and jostling stalks at certain times of the year disperses vast numbers of seeds, so resource managers have resorted to treating individual plants with an approved herbicide in a way that does not harm the surrounding environment.

WOODLANDS

A dark, statuesque **spruce–fir forest** dominates much of Acadia's woodlands, and does well in the cooler, moist environs of Maine's coast. Red spruce trees are tall and polelike, and often cohabitate with fragrant balsam fir. The spruce

FALL FOLIAGE

The timing and quality of Maine's fall foliage owes much to the summer weather that precedes it, but the annual spectacle never disappoints. In early September, as deciduous trees ready themselves for winter, they stop producing chlorophyll, and the green begins to disappear from their leaves. Taking its place are the spectacular pigments—brilliant reds, yellows, oranges, and purples—that paint the leaves and warm the hearts of every "leaf-peeper," shopkeeper, innkeeper, and restaurateur.

The colorful display begins slowly, reaches a peak, then fades—starting in Maine's north in early to mid-September and working down to the southwest corner by mid-October. Peak foliage in Acadia National Park typically occurs in early October, with the last bits of color hanging on almost to the end of the month.

The fall palette is stunning, especially in Acadia. The leaves of white ash turn purple; sumac and sugar and red maples turn scarlet; mountain ash, beech, basswood, and birch trees turn various shades of yellow.

Trees put on their most magnificent show after a summer of moderate heat and rainfall. A summer of excessive heat and scant rainfall means colors will be less brilliant and disappear more quickly. Throw a September or October northeaster or hurricane into the mix, and estimates are up for grabs.

So predictions are imprecise, and you'll need to allow some schedule flexibility to take advantage of optimum color. From early September to mid-October, check the foliage section on the state Department of Conservation's website (www .mainefoliage.com) for frequently updated maps, panoramic photographs, recommended driving tours, and weekly reports on the foliage status (this is gauged by the percentage of "leaf drop" in every region of the state). Between early September and early October, you can even sign up via the website for weekly email reports (Acadia straddles zones 1 and 2 in the report maps). The state's toll-free fall-foliage hotline is 888/624-6345.

Fall-foliage trips are extremely popular and have become more so in recent years, so lodging can be scarce. Plan ahead and make reservations; sleeping in your car can be mighty chilly at that time of year.

---

grows needles only at the canopy, sparing little energy for growing needles where the sun cannot reach. Because the sun barely touches the forest floor, little undergrowth emerges from the bump and swale of acidic, rust-colored needles that carpet the ground, except for more tiny, shade-loving spruce, waiting for their chance to grow tall.

The spruce–fir forest can be uncannily quiet, especially in the middle of the day. The density of the woods and the springy, needle-laden floor seem to buffer noise from without. Listen closely, however, and you may hear the cackle of ravens, the squabble of a territorial red squirrel, or the rat-a-tat of a woodpecker.

Red squirrels are energetic denizens of the spruce–fir forest, scolding innocent passersby or sitting on tree stumps scaling spruce cones and stuffing their cheeks full of seeds. Observant wildlife watchers will find their middens (heaps of cone scales) about the forest. Squirrels are especially industrious (even comical) in autumn as they frantically prepare for the winter by stocking up on food stores, and tear about from branch to branch with spruce cones poking out of their mouths like big cigars.

Woodpeckers favor dead, still-standing trees, shredding the bark to get at the insects infesting the trunk. The pileated woodpecker—a large black-and-white bird with a red cap—is relatively shy, so you are most likely to encounter evidence of its passage (rectangular and oval holes in trees) rather than the bird itself. Other common woodpeckers you might observe are the hairy and the downy.

The face of Acadia's woodlands changed dramatically in 1947. That fall, during a period of extremely dry conditions, a fire began west of the park's present-day visitor center in Hulls Cove. Feeding on tinder-dry woods and grasses, and whipped into an inferno by gale-force winds, the fire roared across the eastern half of Mount Desert Island, miraculously skirting downtown Bar Harbor but destroying numerous year-round and seasonal homes. In all, 17,000 acres burned (10,000 in the park).

Researchers have studied 6,000 years of the park's fire history by pulling core samples from ponds to analyze the layers of pollen and charcoal that have settled in their bottoms over time, the latter indicating periods of fire. The most significant layer of charcoal appeared in the period around 1947, indicating the intensity of the great fire.

The aftermath of the fire—the scorched mountainsides and skeletal, blackened remains of trees—must have been a devastating sight. Loggers salvaged usable timber and removed unsafe snags. Seed was ordered so replanting could begin in earnest. Soils needed to be stabilized and the landscape restored.

Then a curious thing happened the following spring. As the snow melted, green shoots began to poke up out of the soils among the sooty remains. "Pioneer plants," such as lowbush blueberry and Indian paintbrush, took over the job of stabilizing soils. By the time the ordered seeds arrived two years late (demand had been overwhelming, for much of Maine had burned in 1947), nature was already mending the landscape without human intervention. What had been blackened showed promise and renewal in green growing things.

Over the decades since then, a mixed deciduous forest has grown up from the ashes of the fire, supplanting the dominance of the spruce–fir forest on Mount Desert Island's east side. **Birch, aspen, maple, oak, and beech** have embraced wide-open sunny places where shady spruce once thrived. The new growth not only added colorful splendor to the autumn landscape but also diversified the wildlife.

Populations of **white-tailed deer** benefited from all the new browse (and a lack of major predators), and by the 1960s, the island's deer herd soared. Recent studies have shown the population to be healthy and stable—perhaps due to car–deer collisions and predation from the recently arrived eastern coyote.

Coyotes crossed the Trenton Bridge and wandered onto Mount Desert Island in the 1980s. They had been expanding their territory throughout the northeast, handily picking up the slack in the food chain that was vacated when other large predators, such as the northern gray wolf and the lynx, were hunted and trapped out of the state. While coyote sightings do occur, you are more likely to be serenaded by yipping and howling in the night. Their vocalizations warn off other coyotes, or let them keep in touch with the members of their packs.

The **snowshoe hare**, or varying hare, is a main prey of the coyote. The large hind feet of these mammals allow them to stay aloft in the snow and speed away from predators. Camouflage also aids these fleet-footed hares—their fur turns white during the winter and brown during the summer, hence the name "varying hare." Not all hares escape their predators. It is not uncommon to encounter coyote scat full of hare fur along a carriage road or trail.

Also along a carriage road or trail, you might encounter a **snake** sunning itself on a rock. Five species of snakes—including the garter snake, milk snake, and green snake—inhabit Acadia. None of these snakes are poisonous, but they will bite if provoked.

While autumn may cloak Acadia's mountainsides in bright beauty, spring and summer bring relief to Mainers weary of ice storms, shoveling, freezing temperatures, and short, dark days. Spring arrives with snowy clusters of star flowers along roadsides, and white mats of **bunchberry** flowers (dwarf members of the dogwood family) on the forest floor. Birdsong provides a musical backdrop. Twenty-one species of wood warblers migrate to Acadia from South America to nest—among them are the **American redstart, ovenbird, yellow warbler, and Blackburnian warbler.** At the Visitor Center, request a bird checklist, which names 273 species of birds that have been identified on Mount Desert Island and adjacent areas. Then join a ranger for an early morning bird walk. Check the *Beaver Log* for details.

The fire of 1947 may have transformed a portion of Acadia's woodlands, but change is always part of a natural system. While the broad-leafed trees that grew up in the wake of the fire continue to grow and shed leaves as the cycle of nature demands, young spruce trees poke up through duff and leaf litter, waiting in the shade for their chance to dominate the landscape once again.

MOUNTAINS

A hike up one of Acadia's granite-domed mountains will allow you to gaze down at the world with a new perspective. Left behind is the confining forest—the woods, in fact, seem to shrink as you climb. On the south-facing slopes of some mountains, you'll encounter squat and gnarled pitch pines. The fire of 1947 not only was beneficial to the growth of deciduous vegetation but it also aided in the regeneration of **pitch pines,** which rely on heat, such as that generated by an intense fire, to open their cones and disperse seeds.

Wreathing rocky outcrops and trailsides are such shrubs as **low-bush blueberry, sheep laurel (lambkill), and bayberry.** In the fall, their leaves turn blood-red. In the spring, **shadbush** softens granite mountainsides with white blossoms.

Green and gray lichens plaster exposed rocks in patterns like targets. Composed of algae and fungi, lichens were probably among the first organisms to grow in Acadia as the vast ice sheets retreated 20,000 to 10,000 years ago. Sensitive to air pollution and acid rain, lichens have become barometers of air quality all over the world.

On mountain summits, the trees are stunted. These are not necessarily young trees—some may be nearly 100 years old. The tough, cold, windy climate and exposed conditions of summits force plant life to adapt to survive. Growing close to the ground to avoid fierce winds is one way in which trees have adapted to life at the summit.

Other plants huddle in the shallow, gravelly soil behind solitary rocks, such as **three-toothed cinquefoil,** a member of the rose family which produces a tiny white flower in June and July, and **mountain sandwort,** which blooms in clusters June through September.

While adapted to surviving the extreme conditions of mountain summits, plants can be irreparably damaged by feet trampling off-trail, or by removal of rocks to add to cairns (trail markers) or stone "art." One has only to look at

Champlain Mountain summit

the summit area of Cadillac Mountain to see the damage wrought by millions of roving feet: the missing vegetation and the eroded soils. It may take 50 to 100 years for some plant life, if protected, to recover. Some endangered plant species that grow only at summits may have already disappeared from Cadillac due to trampling.

To protect mountain summits and to preserve the natural scene, follow Leave No Trace principles of staying on the trail and on durable surfaces, such as solid granite. Do not add to cairns or build rock art, a form of graffiti that not only damages plants and soils but also blemishes the scenery for other visitors.

Autumn provides a terrific opportunity to ob-

LEAVE THE ROCKS FOR THE NEXT GLACIER

Acadia's relatively small size among national parks (compared to Yosemite, say, or Yellowstone) and high volume of visitors have necessitated a very active campaign to heighten sensitivity to the park's ecosystem. While you're in Acadia (and, for that matter, anywhere else), do your part to "Keep Acadia Beautiful" by adhering to principles (guidelines, really) developed by the national Leave No Trace (LNT) organization, based in Boulder, Colorado (www.lnt.org):

• Plan ahead and prepare.
• Travel and camp on durable surfaces.
• Dispose of waste properly.
• Leave what you find.
• Minimize campfire impacts.
• Respect wildlife.
• Be considerate of other visitors.
• While all seven of these are important, two are especially critical for Acadia:

• **Travel and camp on durable surfaces.** Since there is no backcountry camping in Acadia, and park rangers do their best to monitor the park's three "front-country" campgrounds (two on Mount Desert, one on Isle au Haut), the focus is on hiking—and use of the trails. Stay on existing trails—paying attention to signposts, blazes, and cairns—and don't be seduced by false trails where hikers have begun to stray. Walk single file down the center of a trail to avoid trampling the sensitive vegetation alongside; slow-growing lichens are particularly fragile. Remember, plants grow by the inch and die by the foot. Every footstep can make a difference. If you must step off the trail, step onto a durable surface. Acadia's most fragile sites are the summits and ridges. Especially vulnerable is the summit of Cadillac—it's a matter of sheer numbers. Yes, walk the summit loop for its great

views, but above all, stick to the trail or at least step on solid rock.

• **Leave what you find.** That means take *NO souvenirs.* Save the wildflowers for the next visitors to enjoy, and leave the tidepool creatures where you find them. Above all, don't mess with cairns, the carefully constructed stone trail markers. Resist the urge to build or unbuild or rebuild cairns along the way—in some instances, removal or addition of a single stone can threaten a cairn's stability. It's a safety issue, too—a collapsed cairn becomes a missing link in the trail-marking system. Follow cairns, don't build them. As the slogan has it, "leave the rocks for the next glacier." Imagine if every one of the park's nearly three million visitors each year removed one cobble or rock. (Unfortunately, enough already have. Bar Harbor Airport screeners, under heightened security regulations, have been seeing visitors departing with beach rocks. But what to do with them? Who can say exactly where they came from? Please leave them where you found them.) If you're planning to camp at one of the park campgrounds, bring firewood—you'll see dozens of Firewood for Sale signs along the roads leading to the park. Stop and buy a bundle; it'll set you back only a dollar or two.

Also essential—anywhere, not just in Acadia—is the "carry in, carry out" message. If you're planning a picnic, enjoy it (on a durable surface—there's plenty of granite in Acadia), then remove all evidence of it. Carry trash bags and use them.

To keep wildlife wild, *do not feed* any of the park's wildlife—a problem that's of increasing concern at Acadia. Animals become dependent on humans and risk being hit by cars or otherwise meeting their end.

We all love the park, but we can't love it to death.

serve **raptors** of all kinds. In the fall, during their southward migration, raptors take advantage of northwest winds flowing over Acadia's mountains. Eagles, red-tailed hawks, sharp-shinned hawks, goshawks, American kestrels, peregrine falcons, and others can be spotted. (The peregrine, a seasonal mountain dweller, has been reintroduced to Acadia after a long absence; see the sidebar, *Peregrine Falcons* in the *Acadia on Mount Desert Island* chapter.) From late August to mid-October, join park staff for the annual Hawkwatch atop Cadillac Mountain (weather permitting) for viewing and identifying raptors. Check the *Beaver Log* for details. In 2002, hawkwatchers counted 1,659 raptors from 10 species (down a bit from the annual average of 2,500). The most prevalent species are American kestrels and sharp-shinned hawks.

WILDLIFE-WATCHING TIPS

• Seek out wildlife at dusk and dawn when it is more active. Bring binoculars and a field guide.
• Leave Rover at home—pets are intruders into the natural world, and they will scare off wildlife. If leaving your dog behind is not an option, remember that in the park, pets must be restrained on a leash no longer than six feet. This is for the safety of both the pet and wildlife, and is courteous to other visitors.
• Never approach wildlife, which could become aggressive if sick or feeling threatened. Enjoy wildlife at a distance.
• Do not feed wildlife, not even gulls. Feeding turns wild animals into aggressive beggars that lose the ability to forage for themselves, and often ends in their demise.
• Join walks, talks, hikes, cruises, and evening programs presented by park rangers to learn more about your national park and its flora and fauna. Programs are listed in the *Beaver Log*, readily available at the Hulls Cove Visitor Center, the Sieur de Monts Nature Center, and park campgrounds, as well as online at **www.nps.gov/acad/**
• Visit the Nature Center at Sieur de Monts Spring, where exhibits show the diversity of flora and fauna in the park, and the challenges that resource managers face in protecting it.
  See *Suggested Reading* for a selection of books (including field guides) on Acadia's natural history.
  (*The* Flora and Fauna *section of this chapter was written by Kristen Britain, former writer/editor for Acadia National Park.*)

History

NATIVE AMERICANS

As the great continental glacier receded northwestward out of Maine about 11,000 years ago, some prehistoric grapevine must have alerted small bands of hunter-gatherers—fur-clad Paleoindians—to the scrub sprouting in the tundra, burgeoning mammal populations, and the ocean's bountiful food supply. Because they came to the shore in droves—at first seasonally, then year-round. Anyone who thinks tourism is a recent phenomenon in this part of Maine need only explore the shoreline of Mount Desert Island, where cast-off oyster shells and clamshells document the migration of early Native Americans from woodlands to waterfront. "The shore" has been a summertime magnet for millennia.

Archaeological evidence from the Archaic period in Maine—roughly 8000–1000 B.C.—is fairly scant, but paleontologists have unearthed stone tools and weapons and small campsites attesting to a nomadic lifestyle supported by fishing and hunting (with fishing becoming more extensive as time went on). Toward the end of the tradition, during the late Archaic period, there emerged a rather anomalous Indian culture known officially as the Moorehead phase but informally called the Red Paint People; the name comes from their curious trait of using a distinctive red ocher (pulverized hematite) in burials. Dark red puddles and stone artifacts have led excavators to burial pits in Ellsworth and Hancock, close to Mount Desert Island. Just as mysteriously as they had arrived, the Red Paint

People disappeared abruptly and inexplicably around 1800 B.C.

Following them almost immediately—and almost as suddenly—hunter-gatherers of the Susquehanna Tradition arrived from well to the south, moved across Maine's interior as far as the St. John River, and remained until about 1600 B.C., when they, too, enigmatically vanished. Excavations have turned up relatively sophisticated stone tools and evidence that they cremated their dead. It was nearly 1,000 years before a major new cultural phase appeared.

The next great leap forward was marked by the advent of pottery making, introduced about 700 B.C. The Ceramic period stretched to the 16th century, and cone-shaped pots (initially stamped, later incised with coiled-rope motifs) survived until the introduction of metals from Europe. During this time, at Pemetic (their name for Mount Desert Island) and on some of the offshore islands, Native American fishermen and their families built houses of sorts—seasonal, wigwam-style birch-bark dwellings—and spent the summers fishing, clamming, trapping, and making baskets and functional birch-bark objects.

Anyone who thinks tourism is a recent phenomenon in this part of Maine need only explore the shoreline of Mount Desert Island, where cast-off oyster shells and clamshells document the migration of early Native Americans from woodlands to waterfront. "The shore" has been a summertime magnet for millennia.

ARRIVAL OF THE EUROPEANS

The identity of the first Europeans to set foot in Maine is a matter of debate. Historians dispute the romantically popular notion that Norse explorers checked out this part of the New World as early as A.D. 1000. Even an 11th-century Norse coin found in 1961 in Brooklin (near Blue Hill, the next peninsula west of Mount Desert) probably was carried there from farther northeast.

Not until the late 15th century, the onset of the great Age of Discovery, did credible reports of the New World (including what's now Maine) filter back to Europe's courts and universities. Thanks to innovations in naval architecture, shipbuilding, and navigation, astonishingly courageous fellows crossed the Atlantic in search of rumored treasure and new routes for reaching it.

John Cabot, sailing from England aboard the ship *Mathew,* may have been the first European to reach Maine, in 1498, but historians have never confirmed a landing site. There is no question, however, about the account of Giovanni da Verrazzano, a Florentine explorer commanding *La Dauphine* under the French flag, who reached the Maine coast in 1524. Encountering less-than-friendly Indians, Verrazzano did a minimum of business and sailed onward toward Nova Scotia. (Four years later, he died in the West Indies.) His brother's map of their landing site (probably on the Phippsburg Peninsula, near Bath) labels it "The Land of Bad People." Esteban Gomez, a Portuguese explorer sailing under the Spanish flag, followed in Verrazzano's wake in 1525, but the only outcome of his exploits was an uncounted number of captives whom he sold into slavery in Spain. A map created several years later from Gomez's descriptions seems to indicate he had at least glimpsed Mount Desert Island.

More than half a century passed before the Maine coast turned up again on European explorers' itineraries. This time, interest was fueled by reports of a Brigadoon-like area called Norumbega (or Oranbega, as one map had it), a myth that arose, gathered steam, and took on a life of its own in the decades following Verrazzano's voyage.

By the 17th century, when Europeans began arriving in more than twos and threes and getting serious about colonization, Native American agriculture was already underway, the cod fishery was thriving on offshore islands, Indians far to the north were hot to trade furs for European goodies, and the birch-bark canoe was the transport of

INTRODUCTION

choice when the Penobscots headed down Maine's rivers toward their summer sojourns on the coast.

MOUNT DESERT ISLAND "DISCOVERED"

In the early 17th century, English dominance of exploration west of the Penobscot River (roughly from present-day Bucksport down to the New Hampshire border and beyond) coincided roughly with increasing French activity east of the river—including Mount Desert Island and the nearby mainland.

In 1604, French nobleman Pierre du Gua, Sieur de Monts, bearing a vast land grant for *La Cadie* (or Acadia) from King Henry IV, set out with cartographer Samuel de Champlain to map the coastline. They first reached Nova Scotia's Bay of Fundy and then sailed up the St. Croix River. Midriver, just west of present-day Calais, a crew planted gardens and erected buildings on today's St. Croix Island while de Monts and Champlain went off exploring. The two men and their crew sailed up the Penobscot River to present-day Bangor (searching fruitlessly for Norumbega) and next "discovered" the imposing island Champlain named *l'Isle des Monts Déserts,* because of its treeless summits. Here they entered Frenchman Bay, landed at today's Otter Creek in early September, and explored inlets and bays in the vicinity before returning to St. Croix Island to face the elements with their ill-fated compatriots. Scurvy, lack of fuel and water, and a ferocious winter wiped out nearly half of the 79 men in the St. Croix settlement. In spring 1605, de Monts, Champlain, and other survivors headed southwest again, exploring the coastline all the way to Cape Cod before returning north-eastward and settling permanently at Nova Scotia's Port Royal (now Annapolis Royal).

Eight years later, French Jesuit missionaries en route to the Kennebec River (or, as some allege, seeking Norumbega) ended up on Mount Desert Island. With a band of about three dozen French laymen, they set about establishing the St. Sauveur mission settlement at present-day Fernald Point. Despite the welcoming presence of amiable Indians (led by Asticou, an eminent Penobscot sagamore), leadership squabbles led to building

low tide at Fernald Point, site of the 17th-century St. Sauveur settlement

delays, and English marauder Samuel Argall—assigned to reclaim this territory for England—arrived in his warship *Treasurer* to find them easy prey. The colony was leveled, the settlers were set adrift in small boats, the priests were carted off to the Jamestown Colony in Virginia, and Argall moved on to destroy Port Royal.

Even though England yearned to control the entire Maine coastline, her turf, realistically, still remained south and west of the Penobscot River. During the 17th century, the French had expanded from their Canadian colony of Acadia. Unlike the absentee bosses who controlled the English territory, French merchants actually showed up, forming good relationships with the Indians and cornering the market in fishing, lumbering, and fur trading. And French Jesuit priests converted many a Native American to Catholicism. Intermittently, overlapping Anglo-French land claims sparked messy local conflicts.

In the mid-17th century, the strategic heart of French administration and activity in Maine was Fort Pentagoet, a sturdy stone outpost built in 1635 in what is now Castine (on the next peninsula west of Mount Desert). From Penta-goet, the French controlled coastal trade between the St. George River and Mount Desert Island and well up the Penobscot River. In 1654, England captured and occupied Pentagoet and much of French Acadia, but, thanks to the 1667 Treaty of Breda, title returned to the French in 1670, and Pentagoet briefly became Acadia's capital.

A short but nasty Dutch foray against Acadia in 1674 resulted in Pentagoet's destruction ("level'd with ye ground," by one account) and the raising of yet a third national flag over Castine.

THE REVOLUTION AND STATEHOOD

From the late 17th to the late 18th century, half a dozen skirmishes along the coast—often sparked by conflicts in Europe—preoccupied the Wabanaki (Native American tribes), the French, and the English. In 1759, roughly midway through the Seven Years' War, the British came out on top in Quebec, allowing Massachusetts Governor John Bernard to divvy up the acreage on Mount Desert Island. Two bravehearts—James Richardson and Abraham Somes—arrived with their

PRONOUNCING MOUNT DESERT: THE "SAHARA SCHOOL" VS. THE "ICE CREAM AND CAKE SCHOOL"

N oted maritime author Admiral Samuel Eliot Morison, in *The Story of Mount Desert Island* (published by Little, Brown, 1960) devotes a long footnote to the controversy over the pronunciation of *Desert* in Mount Desert. Here's his wry take on it:

[Explorer Samuel de Champlain's] exact words are: *"Le sommet de la plus part d'icelles est desgarny d'arbres parceque ce ne sont que roches. Je l'ay nommée l'Isle des Monts-déserts."* Right here we may grapple with the problem [of] how to pronounce it in English—whether we should follow what many people call the "Sahara School" and accent the penult, pronouncing it "Mount Dez´-ert," or what opponents call the "Ice Cream and Cake School," pronouncing it "Mount Dez-ert´," with accent on the last syllable. I should say that the spelling "Mount Desart" on *The Atlantic Neptune* and other old maps indicates that, like "clerk," "sergeant," and other words containing "er," it was pronounced "ar," and that the accent was then on the last syllable. Charles Tracy recorded, in his journal of 1855, that the natives called it "Mount Desert." During my youth most of the older inhabitants called it "Mount Dez´-ert" (although inconsistently they called the steamboat of that name the *Mount Dez-ert´*), and [Harvard] President [Charles] Eliot pronounced in favor of the Sahara School. Bishop [William C.] Doane, on the other hand, unwilling to take orders from a Unitarian, always accented the last syllable; and as my parents were Episcopalians we followed the Bishop rather than Cousin Charles. At the time of writing, the penult accenters are much in a minority.

© KATHLEEN M. BRANDES

Somesville was founded by Abraham Somes and James Richardson in 1760.

families in 1760, and today's village of Somesville marks their settlement. Even as the American Revolution consumed the colonies, Mount Desert Island maintained a relatively low profile (politically speaking) into the early 19th century. A steady stream of homesteaders, drawn by the appeal of free land, sustained their families by fishing, farming, lumbering, and shipbuilding. On March 15, 1820, the District of Maine (which included Mount Desert) broke from Massachusetts to become the 23rd state in the Union, with its capital in Portland. (The capital moved to Augusta in 1832.)

ARRIVAL OF THE "RUSTICATORS"

Around the middle of the 18th century, explorers of a different sort arrived on Mount Desert Island. Seeking dramatic landscapes rather than fertile land, painters of the acclaimed Hudson River School found more than enough inspiration for their canvases. Thomas Cole (1801–48), founder of the group, visited Mount Desert only once, in 1844, but his onetime student Frederic

Edwin Church (1826–1900), vacationed here in 1850 and became a summer resident two decades later. Once dubbed "the Michelangelo of landscape art," Church traveled widely in search of exotic settings for his grand landscapes. After his summers on Mount Desert, he spent his final days at Olana, a Persian-inspired mansion overlooking the Hudson.

It's no coincidence that artists formed a large part of the 19th-century vanguard here: The dramatic landscape, with both bare and wooded mountains descending to the sea, still inspires everyone who sees it. Those pioneering artists brilliantly portrayed this area, adding a few romantic touches to landscapes that really need no enhancement. Known collectively as "rusticators," the artists and their coterie seemed content to "live like the locals" and rented basic rooms from island fishermen and boatbuilders. But once the word got out and painterly images began confirming the reports, the surge of visitors began—particularly after the Civil War, which had so totally preoccupied the nation. Tourist boardinghouses appeared first, then sprawling hotels—by the late 1880s, there were nearly 40

FREDERIC EDWIN CHURCH: CONSUMMATE ROMANTIC

O ne of the best-known second-generation members of the Hudson River School— 19th-century painters of vast landscapes, riverscapes, and seascapes—was Frederic Edwin Church. Born in 1826 in Hartford, Connecticut, Church was a contemporary of Winslow Homer, Fitz Hugh Lane, and James McNeill Whistler. By the time he first visited Mount Desert Island in 1850, Church had already studied under Hudson River School founder Thomas Cole and had been admitted to the National Academy of Design in New York. Cole proudly claimed that his one and only protégé had "the finest eye for drawing in the world." Captivated by Mount Desert's bare summits, broad vistas, and rough shoreline, Church produced dramatic, atmospheric paintings of the area.

Among the best known of Church's Mount Desert paintings are *Otter Creek, Mount Desert* (about 1850), *Twilight in the Wilderness* (1860), and *Mount Newport on Mount Desert Island* (ca. 1851–53); the latter fetched $4.2 million at auction in May 2000. (Mount Newport, named for Christopher Newport, captain of the 1607 Jamestown Colony fleet, is now Mount Champlain.)

One reviewer used an apt musical metaphor to describe the range of Church's extraordinary work: "The painter best known nowadays for what might be termed visual symphonies or operas also regularly created concertos, hymns, and smaller works—the equivalents of sonatas, études, and Lieder."

In 1853, Church set out for South America, following the route of German naturalist Alexander von Humboldt through New Granada (now Colombia) and Ecuador, and creating sketches he used for later paintings of the Andean region. Subsequent journeys to South America, the Canadian Maritimes, Mexico, and the Caribbean, as well as extended explorations of Europe and the Middle East in 1867, served as inspirations for Church masterpieces of the Parthenon, Petra, Baalbek, and Jerusalem.

In 1860, Church married Isabel Carnes, with whom he had six children (two died of diphtheria in 1865). Isabel died in 1899.

Debilitated by rheumatism during the last 15 years of his life, Church retreated to Olana, his Persian-inspired mansion on the Hudson River designed by Calvert Vaux (a colleague of noted architect Frederick Law Olmsted). Church died in New York in 1900. In 1966, Olana became a New York State Historic Site, open to the public.

The last major painting from Church's easel was not of Peru or Petra or the Hudson River, nor even of Cadillac Mountain. It was an 1895 portrait of Katahdin, in what is now Maine's Baxter State Park—*Mount Katahdin from Millinocket Camp*, the view from his beloved Camp Rhodora, on Millinocket Lake, which he purchased in 1878.

The best collection of Church paintings—indeed, the best collection of work by the members of the Hudson River School—is at the Wadsworth Atheneum in Hartford, Connecticut (www.wadsworthatheneum.org).

hotels on the island, luring vacationers for summer-long stays.

At about the same time, the East Coast's corporate tycoons zeroed in on Mount Desert, arriving by luxurious steam yachts and building over-the-top grand estates (quaintly called "summer cottages") along the shore northward from Bar Harbor. (Before long, demand exceeded acreage, and mansions also began appearing in Northeast and Southwest Harbors.) Their seasonal social circuit was a catalogue of Rich and Famous Families—Rockefeller, Astor, Vanderbilt, Ford, Whitney, Schieffelin, Morgan, Carnegie—just for a start. Also part of the elegant mix were noted academics, doctors, lawyers, and even international diplomats. The "Gay Nineties" earned their name on Mount Desert Island.

BIRTH OF A NATIONAL PARK

Fortunately for Mount Desert—and, let's face it, for all of us—many of the rusticators maintained

George Bucknam Dorr, the Father of Acadia and its first superintendent

a strong sense of *noblesse oblige*, engaging regularly in philanthropic activity. Notable among them was George Bucknam Dorr (1853–1944), who spent more than 40 years fighting to preserve land on Mount Desert Island and ultimately earned the title "Father of Acadia."

As Dorr related in his memoir (See *Suggested Reading*), the saga began with the establishment of The Hancock County Trustees of Public Reservations, a nonprofit corporation modeled on the Trustees of Public Reservations in Massachusetts and chartered in early 1903 "to acquire, by devise, gift or purchase, and to own, arrange, hold, maintain or improve for public use lands in Hancock County, Maine [encompassing Mount Desert Island as well as Schoodic Point], which by reason of scenic beauty, historical interest, sanitary advantage or other like reasons may become available for such purpose." President of the new corporation was Charles W. Eliot, president emeritus of Harvard. Dorr became the vice president and "executive officer" and dedicated the rest of his life to the cause.

Dorr wrote letters, cajoled, spoke at meetings, arrived on potential donors' doorsteps, even resorted to polite ruses as he pursued his mission.

He also delved into his own pockets to subsidize land purchases. In effect, Dorr was a fundraiser par excellence, a master of "networking" decades before the days of instant communications. Gradually he accumulated parcels—ponds, woodlands, summits, trails—and gradually his enthusiasm caught on. But easy it wasn't. He faced down longtime local residents, potential developers, and other challengers, and he politely but doggedly visited grand salons, corporate offices, and the halls of Congress in his quest.

In 1913, Bar Harbor taxpayers—irked by the increasing acreage being taken off the tax rolls—prevailed upon their state legislator to introduce a bill to annul the corporation's charter. Dorr's effective lobbying doomed the bill, but the corporation saw trouble ahead and devised a plan on a grander scale. Again thanks to Dorr's political and social connections and intense lobbying in Washington, President Woodrow Wilson on July 8, 1916, created the Sieur de Monts National Monument from 5,000 acres given to the government by the Hancock County Trustees of Public Reservations. George B. Dorr acquired the new title of Custodian of the Monument.

After the establishment of the National Park Service in late August 1916, and after Sieur de Monts had received its first congressional appropriation ($10,000), George Dorr forged ahead to try to convince the government to convert "his" national monument into a national park. "No" meant nothing to him. Not only did he schmooze with congressmen, cabinet members, helpful secretaries, and even ex-President Theodore Roosevelt, he also provided the pen (filled with ink) and waited in the president's outer office to be sure Wilson signed the bill. On February 26, 1919, Lafayette National Park became the first national park east of the Mississippi River; George Bucknam Dorr became its first superintendent. (Ten years later, the name was changed to Acadia National Park.)

THE GREAT FIRE OF 1947

Wildfires are no surprise in Maine—where woodlands often stretch to the horizon—but 1947 was unique in the history of the state and of Acadia. A rainy spring led into a dry, hot summer with almost no precipitation . . . and then an autumn with still no rain. Wells went dry, vegetation drooped, and the inevitable occurred—a record-breaking inferno. Starting on October 17 as a small, smoldering fire at the northern end of the island, it galloped south and east, abetted by winds, and moved toward Bar Harbor and Frenchman Bay before coming under control on October 27. More than 17,000 acres burned (including more than 10,000 in Acadia National Park). Sixty-seven magnificent "cottages" were incinerated on "Millionaires' Row," along the shore north of Bar Harbor, with property damage of more than $20 million. Some of the mansions, incredibly, escaped the flames, but most of the estates were never rebuilt. Miraculously, only one man succumbed to the fire. A few other deaths occurred from heart attacks and traffic accidents, as hundreds of residents scrambled frantically to escape the island. Even the fishermen of nearby Lamoine and Winter Harbor pitched in, staging their own mini-Dunkirk to evacuate more than 400 residents by boat.

THE PARK TODAY

If only George Dorr could see today's Acadia, covering more than 46,000 acres on Mount Desert Island, the Schoodic Peninsula mainland, and parts of Isle au Haut, Baker, and Little Cranberry Islands. The fire changed Mount Desert's woodland profile—from the dark greens of spruce and fir to a mix of evergreen and deciduous trees, making the fall foliage even more dramatic than in Dorr's day. If ever proof were needed that one person (enlisting the help of many others) can indeed make a difference, Acadia National Park provides it.

Environmental Issues

You've already read about some of Acadia's major environmental issues, but still others exist. Tops among these are air pollution and overcrowding. Of utmost importance is the matter of "zero impact," addressed by the Leave No Trace philosophy actively practiced at Acadia.

AIR QUALITY

In 2002, a study by the private National Parks Conservation Association revealed that Acadia National Park had the fifth-worst air quality of all the national parks; Acadia allegedly has twice as much haze as the Grand Canyon. Most scientists and environmentalists attribute the problem primarily to smoke and haze from power plants in the Midwest and South. New England is "the end of the line," so to speak, for airborne pollutants, and it's estimated that 80 percent of Maine's pollution arrives from other regions. Maine has the highest asthma rate in the nation, rivers and lakes have high concentrations of mercury, and rainfall at Acadia is notably acidic. Maine's four legislators, and others in the region, have been especially active in their efforts to strengthen the Clean Air Act

Lichens are sensitive to pollution and barometers of air quality.

and improve conditions at Acadia and in the rest of New England.

To heighten public awareness of pollution problems, a new government/private joint program has initiated **CAMNET,** an intriguing monitoring system that provides real-time pollution and visibility monitoring. Acadia is one of the six New England sites with cameras updating images every 15 minutes. Log on to www.hazecam.net for data on current temperature and humidity, wind speed and direction, precipitation totals, visual range, and the air-pollution level (low, medium, or high). The site also includes a selection of photos showing the variations that have occurred in the past

at Acadia. In the "clear day" photo, visibility was pegged at 199 miles! Ozone alerts (according to EPA standards) usually occur at Acadia a couple of times each summer. When they do, rangers put out signs to caution visitors—particularly hikers and bikers—to restrict strenuous activity.

While pollution is an Acadia issue—affecting the park, its vegetation and wildlife, and its visitors—the solution must be a national one. Stay tuned.

PARK CAPACITY

With nearly three million visitors each year, Acadia and National Park Service officials are wrestling with the question, How many people are too many people? Other national parks have initiated visitor limitations, but Acadia has so far not done so. The time may come, however.

The establishment of the propane-powered Island Explorer bus service has greatly alleviated traffic (and thus also auto, SUV, and RV emissions) during the months it operates (late June to Columbus Day), and freed up space in Acadia's parking areas, but will it encourage more visitors?

Cruise-vessel visits in Bar Harbor have multiplied exponentially in recent years, and most passengers spend at least some time in the park, but it's minimal time—often just a carriage ride or a visit to Jordan Pond House or the Cadillac summit. (Bar Harbor merchants, of course, welcome the influx.)

Heaviest use of the park occurs in July and August, with marginally less use in September, yet there are still quiet corners of the park. It's a matter of finding them. The best advice, therefore, is to visit in "shoulder" periods—May and June, late September, early October. You take your chances then with weather and temperature, but if you're flexible and adaptable, it could be the best vacation you've ever had.

On the Road

What's the best way to get to Acadia National Park, you ask? Drop in by parachute. Next best choice? Probably fly from Boston to the Bar Harbor Airport and take a bus or taxi from there to your lodging site. But much depends on where you're starting, when you're coming, how long you plan to stay, and what else you plan to do while you're here. More of that to come.

How long should you stay at Acadia? Well, you can get a feel for the park on a day-long visit, but an ideal minimum stay would be three or four days. Enough time to take a hike or two, visit a museum, bike a stretch of the carriage roads, go whale-watching or sailing, and sample some appealing restaurants.

But why not stay a week so you can explore the park's major outlying sections—the Schoodic Peninsula and offshore Isle au Haut.

You'll have no trouble filling the days with hikes, picnics, shopping, sea kayaking, and gallery-hopping.

Heck, why not wrestle with your vacation calendar and stay even longer—for more hikes, more bike rides, a horse-drawn carriage ride, a few more museums, and a beach day. If the fog rolls in, settle in with a book or hit more galleries and museums and shops.

How will you get around once you get here? Europeans are always shocked at Maine's minimal public transport. The few large-ish cities have bus systems, but there's almost nothing in small towns. The national Amtrak system enters Maine only at its southern tip. Fortunately, buses link the major urban centers, such as Portland and Bangor—with stops in small towns when they happen to be along the way.

overlooking The Bowl, Champlain Mountain

Among less-populated areas, Mount Desert Island stands out, thanks to its fare-free, propane-fueled **Island Explorer** bus system, subsidized by your park fees, Friends of Acadia, L. L. Bean, and local businesses. The good news is that it's a very efficient network; the bad news is that it runs only between late June and mid-October.

So try to come during the Explorer's season, when you can rubberneck all you want from the comfort of a bus seat. No missed turns, no near-misses. Less pollution, less frazzle. If you've arrived by car, leave it at your lodging and hop on the bus.

Travel Strategies

WHEN TO GO

Realistically, Acadia National Park is a three-season park (spring, summer, and fall), even though it's open in winter for cross-country skiing, snowshoeing, snowmobiling (with some restrictions), and even camping. Peak travel time for Acadia is July Fourth to Labor Day, with the absolute peak around the first week in August, when it's insane to show up without a room or campsite reservation. (Why spend valuable vacation time hanging out at information centers or making the rounds of lodgings to find a vacant room or site? Plan ahead.)

Spring tends to be something of a blip in Maine; the park starts reawakening only around mid- to late April, when the entire Park Loop Road has reopened (including the Cadillac Mountain road). Even then, some of the carriage roads tend to be fragile and open only for foot traffic, not for bicycles. Trails can be muddy, and ice still coats some of the rocks, but you'll be rewarded by hardy wildflowers poking up here and there. Until about mid-May, you'll also be spared from annoying blackflies. In May, the weather can be unpredictable—cold and rainy one day, dramatically clear and sunny the next—and some lodgings still haven't opened for the season.

Summer kicks off with a Memorial Day burst in late May, but June is relatively quiet until the end of the month, when schools release their captives. If you yearn to be car-free on Mount Desert, plan to be here in summer, particularly between late June and mid-October, when Acadia's Island Explorer shuttle service operates. (If you're arriving by RV, without a car in tow, the Island Explorer buses are a major asset.) Summer means lots of festivals and fairs, nightlife in Bar Harbor, nature tours, concerts (jazz, classical, pops), carriage rides, hiking, and whale-watching trips,

Fall is fantastic in the park and on the island—it's my favorite season here. Nights are cool (mid-40s to mid-50s), days are (often) brilliant, and the fall-foliage vistas are dramatic (visit www.mainefoliage.com). The grapevine has spread the word, though, so you won't be alone—but the visitor headcount is still far lower than in July and August.

The **Atlantic hurricane season** runs from June 1 to November, and even though Maine is almost literally at the end of the tracks, tropical storms and hurricanes can affect Maine's weather, particularly in September and October. As with any other weather situation in Maine, it's a crapshoot, so always stay on top of weather information when hurricanes start moving northward along the Atlantic coast.

Time Zone

Acadia National Park (as well as the rest of Maine) is in the eastern time zone—the same as New York; Washington, D.C.; Philadelphia, Pennsylvania; and Orlando, Florida. Eastern standard time (EST) runs from the last Sunday in October to the first Sunday in April; eastern daylight time (EDT), one hour later, is in effect otherwise. If your itinerary also includes the Canadian Maritimes, remember that the provinces of New Brunswick and Nova Scotia are on Atlantic time—one hour later than eastern.

Every day during the summer, fast ferries travel between Yarmouth, Nova Scotia, and Bar

Harbor, losing and gaining an hour en route. Their schedules are printed in local time at each terminus—Atlantic time in Nova Scotia, eastern time in Bar Harbor.

SUGGESTED ROUTES

To reduce congestion on the roads of Mount Desert Island during the peak summer months, it would be ideal if everyone arrived by some mode of public transport rather than bringing a car or RV. That hasn't happened yet, but maybe someday it will, as more and more possibilities are becoming available.

Using public transport to get to Acadia, of course, requires more scheduling than just hopping into the car and driving, and in the end it will take more time without a car. But once you get to Mount Desert, you can leave your vehicle at your lodging and explore virtually the entire island with the Island Explorer bus system (only between late June and Columbus Day).

If, for example, you want to reach Acadia from Boston, you can fly to Hancock County/Bar Harbor Airport and pick up the Island Explorer at the airport to go into downtown Bar Harbor. Or you can take the **Amtrak** "Downeaster" train from Boston to Portland, where you can pick up a bus (Concord Trailways or Vermont Transit, in the same complex as the train station) for Bangor. From Bangor, you can take the bus (Vermont Transit) to Bar Harbor.

It would be interesting to know the statistics on how many people drive directly from Boston to Acadia National Park without stopping en route. I'd guess probably not many (perhaps mostly those who have summer homes on Mount Desert Island or nearby). The trip is 268 miles, and not all of that trek is on multilane highway. You can't count on averaging 60 mph, especially in midsummer, when you hit the two-lane roads. Even on the four- and six-lane Maine Turnpike, traffic can choke up at toll booths. Also, you'll need bathroom breaks, snack breaks, maybe a gas fillup—and all of Maine south of Acadia has its own attractions to lure you into detours (L.L. Bean and the Freeport outlet shops are major magnets).

But if you're determined to drive through from Boston, the best route is I-95, through 18 miles of New Hampshire (the Hampton toll booths often cause major backups), into Maine and directly toward Bangor (the Maine Turnpike and I-95 are the same road for some stretches). Take Exit 45-A to I-395 and watch for signs for Route 1-A to Ellsworth and Bar Harbor. *(Do not take Route 1-A to Hampden, or you'll end up on the wrong side of the Penobscot River.)*

Specific information on Bangor, which is the primary gateway to the Acadia region, as well as traveling through Portland via planes, trains, and on bus, is included later in this chapter.

PLANNING YOUR TRIP

Except for local residents, summer folk, or day-tripping Mainers (often with houseguests), most visitors to Acadia National Park also spend time in other parts of Maine—if for no other reason than to make their way here. Thus, you'll want a sense of the big picture, which comes primarily from statewide tourism sources.

Maine Online

The Maine Office of Tourism has established an award-winning website: **www.visitmaine.com**. You'll find chamber of commerce addresses, current weather reports, articles, photos, information on lodgings, and access to countless Maine tourism businesses. The Maine Tourism Association (MTA), a nonprofit organization contracted by the state Office of Tourism, maintains a useful website at www.mainetourism.com. (The MTA also operates the state's information centers.) On the state's comprehensive official website (www.maine.gov), you can reserve campsites in state parks, buy a fishing license, and more. Hundreds of other Maine Web pages are also up and running, so surf away. (The *Internet Resources* section at the back of this book focuses primarily on Acadia National Park and vicinity, but you'll also find a few of the statewide sites.)

Local Chambers of Commerce and Tourism Offices

Tourism is Maine's second-largest source of

revenue (after the forest industry), so almost every community of any size has some kind of information office, although some are staffed by volunteers and open only in summer. Most of these communities also produce annual booklets, brochures, or maps loaded with tourism information. In the smallest towns, local shopkeepers, lodging hosts, and town-office employees are the best alternative information sources. If you haven't planned ahead, ask them for suggestions for places to sleep, eat, shop, and play. No question is too foolish—and you can bet they've heard it before. Addresses (snail mail and Web) and phone numbers of local tourism offices are listed in the Maine Tourism Association's annual *Maine Invites You* magazine, which you can order via its website.

Details on the information centers on Mount Desert Island, including the Acadia National Park Hulls Cove Visitor Center, are included in the *Acadia on Mount Desert Island* chapter.

Maps

Maine is the home of the DeLorme Mapping Company, publisher of *The Maine Atlas and Gazetteer*. Despite an oversize format inconvenient for hiking and kayaking, this 96-page paperbound book just about guarantees that you won't get lost. Scaled at one-half inch to the mile, it's meticulously compiled from aerial photographs, satellite images, U.S. Geological Survey maps, GPS readings, and timber-company maps, and it is revised annually. DeLorme products are available nationwide in book and map stores, but you can also order direct (800/452-5931, www.delorme.com). The atlas is $19.95 and shipping is $4. (Maine residents need to add 5 percent sales tax.)

DeLorme also publishes an annual edition of *The Maine Map and Guide* ($2.95), a standard folding map with detailed insets of major cities and towns, and lots of helpful information on the reverse. The map as well as the large atlas are available directly from DeLorme as well as in Maine supermarkets, convenience stores, gift shops, bookstores, sporting-goods stores, and some tourist offices.

The **National Park Service** produces an Acadia National Park foldout map that is especially useful for trip planning and orientation. The map is available on the island, but it's worth obtaining a copy in advance by contacting the park office (207/288-3338). If you have Acrobat Reader, you can also download the map from the park's website (www.nps.gov/acad/), but the printed version has more information about the park.

Parkman Publications (P.O. Box 826, Bar Harbor 04609, 207/288-0355, bhmaine.com) publishes a map ($2.95) of hiking trails and carriage roads on Mount Desert Island. Not only is the map useful for hikers and bikers, but a percentage of the profits goes to the Friends of Acadia organization. Pick up a copy when you get to Mount Desert Island (for planning, order it by phone beforehand).

The most recent entrant in the map sweepstakes is the foldout *Acadia National Park Trails* topo map published in 2003 by Maine-based **Map Adventures LLC** (51 Elizabeth St., Peaks Island, ME 04108, 207/879-4777, www.mapadventures.com). It includes carriage roads, hiking trails, biking routes, bus stops, and more. It's available for $4.95 at the Hulls Cove Visitor Center, at bookstores, or through the publisher. With a scale of an inch to the mile, the map is especially detailed, useful, and up-to-date.

Acadia and National Park Service Publications

To plan for a park visit, contact Information, Acadia National Park (P.O. Box 177, Bar Harbor, ME 04609, 207/288-3338, www.nps.gov/acad/). Be sure to request a park map, a carriage-road map, a hiking-trail list, and camping information. The park also publishes an access guide, detailing wheelchair accessibility of information centers, campgrounds, shops, cruises, museums, and trails. Other flyers worth requesting cover geology, plants, birds, mammals, and the park's history. A number of these publications appear on the Acadia website, which contains an enormous amount of helpful information for planning your visit, so download information from the website before calling for snail mail. The park's newspaper, the *Beaver Log,* is published four times between spring and fall; for advance planning (such as choosing Park Ranger programs), the issues are downloadable from the website. Reservations for Park Ranger programs can be made by phone up to three days in advance.

WHAT TO TAKE

Clothing and Gear

No matter how hardy you are, you won't be able to make do at Acadia with just bathing suits, shorts, sandals, and cover-ups; the weather is just too unpredictable, even at the height of summer. Of course, Maine *is* the home of L. L. Bean, so if you're driving to Acadia from southern Maine, you could just stop in Freeport and buy an entire vacation wardrobe there. ("Bean's" also has an outlet store in Ellsworth, on the access route to Mount Desert Island, but the inventory consists primarily of discontinued or returned items.) Seriously, though, in summer you'll need to pack shorts, swimwear, rain gear, jeans and other long pants, a sweater or two, warm nightwear, and a warm jacket. For hiking, you'll want sturdy shoes, a brimmed hat, and a waterproof daypack. If you have a yen for freshwater swimming, throw in a pair of water shoes for navigating wet grass and slippery rocks. If you're considering a boat excursion or whale-watching trip, you'll want to hedge your weather bets with a fleece jacket, a hat, and perhaps even gloves. In spring and fall, skip the shorts, swimwear, and water shoes, double up on all the rest, and add a pair of gloves or mittens, a wool hat, and rubber-bottomed shoes or boots. In winter, double up even more, but always make sure to pack clothing you can don or doff in layers. It's far easier to peel off layers than to freeze from lack of them.

The dress code on Mount Desert Island in summer is relaxed and informal. If you feel most

> *No matter how hardy you are, you won't be able to make do at Acadia with just bathing suits, shorts, sandals, and cover-ups; the weather is just too unpredictable, even at the height of summer.*

comfortable changing for dinner, stick to casual chic—nothing fancy. On the other hand, evenings are cool, so shorts won't do, and you'll need a jacket or sweater. Footwear is required in all restaurants. The island has several self-service Laundromats, and most of the campgrounds have laundry rooms, so you shouldn't need to pack masses of underwear.

If you're planning to tent-camp, get out your camping checklist and load up all its items. Other important gear: flashlight, compass and/or GPS, Swiss Army knife, small first-aid kit, binoculars, sunglasses, lip balm, sunscreen, camera (with an extra battery), whistle, small waterproof carryall, plastic water bottle with a belt hook or strap, health-insurance card, hiking maps and guides, and, perhaps most important of all, bug dope! In fact, if you plan to spend any time outdoors in Maine between early May and late September, insect repellent is critical for keeping at bay the state's winged annoyances—especially blackflies, mosquitoes, and midges. Ben's and Cutter's work well, and Avon Skin-So-Soft lotion has become an inadvertent favorite recently (supermarkets and convenience stores seldom carry Avon products, but all carry the clone Skintastic, produced by the manufacturer of Off!). A new product getting good results is Buzz-Off, an all-natural repellent concocted by Alison Lewey, a Passamaquoddy/Maliseet Indian. Home remedies (try at your own risk) include eating garlic, drinking alcohol, or rubbing cider vinegar, tansy leaves, or crushed lemon thyme on your skin.

Not much daunts the blackflies of spring and early summer, but you can lower your appeal by not using perfume, aftershave lotion, or scented shampoo and by wearing light-colored clothing.

ON THE ROAD

The Portland Gateway

For anyone planning to go *just* to Acadia National Park, the primary gateway typically is Bangor. But if you're visiting Acadia as part of a Maine vacation, you might well choose Portland—160–180 miles south of Bar Harbor, depending on your route—as a springboard for getting to Acadia. Portland is about six hours' drive from New York City, about two hours from Boston.

With 64,249 souls (and bedroom satellites that raise Greater Portland to around 200,000), Portland is as big as Maine cities get. This makes for a stimulating, cosmopolitan blend in a most manageable environment—a year-round destination, not just a summer place. Portland is a must-see, a human-level place that offers—among other features—lobsters, lighthouses, and the great outdoors (it is, after all, known as Forest City).

Portland's assets merely start with a striking art museum with a world-class permanent collection; a thriving, handsomely restored harborfront downtown crammed with shops, galleries, and restaurants of every persuasion and flavor; a cultural agenda that can keep you going all day and out all night; a public market modeled on Seattle's Pike Place; several professional sports teams; and countless miles of hikeable, bikeable urban and suburban turf. Meanwhile, along the working waterfront, there's serious business—commercial fishing vessels, long-distance passenger boats, and ferries lugging freight, commuters, and visitors to the islands of Casco Bay.

Portland's downtown, a crooked-finger peninsula projecting into Casco Bay and today defined vaguely by I-295 at its "knuckle," was named Machigonne ("Great Neck") by the Wabanaki, the Native Americans who held sway when English settlers first arrived in 1632. Characteristically, the Brits renamed the region Falmouth (it included present-day Falmouth, Portland, South Portland, Westbrook, and Cape Elizabeth) and the peninsula Falmouth Neck, but it was 130 years before they secured real control of the area. Anglo-French squabbles, spurred by the govern-

Portland Head Light

ments' conflicts in Europe, drew in Wabanaki from Massachusetts to Nova Scotia. Falmouth was only one of the battlegrounds, and a fairly minor one. Relative calm resumed in the 1760s, only to be broken by the stirrings of rebellion centered on Boston. When Falmouth's citizens expressed support for the incipient revolution, the punishment was a 1775 naval onslaught that wiped out 75 percent of the houses. In 1786, Falmouth Neck became Portland, a thriving trading community where shipping flourished until the 1807 Embargo Act. Severing trade and effectively shutting down Portland Harbor for a year and a half, the legislation did more harm to America's fledgling colonies than to the French and British it was designed to punish.

In 1820, when Maine attained statehood, Portland became its capital. The city became a crucial transportation hub with the arrival of the railroad. The Civil War was barely a blip in Portland's history, but the year after it ended, the city suffered a devastating blow: exuberant July Fourth festivities in 1866 sparked a conflagration that virtually leveled the city. The Great Fire spared only the Portland Observatory and a chunk of the West End. Evidence of the city's Victorian rebirth remains today in many downtown neighborhoods.

The city's waterfront revival began in the 1970s and continues today; a once-sorry Congress Street has blossomed as an arts and retail district; public green space is increasing; and an influx of immigrants from Asia, Africa, and Eastern Europe has changed the city's cultural makeup. With the new millennium, Portland is on a roll.

GETTING THERE

By Air

From more than a dozen cities, American Eagle (800/433-7300, www.aa.com), Delta (800/221-1212, www.delta.com), Continental (800/523-3273, www.continental.com), Northwest (800/225-2525, www.nwa.com), United Express (800/241-6522, www.ual.com), and USAirways (800/428-4322, www.usair.com) all arrive at the **Portland International Jetport** (207/774-7301, www.portlandjetport.org). The three-story ter-

minal underwent a multimillion-dollar facelift in 1996 and contains all the amenities—including a restaurant, gift shop, and Avis, Budget, Hertz, and National car-rental agencies (Alamo has an office at the edge of the airport complex). Local and state visitor information is available at a desk (not always staffed; 207/775-5809) between the gates and the baggage-claim area. Baggage-handling offices surround the luggage carousels, but if you have an emergency, contact the Jetport manager at 207/773-8462.

Expect the fare to be about $15 in a metered taxi from the Jetport to the Portland waterfront, $8 to the Portland Transportation Center (Concord Trailways buses and Amtrak), and $9 to the Vermont Transit (Greyhound) terminal at 950 Congress Street. The airport website has a useful **Ground Transportation Guide** with a list of taxi fares and other relevant local information.

The **Portland Explorer bus service** (207/774-9891, www.transportme.org) connects all of Portland's transportation sites—the Jetport, Portland Transportation Center, Vermont Transit, Casco Bay Ferry Lines, and the *Scotia Prince* ferry terminal—following a route that begins on the hour at the Jetport. Cost is $3 one-way or $7 for a day pass.

By Train

After years of negotiations, Amtrak (www.amtrak .com) has dipped its toe into Maine, with four-times-daily round-trips between Boston's North Station and Portland. **The Downeaster,** which stops en route at Wells and Saco (as well as Old Orchard Beach in summer), arrives at the Portland Transportation Center on Thompson Point Road, just west of I-295. A round-trip ticket is $35, but seniors and students receive a 15 percent discount, and children 2–15 ride half-price. From the Transportation Center, Portland's Metro municipal bus service will take you gratis to downtown Portland; just show your Amtrak ticket stub. For information, call Amtrak at 800/872-7245 or visit www.thedowneaster.com.

Amtrak trains from Washington via New York arrive in Boston at South Station (not North Station). Believe it or not, there's no direct link between the two, although it's been promised.

ON THE ROAD

(The Boston-to-Portland Amtrak route was promised for about eight years, so don't hold your breath.) For now, the best solution is to grab a taxi to bridge the gap.

In late 2003, Amtrak and the Concord Trailways bus company launched a unique partnership program. Their $99 "Flexpass" covers six one-way trips between Boston and Portland (or vice versa) on either the bus or the train. You can go one way on the train, one way on the bus—using whichever transport best suits your schedule.

By Bus

Concord Trailways (800/639-3317, www .concordtrailways.com) departs downtown Boston (South Station Transportation Center) and Logan Airport for the 100-mile trip to Portland about 10 times daily, making pickups at all Logan airline terminals (lower level). Rates are very reasonable ($36 round-trip). Portland's bright, modern Trailways terminal is at the Portland Transportation Center on Thompson Point Road, just west of I-295 (Exit 5 northbound, Exit 5A southbound; it's well signposted). The terminal is not particularly convenient to downtown Portland for pedestrians, but as with Amtrak, if you show your Trailways ticket stub to the Metro bus driver (buses stop regularly outside the terminal), you'll have a free ride downtown. If you need to leave a car at the Transportation Center, there's a large lot, with unlimited parking for $2 a day.

Vermont Transit Lines (950 Congress St., Portland, 207/772-6587 or 800/552-8737, www.greyhound.com), a division of Greyhound Bus Lines, serves Maine, the rest of New England, and beyond, connecting with Greyhound routes. The schedule is slightly less convenient than that of Concord Trailways, but rates are slightly lower and you can buy tickets online.

Van Service

Mermaid Transportation (60 Darling Ave., South Portland 04106, 207/772-2509 or 800/ 696-2463, fax 207/772-3919, www.gomermaid .com) operates the best van service between Boston and Portland (and vice versa). Pickup and dropoff, five times daily, are at Portland Jet-

port and Logan Airport, by reservation only. Cost is $50 pp one-way ($95 round-trip); kids under six ride free, bicycles and caged pets are $15 extra. The company also runs daily van service between Manchester, New Hampshire (same price as for Logan; primarily for Southwest Airlines) and the Portland Jetport. (There are *no flights* between Manchester and Portland.)

Highway Access

The major highway access to Portland from the south is the **Maine Turnpike,** which seamlessly connects with the I-95 interstate highway system at the New Hampshire border. I-295, a spur of I-95, runs through Portland, allowing easy access to the Old Port district.

Getting to Acadia

Getting to Acadia National Park from Portland involves some logistical finagling, depending on your choice of transportation.

There is no air service from Portland to Bar Harbor, nor does the Amtrak passenger train go anywhere north of Portland. Thus, bus and car are the only options—unless you'd like to drop $200 for a taxi from Portland to Bar Harbor.

Once you get to Bar Harbor—if you arrive between late June and Columbus Day—you can get around easily with the **Island Explorer** bus service. Other months, you'll want to have a car, or at least a bike, to make the most of your visit.

Vermont Transit (800/552-8737, www .greyhound.com), a division of Greyhound, has one four-hour trip a day in each direction between Portland and Bar Harbor (departing Portland in early afternoon, departing Bar Harbor very early in the morning).

There are several routes for driving from Portland to Mount Desert Island. Route A follows the four-lane Interstate for most of the way, then finishes up on two-lane roads. Route B is fifty-fifty: half Interstate, half two-lane roads. Route C is almost all on two-lane roads—but it's also the most scenic. As with most other Maine auto explorations, it's particularly helpful to use the De-Lorme *Maine Atlas and Gazetteer* ($19.95, www.delorme.com).

Remember that published distances can be deceptive—whereas the Turnpike and the Interstate have 65 and 60 mph limits, you'll never average even 55 mph on the two-lane roads.

For **Route A,** depart Portland northward on the Maine Turnpike (I-495), toward Gray and Lewiston-Auburn. Continue on the Turnpike to just south of Augusta, where it meets I-95. Continue on I-95 to Bangor, where you pick up I-395 eastbound toward Holden and Ellsworth (and Acadia). At the end of 395, you're also at the end of four-lane highways. It's two lanes for the rest of the way. Continue on Route 1A toward Ellsworth, Mount Desert Island, and Bar Harbor. (It's 105 miles from Augusta to Bangor.)

For **Route B,** start out the same way from Portland, on the Maine Turnpike (I-495), pick up I-95 south of Augusta, and then take Exit 30, heading toward Route 3 East. (You'll now be on two-lane roads for the rest of the way.) You'll need to go through downtown Augusta and negotiate two roundabouts before reaching Route 3, on the east side of the Kennebec River. Continue on Route 3 through rolling farmland to Belfast, where it joins Route 1. (You're actually going northeast, but it feels like north.) Continue on Route 1/Route 3 to Ellsworth, and then Route 3 to Bar Harbor.

Route C is the coastal route, where you'll be winding through and skirting small communities the whole way. This route lends itself to (no, requires!) stops—for photos, for exploring, for shopping, for overnights. Stopping only for lunch and restrooms, you'll still need to allow five or six hours from Portland to Bar Harbor. And all bets are off on Friday afternoon in summer, when towns such as Wiscasset and Camden can be major bottlenecks. (They're lovely towns, though—definitely worth a stop.)

To take Route C from Portland, you can start right off on two-lane Route 1, or you can go north on I-295 and I-95 (four lanes) to Brunswick, then cut over when you see the Coastal Route 1 sign. Follow Route 1 the rest of the way—through Bath, Wiscasset, Newcastle, Waldoboro, Thomaston, Rockland, Rockport, Camden, Belfast, Searsport, Bucksport, and on to Ellsworth, where you'll split off onto Route 3 and head for Mount Desert Island.

Between Brunswick and Rockland, down each of the "fingers" east of Route 1, are even more towns and villages—Harpswell, Phippsburg, Georgetown, Boothbay Harbor, Damariscotta, Friendship, and Cushing.

Which brings us to the bottom line: You could spend *weeks* visiting Portland and making your way from there to Acadia!

ON THE ROAD

The Bangor Gateway

The lumber capital of the world in the 19th century, Bangor (BAN-gore), with a population of 31,473, is still northern Maine's magnet for commerce and culture—the big city for the northern three-quarters of the state, including Mount Desert Island. Chief draws now in this region are the 80-store Bangor Mall (and surrounding shops), Bangor International Airport, and the academic, athletic, and artistic activities of the University of Maine campus, in Orono, eight miles northeast. The county seat for Penobscot County, downtown Bangor is awakening from a 1960s slump typical of many urban areas, and today you can stroll alongside Kenduskeag Stream, duck into museums, shops, and restaurants, and spend a comfortable night in the city's heart.

Bangor was incorporated in 1791; when explorer Samuel de Champlain landed here in 1604 (the same year he reached Mount Desert Island), the Queen City bore the Native American name of Kenduskeag, meaning "eel-catching place." (A plaque downtown, next to Kenduskeag Stream, commemorates Champlain's feat.)

In the late 19th century, when the lumber trade moved westward, smaller industries moved into greater Bangor to take up the slack, but a disastrous fire on April 30, 1911, leveled 55 acres of Bangor's commercial and residential neighborhoods, retarding progress for several decades.

© KATHLEEN M. BRANDES

Bangor's Penobscot River skyline

Plenty of elegant architecture from Bangor's lumbering heyday escaped incineration, so if you have time to spare before heading to Acadia National Park, you can still appreciate it by wandering around with a walking-tour brochure available at the Bangor Region Chamber of Commerce (www.bangorregion.com), or take a one-hour Best of Bangor bus tour through the city's seven historic districts, cruising past a giant statue of legendary lumberjack Paul Bunyan, and fine specimens of Victorian, Italianate, Queen Anne, and Greek Revival architecture (See *Exploring Bangor* later in this chapter.)

Horror honcho Stephen King was born in Portland, and has lived in Bangor since 1980, so you may spot him around town (especially at baseball and basketball games). The best-selling author has had his share of odd encounters with off-the-wall devotees—not to mention his 1999 encounter with an out-of-control minivan. So these days, it's best to keep up with him via his website, www.stephenking.com, where you can sign up for email newsletters and download a Maine map labeled with such fictional King locales as Dark Score Lake, Castle Rock, and Lake Kashwakamak.

ACCOMMODATIONS

Despite the revival of Bangor's downtown, beds remain on the scarce side. Most visitors tend to stay in the chain lodgings, closer to the airport and the Bangor Mall. We can only hope for more entrepreneurs to venture downtown.

Downtown

Many of the guests at the **Riverside Inn** (495 State St., Bangor 04401, 207/973-4100 or 800/252-4044, fax 207/947-3591, www.riversidebangor .org) have business at Eastern Maine Medical Center, next door, but the inn is open to everyone (as is the hospital's 24-hour cafeteria). The inn's smoke-free rooms—50 total, including 15 suites—are several notches above generic motel decor. Request a room overlooking the Penobscot River; avoid rooms overlooking the hospital parking lot. Prices are moderate ($80–130, depending on the season) and special discounts are available; no charge for an under-18 child who doesn't need a cot. Phones, a/c, and cable TV. Arrangements can be made for pets. A continental breakfast buffet is included. Open all year.

BANGOR/BREWER

The Charles Inn (20 Broad St., Bangor 04401, 207/992-2820, fax 992-9826, www .thecharlesinn.com) is a National Historic Register hostelry in downtown Bangor. Built in 1873, the four-story hotel underwent extensive restoration in the 1980s (it was the Phenix Inn before it changed hands in 2003). Walls are thick, furnishings are tasteful replicas, and the lobby feels like an English gentlemen's reading room. Request a room overlooking Kenduskeag Stream. Thirty-two doubles (private baths, a/c) go for $89, including breakfast. (One suite/apartment is $139 a night.) Open all year.

Airport and Bangor Mall Areas

Your choice of a hotel or motel near the Bangor Mall or the Bangor Airport may depend on your frequent-flyer memberships. There are lots of options, and most offer free shuttle service to and from the airport.

Linked to the terminal by a skyway, the **Four Points Sheraton Hotel** (308 Godfrey Blvd., Bangor 04401, 207/947-6721 or 800/228-4609, fax 207/941-9761, www.bangorsheraton.com) has 103 rooms ($127–159 d in summer), an average restaurant, and an outdoor pool. Next closest (two miles) to the airport are Marriott's 153-room **Fairfield Inn** (300 Odlin Rd., Bangor

04401, 207/990-0001 or 800/228-2800, fax 207/990-0917, www.marriotthotelreservations .com), with an indoor pool, free HBO and continental breakfast, and reasonable rates ($89–109 d in summer); **Ramada Inn** (357 Odlin Rd., Bangor 04401, 207/947-6961 or 800/445-7787, www.bangorramada.com), with 114 rooms ($139 d), Nautilus, an indoor pool, and business centers; and the 207-room **Holiday Inn** (404 Odlin Rd., Bangor 04401, 207/947-0101 or 800/914-0101, www.holidayinn.com), with a terrific fitness center and pools indoors and out. Kids under 18 stay free, and pets are allowed. Rates are $89–105 d in summer. Next to the Bangor Mall is the 119-room **Hampton Inn** (10 Bangor Mall Blvd., Bangor 04401, 207/990-4400 or 800/998-7829, www.bangorhamptoninn.com), with free movies, local calls, and continental breakfast. Double rooms are $95–115 in summer. **Motel 6** (1100 Hammond St., Bangor 04401, 207/947-6921 or 800/466-8356) and **Super 8 Motel** (462 Odlin Rd., Bangor 04401, 207/945-5681 or 800/800-8000) are also on this side of the city. Pets are allowed at many of the motels.

In Orono

Especially popular with parents of the university crowd is Orono's three-story **Best Western Black Bear Inn** (4 Godfrey Dr., Orono 04473, 207/866-7120 or 800/528-1234, fax 207/866-7433, www.bestwestern.com). Opened in 1990, it has 68 comfortable motel-style rooms and suites with private baths and cable TV. Rates are $105–140 d, including continental breakfast, July–October ($80–140 d other months). Kids under 12 are free; pets are allowed for a small fee. Concertgoers, sports fans, and university visitors fill the rooms during the school year, so book well ahead to get in here then. Open all year. (For more information on Orono, see the sidebars *Exploring Orono and Old Town* and *The University of Maine*.)

En Route to Bar Harbor

When departing Bangor for Bar Harbor, *be sure* to take Route 1A toward Ellsworth (and Bar Harbor), and not toward Hampden and Winterport.

Twelve miles southeast of Bangor (and about 40 miles northwest of Bar Harbor) is **The Lucerne Inn** (Bar Harbor Rd., Rte. 1A, R.R. 3, Box 540, Holden 04429, 207/843-5123 or 800/325-5123, fax 207/843-6138, www.lucerneinn.com), a retrofitted early 19th-century stagecoach hostelry on a 10-acre hilltop overlooking Phillips Lake and the hills beyond. The fall panorama is spectacular. Thanks to a 1920s tourism scheme, the area is known, with a bit of stretching, as Little Switzerland—hence the Lucerne designation. Despite the highway out front, noise is no problem in the antiques-filled, rear-facing rooms. Twenty-one rooms and four suites ($99–199 d July–mid-October, $59–159 other months) have a/c, phones, cable TV, whirlpool tubs, and fireplaces. Outside there's a pool. No pets. The Sunday brunch buffet (9 A.M. –1 P.M.) in the inn's dining room (where moderately priced dinners are served 5–9 P.M. nightly) is a big draw, as is the adjacent golf course. One-night packages, including dinner, are a good idea, as you're in the middle of nowhere and not likely to head out again once you get here.

Campgrounds

On Bangor's western perimeter are two clean, well-managed campgrounds convenient to I-95 and Bangor. The emphasis is on RVs, but tent sites are available. Closest to the city is the 52-site **Paul Bunyan Campground** (1862 Union St., Rte. 222, Bangor 04401, 207/941-1177, paulbunyancampground.com), about three miles northwest of I-95 Exit 47. Facilities at this attractive Good Sampark include a rec hall and huge outdoor heated pool; activities are offered most weekends in midsummer. Leashed pets are welcome (cleanup is required) and noise rules are strictly enforced. Sites (for two adults, two children) are $15 with no hookup, $27 with full hookup. Open mid-April–October.

About two miles farther out on Route 222, **Pleasant Hill Campground** (Rte. 222, 45 Mansell Rd., Hermon 04401, 207/848-5127, www.pleasanthillcampground.com), also a Good Sampark, has 105 sites on 60 acres. Facilities include mini-golf, laundry, play areas, rec room, heated pool, free showers, and a small store. Pets are welcome. Rates are $18–32 (the latter for full hookups), and the campground is open May–mid-October.

FOOD

Although most of Bangor's lodgings are on the outskirts of the city, the best restaurants by far are downtown, and there are enough choices to keep you coming back for seconds.

Bagels and Bread

A downtown landmark since 1978, **Bagel Central** (33 Central St., Bangor 04401, 207/947-1654) is a cheerful spot to meet, greet, and grab some really good handmade bagels (try the blueberry), great deli sandwiches, soups, and more. It's kosher and closed Saturday but open 6 A.M.–6 P.M., Monday–Thursday, 6 A.M.–5:30 P.M. Friday, and 6 A.M.–2 P.M. Sunday.

Just down the street is the other half of the Judeo-Christian tradition, **Franciscan Friars' Bakehouse** (21 Central St., Bangor, 207/947-3770), run by Brother Don and Brother Kenneth. More than 20 kinds of breads emerge from their ovens, with regular "specials." Also available are tasty scones, muffins, cookies, and, at lunchtime, soups and sandwiches. Seats are scarce at the few tables, so expect to do takeout. Bakehouse profits support the friars' missionary work in Mexico. Open 7 A.M.–3 P.M. Wednesday–Friday and 8 A.M.–2 P.M. Saturday.

Downtown Dining

Bangor's best fine-dining experience is at the **New Moon** (49 Park St., Bangor, 207/990-2233), a handsome bistro-style place with brick walls and Art Deco motifs. The menu fits the fusion label, with Thai bouillabaisse, black bean cakes, and a half-dozen other artfully presented entrée options ($17–27). The lobster-and-corn-fritter appetizer ($6.95) is outstanding. Open for dinner Tuesday–Saturday, 5–9 P.M. The bar opens for happy hour at 4 P.M.

Creativity and serendipity are the bywords at **J. B. Parker's** (167 Center St., Bangor, 207/947-0167), a casual, bright, 60-seat restaurant-cum-art-gallery near St. Joseph Hospital.

Entrées are in the $16–22 range, including choices for carnivores and vegetarians. Reservations are essential, especially on weekends. Quiet live music provides background Thursday–Saturday. Open for lunch weekdays and for dinner Monday–Saturday.

Reservations are also essential at **Thistle's** (175 Exchange St., Maliseet Gardens Plaza, Bangor, 207/945-5480, www.thistlesrestaurant.com). Creative continental entrées with a Latin flair ($13–23), plus excellent homemade breads and desserts, have drawn the crowds, especially at lunchtime. A pianist plays quietly in the background evenings Thursday–Saturday. Open 11 A.M.–2:30 P.M. and 4:30–9:30 P.M. Monday–Saturday all year.

Leslie Thistle—former owner of the eponymous Thistle's—has since gone on to co-found (with Shane McCarthy) **Café Nouveau** (84 Hammond St., Bangor, 207/942-3336), the city's first wine bar and a major hit the minute it opened in 2000. The only dilemma here is trying to decide among the 100-plus wines-by-the-glass (specialty beers, too). Tapas-size (but adequate) dinner entrées (served after 4 P.M.) keep the cost down ($10–14). Nice bistro-type ambience in a retrofitted furniture store. Take home a loaf of the house specialty, Thistle Bread, at $2.75. Open 11 A.M.–11 P.M. Tuesday–Thursday, and until midnight Friday and Saturday. No reservations.

A prime spot for view-and-brew, and one of the liveliest venues in town, is the waterfront **Sea Dog Brewing Co.** (26 Front St., Bangor, 207/947-8004, www.seadogbrewing.com), where you can dine on the deck overlooking the Penobscot River in summer. The menu is pub fare with a flair (dinner entrées are $9–16 and burgers and pub sandwiches run $6–7.50), and the award-winning lagers and ales are superb. Try Old East India, Hazelnut Porter, or Old Gollywobbler. Attractively decorated with tongue-and-groove pine on the inside, the 540-seat brewpub serves lunch and dinner 11:30 A.M.–1 A.M. daily. Live music Thursday–Saturday.

The major claim to fame at **Miller's** (427 Main St., Bangor, 207/942-6361) is its 200-item salad bar—all you can eat for $7.95 at lunch, $11.95 at dinner. (It's not included with all entrées.) This veteran 400-seat restaurant is open 11 A.M.–10 P.M. daily all year.

Ethnic Restaurants

Amazingly, the Bangor area supports more than half a dozen Chinese restaurants, of which the best is **Oriental Jade** (55 Stillwater Ave., Bangor, 207/947-6969, www.orientaljade.com), in the Bangor Mall area (next to the Hoyts Bangor Cinema). Established in the late 1970s, Oriental Jade has developed a loyal year-round clientele. No reservations are needed, and it's open 11 A.M.–10:30 P.M. Go for the huge buffet, laid out until 4 P.M. In 1996, the owners opened a branch, **Noodles and Company** (492 Wilson Street, Rte. 1A, 207/989-9898), across the river in Brewer.

Maine's relative scarcity of ethnic restaurants makes cheerful, family-owned **Bahaar Pakistani Restaurant** (23 Hammond St., Bangor, 207/945-5979) especially welcome in the downtown area. Vegetarians find lots of options among the 70-plus reasonably priced appetizers, biryanis, and curries, which you can order hot, hotter, and hottest. Takeout available; full liquor license. Reservations are advisable Friday and Saturday. Open 11:30 A.M.–2:30 P.M. and 5–10 P.M. Monday–Friday; 11:30–3 P.M. and 5–10 P.M. Saturday.

Three blocks from Bahaar, another downtown South Asian option is **Taste of India** (68 Main St., Bangor, 207/945-6865), an enduring local favorite that changed hands in 2002. It's open 11 A.M.–3 P.M. and 5–10 P.M. Monday –Saturday, as well as 5–10 P.M. Sunday. No reservations; beer and wine only.

Ichiban (226 Third St., at Union, Bangor, 207/262-9308) jumped into (and filled) the gap left by the sudden departure of another Japanese restaurant. This one's a winner, with a great attitude, a large menu, and superb sushi. It's open for lunch 11 A.M.–2:30 P.M. and for dinner 4:30 P.M. Monday–Saturday; it opens for dinner at 4 P.M. on Sunday.

Maine Governor John E. Baldacci cut his teeth, as it were, on the Italian specialties at **Momma Baldacci's** (12 Alden St., Bangor, 207/945-5813), his family's restaurant just north of I-95 Exit 48. (If you're downtown, follow Broadway—Route 15—to just beyond the Interstate and turn right onto Alden.) Nowadays, Momma is here only in spirit (she died in 2002), but the place draws a crowd looking for large portions of "tomato Italian" cuisine. Baldacci, formerly a U.S. congressman from Maine's Second District, held frequent "spaghetti suppers" during his congressional and gubernatorial campaigns—tossing pasta and political patter simultaneously. It certainly hasn't hurt the restaurant. Entrées are $6–13. Open 11 A.M.–2 P.M. and 4:30–8 P.M. Monday–Friday and 11 A.M.–8:30 P.M. Saturday all year.

Bangor Airport Area

Across from the airport, **Captain Nick's** (1165 Union St., Rte. 222, Bangor, 207/942-6444) is well known for seafood, including a triple-lobster special, but it also serves up steak, chicken, and pasta. Nothing fancy here, but the fish is definitely fresh. There's live entertainment at 7 P.M. Saturday in the lounge. Reservations are a good idea on summer weekends. It's open 11 A.M.–9:45 P.M. Monday–Thursday, 11 A.M.–10:45 P.M. Friday and Saturday, and 11 A.M.–9 P.M. Sunday; open until 10 P.M. in summer.

Local Color

Convenient to I-95 Exit 44, **Dysart's** (Coldbrook Rd., Hermon 04401, 207/942-4878) is a 60-acre truckers' destination resort—you can grab some grub, shower, shop, phone home, play video games, fuel up, and even sneak a bit of shut-eye. Breakfast is available round the clock, and three tons of baked beans are served every year. A 20-ounce(!!) sirloin goes for $15.95. For real flavor, opt for the truckers' dining room, where the music is country and dozens of bleary-eyed drivers have reached the end of their transcontinental treks. If you're here with a carload of family or friends, order an 18-Wheeler, the mother of all banana splits: 18 scoops of ice cream on a banana bed with a collection of toppings ($13.95). No question, Dysart's is unique. It's been in business since 1967 and stays open 24 hours every day, all year.

In Orono and Old Town

Catering to the notoriously slim budgets of college students, eating establishments in Orono keep their menus affordable. Three of the most popular spots are on "restaurant row"—Mill Street, just off Route 2 (Main Street).

Orono's veteran restaurant is **Pat's Pizza** (11 Mill St., Orono 04473, 207/866-2111), a statewide, family-owned chain founded in Orono in July 1931 by C.D. "Pat" Farnsworth. Then known as Farnsworth's Café, it became Pat's Pizza in 1953. Pizza toppings are endless, even sauerkraut and capers. Subs, calzones, burgers, and "tomato Italian" entrées are also on the menu. Open 6 A.M.–1 A.M. Monday–Saturday and 7 A.M.–1 A.M. Sunday all year.

Tex-Mex is the rule at **Margarita's** (15 Mill St., Orono 04473, 207/866-4863, www.margs .com), sibling of four other Maine restaurants turning out some of the state's best—you guessed it—margaritas. This popular student hangout is open 4 P.M. to 1 A.M. daily all year. Busiest time is happy hour, 4–7 P.M. weekdays. No reservations, but you can call ahead and put your name on the waiting list—a wise idea on weekends. Every full-moon night, there's a restaurant-wide party—with donated prizes and profits given to local charities.

The newest kid on the block is **Thai Orchid** (28 Mill St., Orono 04473, 207/866-4200), cashing in on the Thai trend. Pad Thai, of course, is on the menu ($5.95), as are tons of rice dishes, but so are more unusual items—presented with flair. Duck tamarind is $14, and "dancing squid" is $11.95. Open 11 A.M.–9 P.M. Monday–Thursday and until 10 P.M. Friday and Saturday; 4–9 P.M. Sunday.

Even though the drinking age is 21, every college town manages to have a variation on the pub theme. At the **Bear Brewpub** (36 Main St., Orono 04473, 207/866-2739), try a mug of Bear Brew Blonde, Midnight Stout, or I'll Be Darned Amber Ale. The menu changes daily; try the ribs. On request, they'll give you a free, 10-minute brewery tour. The Bear is open 11:30 A.M.–11 P.M. daily all year.

The color doesn't get much more local than at the **Oronoka Restaurant** (381 Main St., Orono 04473, 207/866-2169), although the customers tend to be not so much locals as college students, airline pilots, and anyone else looking for the funkiest experience in the area. Word-of-mouth does the trick. Service can be slow to insulting to nonexistent, but steaks are humongous in this barn of a place. For a special occasion, call ahead and you'll have a free cake for dessert. The restaurant is open 5 P.M.–midnight Monday–Friday and 1 P.M.–midnight Saturday and Sunday, all year.

Over in Old Town, not much can match the Penobscot River view from the **Chocolate Grille** (301 Main St., Old Town 04468, 207/827-8971, www.chocolategrille.com), which urges diners to "celebrate the American bar and grille." (I always thought a grille was on the front end of a car.) Burgers and sandwiches run $6–9 (try the chicken prosciutto on focaccia) and dinner entrées are in the $10–19 range (pasta, seafood, and even a garlic-and-herb-stuffed prime rib). Portions are hefty. Save room for a chocolate soufflé. "The Grille" is open 11 A.M.–12:30 A.M. Monday–Saturday and 11 A.M.–10 P.M. Sunday. Reservations are wise on weekends. In 2003, another Chocolate Grille opened on Main Street (Rte. 1) in Searsport—with the same menu but, alas, with no view.

EXPLORING BANGOR

If you're passing through Bangor en route to Acadia, and decide to stay awhile, you can explore the city by picking up the Bangor Historical Society's free walking-tour brochure at the chamber of commerce (or the Bangor Museum gift shop) and following the signs. Numbered signs mark stops on the east-side tour, lettered signs mark those on the west-side tour. The west-side tour takes slightly longer and is more spread out; Stephen King's Italianate villa (not identified by name in the brochure) is one of the stops on this route.

A distinctive westside landmark is the National Historic Register **Thomas Hill Standpipe,** a squat, shingle-style 1897 water tower on one of the city's highest points. One of seven

ON THE ROAD

THE UNIVERSITY OF MAINE

Visitors with who have the time en route to Acadia will find the 660-acre campus of the University of Maine (www.umaine.edu) in Orono well worth a visit. This venerable institution was founded in 1862 as the State College of Agriculture and Mechanical Arts. It received its current designation in 1897 and now awards bachelor's, master's, and doctoral degrees.

One of the newer buildings, built in 1986, is the architecturally dramatic **Maine Center for the Arts,** the year-round site of concerts, dramas, and other events with big-name performers. The box office for the 1,629-seat Hutchins Concert Hall is open 9 A.M.–4 P.M. weekdays; 207/581-1755 or 800/622-8499 (ticket orders). Tickets are also available online at www.MaineCenter-fortheArts.org.

Cleverly occupying part of the center is the small **Hudson Museum** (5746 Maine Center for the Arts, Belgrade and Beddington Rds., University of Maine, Orono 04469, 207/581-1901, www.umaine.edu/hudsonmuseum), spotlighting traditional and contemporary world cultures in a series of well-designed galleries on three floors. Frequent special exhibits augment an eclectic 8,000-item archaeological and ethnographic collection that includes Peruvian silver stickpins, African fetish dolls, Navajo looms, and the superlative Palmer Gallery of Pre-Hispanic Mexican and Central American Culture. An interactive corner in the Penobscot Primer Project lets visitors learn a few words in the Penobscot (Native American) language, and a small shop (207/581-1903) stocks unusual global gifts. Admission is free. The museum is open 9 A.M.–4 P.M. Tuesday–Friday and 11 A.M.–4 P.M. Saturday. It's also open about an hour prior to performances in the adjoining Hutchins Concert Hall.

The solar system takes center stage at the **Maynard F. Jordan Planetarium** (5781 Wingate Hall, Munson Rd., University of Maine, Orono 04469, 207/581-1341, fax 581-1314, hotline 207/581-1348, umainesky.com), on the second floor of Wingate Hall (close to the Maine Center for the Arts). Multimedia presentations and laser-light shows, usually lasting an hour under a 20-foot dome, help explain the workings of our universe and bring astronomy to life. Comet collisions and rocketing asteroids keep the kids transfixed. Unless there's a dramatic cosmic event, there are no summer programs. During the school year, programs usually occur at 7 P.M. Fridays and at 2 P.M. Sundays. You'll need to call ahead to confirm the schedule and reserve space in the 45-seat audito-

tanks used by the Bangor Water District, the tower holds 1.75 million gallons. The view from the observation platform is stupendous, but unfortunately it's open to the public only four times a year (usually March, May, July, and October). Contact the Water District (207/947-4516) for dates and times.

On Main Street, next to the Bangor Region Chamber of Commerce office, stands a 31-foot-high statue of the mythical lumberjack Paul Bunyan, allegedly born in Bangor on February 12, 1834. Built of steel and fiberglass and weighing 3,200 pounds, the colorful statue was erected in 1959, during the city's 125th anniversary. Inside the base is a time capsule due to be opened in 2084. Kids can run and play in adjacent **Paul Bunyan Park.**

Tours

If you'd rather not guide yourself, take the **Downtown Bangor Architecture Tour,** departing at noon each Thursday from mid June–August. Cost is $5 adults, $4 seniors, free for children. Tickets are available at the chamber of commerce and at the Bangor Museum, where the tour begins.

What better way to explore Stephen King's hometown than by reserving a space for **Downtown Bangor by Lamplight: A Ghostly Candlelight Walking Tour.** Tours occur on full-moon nights July–September, and at 7 P.M. each Thursday in October. You'll start out from the Thomas A. Hill House, but reserve through the Bangor Museum (207/942-1900). Cost is $5 adults, $4 seniors, free for children.

rium. Pick up tickets 15 minutes beforehand. Admission to scheduled events is $4 adults, $3 seniors and students (no credit cards). The best place to park is in the Steam Plant parking lot, on College Avenue (Rte. 2A).

At the eastern edge of the campus, the six-acre **Lyle E. Littlefield Ornamentals Trial Garden** (Rangeley Rd., University of Maine, Orono 04469, 207/581-3112) contains more than 2,500 plant species, many being tested for winter durability. The best time to come is early June, when crab apples and lilacs put on their perennial show. The garden is open daily, all year, sunrise to sunset; bring a picnic.

Other campus sites for horticulture fans are the 10-acre riverside **Fay Hyland Arboretum**, on the western edge of campus (207/581-2976), and the **Roger Clapp Greenhouses,** in the center of campus, open 8 A.M.–4:30 P.M. weekdays (207/581-3112).

About midcampus (close to Sebago Rd.) is the **Page Farm and Home Museum** (207/581-4100, www.ume.maine.edu/~pfhm/), located in a late-19th-century barn older than the university itself. Three floors of exhibits cover household items (in re-created rooms), farm equipment, and ice-harvesting and veterinary tools—a slice of

19th-century rural life. Also part of the museum are a one-room schoolhouse, a blacksmith shop, a gift shop (in a replica general store), and gardens featuring heirloom plants. In mid-May, the museum holds a weekend sale of familiar and esoteric herbs. A six-pack of plants goes for about $2.25, and proceeds support the museum's garden programs. During Maine's annual Open Farm Day (last Sunday in July, when farms around the state hold open houses), the museum hosts a potluck retro picnic, focusing on food of yesteryear (pre-1940). Bring your own blanket and old-fashioned (not old) food to share. It's a fun event (9 A.M.–4 P.M.), with all kinds of activities and demonstrations. The museum is open 9 A.M.–4 P.M. daily in summer; it's open the same hours Tuesday–Saturday during the school year. Admission is free.

Campus **parking** is a major sticking point at the university, so you'll need a visitor parking permit for a daytime visit. A one-day permit (free) is available at the Public Safety office on Rangeley Road, on the eastern edge of the campus. (From Route 2, coming from downtown Orono, turn left onto Rangeley Road and watch for the Public Safety building on your right.) You won't need a permit at night or on weekends.

If time is limited, at least try to catch one of the **Best of Bangor bus tours** (9:30 A.M.–noon each Tuesday and Saturday, early June–August) through the city's historic districts, which are sponsored by the **Bangor Historical Society.** The tour—narrated by "Teddy Fields," a 19th-century Irish immigrant who made it big in the Gold Rush before returning to Bangor—includes visits to the Thomas A. Hill House and the Bangor Museum. Cost is $20 adults, $15 seniors, $8 children. Buses depart from the Bangor Museum, where you can buy tickets.

Museums

Seemingly overnight (well, over a three-year span), Bangor's up-and-coming downtown has sprouted museums—the University of Maine

moved its art museum here, the Bangor Historical Society has a new space, and there's a splendid children's museum.

In 2003, the Bangor Historical Society celebrated the opening of the 4,500-square-foot **Bangor Museum and Center for History** (6 State St., Bangor 04401, 207/942-1900, www .bangorhistorical.org) in the Eastern Trust Building beside Kenduskeag Stream. Designed to house and display an extensive collection stored away for years, the museum will have thematic annual exhibits, of which the first was "From Away: Exploring Bangor's Cultural Heritage." The museum is open 10 A.M.–4 P.M. Tuesday–Saturday; admission is free.

Also owned by the Bangor Historical Society, and used as its headquarters, is the Greek

EXPLORING ORONO AND OLD TOWN

Home of the University of Maine, **Orono** is part college town, part generic Maine village—and a fine example of the tail wagging the dog. More than 10,000 university students converge on this Bangor suburb every year, fairly overwhelming the town's 9,112 year-round residents.

Called Stillwater when it was settled by Europeans in the 1770s, the town adopted the name of Penobscot Indian chief Joseph Orono and incorporated in 1806. By 1840—just as with Bangor, eight miles to the southwest—prosperity descended, thanks to the huge Penobscot River log drives spurring the lumber

COURTESY MAINE OFFICE OF TOURISM

Horses pull a wagon tour across the covered bridge at Leonard's Mills, Bradley.

industry's heyday. A stroll along Orono's Main Street Historic District, especially between Maplewood Avenue and Pine Street, attests to the timber magnates' success; the gorgeous homes are a veritable catalog of *au courant* architectural styles: Italianate, Greek Revival, Queen Anne, Federal, and Colonial Revival. Contact Orono's municipal office for a free copy of *A Walking Tour of Orono,* a dated but still useful booklet on the town's cultural and architectural history.

There are other sights worth a look. Located in the former St. Mary's Catholic Church, the **Old Town Museum** (138 S. Main St., P.O. Box 375, Old Town 04468, 207/827-7256, www.oldtown.org/museum) has well-organized exhibit areas focusing primarily on Old Town's pivotal role in the 19th-century lumber industry. Other displays feature woodcarvings by sculptor Bernard Langlais, an Old Town native, and an excellent collection of Native American sweetgrass baskets. Each year, temporary exhibits add to the mix. Try to attend one of the regular Sunday-afternoon (2 P.M.) programs—anything from carving, weaving, beadwork, and quilting demonstrations to handbell concerts and historical lectures. Admission is free for the museum and its programs. The museum is open Wednesday–Sunday 1–5 P.M., June–September, except for the week of Independence Day.

Indian Island's **Penobscot Nation Museum** (5 Center St., Indian Island 04468, 207/827-4153, www.penobscotnation.org/museum/), a fledgling

facility, has exhibits of baskets, beadwork, tribal dress, antique tools, and birch-bark canoes. The museum theoretically is open 10 A.M.–3 P.M. Monday, Wednesday, Thursday, Saturday, and Sunday, but the schedule is very unpredictable, so call ahead to check on opening hours. (The museum is on the right soon after you cross the bridge to Indian Island from Old Town.)

In the island's Protestant cemetery is the grave of **Louis Sockalexis,** a Native American baseball star at the turn of the 20th century. Allegedly, his acceptance onto Cleveland's baseball team spurred management to dub them the Indians—a name that obviously has stuck.

As you drive around the island, you'll see several homemade signs outside the homes of basketmakers and other craftspeople. Stop in and take a look—you just might find a treasure to take home.

Officially known as the **Maine Forest and Logging Museum,** 265-acre Leonard's Mills re-creates a late-18th-century logging village, with a sawmill, blacksmith shop, covered bridge, log cabin, and other buildings. The site is accessible late April–October, sunrise to sunset, but the best times to visit are during the museum's special-events days: 10 A.M.–3 P.M. Saturday July–September—when dozens of museum volunteers don period dress and bring the village to life. Demonstrations, beanhole bean dinners, hayrides, antique games, and even 1790s political debates are all part of the mix. The season's biggest events are **Living History Days,** a two-day festival the first full weekend in July and the first weekend in October. Admission to special programs is $5 adults, $1 children 12 and under; other times, admission is $2, payable on the honor system. For more info, contact the Maine Forest and Logging Museum (P.O. Box 456, Orono 04473, 207/581-2871, fax 827-3641, www.leonardsmills.com). The museum is on Penobscot Experimental Forest Rd., in Bradley, 1.3 miles southeast of Route 178. It's directly across the river from Orono, but the only bridges are north (Old Town/Milford) and south (Bangor/Brewer).

The world's oldest continuously operating canoe manufacturer, **Old Town Canoe Company,** still has its big old 200,000-square-foot factory on Middle Street, close to the Penobscot River in downtown Old Town. Incorporated in 1904, the company was turning out as many as 400 boats a month two years later. In 1915, the list of dealers included Harrod's in London and the Hudson's Bay Company in far northern Canada, and Old Town supplied canoes to expeditions in Egypt and the Arctic. Now Old Town is a division of Johnson Outdoors (part of the Johnson Wax empire). Quality is high at Old Town, so their boats are pricey, but you can visit the **Old Town Canoe Visitor Center** (239 Main St., Old Town 04468, 207/827-1530, www.oldtowncanoe.com) and look over the supply of "factory-blemished" canoe and kayak models. You're likely to end up with a real bargain—usually at least 20 percent discounts. There's also a full line of paddles, jackets, compasses, and other accessories. The shop is open 9 A.M.–6 P.M. Monday–Saturday and 10 A.M.–3 P.M. Sunday, March–November; 9 A.M.–5 P.M. Monday–Saturday, November–February.

The **Wabanaki Arts Center Gallery** (240 Main St., P.O. Box 3253, Old Town 04468, 207/827-0391, www.umaine.edu/hudsonmuseum/miba) is a project of the nonprofit Maine Indian Basketmakers Alliance (MIBA). The attractively laid-out gallery/shop sells superb sweetgrass and brownash baskets, as well as sculpture and handcrafted jewelry. Also available are copies of *A Wabanaki Guide to Maine: A Visitor's Guide to Native Ameri-*

can Culture in Maine ($10), an 86-page handbook to cultural sites and resources related to Maine's Passamaquoddy, Maliseet, Micmac, and Penobscot tribes. The gallery is open 10 A.M.–5 P.M. Monday–Wednesday, Friday, and Saturday. It stays open until 7 P.M. Thursday.

Parks and Preserves

The best times to visit **Sunkhaze Meadows National Wildlife Refuge** (Milford, mailing address 1033 S. Main St., Rte. 2, Old Town 04468, 207/827-6138, www.sunkhaze.org) are in the spring (when the water is high and nearly two dozen warbler species appear) and during the autumn waterfowl migration. But hunting is allowed in the refuge in the fall, so wear a hunter-orange hat and/or vest (except on Sunday, when hunting is banned statewide). More than 200 bird species have been spotted here; moose and beaver are common. There are four nature trails (the Johnson Brook Trail has a boardwalk), and a platform overlooking Maine's second-largest peat bog (wear boots or waterproof shoes). The best way to explore the refuge is to paddle the five-mile stretch of Sunkhaze Stream that bisects the refuge. Allow about six hours for this expedition, putting in on Stud Mill Road (park in the lot at the Ash Landing trailhead; do not park on the Stud Mill Road) and taking out on Route 2. (You'll need two vehicles for this.) Don't forget insect repellent. Access is via the unpaved Stud Mill Road or County Road, north of Milford. No staff or facilities are available at the 10,300-acre refuge; visit or call the Old Town office for information and a map, or visit the website. The office usually is open 7:30 A.M.–4 P.M. Monday–Friday. The turnoff to the refuge is about five miles north of I-95 Exit 51 (Stillwater); go north on Route 2A and cross the Penobscot River to Milford. In winter, refuge trails are open for cross-country skiing and snowmobiling.

In 2003, a mile-long boardwalk was inaugurated to provide access to the almost primeval wonderland known as the **Orono Bog,** a mile-square offshoot of the Bangor City Forest, which straddles the Bangor/Orono boundary. You get to the boardwalk from Bangor the same way you
(continued on next page)

ON THE ROAD

EXPLORING ORONO AND OLD TOWN (cont'd)

get to the City Forest: Stillwater Avenue (Rte. 2A) past the Bangor Mall (toward Orono) and after about a mile, turn left onto Tripp Drive just before the Orono town line. Watch for Bangor City Forest and Orono Bog signs. (If you're coming from Orono, take Stillwater Ave., Rte. 2, southward toward Bangor and turn right onto Tripp Drive just after you cross the Orono line into Bangor.) Park in the City Forest lot, slather on some insect repellent, and take the East Trail a short distance to the boardwalk (pick up info from the kiosk). As you walk deeper into the peat bog—estimated to be 10,000 years old—seven interpretive signs explain some of the bog's intriguing natural history. Rhodora bushes are the spring highlight, and wild orchids are blooming in July. Birders should be sure to bring binoculars. The wheelchair-accessible boardwalk is open 7 A.M.–7 P.M. daily in summer, 8 A.M. to 5 P.M. in the spring and fall. Bicycles and dogs are prohibited. For more information, visit www.oronobogwalk.org.

Revival **Thomas A. Hill House** (159 Union St., Bangor 04401, 207/942-5766), built by a wealthy attorney in 1836. Listed on the National Register of Historic Places, the handsome brick building on the corner of High Street has been restored to Victorian elegance, with period furnishings, Maine paintings, and special exhibits. Hour-long guided tours occur 10 A.M.–4 P.M. Tuesday–Saturday, April to mid-December. Admission is $4 adults, $3 seniors, and free for children 12 and under (little kids may get squirmy here).

Squirmy kids are *never* a problem at the **Maine Discovery Museum** (74 Main St., Bangor 04401, mailing address P.O. Box 64, Bangor 04402, 207/262-7200, www.mainediscoverymuseum.org). Opened in January 2001 after several years of planning, fundraising, and construction, the museum occupies more than 22,000 square feet on three floors of the former Freese's Department Store. Seven permanent interactive exhibit areas feature nature, geography, art, science, anatomy, Maine children's literature, and music. It all awaits in this multimillion-dollar facility—the largest children's museum north of Boston. Kids can operate pulleys, open locks and dams, create paintings or sculptures, and explore a beaver dam from the underside. Most exciting are the global adventures in a Peruvian classroom, a Ghanaian market, and an Australian outback campsite. Special programs are scheduled for children and families throughout the year. Ad-

mission is $5.50. The museum is open noon–5 P.M. Monday, 9:30 A.M.–5 P.M. Tuesday–Saturday, and 11 A.M.–5 P.M. Sunday.

Children also love the **Cole Land Transportation Museum** (405 Perry Rd., Bangor 04401, 207/990-3600, www.colemuseum.org), a sprawling facility on the city's outskirts founded by Bangor trucking magnate Galen Cole. More than 200 19th- and 20th-century vehicles—just about anything that has ever rolled across Maine's landscape—fill the museum. Besides vintage cars, there are fire engines, tractors, logging vehicles, baby carriages, even a replica railroad station. A gift shop stocks transportation-related items. Admission is $5 adults, $3 seniors, free for anyone under 19. The museum, located near the junction of I-95 and I-395, is open 9 A.M.–5 P.M. daily May–mid-November.

The University of Maine moved the art museum downtown from its Orono campus in late 2002 to gain more exhibit space. And what a space it is—the historic Norumbega Hall, a Sears store in its previous life. Located across from Bangor City Hall and backing up to Kenduskeag Stream, the **University of Maine Museum of Art** (40 Harlow St., Bangor 04401, 207/561-3350, www.umma.umaine.edu) has a rich permanent collection of nearly 6,000 artworks, devoted primarily (but definitely not exclusively) to such Maine artists as Winslow Homer, John Marin, Marsden Hartley, and Andrew Wyeth. UMMA is one of seven stops on the **Maine Art Museum Trail,** highlighting the state's best collections. The museum is open 9 A.M.–6 P.M. Tuesday–Saturday and 11 A.M.–5 P.M. Sunday. Admission is $3. (There's ample parking, but be aware that Harlow Street is one-way in front of the museum.)

Arts and Entertainment

More than a century ago, when cabin-feverish lumberjacks roared into Bangor for R&R, they were apt to patronize Fan Jones's notorious "establishment" on Harlow Street. Needless to say, things have changed. Adult entertainment is still available in the city, but the focus is very much on higher-brow stuff.

The **Bangor Symphony Orchestra** (207/942-5555 or 800/639-3221, www.bangorsymphony.com), founded in 1896, has an enviable reputation as one of the country's oldest and best community orchestras. During the regular season, late September to mid-May, monthly concerts are presented weekends at the University of Maine's Maine Center for the Arts, in Orono. Individual concert tickets are $12–37 for adults. *The Nutcracker Ballet* is performed on an early December weekend.

The biggest local film multiplex is **Hoyts Bangor Cinemas 10** (557 Stillwater Ave., Bangor 04401, next to the Bangor Mall, 207/942-1303). Three or four of the 10 screens usually have matinees, with lower prices than evening flicks. Also in the mall area, **Movie City 8 Cinemas** (268 Odlin Rd., Bangor 04401, 207/941-0000) has eight screens and bargain-basement ticket prices ($6 for art and foreign films, $3 for first-run flicks). On Thursday, bring your own bowl and get free popcorn.

Festivals and Events

In April (usually the third Saturday), the **Kenduskeag Stream Canoe Race** is an annual (since 1969) 16.5-mile spring-runoff race sponsored by Bangor Parks and Recreation (207/947-1018). It draws upwards of 700 canoes and thousands of spectators and finishes in downtown Bangor. The best location for spotting action is Six Mile Falls. Take Broadway (Rte. 15) about six miles northwest of downtown.

Late July into early August, the **Bangor State Fair,** held in Bass Park, is a huge 10-day affair with agricultural and craft exhibits, a carnival, fireworks, sinful food, and big-name live music. This is a big deal and attracts thousands from all over northern Maine.

Parks and Recreation

Parks pop up everywhere in Bangor—from vest-pocket oases to a downtown pedestrian mall to a sprawling garden cemetery. Beyond the city in all directions (but particularly north) lie preserves and countless recreational opportunities.

In a state where burial grounds usually command views to die for, the standout is **Mount Hope Cemetery,** consecrated in 1836 and easily Maine's loveliest. Among the prominent Mainers interred here is Civil War–era U.S. Vice President Hannibal Hamlin. The movie based on Stephen King's 1983 novel *Pet Sematary* was filmed here. Inspired by the design of Mount Auburn Cemetery in Cambridge, Massachusetts, 254-acre Mount Hope is more park than cemetery—with gardens, ponds, bridges, paved paths, lots of greenery, a few picnic tables, and wandering deer. Hence, even if the idea seems a bit macabre, Mount Hope (open 7:30 A.M. to sunset daily all year)falls under the category of Parks and Recreation. The Bangor Historical Society (207/942-5766) sponsors an hour-long guided walking tour of the cemetery at 2 P.M. on the first Saturday of the month, June–October. Cost is $5 adults, $4 seniors, free for children. The entrance to the green-fenced cemetery is at 1038 State St. (Rte. 2), about .25 mile east of Hogan Road. Tours begin at the Mount Hope superintendent's office.

Built over the meandering Kenduskeag Stream, right downtown, are two block-long parks: **Norumbega Parkway,** with a war memorial and benches, and **Hamlin Mall,** with cannons, the Champlain landing plaque, and a bronze statue of Hannibal Hamlin.

A waterfall and a fountain are the focus at **Cascade Park** (State St., Rte. 2, .3 mile east of Eastern Maine Medical Center), where you can collapse on a bench or grab a picnic table and chill out.

The best kid place is **Hayford Park** (115 13th St., off Union St.), northwest of downtown, where the Gothic-looking **Bangor Creative Playground,** designed by Robert Leathers, has a maze of entertaining wooden structures to climb in, on, and around. Next to it is the state-of-the-art, 1,500-seat Shawn T. Mansfield baseball stadium, locally dubbed the Field of Screams, since it was underwritten by baseball enthusiast Stephen King.

The best way to check on locations and opening times for municipal swimming pools, tennis courts, and skating rinks is to contact the **Bangor Parks and Recreation Department** (207/947-1018).

At 650 acres, **Bangor City Forest** is three-fourths the size of New York's Central Park—and that's pretty much where the comparisons end. More than 10 miles of trails wind through the City Forest, a tranquil wildlife preserve just down the road from the bustling Bangor Mall. You're likely to spot deer, wild turkeys, beaver, red squirrels, and birds that range from warblers to waterfowl. You might even see a moose, but don't bet on it. The trails are open to hikers and mountain bikers. Be sure to use insect repellent—especially if you continue across the Bangor city line and into the Orono Bog. To reach the City Forest, take Stillwater Avenue about 1.5 miles northeast of the Bangor Mall and watch for the left turn onto Tripp Drive. Continue to the City Forest parking area; trail maps are available at the information kiosk.

After you've done the trails and walking tours of Bangor, you'll need to get out of town for anything in the way of vertical hiking. In Dedham, 12 miles southeast of Bangor (on the way to Acadia), a favorite hike goes up **Bald Mountain** (sometimes called Dedham Bald Mountain) to the disused fire tower on the bald summit. On a clear day, climb the tower for panoramic views to both Katahdin and Cadillac Mountain. Allow about two hours round-trip if you plan to picnic and climb the tower. To reach the trailhead from downtown Bangor, take Route 1A (Wilson St.) through Brewer for about 8.5 miles from the Penobscot River bridge to the Route 46 junction. Just beyond the junc-tion, turn right onto Upper Dedham Road. Go about 2.5 miles and, just after a stream, bear left onto Dedham Road. Continue about 3.5 miles to the parking area (on left). The trail leads up from here, over a few steep, ledgy spots. It's well worth the climb, especially during fall-foliage season.

South of Bangor/Brewer (although it feels like you're heading east) is the Maine Audubon Society's **Fields Pond Audubon Center** (216 Fields Pond Rd., Holden 04429, 207/989-2591, www.maineaudubon.org). About four miles of footpaths wind through 192 acres of woods, fields, marshes, and lakeshore—all open daily, year-round, sunrise to sunset. (Wear waterproof shoes or boots; some parts of the trails can be wet.) Headquarters is the L. Robert Rolde Nature Center building, where you can pick up brochures and maps. A full schedule of programs occurs here throughout the year, including lectures, nature walks, canoeing, slide talks, and a summer day camp for youngsters 7 to 12. Program costs (except for the day camp) average $5 per person. A nature store carries books, cards, and gifts. The Rolde building is open 10 A.M.–4 P.M. Thursday–Saturday and 1–4 P.M. Sunday.

Three Bangor-area bike shops spearhead the bicycling activity in this part of Maine. They sponsor road and offroad group rides, most briskly paced, April–October, in the Bangor area. Helmets are required. For the most up-to-date schedule of bicycling events, check out the website of the Bicycle Coalition of Maine, www.BikeMaine.org.

North of I-95 (and east of the Bangor Mall), next to the Olive Garden restaurant, is **Ski Rack Sports** (24 Longview Dr., Bangor, 207/945-6474 or 800/698-6474), with a huge selection of mountain and road bikes and fast repair service (24-hour turnaround). If you haven't brought your bike, this is the best place to rent one. The shop, which also carries kayaks and other sporting gear, is open 10 A.M.–6 P.M. Monday–Thursday and Saturday, 10 A.M.–8 P.M. Friday, and noon–4 P.M. Sunday all year. Group rides are usually at 6 P.M. Monday, Wednesday, and Thursday evenings, and on Sunday mornings.

Across the Penobscot River is well-stocked **Pat's Bike Shop** (373 Wilson St., Rte. 1A, Brewer 04412, 207/989-2900), which has been in business since 1973. Pat's has no rentals but does repairs and sponsors group rides at 6 P.M. Monday and Wednesday and 8:30 A.M. Sunday. The shop also sells snowshoes and skateboards. It's open 10 A.M.–6 P.M. Monday–Friday and 9 A.M.–5 P.M. Saturday.

Upriver, **Rose Bicycle** (9 Pine St., Orono 04473, 207/866-3525 or 800/656-3525 in Maine, www.rosebike.com), better known as Rose Bike Shop, caters to the university crowd. The shop is open 9 A.M.–5 P.M. Monday and Friday, 9 A.M.–7 P.M. Tuesday–Thursday, and 9 A.M.–4 P.M. Saturday in the summer. It is closed Sunday and Monday in the winter. Group rides are Monday, Wednesday, and Friday, usually at 6 P.M. No rentals, but there are free route maps.

Considered a standout among public courses, the **Bangor Municipal Golf Course** (35 Webster Ave., Bangor 04401, 207/941-0232) has 18 holes dating from 1964 and a newer (and tougher) nine holes. Stretching over both sides of Webster Avenue, the course is also on the Bangor Airport flight path; don't flinch when a jet screams overhead. Tee times are needed only for the newer nine, but plan to arrive early in midsummer (the course opens at 7 A.M.). Open mid-April to mid-November. The clubhouse (with pro shop and snack bar) is .4 mile south of Hammond St. (Rte. 2), on the southwest side of town.

Twelve miles southeast of Bangor, adjacent to the Lucerne Inn, the nine-hole **Lucerne-in-Maine Golf Course** (Bar Harbor Rd., Rte. 1A, Holden 04429, 207/843-6282, www.lucernegolf.com) is worth a visit just for the spectacular views. The course is open mid-May–September, the fall foliage is fabulous, and greens fees are moderate. A tunnel under the busy highway connects two sections of the course.

Shopping

Since Bangor is the commercial hub for all of northern (and some of central) Maine, it's loaded with shopping opportunities both downtown and at the Bangor Mall, on the fringes of the city.

A handsome brick wall serves as a backdrop for paintings at the **Clark House Gallery** (128 Hammond St., Bangor 04401, 207/942-9162, www.clarkhousegallery.com), a sure sign of downtown Bangor's cultural revival. Gallery director Susan Maasch has mounted respected shows, featuring about 30 New England artists, about once a month since she opened in 1996. Also in the gallery are sculpture, jewelry, ceramics, and glassware. Hours are 10 A.M.–3 P.M. Tuesday–Saturday March–December, or by appointment.

Two independent bookstores in downtown Bangor have carved out their own niches, helping them compete with the Borders superstore at the Bangor Mall.

"Where is human nature so weak as in a bookstore?" reads a sign at **BookMarc's Bookstore and Café** (78 Harlow St., Bangor 04401, 207/942-3206, www.bookmarcs.com), northern Maine's largest independent bookstore. Indulge your literary weakness at Marc Berlin's shop with lots of children's and young-adult titles, esoteric journals, and almost everything by Stephen King. After that, sit down in the adjoining café and succumb to gourmet coffee, vegetarian lunches, and pastries. The store, located opposite Bangor City Hall and close to the University of Maine Museum of Art, is open 9:30 A.M.–5:30 P.M. weekdays, 10 A.M.–4 P.M. Saturday, and 10 A.M.–2 P.M. Sunday all year.

Just around the corner from BookMarc's is **Lippincott Books** (36 Central St., Bangor 04401, 207/942-4398, www.abebooks.com/home/lipbks/), a longtime antiquarian-book resource with more than 30,000 preowned books. Specialties are Maine titles and nonfiction volumes on Native Americans and Canada, but you'll find lots of surprises. The eclectic shop is open 10 A.M.–5:30 P.M. Monday–Friday, 10 A.M.–5 P.M. Saturday, and 10 A.M.–3 P.M. Sunday all year.

Also in downtown Bangor is **Pro Libris** (12 Third St., Bangor 04401, 207/942-3019), billing itself as a "readers' paradise." With 30,000 used paperbacks and hardcovers, that's just about right. Call ahead to be sure they're open.

Betts Bookstore (584 Hammond St., Bangor 04401, 207/947-7052, fax 947-6615, www.bettsbooks.com), in business since 1938, specializes in Stephen King. All of his books are here (and available by mail), including autographed copies and $7,500 limited editions, plus King posters and T-shirts, and models of his house. King groupies will love this place. The store is open 9 A.M.–4 P.M. Monday–Friday and 9 A.M.–3 P.M. Saturday.

Believe it when **The Grasshopper Shop** claims to be the state's largest boutique—it sprawls over two floors in downtown Bangor (1 W. Market Sq., Bangor 04401, 207/945-3132, www.grasshoppershop.net). Steer kids toward the T-shirts, music, and toys. Adults will find unstodgy imported clothing, housewares, jewelry, gifts, and cards. Other branches are located at the Bangor International Airport; in downtown Ellsworth, near Bar Harbor; in Stonington (Deer Isle, seasonal); and in Rockland (year-round). The downtown Bangor shop is open daily, all year, with varying hours depending on the season.

Also in the heart of downtown, **Epic Sports** (6 Central St., Bangor 04401, 207/941-5670, www.epicsportsofmaine.com), formerly Cadillac Mountain Sports, carries all the garb and gear you'll need for hiking, kayaking, biking, camping, and more. The store's owners are active in the non-sweatshop Clean Clothes Campaign. Open 9 A.M.–8 P.M. Monday–Saturday and 9 A.M.–5 P.M. Sunday.

The year-round **European Farmers' Market,** held at Sunnyside Florists and Greenhouses (117 Buck St., Bangor, 207/326-4741), features an eclectic array of unusual goodies—from Vietnamese cooked food to fresh pasta. Also available are wild mushrooms, European pastries, farm-raised venison, and goat cheese. The market operates 9:30 A.M.–1 P.M. every Saturday, across from the Bangor Auditorium parking lot. Buck Street is off Main St. (Route 1A), just north of Bass Park.

The largest mall north of Portland is the 80-store **Bangor Mall** (Hogan Rd. and Stillwater Ave., just north of I-95 Exit 49, 207/947-7333, www.bangormall.com), with such household names as J. C. Penney, Filene's, The Gap, Disney, and Sears. There are two ATMs and several

chain restaurants. The mall is open 9 A.M.–9 P.M. Monday–Saturday and 11 A.M.–6 P.M. Sunday. When the mall closes for the evening, lots of shoppers head just down the road to the giant Borders book and music store (116 Bangor Mall Blvd., 207/990-3300), which has live entertainment, coffee, and night-owl hours on Friday and Saturday.

GETTING THERE
Airport
Bangor International Airport (BGR) (287 Godfrey Boulevard, 207/947-0384 or 866/359-2264, www.flybangor.com) is northern and eastern coastal Maine's hub for flights arriving from Boston and points beyond. Bangor is the closest large airport for getting to Bar Harbor, Acadia National Park on Mount Desert Island, as well as the park's other outposts. About half a million passengers annually move through Bangor International, a user-friendly facility on the outskirts of the city. The airport's director is Rebecca Hupp, 207/947-0384.

Despite the "International" in the airport's name, passenger service from international destinations to Bangor tends to be limited to charter airlines, which sometimes arrive here to clear customs (and refuel) and then continue on to points south and west. More typically, international visitors arrive in Bangor via New York or Boston gateways. The only regularly scheduled international destination is Halifax, Nova Scotia. (Well, yes—U.S. citizens often forget that Canada *is* another country.)

Major scheduled airlines with frequent jet service to and from Bangor are **Delta, U.S. Airways, American Eagle, Continental Connection** and **Northwest Airlines.** Destinations include Boston, New York (LaGuardia), Washington (Reagan), Philadelphia, Pittsburgh, Cincinnati, Detroit, and Albany. **Pan Am** provides direct jet service to and from Orlando, Florida. **Boston-Maine Airways** (a subsidiary of Pan Am) connects Bangor with Manchester, New Hampshire (especially helpful for connecting with Southwest Airlines flights), and Halifax, Nova Scotia. Bad weather in Portland or Boston also can create unexpected domestic and international arrivals at Bangor's less-foggy airfield.

The airport's lower level has an interactive information kiosk, where you can contact local hotels and motels for rooms and airport shuttle service.

Bus and Taxi Services

Concord Trailways (1039 Union St., Route 222, Bangor 04401, 800/639-3317 or 945-4000, www.concordtrailways.com) provides daily bus service year-round from Logan Airport in Boston to Bangor. No reservations are accepted, but you can purchase tickets ($65 round trip) online. The Concord Trailways station in Bangor is near I-95 Exit 47, less than a mile from the airport, but plan to take a taxi for that short distance.

Vermont Transit (800/552-8737, www.greyhound.com), a division of Greyhound, operates a once-a-day seasonal bus service between Bangor (Bangor Bus Terminal, 158 Main St.) and downtown Bar Harbor. You can buy tickets online for Vermont Transit.

Round-the-clock **taxi service** is provided by Airport/River City Taxi, 207/947-8294 or 800/997-8294, and Town Taxi, 207/945-5671 or 800/750-9935.

Car Rentals

Avis, Budget, Hertz, and **National** car rental companies all have desks at Bangor Airport. In July, August, and September, it's essential to reserve a car a week or two before your arrival. Bangor is slightly less than 50 miles from Bar Harbor, but you'll be traveling almost entirely on two-lane roads; in summer, figure on an hour at the very least.

RV Rentals

Rec Time USA (84 Main St., Rt. 1A, Holden 04429, 207/989-4678 or 866/773-2846, www.rectimeusa.com) is a national firm with a local office renting pop-ups ($99–119 a night or $359–499 a week in summer; $79–99 a night or $299–329 a week off-peak), 30-foot campers ($200–250 a night or $1,200–1,500 a week in summer; $135–175 a night or $800–1000 a week

off-peak), and canoes ($15 a night with camper rental). Reserve in advance and they'll pick you up at Bangor International Airport.

INFORMATION AND SERVICES

The **Bangor Region Chamber of Commerce** (519 Main St., P.O. Box 1443, Bangor 04401, 207/947-0307, fax 990-1427, www.bangorregion.com) is located next to the Paul Bunyan statue and close to the Civic Center complex. The office is open 8 A.M.–5 P.M. weekdays all year. The visitor information center, in the same building, is open 8 A.M.–7 P.M. Monday–Saturday and noon–5 P.M. Sunday, June–September.

Two **Maine Visitor Information Centers** are located just south of Bangor on I-95, one on each side of the highway. The modern gray-clapboard buildings have racks of statewide information, agreeable staffers, clean restrooms, vending machines, and covered picnic tables. Northbound, the center is at mile 175 (207/862-6628); southbound, it's at mile 179 (207/862-6638). They're open 9 A.M.–5 P.M. all year, with later hours in summer.

Claiming one of the state's best reference sections, with a staff of librarians fielding about 30,000 questions a year, the **Bangor Public Library** (145 Harlow St., Bangor 04401, 207/947-8336, www.bpl.lib.me.us) also provides interlibrary loans throughout the state. A large, metered parking lot is just across the street. The handsome 1912 structure, built after the 1911 fire and renovated at a cost of $8.5 million in the mid-1990s, is open Monday–Saturday all year.

The *Bangor Daily News* (207/990-8000 or 800/432-7964, www.bangornews.com) carries the densest coverage of Bangor and northern Maine, plus national and international news. The Thursday edition has extensive calendar listings.

Bangor Photo (559 Union St., Bangor, 207/942-6728, www.bangorphoto.com), in business since 1976, has a wide range of services, including passport photos, one-hour prints and E-6 slide processing, and new and used gear. The shop, on the corner of 14th Street, is about midway between downtown and the airport. It's open

8:30 A.M.–6 P.M. Monday–Friday and 9 A.M.–
4 P.M. Saturday all year.

Emergencies

Maine's second-largest (after Portland) medical
center is **Eastern Maine Medical Center** (489
State St., P.O. Box 404, Bangor 04402, 207/
973-7000, www.emmc.org). Round-the-clock
emergency-room service (207/973-8000), a walk-
in clinic (207/973-8030), and a state-of-the-art
children's wing are among the first-rate features
here. **St. Joseph Hospital** (360 Broadway, Bangor, 207/262-1000, www.stjoeshealing.org), a
Catholic facility, also has a 24-hour emergency
department (207/262-5000).

For **police, fire, or ambulance services,** dial
911.

Colonel Black Mansion, Ellsworth

ELLSWORTH AND TRENTON

You can't get to Mount Desert Island/Acadia National Park without going through Ellsworth and
Trenton. Trenton (pop. 1,370), linked by a bridge
to Mount Desert, is little more than a six- or
seven-mile strip of restaurants, lodgings, shops,
and activities along Bar Harbor Road (Rte. 3)—
the funnel to Mount Desert.

Bar Harbor Road is something of an Achilles
heel—often a summertime bottleneck as it fun-
nels all traffic to Mount Desert Island. This became all too clear in June 2003, when a wealthy
island summer resident had a mature apple tree
moved from Ellsworth—via Trenton, of course—
to his Northeast Harbor home. With no passing room to spare on the narrow two-lane roads,
and the need to raise phone, cable, and electric
wires along the entire route for the 20-foot-high
tree, the traffic backed up halfway to Bangor—a
costly 12-hour nightmare. Public works and local
government officials learned a hard lesson, residents and commuters earned a public apology in
the newspapers, and wags vowed to sneak in and
sample those expensive apples if and when the
tree bears fruit in its new soil.

Ellsworth (pop. 6,456) is a long-established
community and the Hancock County seat. The
city has mushroomed with the popularity of
Acadia National Park. In fact, it's worth a stop,

including handsome architectural remnants of
the city's 19th-century lumbering heyday (which
began shortly after its incorporation in 1800).
Brigs, barks, and full-rigged ships—built in
Ellsworth and captained by local fellows—
loaded lumber here and carried it round the
globe. Despite a ruinous 1855 fire that swept
through downtown, the lumber trade thrived
until late in the 19th century, along with facto-
ries and mills turning out shoes, bricks, boxes,
and butter.

If you have time, try to visit **The Black House**
(also called the Woodlawn Museum), on the
outskirts of Ellsworth (Rte. 172), open Tuesday–Sunday mid-May–October. Very little has
changed in the house since George Nixon Black
donated it to the town in 1928. Completed in
1828, the Georgian house is a marvel of preser-
vation, one of Maine's best, filled with original
Black family antiques and artifacts. Even kids
appreciate all the unusual stuff. Afterward, you
can picnic on the manicured grounds, explore
two sleigh-filled barns, the Memorial Garden,
and the two miles of mostly level trails in the
woods up beyond the house. Restrooms are next
to the parking area.

Accommodations

National chain (Comfort Inn, Holiday Inn, Trav-
elodge) and independent motels line High Street

(Rtes. 1 and 3), a densely commercial stretch in Ellsworth, and continue southward through Trenton toward Mount Desert Island. Most of the motels and cabin complexes along the Trenton stretch are smaller, family-owned operations—not fancy, but their rates are far lower than what you'd find on Mount Desert. (Bar Harbor is 20 miles from downtown Ellsworth.)

If you can handle sleeping in the middle of a shopping mall, the best of the Ellsworth chain motels is the **Holiday Inn** (215 High St., Rte. 1, Ellsworth 04605, 207/667-9341 or 800/401-9341, fax 207/667-7294, www.holidayinn.com). Request a room facing the mall, not the highway. The 103-room motel has a/c, phones (and dataports), cable TV, laundry, a serious fitness center, indoor tennis courts, restaurant, and heated indoor pool. Doubles are $85–150, depending on the season. Kids and pets are welcome. Open all year.

About a mile north of the Holiday Inn, heading Down East out of Ellsworth (not on the road to Acadia), **White Birches** (Rte. 1, P.O. Box 743, Ellsworth 04605, 207/667-3621 or 800/435-1287, www.wbirches.com) is a clean, generic motel with 67 rooms ($45–100 d, depending on the season), popular with tour groups. A big plus for golfing guests: free use of the course. Request a room overlooking the course. The motel's family-oriented **Czy Gil's Restaurant** does a breakfast buffet and dinner (entrées $8–15), plus lunch in summer. Rooms have phones and cable TV; some have a/c. Pets and kids are welcome. Open all year.

Food

Order breakfast anytime at **The Riverside Café** (151 Main St., Ellsworth 04605, 207/667-7220). Juices are fresh (if a bit pricey), buckwheat pancakes are outstanding, but try the veggie benedict, with spinach and tomato. Lunch menu includes homemade soups, salads, sandwiches, grilled sandwiches, and high-cal desserts; skip the fried-seafood platters. Sunday brunches (summer and fall only) are legendary. And the café's name? It used to be down the street, overlooking the Union River. Open 5 A.M.–3 P.M. Monday–Friday, 7 A.M.–3 P.M.

Saturday all year; it's also open 7 A.M.–2 P.M. Sunday, June–mid-October.

On the Main Street spur heading east from Ellsworth (also called Washington Junction Road), **Larry's Bakery** (241 Main St., Ellsworth 04605, 207/667-2557) may look unassuming, but *everyone* goes there for bread, rolls, pies, and Saturday night's baked beans. No preservatives are used. No credit cards. Open 6 A.M.–5 P.M. Monday–Saturday all year.

There are also some good ethnic restaurants. In Ellsworth, go to **Frankie's Café & Good Stuff** (40 High St., Rte. 1, in the Cadillac Mountain Sports building, 207/667-7701) for excellent Mediterranean/vegetarian specialties—veggie-rice pie, spanakopita, brie pasta pie, sesame-butter-topped bagels. Pâté and meat sandwiches are available. Everything's very casual. Only a handful of tables, so order food to go if it's crowded (which it often is). Open 8 A.M.–7 P.M. weekdays, 9 A.M.–5 P.M. Saturday.

While Frankie's is best for lunch, look for a lunch or dinner Mediterranean-bistro feast at **Cleonice** (112 Main St., Ellsworth 04605, 207/664-7554), in a historic building in downtown Ellsworth. (It helps if you learn how to pronounce it: "klee-oh-NEESE.") The restaurant is named for Cleonice Renzetti, the chef/owner's mother. Chef Rich Hanson (his father, obviously, wasn't Italian) had years of experience at the former Jonathan's Restaurant in Blue Hill, and it shows. The tapas and meze selection alone is worth the trip—covering the Mediterranean circuit (spanakopita, hummus, Manchego cheese with pear sauce, and even brandade de morue)—at $3–7.50 a portion. The Tunisian spiced lemonade is outstanding ($7 a carafe), especially with lunch (sandwiches $5.50–7.50; vegetarian moussaka $9; crab-meat-and-kasseri fondue $10). The place—with wooden booths, a huge wooden bar dating from 1938, and Med decor—really *feels* like a bistro. Dinner entrées are $16.50–19. Cleonice is open for lunch and dinner Tuesday–Saturday, all year.

Mediterranean seems to be the *cuisine du jour* in Ellsworth. Another fine contender is **Turriglio's Ristorante Italiana** (59 Franklin St.,

winter at the Trenton Bridge Lobster Pound: a lobster-crate "Christmas tree"

© KATHLEEN M. BRANDES

Ellsworth 04605, 207/667-0202), owned by Manhattan escapee Matthew Parker (also Italian on his mother's side). The Little Italy décor runs to vintage posters, antique radios, and photos of Rome in this storefront place (a few steps off Main Street). The antipasto is huge, pasta dishes are creative, and the Italian wine list is impressive. Entrées are in the $11–21 range. Open Tuesday–Sunday, 5–9 P.M.; reservations advisable on weekends.

The Mex (185 Main St., Ellsworth 04605, 207/667-4494, www.themex.com) has been a popular local eatery since 1979. The menu is punnily entertaining ("Juan-derful Beginnings") and you won't go hungry. Lots of vegetarian choices. Entrées are $7–16. Take home a bottle of the fiery hot sauce. Open 11 A.M.–9 P.M. Monday–Friday and until 10 P.M. weekends all year.

Ellsworth even has a Thai restaurant. **The Bangkok Restaurant** (321 High St., Rte. 3, Ellsworth, 207/667-1324), does a creditable job, and the always-popular pad Thai is a winner. Entrée range is $7–16. No MSG is used. Open 11 A.M.–3 P.M. and 4–9 P.M. Monday–Saturday, 4–9 P.M. Sunday all year.

Route 3 (Bar Harbor Rd.), between Ellsworth and Mount Desert Island, is lined with eateries, including a couple of lobster "pounds." One of the best-known and longest-running (since 1956) of these lobster-in-the-rough places is **Trenton Bridge Lobster Pound** (Rte. 3, Bar Harbor Road, Trenton 04605, 207/667-2977, fax 207/667-3412), on the right, next to the bridge leading to Mount Desert Island. Watch for the "smoke signals"—steam billowing from the huge vats; the lobster couldn't be much fresher. The pound is open 11 A.M.–7:30 P.M., Monday–Saturday Memorial Day–Columbus Day. They also ship lobsters throughout the year.

Getting There

The **Hancock County/Bar Harbor Airport (BHB)** (Rte. 3, Bar Harbor Rd., Trenton 04605, 207/667-7171, www.bhbairport.com), 12 miles from downtown Bar Harbor, is well located for anyone headed for Mount Desert Island, but this isn't a big-jet airport—in case you're squeamish about small planes. (Despite its name, the airport is located in Trenton, just north of Mount Desert Island.) **USAirways/Colgan Air** (207/667-7171 or 800/428-4322, www.colganair .com or www.usairways.com) operates daily commuter-plane service from Boston to Bar Harbor Airport, with a stop in Owls Head, near Rockland (Knox County Municipal Airport). Flight time from Boston to Trenton is about 80 minutes. (Driving time from Boston to Trenton would be a minimum of six hours, usually longer.) The airline will also arrange other connections beyond Boston. Hertz (year-round) and Budget (May–October) have rental-car offices at the Bar Harbor Airport; in summer, be sure to reserve a car well in advance.

The **Island Explorer** bus system, which primarily serves Mount Desert Island with its fleet of propane-fueled, fare-free vehicles, has one route linking the Hancock County/Bar Harbor Airport with downtown Bar Harbor. Operated by Downeast Transportation, the Island Explorer runs between late June and Columbus Day (more information is available in the *Acadia on Mount Desert Island* chapter). If you need van service, check with the airport-terminal desk of **Airport and Harbor Car Service** (207/667-5995 or 888/814-5995, www.mymainecarservice.com), which also will do runs to Bangor International Airport. In the middle of summer, a reservation is essential for trips to and from Bangor.

Tips for Travelers

TRAVELING BY RV

Bringing a recreational vehicle (RV) to Mount Desert Island and Acadia National Park creates something of a conundrum. No question, the vehicles are convenient for carting kids and gear, but they're a major source of traffic problems on the island, and especially within the park. All of the island's roads are two lanes, and even though the island offers more designated bike lanes than almost anywhere else in Maine, bikes and RVs often have to share the road. RV parking is very limited, and even banned in some locales (such as downtown Bar Harbor). Ideally, you should consider bringing an RV to Acadia only between late June and Columbus Day—when you can park the vehicle in one of the island's dozen commercial campgrounds and travel around the island via the Island Explorer shuttle service.

Incidentally, be aware that the maximum trailer (or RV) length in the national park's two campgrounds is 35 feet, maximum width is 12 feet, and only one vehicle is allowed per site. Neither park campground has water or electric hookups. (More details on the two campgrounds appear at the end of the *Acadia on Mount Desert Island* chapter.)

Plans are in the works (but no date has been set) to provide parking facilities and a shuttle stop at the northern end of Mount Desert Island, which promises to be a major plus for day-trippers with RVs. Until then, however, you can park on a space-available basis near the park's Hulls Cove Visitor Center and in a designated area on Lower Main Street (watch for signs) in Bar Harbor.

TRAVELING WITH CHILDREN

Acadia National Park isn't a turn-the-toddlers-loose kind of place (too many cliffs and other potential hazards), but for school-age youngsters and cooperative teenagers, it's a fabulous family-vacation destination. There are family-oriented kayak tours, Park Ranger tours, whale-watching trips, hiking and biking trails, carriage rides, and boat excursions. There's saltwater (literally breathtaking for adults, but not for kids) swimming at Sand Beach and freshwater swimming at several lakes and ponds. Incredibly, McDonald's and Burger King haven't invaded Mount Desert Island (although Subway has), but Bar Harbor and other towns have plenty of pizza and lobster joints, as well as two cinemas (one year-round, one seasonal) and several museums for rainy days.

Be forewarned that in-line skates and skateboards are not allowed anywhere within the park. The island communities surrounding the park are all small and—especially at the height of summer—congested. In-line skates can come in handy, but use them sensibly; skateboards, on the other hand, are a major hazard in these villages. Bikes are *not* allowed on any of the park's hiking trails, but the car-free carriage-trail network is ideal for biking.

How about doing a family volunteer stint? Consider spending a morning on a trail-maintenance crew (8:30–noon, Tuesday, Thursday, and Saturday, June–Columbus Day). Bring water and a bag lunch for a post-work picnic—the camaraderie is contagious. The nonprofit Friends of Acadia organization chalks up more than 7,000 volunteer hours every year. Check the website before you come (www.friendsofacadia.org), or

ON THE ROAD

COURTESY MAINE OFFICE OF TOURISM

ON THE ROAD

along Acadia's Park Loop Road

call 207/288-3934 when you get here for the recorded schedule of work projects. (Volunteer crews meet at Park Headquarters on Rte. 233, Eagle Lake Road.)

TRAVELING WITH PETS

If you're used to traveling with your cat or dog, you should be accustomed to playing by the rules. In Acadia National Park, dogs are allowed *only* on leashes, and they are banned from several park locations: Sand and Echo Lake beaches, Duck Harbor Campground (on Isle au Haut), park buildings, and any of the "ladder" hiking trails, which have iron foot- and handholds. (When you see the ladder trails, you'll understand why pets are forbidden.) Don't take pets on the Park Ranger tours, and do *not* leave your dog unattended (especially in an RV at one of the campgrounds). Be considerate of your pet as well as of other visitors. Of course, guide dogs are exempted from all rules.

To make the best of a visit to Acadia—so you can hike and bike and kayak without worrying about your pet—you might want to reserve ken-

nel space for part of your stay. Mount Desert Island has the **Acadia Woods Kennel** (Crooked Road, Bar Harbor 04609, 207/288-9766, variable rates); on the mainland in nearby Ellsworth is **Downeast Boarding Kennel** (275 High St., Rte. 3, Ellsworth 04605, 207/667-3062, variable rates). In July and August, be sure to call well in advance for a reservation. If you'd prefer to have a dog-sitter come to your hotel or campground, contact Wendy Scott at **Bark Harbor, Inc.** (200 Main St., Bar Harbor, 207/288-0404, www.barkharbor.com). She'll recommend someone who can help. If at all possible, call before you arrive to make arrangements, and when you get here, visit the store—a Toys R Us for pet owners.

ACCESSIBILITY

Acadia National Park has been conscientious about providing as much accessibility as possible to people with disabilities. For a start, the Hulls Cove Visitor Center (the park's spring, summer, and fall information center) has a special parking area for easy wheelchair access, bypassing the 52 steps from the main parking area. When you get

GETTING AWAY TO NOVA SCOTIA

Bar Harbor is the starting point for the summertime car-and-passenger ferry to **Yarmouth, Nova Scotia,** which shaves more than 600 miles off the driving route. From mid-May to mid-October, the high-speed 900-passenger catamaran called *The Cat,* owned by Bay Ferries, zips to Yarmouth in 165 minutes, departing Bar Harbor at 8 A.M. daily. (Remember that Yarmouth is on Atlantic time.) In July and August, there's also a 4 P.M. run every day except Wednesday. Not without controversy when it first went into service, *The Cat* was criticized for creating harbor wakes, and even received speeding tickets, but after several years of operation, it seems to be a big hit. The ferry—rather like a very comfortable floating bus—has onboard food service, a small casino, a duty-free shop, and a TV/cinema lounge.

One-way fare for a car is $120 at the height of the season. Adult passengers are $55, seniors $50, children 5–12 are $25, free for children under five. One-way family fare (two adults and up to four children) is $255 in summer. A bicycle is $10. No pets in the passenger areas; special kennels are available for pets. Vehicle reservations are wise, and you can book everything online. If you're taking your car, plan to arrive at the ferry terminal in Bar Harbor an hour before departure.

In summer, you can even go to Yarmouth for the day, without a car, departing at 8 A.M. and returning on the later ferry, reaching Bar Harbor about 10:30 P.M. Round-trip fare for the day cruise to Canada is $59 in July and August (as well as Tuesday and Thursday in September), $25 for children; the family rate is $160.

Special packages are available if you want to stay longer and explore Nova Scotia.

For a current schedule and other fare information, contact **Bay Ferries** (207/288-3395 or 888/249-7245, www.catferry.com). In summer, Nova Scotia's **Yarmouth County Tourism Association** (207/288-9432 or 902/742-5355) staffs an information office at the ferry terminal (121 Eden St., Rte. 3, Bar Harbor 04609). In downtown Bar Harbor (65 Main St., corner of Cottage St.), Yarmouth Tourism and *The Cat* staffers share an office where you can get information and make reservations.

If you're taking the day cruise, consider making arrangements in advance with **Discover Acadia Vacations** (P.O. Box 40, Port Williams, NS, Canada B0P 1T0, 902/542-1184 or 888/277-3144, fax 542-1107, www.novascotiatours.com). This enterprising operation—run by Meg Scheid and Patricia Bernier—will pick you up in a van at the ferry dock in Yarmouth and show you the natural, cultural, and historical sights of the area, originally part of historical Acadia (remember Longfellow's epic poem *Evangeline?*). Meg is a former Acadia National Park interpreter and the author of *Discovering Acadia* (See *Suggested Reading;* her book is about Acadia National Park, not the historical Acadia); Patricia formerly worked for the Yarmouth County Tourism Association. Their combination of talents and interests works perfectly in this enterprise. Their tour schedule coincides with *The Cat's* season (mid-May to mid-October). In July and August, when you'll have six hours between boats, they organize a superb six-hour tour, including an authentic Acadian meal, for $62 a person; other months, when the layover is only two hours, they do an excellent two-hour tour for $20, including a light snack.

Their reputation is getting around, so book well ahead if you plan to do this. Meg and Patricia can also help you make arrangements for longer stays.

ON THE ROAD

into the center, request a **Golden Access Passport,** which provides free lifetime entry to any national park (and half-price park campsites) for any citizen or permanent resident who is permanently disabled. (If you've broken your leg or have another temporary disability, you're not eligible.) The passport is also available at the park's two campgrounds, at park headquarters, and at the Sand Beach and Bar Harbor Village Green ticket booths.

Also at the Hulls Cove Visitor Center, pick up a copy of the *Acadia National Park Access Guide,* which provides detailed accessibility information (including parking, entry, restrooms, pay phones, and water fountains) for the park's visitor centers, the two campgrounds, picnic areas, beaches, and gift shops, as well as carriage rides, some boat cruises, and nonpark museums on Mount Desert Island. A few of the Park Ranger programs are wheelchair-accessible, as are all of the evening programs at the park's two campgrounds. Access to the carriage-road network depends on your ability (there are some steep grades); even the easiest trails may require some assistance. Each of the Island Explorer shuttle buses—operating between late June and Columbus Day—has room for at least one wheelchair.

Parking lots at some of the park's most popular locales (such as Thunder Hole, the Cadillac summit, and Jordan Pond House) have designated handicapped spaces.

The Hulls Cove Visitor Center rents cassettes (and tape players) and CDs for a self-guided auto tour of the Park Loop Road and beyond (the entire tour covers 56 miles on the island). Wheelchair rentals are handled by **West End Drug Co.** (105 Main St., Bar Harbor 04609, 207/288-3318).

To plan your Acadia trip in advance, order a Golden Access Passport online, then download the accessibility information from the park's website (www.nps.gov/acad/accessibility.htm). If you're reserving a campsite online (reservations.nps.gov/) for the Blackwoods Campground—up to four months before your arrival—you'll need the Golden Access Passport beforehand.

For additional accessibility information, call 207/288-3338 (voice) or 207/288-8800 (TTY). For emergencies in the park or elsewhere on Mount Desert Island, dial 911. (If you call the main park number during working hours regarding an emergency, a recorded message will tell you to hang up and dial 911.)

FOREIGN TRAVELERS

Entering the United States

Citizens of more than two dozen countries can enter the United States for holidays or business for 90 days via the Visa Waiver Program (see regulations at travel.state.gov/vwp). Countries participating in the program are Andorra, Australia, Austria, Belgium, Brunei, Denmark, Finland, France, Germany, Iceland, Ireland, Italy, Japan, Liechtenstein, Luxembourg, Monaco, Netherlands, New Zealand, Norway, Portugal, San Marino, Singapore, Slovenia, Spain, Sweden, Switzerland, and the United Kingdom. You'll need a return (plane or boat) ticket, as well as a machine-readable passport. (The return-ticket rule does not apply to overland border crossings from Canada.)

Citizens of countries other than those in the VWP need to be aware that the United States has become exceedingly security-conscious and has tightened the scrutiny of visa applications and the issuance of visas, making delays inevitable—and frustrating. If you need a visa, *plan well ahead!*

Foreigners visiting Acadia National Park typically arrive in the United States via major ports of entry, such as Boston or New York, and then continue to Maine; a smaller number arrive in Maine by road via Canada (New Brunswick or Quebec) or in Bar Harbor via *The Cat,* a fast catamaran ferry from Yarmouth, Nova Scotia. (The only customs facilities on Mount Desert Island are at The Cat Ferry Terminal in Bar Harbor. See the sidebar *Getting Away to Nova Scotia.*)

Canadians do not need visas to enter the United States, but valid identification (birth certificate or passport) is required. Duty-free limits for Canadians returning home are C$20 after a 24-hour stay, C$100 after 48 hours, and C$300 after seven days (not counting the departure day). The first two exemptions can be claimed any number of times; the $300 exemption is valid only once per year.

Canadians visiting the United States for at least 72 hours may take back gifts valued as high as US$100, but no more than twice a year. Here's an odd regulation, obviously easy to circumvent: Canadians can carry one liter of beer, wine, or liquor as a personal effect but not as a gift.

Visitors are also allowed to bring in 200 cigarettes, 50 cigars (though not Cuban ones), or 4.4 pounds of tobacco. Duty assessed on items over and above the personal exemptions is 3.5 percent.

There is no limit on the amount of money or value of traveler's checks a nonresident may bring into the United States. If the amount exceeds $10,000, however, it's necessary to fill out an official report form.

No fruit, vegetables, or plant materials can be taken across the border in either direction. A stern-faced U.S. customs official once confiscated a flourishing 20-year-old jade plant that a friend of mine was carting across the border from Canada, and I suspect it's still adorning his living room.

Other banned items—some self-evident, some not—include drugs and drug paraphernalia (except medically authorized), firearms, and most meat and poultry products (including dried meat). For more detailed information, check the website of the Customs and Border Protection division of the Department of Homeland Security (www.cbp.gov).

Money and Currency Exchange

Since Maine's Down East (geographically, northeast) coast borders Canada, don't be surprised to see a few Canadian coins mixed in with American ones when you receive change from a purchase. In such cases, Canadian and U.S. quarters are equivalent, although the exchange rate is in fact drastically different. Most services (including banks) will accept a handful of Canadian coins at par, but you'll occasionally spot No Canadian Currency signs. Until the early 1980s, the two currencies were exchangeable one for one, but they've been drawing apart ever since. By 2003, one Canadian dollar was worth only 69 U.S. cents.

It's not absolutely necessary to exchange currency when traveling between the United States and Canada, but Canadian dollars are worth far less in the United States (and U.S. dollars are worth far more in Canada). Also, the farther south of Canada you roam, the more likely you'll find resistance to Canadian currency in restaurants and shops. It's easier to convert it.

Other foreign currencies are not easily convertible (without losing in the exchange) at the small local banks on Mount Desert Island. Acadia National Park has no ATMs (automated teller machines) within its boundaries, but there are ATMs in Bar Harbor and other communities on Mount Desert Island. It's best to bring a Visa or EuroCard (MasterCard) and/or traveler's checks in U.S. dollar amounts (preferably $50 or under, for ease of cashing in Maine). You can use credit cards in most shops, hotels, and restaurants, but a few B&Bs and small cafés don't accept them.

Health and Safety

There's too much to do and see in Acadia National Park to spend even a few hours laid low by illness or mishap. Be sensible—get enough sleep, wear sunscreen and appropriate clothing, know your limits and don't take foolhardy risks; heed weather and warning signs, carry water and snacks while hiking, don't overindulge in food or alcohol, always tell someone where you're going, and watch your step. If you're traveling with children, quadruple your caution.

MEDICAL CARE

Emergencies

The **Mount Desert Island Hospital** (10 Wayman Ln., Bar Harbor 04609, 207/288-5081, www.mdihospital.org) has round-the-clock emergency-room services with doctors and dentists on duty or on call. The next nearest hospital, even larger, is **Maine Coast Memorial Hospital** (50 Union St., Ellsworth 04605, 207/664-5311 or 888/645-8829, emergency room 207/664-5340, www.mainehospital.org).

The hospital is 20 miles north of Bar Harbor. The region's largest hospital is **Eastern Maine Medical Center** (489 State St., Bangor 04402, 207/973-7000 or 877/366-3662, emergency room 207/973-8000, www.emmc.org); Bangor is 50 miles from Bar Harbor. EMMC also is one of two Maine bases for LifeFlight of Maine, operating medical air-rescue helicopters statewide.

Alternative Health Care

Nontraditional health-care options are available on Mount Desert Island as well as on the Blue Hill Peninsula and Deer Isle. After some overambitious hiking or biking expeditions, a massage might be in order. Holistic practitioners, as well as certified massage therapists and acupuncturists, are listed in the Yellow Pages of local phone books. Also, check the bulletin boards and talk to the managers at the health-food stores in Bar Harbor, Ellsworth, and Blue Hill. They always know where to find homeopathic doctors.

GEORGE DEWOLFE, COURTESY FRIENDS OF ACADIA

A misstep along Acadia's rugged shoreline could ruin your entire day.

Pharmacies

The major pharmacy chain in and near Acadia is **Rite-Aid;** Hannaford and Shop 'n Save supermarkets also have pharmacy departments. Mount Desert Island has independent drugstores in each of its towns. All carry prescription and nonprescription (over-the-counter) medications. There are no round-the-clock pharmacies. Some independent pharmacists post emergency numbers on their doors and will go out of their way to help, but your best bet for a middle-of-the-night medication crisis is the hospital emergency room.

If you take regular medications, be sure to pack an adequate supply, as well as a new prescription in case you lose your medicine or unexpectedly need a refill.

LYME DISEASE

A bacterial infection that causes severe arthritis-like symptoms, Lyme disease (named after the Connecticut town where it was first identified, in 1975) has been documented in Maine since 1986. (In Europe, the disease is known as borreliosis, after the *Borrelia burgdorferi* bacterium that causes it.) In 2003, 219 cases of Lyme disease were reported in Maine— a huge increase from the *three* cases reported in 1989. No reliable statistics exist on visitors who have left the state and experienced delayed onset of the disease—a frequent occurrence. Health officials monitor the situation carefully and issue warnings during prime tick season—mid-May into August. Atlanta's Centers for Disease Control and Prevention (www.cdc.gov) has cited the wooded, marshy areas of Maine's southernmost counties as the highest-risk areas, but incidences of Lyme disease have been reported in Acadia National Park.

Lyme disease is spread by bites from tiny deer ticks (not the larger dog ticks; they don't carry it), which feed on the blood of deer, mice, songbirds, and humans. Symptoms include joint pain, extreme fatigue, chills, a stiff neck, headache, and a distinctive ring-like rash. In the past, early-stage treatment has involved a fairly expensive round of antibiotics, but considerable success has been reported from treatment with doxycycline or amoxicillin. Except for the rash, which occurs only in about 80 percent of victims, the symptoms mimic those of other ailments, such as the flu, so the disease is hard to diagnose. The rash, which expands gradually and usually is not painful, may appear one or two weeks after a bite. If left untreated, Lyme disease eventually can cause cardiac and neurological problems and debilitating arthritis. Preventive measures are essential. (LYMErix, a vaccine approved by the FDA in 1998, was withdrawn from the market in 2002.)

The best advice is to take precautions: wear a long-sleeved shirt and long pants, and tuck the pant legs into your socks. Light-colored clothing makes the ticks easier to spot. Buy tick repellent at a supermarket or convenience store and use it liberally on your legs. Spray it around your cuffs and beltline. While you're hiking, stay away from long grasses and keep to the center of trails. (You should do this anyway—part of the Leave No Trace philosophy—to preserve Acadia's fragile ecosystem.) After any hike, check for ticks—especially behind the knees, and in the armpits, navel, and groin. Monitor children carefully. If you find a tick or suspect you have been bitten, head for the nearest hospital emergency room. If you spot a tick on you (or anyone else), try to remove it with tweezers and save it for analysis, since not all deer ticks are infected with the bacterium.

RABIES

Incidents of rabies—a life-threatening, nerve-attacking disease for which there is no cure unless treated immediately—have increased dramatically in Maine since 1994. The biggest jumps were among rabid skunks and raccoons. No human has ever survived a case of rabies, and the disease is horrible, so *do not* approach, or let any child approach, any of the animals known to transmit it: raccoons, skunks, squirrels, bats, and foxes. Domestic dogs are required to have biennial rabies inoculations, thus providing a front line of defense for humans. If you're bitten by any animal, especially one acting suspiciously, head for the nearest hospital emergency room.

The virus travels along nerve roots to the brain, so a facial bite is far more critical, relatively speaking, than a leg bite. Treatment (a series of injections) is not as painful as it once was, but it's very expensive—and, I might add, much better than the alternative. For statewide information about rabies, contact the Maine Disease Control Administration in Augusta, 207/287-3591.

ALLERGIES

If your medical history includes extreme allergies to shellfish or bee stings, you already know the risks of eating a lobster or wandering around a wildflower meadow. However, if you come from a landlocked area and are new to crustaceans, you might not be aware of the potential hazard. Statistics indicate that only about 2 percent of adults have a severe shellfish allergy, but for those victims, the reaction can set in quickly. Immediate treatment is needed to keep the airways open. If you have a history of severe allergic reactions to *anything*, be prepared when you come to the Maine coast dreaming of lobster feasts. Ask your doctor for a prescription for EpiPen (epinephrine), a preloaded, single-use syringe—enough to tide you over until you can get to a hospital.

SEASICKNESS

Samuel Butler, the 19th-century author of *Erewhon*, wrote, "How holy people look when they are sea-sick." And he wasn't kidding. Seasickness conjures visions of the pearly gates and an overwhelming urge for instant salvation. Fortunately, even though the ailment seems to last forever, it's only temporary—depending on where you are, what remedies you have, and how your system responds. If you're planning to do any boating in the waters around Acadia National Park—particularly sailing or whale-watching—

> *Samuel Butler, the 19th-century author of* **Erewhon,** *wrote, "How holy people look when they are sea-sick." And he wasn't kidding. Seasickness conjures visions of the pearly gates and an overwhelming urge for instant salvation. Fortunately, even though the ailment seems to last forever, it's only temporary.*

you'll want to be prepared. (Being prepared, in fact, may keep you from succumbing, since fear of seasickness just about guarantees you'll get it.)

Seasickness allegedly stems from an inner-ear imbalance caused by boat motion, but researchers have had difficulty explaining why some people on a vessel become violently ill and others have no problem at all.

To prevent seasickness, try to stay in good shape. Get enough sleep and food, and keep your clothing warm and dry (not easy, of course, on a heeling sailboat). Some veteran sailors swear by salted crackers, sips of water, and bites of fresh ginger. If you start feeling queasy, keep your eyes on the horizon and stay as far away as possible from odors from the engine, the galley, the head, and other seasick passengers. If you become seasick, keep sipping water to prevent dehydration.

Dramamine, Marezine, and Bonine, taken several hours before a boat trip, have long been the preventives of choice. They do cause drowsiness, but anyone who's been seasick will tell you he or she would rather be drowsy. Another popular preventive is the scopolamine patch (available by prescription under the trademark Transderm Scop), which gradually releases medication into the bloodstream for up to three days. Behind an ear or a knee is the best location for the little adhesive disc. Wash your hands after you touch it—the medication can cause temporary blurred vision if you inadvertently rub your eyes. Children, pregnant women, and the elderly should not use scopolamine. Discuss the minor side effects with the physician who gives you the prescription.

Some people swear by the pressure bracelet, which operates somewhat on the principle of acupressure, telling your brain to ignore the fact that you're not on terra firma. Great success has been reported with these prophylactics in the last decade. Before embarking, especially if the weather is at all iffy, go ahead and put on a patch or a bracelet. Any such preventive measure also improves your mental attitude, relieving anxiety.

SUNSTROKE

Since Acadia National Park lies above the 44th parallel, sunstroke is not a major problem, but don't push your luck by spending an entire day frying on Sand Beach or the granite shoreline. Not only do you risk sunstroke and dehydration, but you're also asking for skin cancer down the road. Early in the season, slather yourself, and especially children, with plenty of PABA-free sunblock. (PABA can cause skin rashes and eruptions, even on people not abnormally sensitive.) Depending on your skin tone, use sun protection factor (SPF) 15 or higher. If you're in the water a long time, slather on some more. Start with 15 to 30 minutes of solar exposure and increase gradually each day. When you're hiking, carry water. If you don't get it right, watch for symptoms of sunstroke: fever, profuse sweating, headache, nausea or vomiting, extreme thirst, and sometimes hallucinations. To treat someone for sunstroke, find a breezy spot and place a cold, wet cloth on the victim's forehead. Change the cloth frequently so it stays cold. Offer lots of liquids—strong tea or coffee, fruit juice, water, soft drinks (no alcohol).

HYPOTHERMIA AND FROSTBITE

Wind and weather can shift dramatically in Maine, especially at higher elevations, creating prime conditions for contracting hypothermia and frostbite. At risk are hikers, swimmers, canoeists, kayakers, sailors, bicyclists, and even cross-country skiers.

When body temperature plummets below the normal 97° to 98.6°F, hypothermia is likely to set in. Symptoms include disorientation, a flagging pulse rate, prolonged shivering, swelling of the face, and cool skin. Quick action is essential to prevent shock and keep body temperature from dropping into the 80s, where cardiac arrest can occur. Emergency treatment begins with removal of as much wet clothing as possible without causing further exposure. Wrap the victim in anything dry—blankets, sleeping bag, clothing, towels, even large plastic trash bags—to keep body heat from escaping. Be sure the neck and head are covered. Or practice the buddy system—climb into a sleeping bag with the victim and provide skin contact. Do not rub the skin, apply hot water, or elevate the legs. If he or she is conscious, offer high-sugar snacks and nonalcoholic hot drinks (but, again, no alcohol; it dilates blood vessels and disrupts the warming process). As quickly as possible, transport the victim to a hospital emergency room.

When extremities begin turning blue or gray, with red blotches, frostbite may be setting in. As with hypothermia, add warmth slowly but do not rub frostbitten skin. Offer snacks and warm, nonalcoholic liquids.

To prevent hypothermia and frostbite, dress in layers and remove or add them as needed. Wool, waterproof nylon (such as Gore-Tex), and synthetic fleece (such as Polartec) are the best fabrics for repelling dampness; cotton does not do the job. Polyester fleece lining wicks excess moisture away from your body. If you plan to buy a down jacket, be sure it has a waterproof shell; down will just suck up the moisture from snow and rain. Especially in winter, always cover your head, since body heat escapes quickly through the head; a ski mask will protect ears and nose. Wear wool- or fleece-lined gloves and wool socks.

Even during the height of summer, be on the alert for mild hypothermia when children stay in the ocean too long. Bouncing in and out of the water, kids become preoccupied, refuse to admit they are cold, and fall prey to wind chill.

Acadia on Mount Desert Island

Rather like an octopus, or perhaps an amoeba, Acadia National Park extends its reach here and there and everywhere on Mount Desert Island. The park was created from donated parcels—a big chunk here, a tiny chunk there—and slowly but surely fused into its present-day size of more than 46,000 acres. Permanent boundaries do exist (Congress certified them as permanent in 1986), but they can be confusing to visitors. One minute you're in the park, the next you've stepped into one of the island's towns. This symbiotic relationship reminds us that Acadia National Park, covering a third of the island, is indeed the major presence here on Mount Desert. It affects traffic, indoor and outdoor pursuits, and, in a way, even the climate.

Acadia's history is unique among national parks and indeed fascinating. Several books have been written about some of the high-minded (in the positive sense) and high-profile personalities who provided the impetus (and wherewithal) for the park's inception and never flagged in their interest and support. Just to spotlight a few, we can thank the likes of George B. Dorr, Charles W. Eliot, and John D. Rockefeller, Jr., for what we have today.

Cadillac Mountain from Otter Cove

ACADIA HIGHLIGHTS

The highlights listed here are all within the park acreage on Mount Desert Island. (The park also occupies territory on the Schoodic Peninsula and Isle au Haut, and on several islands in the bay.) All of the locations mentioned are accessible from various parts of the island via the very convenient propane-powered **Island Explorer** bus system, which originates in downtown Bar Harbor. Be sure to take advantage of this cost free, hassle free service, operating on many routes around the island from late June to Columbus Day. The Island Explorer also has a free bus route on the Schoodic Peninsula section of the park, which you can reach via the **Bar Harbor Ferry,** departing from the Bar Harbor Inn Pier (adults $24 round-trip, kids $15, bikes $5). No cars are allowed on the ferry.

Hulls Cove Visitor Center: Here's where your visit should begin. Watch the 15-minute video about the park, sign up for a Park Ranger tour, use the restrooms, buy a trail map, and ask the rangers all the questions you've stored up. (Chances are, you won't stump them—especially the longtimers.) If you're here only for the day, park your car here and use the Island Explorer bus to get around the island.

Cadillac Mountain: Acadia's prime feature is the tallest point (1,530 feet) on the eastern seaboard, allegedly where the sun's first rays land (between early October and early March). Sunsets here are gorgeous, too, but don't expect romantic solitude—the Cadillac summit is a megapopular spot from sunrise to sundown. At the height of summer, wall-to-wall tour buses fill the parking spots.

Carriage-Road System: On the eastern side of Mount Desert Island, 57 miles of meandering, broken-stone roads with 17 handsome stone bridges welcome walkers, bikers, horseback riders, snowshoers, and cross-country skiers. (Bikes are allowed on only 45 of the 57 miles of the network; 12 miles are private, open only to walkers and horseback riders.) Electric wheelchairs are the only motorized vehicles allowed on carriage roads.

Hiking Trails: Besides the carriage roads, the park has about 130 miles of easy, moderate, and rugged trails just for hikers. Bicycles are *not* allowed on hiking trails; pets (which must be leashed) are allowed only on trails without ladders.

Naturalist Programs: Park rangers present lectures and lead one- to three-hour walks and hikes throughout the summer season. Most are free, some require reservations; many are specially geared to children or families (at least one adult must accompany children). They range from easy to strenuous, and some are accessible for people with disabilities. Sign up for "Acadia's Birds," or perhaps "Mr. Rockefeller's Bridges," or "Written in the Rocks"—they're all enlightening. The complete schedule is published in the park's *Beaver Log* tabloid-format newspaper; for trip planning, you can download it ahead of time from www.nps.gov/acad. For ranger-tour reservations, call 207/288-8832 (up to three days in advance). Park rangers also accompany several natural and cultural history cruises, all requiring reservations and fees. Pets are banned from ranger programs.

Park Loop Road: The best capsule experience of Acadia is the paved, 20-mile Park Loop Road, followed clockwise (part of it is one-way). The road to the Cadillac Mountain summit adds another seven miles, round-trip, to this total. Island Explorer bus routes cover different parts of this loop, although none of its routes include the Cadillac summit. Among the sights on or close to the loop: Sand Beach, Thunder Hole (best visited when the surf is wild), Otter Cliffs (a giant headland), Sieur de Monts Spring (nature center, museum, and gardens), and Eagle Lake. (See the *Driving Tour* section in this chapter for more on the Park Loop Road.)

Bass Harbor Head Light: This cliffside lighthouse within park boundaries at the southern tip of Mount Desert Island (beyond Southwest Harbor) is a prime photo-op site. Not far away (east on Route 102A) are trailheads for two lovely, interesting paths to the shore (Ship Harbor and Wonderland).

MOUNT DESERT ISLAND

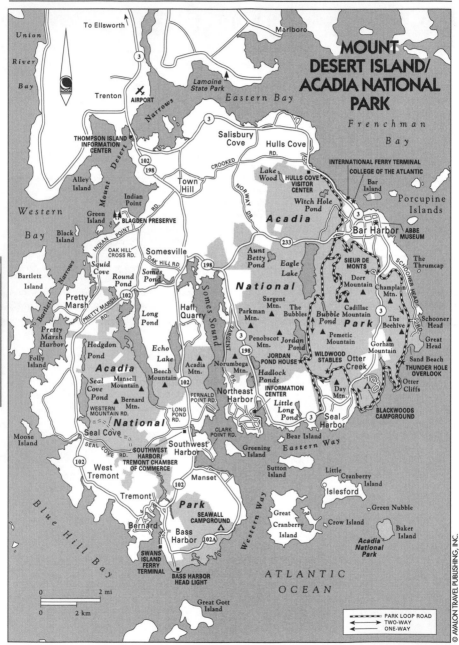

MOUNT DESERT ISLAND/ ACADIA NATIONAL PARK

MOUNT DESERT ISLAND

Exploring the Park

The sidebar *Acadia Highlights* provides an overview of what to see and do in the park, but there's so much more. First things first—the information centers.

INFORMATION CENTERS

There are two major centers on Mount Desert Island for Acadia National Park information. Some Acadia information is also available from the Bar Harbor Chamber of Commerce's two offices, the Southwest Harbor Chamber of Commerce, and the Mount Desert Chamber in Northeast Harbor.

Also, in Trenton, en route from Ellsworth on Route 3, and shortly before you reach Mount Desert, you'll see (on your right) the Acadia Information Center (Rte. 3, Trenton; P.O. Box 139, Mount Desert 04660, 207/667-8550 or 800/358-8550, www.acadiainfo.com). The privately owned seasonal center contains brochures, displays, and an interactive TV—all subsidized by the advertisers who participate in this operation. It is not an official park center, but the staff is knowledgeable and helpful. You'll also find info on Down East Maine, the Canadian Maritime provinces, and the ferry from Bar Harbor to Yarmouth, Nova Scotia, as well as free phones for local calls. It's open 10 A.M.–8 P.M. mid-May to mid-October.

Thompson Island Visitor Center

As you cross the bridge from Trenton toward Mount Desert Island, you might not even notice that you arrive first on tiny Thompson Island, site of a visitor center established jointly by the chambers of commerce of Mount Desert Island's towns and Acadia National Park.

The rustic building (on your right) has walls lined with brochures for accommodations, restaurants, and activities. There are also restrooms. Across Route 3 is a picnic area overlooking Mount Desert Narrows.

If you've arrived without a place to stay (particularly in July and August), the welcoming

© KATHLEEN M. BRANDES

ACADIA NATIONAL PARK

MOUNT DESERT ISLAND

staffers here are incredibly helpful—they keep track of lodging vacancies throughout Mount Desert Island and will go to great lengths to funnel you somewhere. In high season, don't expect to be overly choosy, though—room rates are high, vacancies are few, and you take your chances.

The center opens for the season in late May and is open daily, 10 A.M.–8 P.M. Everything wraps up soon after Columbus Day, when the center closes for the season.

At the height of summer, a park ranger usually is posted here on Thompson Island to answer questions and provide basic advice on hiking trails and other park activities, but consider this a stopgap—be sure also to continue on to the park's main visitor center.

PARK ENTRANCE FEES

A single glance at the map of Mount Desert Island immediately raises the question: How do you sell passes and count heads in a park that has patches of land here and there and everywhere—even on a section of the mainland and offshore islands? The answer? Not easily.

So . . . let's look at the picture another way. Thanks to action by Congress, about 80 percent of the fees Acadia collects are now returned to the park for much-needed maintenance and educational projects. The private Friends of Acadia organization and other donors often match these funds to make the money even more effective. Thus, consider just a few of the projects your pass helps fund:

- Trail and carriage-road reconstruction and rehabilitation
- The Island Explorer bus system
- New and improved restroom facilities
- Repairs to historic stone bridges
- New and improved informational exhibits
- Rock wall reconstruction
- Campground rehabilitation

At many of the project sites, you'll see brown Park Service signs—This Project Funded by Your Park User Fee—think of it as Acadia's thank-you note for your support.

Where to Buy Your Park Pass

- **The Hulls Cove Visitor Center,** the park's visitor information center from May through October. (No entrance fees are collected November through April.)
- The Acadia National Park information office opposite the **Village Green** in downtown Bar Harbor. It also faces the hub for the propane-powered Island Explorer bus system.
- The **Sand Beach Park Entrance Station,** on the Park Loop Road, between the Schooner Head Overlook and Sand Beach.
- The **Blackwoods and Seawall Campgrounds,** the park's only camping areas.
- **Acadia Park Headquarters** (Eagle Lake Rd., Rte. 233, Bar Harbor), open weekdays in summer.
- If you're coming to Acadia from southern Maine, you can also buy the one-week Acadia pass at the **L.L. Bean** store in Freeport, some 145 miles south of Acadia. Keep in mind, though, that the pass is good for seven days and becomes effective the day you buy it (not the first day you use it). Unless you're going directly from the store to Acadia, you might want to wait and buy your pass on Mount Desert Island if you're planning to spend a full

Hulls Cove Visitor Center

The modern Hulls Cove Visitor Center (Rte. 3, Hulls Cove, 207/288-3338) is eight miles southeast of the head of Mount Desert Island, and well signposted. Here you can buy your park pass ($20 per vehicle, good for a week) rendezvous with pals, make reservations for ranger-guided natural- and cultural-history programs, watch a 15-minute film about Acadia, study a relief map of the park, buy books and park souvenirs, rent or buy cassette guides, admire the view of Frenchman Bay, and use the restrooms. Pick up a copy of the *Beaver Log,* the tabloid-format park newspaper that lists the schedule of park activities, plus tide calendars and the entire schedule for the excellent **Island Explorer** shuttle bus system which operates from late June

to Columbus Day. The Island Explorer is supported by park entrance fees, as well as by Friends of Acadia and L.L. Bean.

Parking usually is ample at the Visitor Center, although the lot gets mighty full in midsummer, when as many as 9,000 people a day visit the center. Day-trippers also use the lot to leave their cars and hop on the Island Explorer bus. The bus stops at the base of the winding stairway from the parking lot to the center, which is open 8 A.M.–4:30 P.M. mid-April through October and 8 A.M.–6 P.M. July and August.

Acadia Park Headquarters

From November to April, information is available at **Acadia National Park Headquarters** on Eagle Lake Road (Route 233), about 3.5

week in the park. (If you're planning to spend more than a week, invest in the Acadia Annual Passport—details follow.)

Park Fees and Passes

• **Entrance fee:** $20 per vehicle (whether car or RV), covering everyone in the vehicle, valid for seven days. The motorbike fee is $10, also valid for seven days.

• **Acadia Annual Passport:** $40, valid for one year from the day you buy it. If you're hoping to be in Acadia more than a week in any given year, you'll easily amortize this fee.

• **National Parks Pass:** $50, allowing unlimited entrance for one year to all national parks with entrance or vehicle fees. You can buy this online anytime after mid-April at http://buy.nationalparks.org, or call toll-free, 888/467-2757. For an additional $15, you can get a **Golden Eagle** hologram to apply to the National Parks Pass, thus allowing you to enter—besides all the national parks—all

sites managed by Fish and Wildlife, the Forest Service, and the Bureau of Land Management (BLM).

• **Golden Age Passport:** $10, for U.S. citizens and permanent residents who are 62 or older, allowing lifetime entrance to the more than 300 national parks, historic sites, and monuments. It also entitles you to half-price camping. This is an incredible bargain, but the downside is that you have to become old enough to earn it! Purchase has to be made in person, with proof of age (driver's license, passport, etc.). The pass covers everyone in the passholder's vehicle.

• **Golden Access Passport:** free for any U.S. citizen or permanent resident who is blind or permanently disabled (a temporary disability, such as a broken arm or leg, does not qualify). It allows lifetime entrance to all national parks, as well as Fish and Wildlife, Forest Service, and BLM sites. It also allows half-price camping. The pass covers everyone in the vehicle accompanying the passholder.

© KATHLEEN M. BRANDES

the Acadia and Island Explorer information office in downtown Bar Harbor

miles west of downtown Bar Harbor. These months, the HQ office is open 8 A.M.– 4:30 P.M. daily except Thanksgiving, Christmas, and New Year's Day. During the summer, park publications are also available here, but the office is open only weekdays.

Park Headquarters is also the meeting point for the three-times-weekly volunteer work projects organized by the park and Friends of Acadia.

EMERGENCIES IN THE PARK

If you have an emergency while in the park, **call 911.** (The park's general information number is 207/288-3338.) If you're in a remote location, it

helps if you're carrying a cell phone, but *please* keep it turned off while hiking or biking; save it for an emergency. The nearest hospital is in downtown Bar Harbor (Mount Desert Island Hospital, with a 24-hour emergency room). The nearest major medical center is in Bangor (Eastern Maine Medical Center), via a congested route that can take an hour or longer at the height of summer. (Bangor, however, is one of the state's bases for a LifeFlight medevac helicopter.) Best advice for averting emergencies: Be cautious and sensible in everything you undertake in the park. Wear a helmet while biking. Don't hike alone or go off the trails—nearly every year, someone is seriously

MOUNT DESERT ISLAND

injured or killed falling from the cliffs. Keep a sharp eye on children.

DRIVING TOUR

The ideal way to fully appreciate Acadia is to hike the miles of trails, bike the carriage roads, canoe the ponds, swim in Echo Lake, and camp overnight. It seems rather a shame to treat Acadia as a drive-through park, but circumstances—time, health, and other factors—sometimes dictate that.

Logically, then, a driving tour in Acadia would follow the 27-mile **Park Loop Road.** It begins at the Visitor Center, winds past several of the park's scenic highlights (with parking areas), ascends to the summit of Cadillac Mountain, and provides overlooks to magnificent vistas. Allow a couple of hours so you can stop along the way.

A drive-it-yourself tour booklet, *Motorist Guide: Park Loop Road* ($1.50), is available at the Thompson Island and Hulls Cove Visitor Centers. Start at the parking lot below the Hulls Cove Visitor Center and follow the signs; part of the loop is one-way, so you'll be doing the loop clockwise. Traffic gets heavy at midday in mid-

summer, so aim for an early morning start if you can. Maximum speed is 35 mph, but be alert for gawkers and photographers stopping without warning. If you're out here at midday in mid-summer, don't be surprised to see cars and RVs parked in the right lane in the one-way sections; it's allowed when the designated parking lots are filled (and even when they aren't).

Along the route are trailheads and overlooks, as well as **Sieur de Monts Spring** (Acadia Nature Center, Wild Gardens of Acadia, Abbe Museum summer site, and the convergence of several spectacular trails), **Sand Beach, Thunder Hole, Otter Cliffs, Fabbri picnic area** (there's one wheelchair-accessible picnic table), **Jordan Pond House, Bubble Pond, Eagle Lake,** and the summit of **Cadillac Mountain.** Just before you get to Sand Beach, you'll see the Park Entrance Station, where you'll need to purchase a pass if you haven't already done so. (If you're here during nesting/fledging season—April to mid-August—be sure to stop in the Precipice Trailhead Parking Area; see the *Peregrine Falcons* sidebar.)

If you still have time for and/or interest in more driving after you've done the loop, take a spin around the rest of the island. Exit the Park

one of the distinctive stone bridges along the Park Loop Road

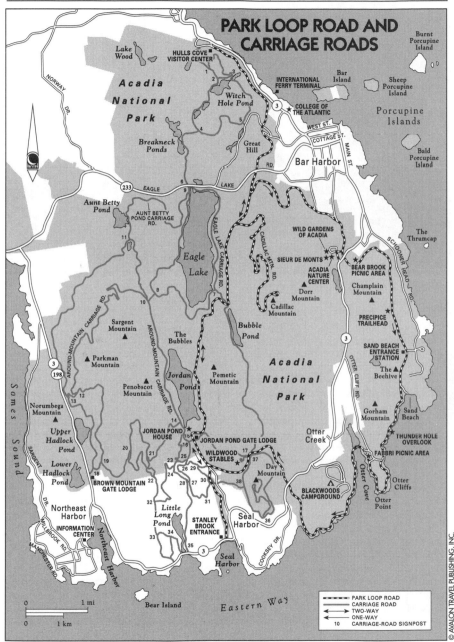

PARK LOOP ROAD AND CARRIAGE ROADS

Lake Wood

Acadia National Park

HULLS COVE VISITOR CENTER

Burnt Porcupine Island

Witch Hole Pond

INTERNATIONAL FERRY TERMINAL

Bar Island

Sheep Porcupine Island

NORWAY DR.

COLLEGE OF THE ATLANTIC

WEST ST.

COTTAGE ST.

MAIN ST.

Porcupine Islands

Breakneck Ponds

Great Hill

RD.

Bar Harbor

Bald Porcupine Island

233 EAGLE

LAKE

Aunt Betty Pond

AUNT BETTY POND CARRIAGE RD.

WILD GARDENS OF ACADIA

The Thrumcap

SCHOONER HEAD RD.

Eagle Lake

EAGLE LAKE CARRIAGE RD.

CADILLAC MTN. RD.

SIEUR DE MONTS

ACADIA NATURE CENTER

BEAR BROOK PICNIC AREA

Champlain Mountain

Dorr Mountain

Cadillac Mountain

PRECIPICE TRAILHEAD

Sargent Mountain

AROUND-MOUNTAIN CARRIAGE RD.

The Bubbles

Bubble Pond

Acadia National Park

SAND BEACH ENTRANCE STATION

3

The Beehive

Parkman Mountain

AROUND-MOUNTAIN CARRIAGE RD.

Jordan Pond

Pemetic Mountain

OTTER CLIFF RD.

3

198

Penobscot Mountain

Norumbega Mountain

Gorham Mountain

Sand Beach

Upper Hadlock Pond

JORDAN POND HOUSE

JORDAN POND GATE LODGE

Otter Creek

THUNDER HOLE OVERLOOK

FABBRI PICNIC AREA

Lower Hadlock Pond

WILDWOOD STABLES

Day Mountain

Otter Cove

Otter Cliffs

BROWN MOUNTAIN GATE LODGE

BLACKWOODS CAMPGROUND

Otter Point

Northeast Harbor

INFORMATION CENTER

MILLBROOK RD.

Little Long Pond

STANLEY BROOK ENTRANCE

Seal Harbor

SARGENT DR.

MANCHESTER RD.

Northeast Harbor

3

Seal Harbor

COOKSEY DR.

Somes Sound

0 1 mi
0 1 km

Bear Island

Eastern Way

PARK LOOP ROAD
CARRIAGE ROAD
TWO-WAY
ONE-WAY
10 CARRIAGE-ROAD SIGNPOST

MOUNT DESERT ISLAND

© AVALON TRAVEL PUBLISHING, INC.

MOUNT DESERT ISLAND

© KATHLEEN M. BRANDES

Jordan Pond Gate Lodge

Loop Road (near Bar Harbor) onto Route 233, heading west. (See the *Mount Desert Island Communities* chapter for potential sights along the way.) Continue to Route 198 and go left (south). In just over a mile, watch for a smallish sign for **Sargent Drive**. (*Note:* Only cars are allowed on this road, no RVs.) Take Sargent Drive, skirting gorgeous **Somes Sound**, into Northeast Harbor.

Leave Northeast Harbor via Route 198, northward, until you reach the head of Somes Sound. Go left around the head of the sound, to **Somesville**, a gem of a historic hamlet, then continue southward on Route 102 to Southwest Harbor. If you have time, take the Route 102A loop, with a chance to see **Bass Harbor Head Light**—you'll want to walk from the parking lot to get the best view. Otherwise, continue on Route 102 to Tremont (maybe detour into Bernard for great lobster on the wharf), then clockwise around to West Tremont, Seal Cove, Pretty Marsh, and back to Somesville. From there, you can go directly north to leave the island via Route 102/198, or go to Bar Harbor by heading eastward (follow signs).

GUIDED TOURS

The variety of guided activities in the park and nearby is astonishing—park ranger walks and talks and cruises, bus tours, bicycling tours, sea kayaking tours, birding expeditions, guided hikes, horse-drawn carriage rides, and even deluxe camping outfitters. (Besides these, see *Rock Climbing* for info on two Bar Harbor firms that specialize in guided rock climbing and bouldering.)

Park Ranger Programs

When you stop at the Hulls Cove Visitor Center and pick up the current issue of the park's *Beaver Log* newspaper (or download it ahead of time at www.nps.gov/acad/), you'll find a whole raft of possibilities for learning more about the park's natural and cultural history.

The Park Ranger programs, lasting one to three hours, are great—and most are free. During July and August, there are about 100 programs each week, all listed in the *Log*. Included are early-morning (7 A.M.) birding walks; mountain hikes (moderate level); tours of the historic

THE CAR-FREE PARK

Every way you look at it, the **Island Explorer** bus system seems to be a success. Since 1999, when the fare-free propane-fueled buses began running on an experimental basis throughout Mount Desert Island, ridership has more than doubled, more than 316,000 car and RV visits were eliminated, and pollutants were reduced by an estimated 24.4 tons.

Each year since the service began, expansion has occurred, with increased stops and routes, and 2003 saw a six-week extension in the fall schedule, thanks to a million-dollar grant from L.L. Bean. Service now begins in late June and lasts until Columbus Day (the Schoodic Peninsula route, established on a trial basis in 2003, stops on Labor Day).

"The little bus system that could," as Friends of Acadia president Ken Olson calls it, transports passengers to ferry landings, saves hikers and bikers from backtracking, gets commuters to work, and generally has revolutionized the summertime traffic patterns on Mount Desert Island.

Why spend valuable vacation time looking for a place to park your car? Why be disappointed when you reach a hiking trailhead and find the parking lot full? Take the bus. Feeling unsteady and un-

able to hike or bike? Tour the park and the island on the bus. Each bus can handle two bikes and a wheelchair.

The fleet is operated by the nonprofit Downeast Transportation (www.exploreacadia.com), with support from your park entrance fees, Friends of Acadia, and area towns and businesses.

The Island Explorer hub is the Bar Harbor Village Green, where all of the routes (except Schoodic) begin or end. Between late June and Labor Day, service begins at 6:45 A.M., although not every route starts that early. But, like the Energizer bunny, the buses keep going and going and going . . . until late into the summer evening (last bus leaves downtown Bar Harbor about 11 P.M. for the campgrounds in the northern end of the island). A geolocator system provides tracking information at the Village Green and at the Hulls Cove Visitor Center.

Specific stops are listed on the schedule, but drivers will pull over and pick you up or drop you off anywhere they feel it's safe. Don't hesitate to request a stop or flag down a bus.

So pick up a schedule—copies are everywhere on Mount Desert—and use the Island Explorer to explore the island!

Carroll Homestead, a 19th-century farm; Cadillac summit natural-history tours; children's expeditions to learn about tide pools and geology (an adult must accompany kids); trips for the wheelchair-borne; and even a couple of tours a week in French. Some tours require reservations, some do not. (Reservations can be made up to three days in advance.) Reservations and fees are required for several different boat cruises with park rangers who provide natural-history narration (the specific cruises tend to vary from year to year).

Park rangers also give the evening lectures during the summer in the amphitheaters at Blackwoods and Seawall Campgrounds.

And the good news is that between late June and mid-October, you can join almost every ranger program via an Island Explorer bus.

Bus and Trolley Tours

The veteran of the Bar Harbor–based bus tours is **Acadia National Park Tours** (tickets at Testa's Restaurant, Bayside Landing, 53 Main St., P.O. Box 52, Bar Harbor 04609, 207/288-3327, www.acadiatours.com), operating May through October. A 2.5-hour, naturalist-led tour of Bar Harbor and Acadia departs at 10 A.M. and 2 P.M. daily from downtown Bar Harbor (Testa's is across from Agamont Park, near the Bar Harbor Inn). Reservations are wise in midsummer and during fall-foliage season (late September and early October); pick up reserved tickets 30 minutes before departure. Cost is $20 adults, $10 children under 12.

If there's a time crunch, take the one-hour trolley-bus tour operated by **Oli's Trolley** (P.O. Box 794, Bar Harbor 04609, 207/288-9899, www.acadiaislandtours.com), which departs downtown Bar Harbor five times daily (between 10 A.M. and 6 P.M.) in July and August, including Bar Harbor mansion drive-bys and the Cadillac summit. Starting point is the Oli's Trolley Ice Cream Shop, 58 Cottage Street, across from the post office. (Tickets are also available at Harbor Place, the waterfront marketplace near the Bar Harbor Inn.) Dress warmly if the air is at all cool; it's an open-air trolley. Cost is $15 adults, $10 children under 12. Reservations are advisable. The trolley also does 2.5-hour park tours at 10 A.M. and 2 P.M. May through October. Tickets are $20 adults, $10 children under 12. The bus and trolley routes both include potty stops.

Bicycling Tours

VBT (formerly Vermont Bicycle Touring; 614 Monkton Rd., Bristol, VT 05443, 800/245-3868, www.vbt.com), in business since the mid-1970s, offers well-organized six-day tours of Acadia and two offshore islands (Swans and Little Cranberry), with dinners and overnights at comfortable inns—usually the Bar Harbor Inn and the Claremont Hotel. The difficulty level is easy to moderate, covering 13–26 miles a day. Maximum group size is 18. The trips operate early June to mid-October, for $1,495 pp, not counting the cost of getting here. (The early June trips are about $200 cheaper; the September and early October trips—fall foliage season—are $100 more.)

PARK RULES

All parks have rules, and Acadia is no exception. Most are just common sense; some are specific to Acadia's situation and needs.

• It's forbidden to disturb or remove any public property—plants, minerals, artifacts, animals, etc. This extends to the rocks on the beach, and you'll see signs here and there reminding you of that.

• Pets are allowed in Acadia, with some exceptions, but they must be leashed or physically restrained. Voice control is not accepted. They must not be left unattended. Pets are not allowed on Sand Beach, the beach at Echo Lake, or in the Duck Harbor campground on Isle au Haut. They are also banned from the park's ladder trails and from the visitor centers and other public buildings. Pets should not be taken on Park Ranger tours. (Service dogs, of course, are always exempted from the rules.)

• In-line skating and skateboarding are not allowed in the park.

• Bicycles are not allowed on any hiking trails. They're allowed on 45 miles of park carriage trails, but *not* on 12 miles of signposted (Green Rock Company) private carriage roads.

• Motorcycles and motorbikes are not allowed on park trails and carriage roads; ATVs are not al-

© KATHLEEN M. BRANDES

lowed anywhere in the park. Electric wheelchairs *are* allowed on the carriage roads.

• Camping is allowed only at the park's two campgrounds on Mount Desert Island and one on Isle au Haut. There is no backcountry camping in the park or anywhere else on Mount Desert Island, but the island has a dozen commercial campgrounds.

• Camp stoves and grills are allowed only in designated campgrounds and picnic areas; fires are allowed only in fire rings and fireplaces at these sites.

• Alcohol use is not allowed at Sand Beach or Echo Lake beach.

• Hunting is not allowed in the park.

For bicycling on your own, see Biking, below. For bike rentals, see the sections on Bar Harbor and Southwest Harbor in the *Mount Desert Island Communities* chapter.

Sea Kayaking Tours

Most of the sea kayaking tours are in the waters around Mount Desert, particularly Bar Harbor, so they don't strictly qualify as park tours. For information on the various sea kayaking outfitters and tour operators, see the *Getting Afloat* sections in the *Mount Desert Island Communities* chapter.

Birding and Nature Tours

For private tours of the park and other parts of the island, contact Michael Good at **Down East Nature Tours** (P.O. Box 521, Knox Road, Town Hill, Bar Harbor 04609, 207/288-8128, www.mainebirding.net/downeast). A biologist with a special interest in birds, he'll take neophyte birders on a four-hour tour they won't forget. What better place to begin a life list than Acadia National Park? Birding tours occur daily, rain or shine, starting about $25 pp, but prices vary according to the destination and length of tour (two or four hours, or all day); maximum group is eight people. Lodging pickup is available. Bring your own binoculars, but Michael supplies a spotting scope.

Hiking Itineraries

If you're happy to hike on your own but you'd like to have someone suggest and plan routes geared to your abilities (especially if you have a group), contact Earl Brechlin at **Base Camp Outfitters** (207/288-4859, www.justmaine.com/brechlin/basecamp/). He's the author of several books on Acadia, Bar Harbor, and Mount Desert (See *Suggested Reading*), a newspaper editor, and a Registered Maine Guide. He'll suggest hikes and provide insider advice. Cost depends on the many possible variables—group size, number of hikes, amount of help needed.

Carriage Tours

A fabulous way to recapture Acadia's early carriage-roads era is to take one of the horse-drawn open-carriage tours run by Ed Winterberg's **Carriages in the Park,** departing from Wildwood Stables, .5 mile south of the Jordan Pond House, on the Park Loop Road (P.O. Box 241, Seal Harbor 04675, 207/276-3622, www .acadia.net/wildwood). Don't pooh-pooh this as too touristy—on a gorgeous day, the vistas are everything, and you won't be disappointed. Half a dozen one- and two-hour trips start daily at 9:30 A.M., mid-June to Columbus Day. Reservations are encouraged, especially at the height of summer. The best outing is the two-hour **Sunset at the Summit** to the top of Day Mountain, departing at 6:30 P.M. in June, 6:15 P.M. in July, and 6 P.M. in August. Cost is $17.50 adults, $16.50 seniors and $8 children 6–12. Other routes are $13.50–17.50 per adult. If you take the two-hour carriage ride to Jordan Pond House, departing daily at 1:15 P.M. ($15.50 adults, not counting food and beverage), you're guaranteed a reserved lawn chair for tea and popovers.

If you have a group of six or fewer, you can arrange for a private carriage-road tour of two–four hours ($90 an hour). Wildwood has no trail rides, but you can bring your own horse and stable it here at $20 a night for a box stall. (A basic campground has sites for stall renters for $10 a night.)

Camping Tours

Most campers are self-sufficient do-it-yourselfers, so what's this? A camping outfitter that does it all for you, African-safari–style. Consider how you feel sometimes after a long day of hiking or biking or kayaking—no energy to organize dinner? Consider the planning that goes into a camping trip—organizing menus, packing pots and gear and all the other "stuff." If your life is so hectic you can't get it together, you might be working a job that produces disposable income. So if your budget allows, and you like to camp, leave all the details to **Krismark Outfitters** (202 U.S. Rte. 1, Box 349, Falmouth 04105, 888/746-2267, www.krismarkoutfitters.com). Their slogan is "the best camping trip you never had to plan." A three-day "Acadia Weekender," including camp setup and breakdown, meals, and a kayak or bike tour, runs $295–345 adults, $120–150 kids (children not allowed on some trips). They'll also do custom trips, with varied itineraries. Campsites are at the Smuggler's Den Campground.

Sights

The **Park Loop Road** will lead you to the major sights on the east side of the park—Sieur de Monts Spring, Sand Beach, Thunder Hole, Otter Cliffs, and the summit of Cadillac Mountain—but then there's also the fantastic carriage-road system. As you explore the rest of the park acreage on Mount Desert, particularly its west side, you'll come upon still more surprising spots.

SIEUR DE MONTS SPRING

About two miles from Bar Harbor and close to the often-busy Park Loop Road, Sieur de Monts Spring is an oasis in a tranquil woodland setting. Named after 17th-century French explorer, Pierre du Gua, Sieur de Monts, the spring is the centerpiece of a 10-acre parcel donated in 1916 for a future national park by George Bucknam Dorr, the Father of Acadia. It was Dorr who erected the pretty Italianate Spring House and dubbed this "The Sweet Waters of Acadia"—after the Sweet Waters of Europe and the Sweet Waters of Asia, two springs that had deeply impressed him on a visit to Constantinople. (The water here, incidentally, is not safe to drink—nor, for that matter, is the water in those Istanbul springs.)

Also here is the Acadia **Nature Center,** containing exhibits on flora and fauna and explanations of the ongoing efforts to preserve the park's natural resources. The center is open mid-May through mid-October (9 A.M.–5 P.M. daily in July and August). Admission is free.

Below the Nature Center, take time to walk through the **Wild Gardens of Acadia,** touted as "an outdoor field guide" to the island's plant life. Maintained by the Bar Harbor Garden Club, the Wild Gardens are divided into a dozen different habitats containing more than 400 species of wildflowers. The gardens are open mid-May to mid-October: 9 A.M.–5 P.M. in July and August, shorter hours early and late in the season.

An important feature of this lovely area is the privately run **Abbe Museum** (207/288-3519, www.abbemuseum.org), the original home of Dr. Robert Abbe's extensive personal collection of prehistoric and historic archaeological artifacts, some dating back 11,000 years. Built in 1928, the museum outgrew this National Historic Register building and now has a handsome year-round structure in downtown Bar Harbor. The Sieur de Monts Spring site, with exhibits on Maine archaeology and the history of the museum, is open Memorial Day Weekend to mid-October: 9 A.M.–5 P.M. July and August, 10 A.M.–4 P.M. in spring and fall. Admission is $2 adults, $1 children 6–15; free admission for Native Americans and children under six.

Jesup Trail signpost, toward Sieur de Monts

MOUNT DESERT ISLAND

The Sieur de Monts Spring area provides access to several Acadia trails. To the west of the Spring House are strenuous trails leading up **Dorr Mountain** (originally Dry Mountain, then Flying Squadron Mountain). To the north is the easy **Jesup Path**—two to three miles in this valley between Dorr Mountain and Huguenot Head. The Jesup Path (also called the Jesup Trail) is particularly spectacular during the fall foliage season. You can also access the Tarn and Hemlock Trails at Sieur de Monts.

SAND BEACH

Below the Park Loop Road and the newly spiffed-up Park Entrance Station, Sand Beach is the park's only large sandy beach on salt water— *cold* salt water. Well, it's not really sand, as a sign posted here will tell you—it's composed of zillions of crushed shells, pulverized so they look like sand. If you haven't purchased your park entrance pass by this point, you'll need to do it here. Via the Island Explorer bus, Sand Beach is about 25 minutes from Bar Harbor (a bit less than that by car before and after the bus season).

© KATHLEEN M. BRANDES

MOUNT DESERT ISLAND

Thunder Hole—with no crowds and no thunder

THUNDER HOLE

Thunder Hole gets pumped up as a spectacular attraction, and it is—but only if your timing is right. When the wind is coming from the south or southeast, when a storm has churned up the sea, or when the tide is rushing inward— then you'll hear (and feel) how Thunder Hole got its name. As the water rushes into a narrow slot in the rocks, it creates a powerful roar, shoots into the air, and often showers the closest bystanders.

If your schedule can be flexible, check the tide tables in the local paper (or in the park's *Beaver Log* newspaper) and try to be here for the incoming tide, preferably about midtide.

A note of caution: Because of the seaspray, the steps leading down toward Thunder Hole often are very slippery. Take particular care with small children and anyone who tends to be unsteady.

JORDAN POND HOUSE

Afternoon tea at the rustic Jordan Pond House was a summer tradition in the late 19th century, and it's still on everyone's list of Acadia highlights. You can even arrive by carriage and re-create the car-free era. While tea (with hot-from-the-oven popovers and strawberry jam) is the most popular choice here, the restaurant— now in a modern building—also serves lunch and dinner, between mid-May and mid-October. From late June to Columbus Day, the Island Explorer bus will get you here in 20 minutes from Bar Harbor. (In summer, the last bus for Bar Harbor leaves the restaurant at 8:50 P.M.)

CADILLAC MOUNTAIN

As the highest point (1,530 feet) in Acadia, the Cadillac summit receives the day's first ray of

JORDAN POND HOUSE

In the late 19th century, when Bar Harbor was in the throes of becoming "the great new place" to escape the heat of Washington, New York, Philadelphia, and the Midwest, gentle ladies and men patronized an unassuming farmhouse/teahouse on the shores of Jordan Pond. By 1895 or 1896, under the stewardship of Thomas McIntire, it became Jordan Pond House—a determinedly rustic establishment, with massive fieldstone fireplaces, serving afternoon tea and leisurely luncheons during the summer and fall.

And rustic it remained, well into the late 20th century—until leveled by a disastrous fire in the summer of 1979. At that point, it was owned by Acadia. John D. Rockefeller, Jr., had bought it in the 1930s and donated it to the park in the early 1940s. Since then, it's been managed on behalf of the park by concessionaires—currently the Acadia Corporation (which also operates gift shops in several locations).

Today, Jordan Pond House, the only restaurant within Acadia National Park, must rely on its framed antique photos to conjure up a bit of nostalgia for the bygone era. The building is modern and open, the pace in summer is frenetic, and the food is average. But the view from the lawn over Jordan Pond and the astounding Bubbles is incredible. Surely *it* hasn't changed.

So . . . at least once, brave the crowds and have afternoon tea on the lawn at Jordan Pond House. Order tea or Oregon chai or even cappuccino and fresh popovers (two) with extraordinary strawberry jam. That package will set you back $7.50–8.75, but how much would you pay for the view?

Lunch (salads, sandwiches, and entrées include a popover) and afternoon tea are served from 11:30 A.M.–5:30 P.M. daily, inside or on the lawn. Dinner (entrées $15–20) begins at 5:30 P.M.—inside or on the porch. The reservation system is unique: call 207/276-3316, any time from 9:15 A.M., which puts you "on the list." You'll probably have to wait when you arrive, so stop in the gift shop for a jar of jam to take home.

Perhaps because of all the sweet drinks and jam served outdoors, patrons at the lawn tables sometimes find themselves pestered by bees. They don't usually sting unless you pester them back, but if you're hyperallergic to bee stings, or are with anyone who is, be alert.

Jordan Pond House, on the Park Loop Road, is open 11:30 A.M.–8 P.M. mid-May to mid-October (until 9 P.M. July and August). From late June to Columbus Day, it's easy to reach via the Island Explorer bus, and several park hiking trails originate or pass near here.

If you need a popover fix when you return home, you can always buy a package of the mix along with the jam in the gift shop, but if you don't, here's the Jordan Pond House recipe:

Jordan Pond House Popovers

2 large eggs
1 cup whole milk
1 cup all-purpose flour (presifted)
1/2 teaspoon salt
1/8 teaspoon baking soda

Preheat oven to 425° F. Beat eggs with electric mixer at high speed three minutes. Reduce mixer speed to lowest setting and very gradually pour in half the milk. In separate bowl, combine sifted flour, salt, and baking soda and sift again.

With mixer still running at slowest speed, add dry ingredients to egg-and-milk mixture. Turn off mixer and use rubber spatula to blend mixture thoroughly.

Set mixer to medium speed and very gradually pour in remaining milk, blending one minute. Raise mixer speed to highest setting and beat 10 minutes.

Strain batter through fine-mesh strainer to remove lumps, then pour into well-buttered popover or custard cups. Bake 15 minutes. Without opening oven, reduce heat to 350° and bake 15 more minutes (20 minutes if oven door has a window).

Serve immediately, with fresh jam and room-temperature butter.

Hint: Popovers turn out significantly better if baked in ovenproof cups rather than in metal or glass.

Recipe makes two popovers. Increase as desired, but be sure to measure carefully.

sunlight between early October and early March. A couple of trails will get you to the Cadillac summit (including one from Blackwoods Campground), and you can get a good mountain-bike workout on the road (bikes aren't allowed on trails), but in the end, most summiteers tend to get there by car—a seven-mile round-trip via paved road. (The Island Explorer bus does not go to the Cadillac summit.)

Formerly named Green Mountain, Cadillac was topped by the wooden Summit Hotel, built by an ambitious developer who eventually fell on hard times and went into bankruptcy. Some might say he deserved it, for blighting the landscape. Before his decline in the late 19th century, however, his 6,000-foot Green Mountain Cog Railway transported guests to the summit, where the view was just as spectacular as it is today. (Photos of the Cog Railway era are part of the collection at the Bar Harbor Historical Society, on Ledgelawn Street.) The summit road was built in 1931.

At the height of summer, sunrise, midday, and sunset are the busiest times on the summit; if you're not looking for bragging rights about sun-rise or sunset, try to be here an hour or two after sunrise or an hour or two before sunset.

At the top are head-swiveling vistas and a gift shop and restrooms. Be sure to walk the paved, .3-mile Summit Trail loop for the full effect, but *please stay on the trail* to preserve the summit's fragile plants and soil.

From late August to mid-October, the park runs the **Hawkwatch** program near the Cadillac summit. (The observation site is on the Cadillac North Ridge Trail, about 600 feet from the summit parking lot.) Each day during the Hawkwatch, 9 A.M.–2 P.M., weather permitting, park interpreters are on hand to help you identify the various species of hawks, falcons, eagles, and ospreys that migrate through Acadia each fall. More than 3,000 visitors participated in 2003. Since the Hawkwatch project began in 1995, the annual raptor count here during the migration season has averaged about 2,500.

THE CARRIAGE-ROAD SYSTEM

Bare summits, woodlands, gemlike ponds, 17 handsome stone bridges, and dazzling vistas—

carriage-road entrance gate near Jordan Pond

MOUNT DESERT ISLAND

MR. ROCKEFELLER'S ROADS

I magine being able to build your own network of pathways where you could step into a horse-drawn carriage and meander through matchless terrain. Petroleum heir John D. Rockefeller, Jr., did just that on Mount Desert Island—and, thanks to him, we can all walk and bike these roadways, and even go for our own horse-drawn carriage rides.

The story of Acadia's car-free carriage roads has been told and retold, but Rockefeller's grand-daughter, Ann R. Roberts, had the inside track when she wrote *Mr. Rockefeller's Roads: The Untold Story of Acadia's Carriage Roads & Their Creator* (see *Suggested Reading*). Her book relates a fascinating saga of benevolence and sensitivity and talent and organization. The carriage-road system is one of Acadia's most valued cultural resources—listed since 1979 on the National Register of Historic Places.

Between 1913 and 1940, Rockefeller was involved in the purchase of acreage and the design and construction of more than 57 miles of carriage roads on Mount Desert. (Forty-five miles of these roads are now within Acadia National Park boundaries and 12 on private land but open to the public.) And "involved" is the operative word here. Not only did he conceptualize the project, finance it, and consult on every aspect of the road and bridge designs, he was on hand during the construction and landscaping phases. No detail escaped his scrutiny.

Rockefeller's passion for road engineering and landscaping came from watching and working with his father, John D. Rockefeller, Sr., who planned carriage roads and rustic stone bridges for the family's estate near Cleveland. Later, father and son created carriage roads through Pocantico Hills, their vast Hudson River estate. Lessons learned from those undertakings laid the groundwork (literally and figuratively) for the even more ambitious project on Mount Desert.

Rockefeller Jr. first visited Mount Desert as a Brown University student in 1893, but it was his 1908 trip to Seal Harbor—with his wife Abby—that shaped his lifelong love for the island. In 1910, they bought "The Eyrie," a Seal Harbor estate that still remains in the family, and he soon began the other land acquisitions that continued until 1940. Around 1913, he began laying out his astonishing network of carriage roads, stepping up the pace in 1916 when he hired Charles P. Simpson as his chief engineer. In 1922, Simpson turned over the task to his son Paul ("Chip"), who remained chief engineer until 1940. Renowned landscape architect Beatrix Farrand worked with Rockefeller on roadside plantings, and dozens of other people—noted and not-so-noted—became part of the team at some point during the nearly three-decade-long project.

you'll see them all as you walk or bike the fantastic 57-mile carriage-road network that makes Acadia unique among America's national parks.

Forty-five miles of the broken-stone roads—all on the east side of the island, between the Hulls Cove Visitor Center in the north and Seal Harbor in the south—are open for walking, bicycling, and horseback riding (and in winter for cross-country skiing and snowshoeing). Twelve additional miles, on private land owned by the Green Rock Company, are open for walking and horseback riding but not biking (be alert for the No Bikes signs when you're cycling; all of the private roads are south of the Jordan Pond House).

PRETTY MARSH PICNIC AREA

Picnic spots are everywhere on Mount Desert, but an Acadia National Park site that many people miss is the Pretty Marsh Picnic Area, overlooking Pretty Marsh Harbor, on the opposite side of the island from Bar Harbor. Dense woods shelter grills and tables, and you can walk down to the shoreline and even launch a sea kayak. Kids love this place, but be prepared with insect repellent. The picnic area is just west of Route 102 (Pretty Marsh Rd.), on the westernmost shore. (Pretty Marsh is not on an Island Explorer bus route; you'll need a car or bike to get there.)

Distinctive features of the roads are 17 handsome rough-stone bridges (with single, double, and triple arches; no two alike), 16-foot-wide broken-stone roadbeds that required more man-hours than anyone could count, and tasteful carved trail markers. A holdover from Rockefeller's previous carriage-road experience was the use of roadside borders of squared-off granite coping stones—known at Acadia as "Mr. Rockefeller's teeth."

And then there are the two stone gate lodges (or gate houses)—Brown Mountain Gate Lodge and Joordan Pond Gate Lodge—heralding entrances to the original carriage-road system. (Many more access points exist today.) Designed by Grosvenor Atterbury in a whimsical French Romanesque style, the handsome structures are startling, to say the least. It's hard not to smile when you come upon them (near Northeast Harbor, and near Jordan Pond, respectively). During the carriage-road building, engineer Paul Simpson and his family occupied the Jordan Pond Gate Lodge.

Until his death in 1960 (when Acadia assumed responsibility for 45 miles of the carriage-road system), John D. Rockefeller, Jr., continued his magnanimity by financing the maintenance of the carriage-road network. By the early 1990s, however, the roads, bridges, and drainage systems had seriously deteriorated, and the fabulous vistas had become overgrown. Enter Friends of Acadia, an amazing nonprofit organization that helped the park obtain federal funding and then maximized the grant with matching private funds—generating enough to cover the $6 million facelift and begin a carriage-road endowment. Thanks also to the impetus of Friends of Acadia, work began in 2003 to repair more than two dozen bridges and nearby sections of historic hiking trails—an estimated $3 million project.

As one carriage-road admirer put it: "The roads are just the way God would have made them if he only had the money."

MOUNT DESERT ISLAND

© KATHLEEN M. BRANDES

This carriage-road sign features the historic Bubble Pond Bridge, built in 1928 of compressed rock.

Hiking

It would take weeks of nonstop all-day hiking to cover every trail in the Mount Desert Island acreage of Acadia National Park. And it would consume most of this book to write about them. Not a bad idea—but few of us have enough free time to manage such a feat. (Island resident Tom St. Germain, author of *A Walk in the Park,* somehow finds time to hike each of the trails at least once a year. More power to him!) Best to do as much as you can when you're here—and return as often as possible to do more!

What follows, therefore, is a selection of choice hikes, ranging from very easy to strenuous. Evaluate your schedule, your skills and/or limitations (especially the capabilities of your least-sturdy hiking partners), gather your gear, pack a picnic, and head out. (If you don't feel like doing your own planning, or you'd prefer a guide to provide cultural and natural historical information, see *Guided Tours.*)

As you take your first step on your first park trail, however, keep in mind the Leave No Trace philosophy that governs all recreation in the park—but especially hiking. Stick to it for yourself, your family, and the generations to come.

Until the establishment of the **Island Explorer** bus system, hikers had to do loop trails in Acadia in order to return to their cars or bikes, or they had to make elaborate arrangements for pickup or shuttling. The bus schedule now has created all kinds of other options. It allows you to skip the backtracking—and in some cases lets you pick up transport along the way if you (or the kids) wear out earlier than expected. (Of course, this holds true only for the bus season—late June to Columbus Day, and the schedule is reduced between Labor Day and Columbus Day.) Even if your destination/locale isn't on the bus schedule, you can request a stop or flag down a bus anywhere that it's safe for the driver to pull over. The bus schedules vary slightly each year. Pick up the latest schedule at the Hulls Cove Visitor Center or download it before you leave home (www .exploreacadia.com). Then take advantage of the system while you're on Mount Desert Island.

All of the hikes described here follow Acadia National Park hiking trails. (See the *Bar Harbor and Vicinity* section in the *Mount Desert Island Communities* chapter for info on the intown Shore Path, which is not part of the park.) The separate but sometimes interconnected carriage roads, which also are open to hiking (more like strolling, in many cases)—as well as horseback riding and bicycling—are described later, under *Biking.*

The hikes that follow are divided into two sections—the east side of Mount Desert Island and the west side. Because Somes Sound almost bisects the island, none of the trails cross from one side of the island to the other, and almost every one of the peaks' ridgelines runs in a north-south (or south-north) direction. The hikes are described below in the order of difficulty, from very easy to strenuous; lengths of hikes vary within each category (length, of course, doesn't always determine the difficulty). Ratings are based on park advisories and personal experience.

While you plan, bear in mind that most visitors tend to spend more time on the east side of the island, for a variety of reasons—more trails, a range of easy-to-moderate trails, the carriage-road network, the auto road to Cadillac's summit, the Park Loop Road, the park's only restaurant (Jordan Pond House), and so on. So heading for the west-side trails, even at the height of summer, can provide you with quieter spaces and some truly great hikes. The 2002 trails census (taken on the first weekend in August, arguably the busiest of the summer) counted 5,225 hikers on east-side trails and 2,717 hikers on west-side trails. The numbers tell the story.

EAST-SIDE TRAILS
Ocean Trail
• Distance: 4 miles round-trip
• Rating: Very easy
• Trailhead: Take the Park Loop Road to either the Sand Beach or the Otter Point parking lot. The Island Explorer bus stops at Sand Beach

TIPS FOR DAY HIKING

Since Acadia has no backcountry camping, all the hikes in the park are day hikes—guaranteeing, at least, a load off your back! You'll need far less gear for a half-day or daylong hike, but don't be complacent or stupid—use common sense and be prepared for emergencies. That way, they probably won't happen.

Experienced hikers and backcountry campers won't need my advice here, but a few reminders never hurt, and it's worth noting the "maps and guides" information, specific to Acadia.

In general, the gear you carry (and the size of your day pack) depends on your plans for the day—following a short nature trail then calling it quits; hiking for a few hours then stopping for a swim; hiking all day with a noontime picnic—lots of options. Here's a checklist that should help you get organized (divvy up the items if you're hiking with friends or family):

• **Identification,** such as a driver's license. Even if you don't carry your regular wallet, be sure you have your health-insurance card.

• **Maps and guides.** Purchase a trail map at the park's visitor center. The National Park Service map of Acadia that's available free at the visitor center will give you the lay of the land and useful general info, and it's serviceable if you're planning only to drive or bike the Park Loop Road, but *do not* rely on it for hiking. The map published by Jim Witherell is particularly good (contour interval 20 feet), as is the Parkman Publications map, published in conjunction with Friends of Acadia (contour interval 50 feet). On the east side of the island, even if you are planning to stick to the hiking trails, *be sure* also to carry a map of the park's carriage trails to avoid confusion where carriage and hiking trails meet and cross.

Purchase and use a trail guide as well. I recommend *A Walk in the Park,* by Tom St. Germain ($11.95) and/or *Hiking Acadia National Park,* by Dolores Kong and Dan Ring ($16.95). Both provide useful detailed maps and elevations for each hike. Also valuable is the Appalachian Mountain Club's *Discover Acadia National Park,* by Jerry and Marcy Monkman ($16.95), which comes with a foldout map (contour interval 100 feet). Besides hikes, the Appalachian Mountain Club guide includes information on bike and paddling routes as well as other recreational activities in the park.

Between late June and Columbus Day, carry a copy of the **Island Explorer bus schedule,** which you can find almost anywhere on the island (or download it before you leave home: www .exploreacadia.com). Stuff it in your day pack, even if you're getting to your trailhead by car. If someone in your hiking party wants to quit early, you'll want to know the nearest spot (and time) to catch a bus.

• **Water and food.** Even though some ponds in the park are used as drinking-water sources for surrounding towns, it's treated before they get it. Don't risk intestinal problems; carry your own water. If you're worried about carrying weight, include iodine tablets if you can stand the taste. To avoid excessive thirst, don't bring salty snacks—carry gorp or energy bars (without chocolate, so you don't have to deal with a melting mush). If you're carrying picnic fare, don't be overambitious (or overgreedy) if you're planning a strenuous hike. Be sure to pack any mayo-based food in a flexible insulated bag; peanut-butter-and-jam (jelly for the kids) sandwiches are a safer bet.

• A couple of wastebasket-size **trash bags**—carry in, carry out. A spare bag can also come in handy for protecting maps, camera, binoculars, etc., in the event of a sudden squall (not unheard-of during a Maine summer).

• A **compass or GPS,** particularly if you're directionally challenged or are planning a lengthy hike (or both). If you own a cell phone, carry it, but *turn it off* and use it *only* in an emergency. Wireless service can be iffy in some parts of Acadia; check when you arrive.

• A small **first-aid kit** (in a waterproof or zip-top bag) containing a few basic items: adhesive bandages, aspirin or acetaminophen, ibuprofen, perhaps an Ace bandage. Even though bees don't tend to be a problem in Acadia (except perhaps on the lawn at Jordan Pond House), be sure you're carrying a prefilled epinephrine syringe to prevent anaphylaxis if you're allergic to bee stings (or, for that matter, shellfish). Include a few wooden matches and a whistle in case of emergency.

(continued on next page)

MOUNT DESERT ISLAND

MOUNT DESERT ISLAND

TIPS FOR DAY HIKING (cont'd)

- **Moist towelettes** for various cleanup tasks, or for cleansing minor scrapes.
- **Swiss Army knife.** Carry the kind with a corkscrew if you're planning on having wine with a picnic. Or you could decant white wine into a plastic water bottle to save weight—but go easy on the alcohol. Not only will it dehydrate you, but you're likely to be more prone to tripping and falling.
- A full-brimmed hat and decent hiking shoes (not sandals, which provide no ankle support).
- **Sunblock, lip balm** (the kind with UV protection), and **insect repellent.** Buzz-Off, a new natural repellent, is a good choice, especially for children. Ben's and Cutter's tend to be widely available.
- **Camera** (and a spare battery) and **binoculars.** Take plenty of film if you're planning to be out all day. Most of the island's summits are bare, allowing fabulous views—photo ops are everywhere in Acadia.
- A **mini-flashlight** and spare batteries (just in case).

- Depending on your plans for the day, carry a change of socks, a rain jacket and/or windbreaker, maybe a fleece vest, perhaps a swimsuit for a hike such as Penobscot and Sargent Mountains, where you can pause for a swim in Sargent Pond.

Important: Don't hike alone, or if you do, tell someone—a friend, a relative, your lodging manager, a campground ranger, your shrink, anyone—or leave a note to say where you are headed. If for any reason you don't return, the park rangers at least will know where to start looking.

Reminders: Bikes are banned from *all* hiking trails. Dogs must be leashed (not always convenient on strenuous scrambles), and they are banned from Sand Beach and hiking trails with ladders ("ladder trails"). Best advice: Don't bring a dog. If you do, hike only the shorter, easier trails—and *DO* come equipped to clean up after your pet.

And a *health note:* Lyme disease has been reported here, so when you return from hiking, check for ticks.

and Otter Cliffs Parking Areas, so you can begin the walk at either end. If you want to do the trail once, rather than backtracking, get off the bus at one end or the other, then pick up another bus when you're ready to continue onward—mix and match, if you will.

Because this trail is so easy, and easy to reach, it's extremely popular. In fact, lovely as it is, you'd have to be crazy to be on it between 10 A.M. and 3 P.M. at the height of summer. At the risk of divulging the solution, the last time I walked it, at 7 A.M. on a bright June day, I had the path all to myself—a minor miracle, actually—and the tide was at just the right height for Thunder Hole to live up to its name.

The first bus doesn't arrive at Sand Beach until 9:25 A.M., so if that's your mode of transport, consider doing this trail later in the day at the height of summer.

The trail runs close to the shore for about half of its length and takes in several of the Park Loop Road's highlights—Sand Beach, Thunder Hole, Otter Cliffs, and the giant sea stack in Monument

Cove—not to mention gorgeous sea-level views of Frenchman Bay.

Along here, it's especially tempting to "liberate" rocks from the shore—resist the urge. Remember the slogan, "Leave the rocks for the next glacier." If you forget, a few judiciously placed national park signs will remind you.

Great Head Trail

- Distance: 1.4 miles round-trip
- Rating: Easy to moderate
- Trailhead: Take the Park Loop Road to the Sand Beach Parking Area—the lower one is closer to the beach, but it fills up first. Walk down the steps to the beach and across it to the far (eastern) side, where you'll see the trailhead marker. You'll need to cross a rivulet here to reach the trailhead. If you're not here at low tide, and you don't have waterproof shoes, remove your shoes so you won't be hiking with wet feet.

First take the trail to the right, which climbs a few dozen steps (the "moderate" part), then

© KATHLEEN M. BRANDES

The Great Head Trail starts at the far side of Sand Beach.

continue right toward the headland ("head"), from which you can see the beach and the prominent mound of The Beehive. Out in Frenchman Bay is Egg Rock Light and beyond is Schoodic Point. Continue on the trail counterclockwise, following the perimeter of the head, perhaps pausing for a picnic near the ruins of a mid-19th-century stone teahouse. Continue the loop around the head, then return back to Sand Beach.

You can reach Sand Beach (and therefore the Great Head Trail) via the Island Explorer bus, but since the Park Loop Road is one-way at this point, you won't be able to return to Bar Harbor the way you came. You'll need to grab a bus and continue its loop back to Bar Harbor, but the time is the same: 25 minutes from Bar Harbor to Sand Beach, 25 minutes back to the Village Green from Sand Beach.

Option: Another way (easier) to hike Great Head is to begin on the north side of the head and go in a clockwise direction. Take Main Street (Route 3) southward out of Bar Harbor, and at about .8 mile after the athletic field, bear left onto Schooner Head Road, which roughly parallels the Park Loop Road. Continue just beyond the turn for the Schooner Head Overlook, park at the dead end, and begin your hike from this end of Great Head. There are actually two loops, which could end up taking you 1.8–2 miles. Keep bearing left (clockwise) so you'll skirt the perimeter of Great Head.

Jordan Pond Loop Trail

- Distance: 3.3 miles round-trip
- Rating: Easy to moderate
- Trailhead: By car from Bar Harbor, take the Park Loop Road (the two-way west side of the loop) to the Jordan Pond parking lot. An Island Explorer bus follows the same route. (In midsummer, another auto option is to take Route 3 south from Bar Harbor to Seal Harbor, then take the Stanley Brook entrance to the park, going north toward Jordan Pond.) Park and head toward the boat-launching ramp; you'll see the trailhead to the right.

This mostly level counterclockwise circuit of Jordan Pond is a great way to walk off a Jordan Pond House lunch (including those popovers). Or do the hike first and reward yourself with afternoon tea. Start on the east side, the easiest; the west side has the only moderate section—

rocky and rooty and, depending on recent weather, possibly a bit squishy. Log bridges have been installed in a number of spots.

Jordan Pond is part of the island's drinking-water supply, so no swimming (or even wading) here.

As if the summer setting here weren't enough, this trail is even more beautiful in the fall, when stands of birches add gold to the palette. Plus the trail is far less crowded in late September and early October (except perhaps for Columbus Day weekend).

Option: The giant glacial erratic known as **Bubble Rock** is enough of a phenomenon that you may want to detour from the shore trail to see it—via the Bubble Rock Trail (at the northeast corner of the pond). It's a slightly steep .8-mile round-trip, up and back on the trail. At the risk of perpetuating a cliché, I'll add that the classic photo here is a Sisyphus imitation—the

WITH A LITTLE HELP FROM OUR FRIENDS. . .

As we watch federal funding for national parks lose headway year after year, every park in America needs a safety net like **Friends of Acadia (FOA),** a dynamic organization headquartered in Bar Harbor. Historic stone bridges need repairs? FOA raises the funds. Propane-powered shuttle-bus service needs expanding? FOA finds a million-dollar donor. Well-used trails need maintenance? FOA organizes volunteer work parties. New connector trails needed? FOA gets them done. No vacuum seems to go unfilled.

FOA—one of Acadia National Park's greatest assets—is both reactive and proactive. It's an amazingly symbiotic relationship. When informed of a need, the Friends stand ready to help; when they themselves perceive a need, they propose solutions to park management and jointly figure out ways to make them happen. It's hard to avoid sounding like a media flack when describing this organization.

Friends of Acadia was founded in 1986 to preserve and protect the park for resource-sensitive tourism and myriad recreational uses. Since 1995, FOA has contributed more than $3 million to the park and surrounding communities for trail upkeep, carriage-road maintenance, and other conservation projects. Plus FOA cofounded the Island Explorer bus system and instigated the Acadia Trails Forever program, a joint park–FOA partnership for trail rehabilitation. In 2003, for instance, FOA and the park announced the reopening (after considerable planning and rebuilding) of the Homans Path, on the east side of Dorr Mountain. The trail, built around 1916 and named after Eliza Homans, a generous benefactor, fell into disuse in the 1940s. It ascends via a granite stairway to a ledge with a commanding view of the Great Meadow and Frenchman Bay.

You can join FOA and its 3,000 members and support this worthy cause for $35 a year, or $100 for a family (43 Cottage St., P.O. Box 45, Bar Harbor 04609, 207/288-3340 or 800/625-0321, www.friendsofacadia.org). You can also lend a hand (or two) while you're here. FOA and the park organize volunteer work parties for Acadia trail, carriage-road, and other outdoor maintenance three times weekly between June and Columbus Day: 8:30 A.M.–noon Tuesday, Thursday, and Saturday. Call the recorded information line (207/288-3934) for the work locations, or 288-3340 for answers to questions. The meeting point is Park Headquarters (Eagle Lake Rd., Rte. 233, Bar Harbor), about three miles west of town. This is a terrific way to give something back to the park, and the camaraderie is contagious. Be sure to take your own water, lunch, and bug repellent. Dress in layers and wear closed-toe shoes. More than 7,000 volunteer hours a year go toward this effort.

Each summer, Friends of Acadia also sponsors a handful of **Ridge Runners,** who work under park supervision and spend their days out and about on the trails repairing cairns, watching for lost hikers, and handing out Leave No Trace information.

If you happen to be in the region on the first Saturday in November, call the FOA office to register for the annual carriage-road cleanup, which usually draws 250 or so volunteers. Bring water and gloves; there's a free hot lunch at midday for everyone who participates. It's dubbed Take Pride in Acadia Day—indeed an apt label.

MOUNT DESERT ISLAND

mythological fellow relentlessly pushing the boulder up a mountain, only to have it roll back. Fortunately, this one doesn't move, since it's the size of an SUV. There must be thousands of photo albums (and probably CDs) all over the world containing this image. Needless to say, kids love it.

Note: In the summer of 2003, trail areas around Jordan Pond House and Jordan Pond were upgraded for wheelchair access, part of a major public-private collaborative effort to increase accessibility in the park. The improved access is on the east side of Jordan Pond.

Gorham Mountain Trail
- Distance: 2 miles round-trip
- Rating: Moderate
- Trailhead: On the one-way section of the Park Loop Road, continue past Sand Beach and Thunder Hole to the Gorham Mountain Parking Area. (The Island Explorer bus can drop you off here, or walk a short distance along the Ocean

sunrise, Gorham Mountain

Trail after getting off the bus at the Thunder Hole stop.) The trailhead is at the back of the parking lot.

The round-trip distance specified here covers the trail directly to the summit, then a return the same way with a short detour via Cadillac Cliffs. (You can also continue onward from the Gorham summit, following part of the Bowl Trail down to the Park Loop Road, then walk along the Ocean Trail back to your car—if you've left it in the Gorham lot.)

The Gorham Mountain Trail is another hike that requires not a great deal of effort to produce maximum rewards, and it's an excellent family hike—kids love the Cadillac Cliffs.

Follow cairns across ledges up from the trailhead to a fork, where you'll see a plaque commemorating Waldron Bates, the ingenious pathmaker who instigated the strategic use of granite staircases and iron ladders for Acadia's trails.

Bates was a lawyer for his day job, but his summer avocation as head of the Roads and Paths Committee for the Bar Harbor Improvement Association (1900–1909) gave him the greatest pleasure. Think of him as you navigate the Cadillac Cliffs Trail, one of his projects.

For now, though, bear left (saving the Cadillac Cliffs route for the return) and head for the open-ledge summit (525 feet, third-lowest of Acadia's peaks). A signposted cairn marks the spot. From here, you'll see Sand Beach, Egg Rock Light in Frenchman Bay, the Beehive, Champlain Mountain, and lots more—a fabulous view.

Return via the same route, but make the short detour left onto the U-shaped Cadillac Cliffs Trail, featuring stairs, rocky footing, granite "tunnels," and even an ancient sea cave, now high and dry. (This sea cave once was filled with beach cobbles, but slowly, slowly it's been cleaned out by hikers—a prime example of the damage done by removing "just one.")

Penobscot and Sargent Mountains
- Distance: 6 miles round-trip
- Rating: Moderate to difficult
- Trailhead: Park your car in the overflow lot at Jordan Pond House, go left of the restaurant and look for the carved trail signpost.

MOUNT DESERT ISLAND

You'll cross Jordan Stream and a carriage road before starting on the rough part—heading upward rather steeply with rocky, ledgy underfooting. Handholds have been installed in strategic spots. (This part is even less fun on the return route.) But the rewards are worth the effort. Continue on to the Penobscot summit (1,194 feet, fifth-highest in the park), with wide-open views. In August, you'll have wild blueberries (but leave some for others) en route to the top.

The best feature of this hike is that you get to reach one summit then go for a swim in gorgeous little Sargent Pond before tackling the next one. From Penobscot's summit, it's only 10 minutes downhill to the pond. (If you're retracing your route, you can even have a second swim on the way back.) This is a long hike, however; if you're hiking with kids, be sure they're up to the challenge. For that matter, be sure *you* are.

From Sargent Pond, head upward on the South Ridge Trail to the summit of Sargent Mountain (1,373 feet, second-highest in the park).

Don't rush the return—the vistas are superb up here—but when you're ready, go back the same way.

Shortest and easiest of the park's trails, Wonderland is more a walk than a hike. Most of the route is wooded—trees gnarled from the wind, branches laden with moss—with the rugged shoreline and a small cobble beach as your reward at the end.

Other Recommended East-Side Trails

In the *easy* category, consider **Jesup Path,** two to three miles through the lovely area around Sieur de Monts Spring. Also, the **Seaside Path** (or Seaside Trail) runs about two miles through the woods (use insect repellent) between Seal Harbor and the Jordan Pond House. Use the Island Explorer bus to make this a one-way hike, or retrace your route for a longer hike.

A choice hike in the *moderate* category is **Conner's Nubble,** with super views down to Eagle Lake and the mountains off to the east. In the *moderate-to-strenuous* range, try **Parkman Mountain**—not too strenuous but enough to make it worthwhile, especially with the views from the

bald summit—what you might call an "all-purpose hike."

See *Park Camping* later in this chapter for info on hiking the **Cadillac South Ridge Trail** from Blackwoods Campground.

Beehive and Precipice Trails

These two "ladder trails" (where no pets are allowed) are the park's toughest routes, with sheer faces, iron ladders, and strenuous ratings. As already mentioned, Champlain Mountain's Precipice Trail often is closed (usually mid-April into August) to protect nesting peregrine falcons. If challenges are your thing, you're not acrophobic, and these trails are open (check beforehand at the Hulls Cove Visitor Center), go ahead. Avid hikers consider the Beehive a "must-do." But a fine alternative in the *strenuous* category is the **Beachcroft Trail** on Huguenot Head, leading up the west side of Champlain. Also called the Beachcroft Path, the trail is best known for its 1,500 beautifully engineered granite steps, built by the Civilian Conservation Corps (CCC). Round-trip is about 2.2 miles, or you can continue a loop at the top, taking in the Bear Brook Trail, for about 4.4 miles. The parking area is just north of Route 3, near Sieur de Monts Spring, and just west of the Park Loop Road, near the Jackson Laboratory (or take the Island Explorer bus).

WEST-SIDE TRAILS
Wonderland

- Distance: 1.4 miles round-trip
- Rating: Very easy
- Trailhead: The Wonderland trail begins on the south side of Route 102A, a mile west of the Seawall Campground. Walk from Seawall; if you're staying elsewhere, ask the Island Explorer bus driver to drop you off (it's not a regular stop).

PEREGRINE FALCONS

One of Acadia's great success stories is that of a seasonal mountain dweller, the **peregrine falcon**. DDT and other pollutants caused a decline in the falcons until the last breeding pair in Acadia was observed in 1956. (Before DDT, peregrines were depleted by trappers, hunters, and nest robbers.) The peregrine was listed as a federal endangered species in the early 1970s and removed from that list in 1999; it remains an endangered species in Maine. In the 1980s, biologists worked to reintroduce the falcons to Acadia. Their efforts proved successful when, in 1991, a breeding pair of falcons settled on the east-facing cliffs of Champlain Mountain and produced young. Since then, there have been up to three breeding pairs of falcons nesting in Acadia (at Champlain, Jordan Cliff, and Beech Cliff).

Their nests, or scrapes, are but shallow ledges on cliffsides, which provide them with an unimpeded view of potential prey (other birds) below. Their high-speed pursuits of prey thrill those who are lucky enough to witness them.

During the spring and summer, park staff are stationed at the Precipice Trail Parking Area each morning (weather permitting), from 9 A.M. to noon, with spotting scopes to help anyone who stops by to view the peregrines and their scrape, and to provide information about their habits. Check the park newspaper, the *Beaver Log,* for the latest information.

During breeding and fledging season (April to mid-August), the trailhead for the **Precipice Trail** is gated, with an informational sign explaining the history and status of peregrines in the park. (When you arrive, other trails may be closed for the same reason; check at the Hulls Cove Visitor Center.)

(Contributed by Kristen Britain)

Shortest and easiest of the park's trails, Wonderland follows an old fire road and is more a walk than a hike—a great starter-upper for a family ensconced at Seawall Campground. Most of the route is wooded—trees gnarled from the wind, branches laden with moss—with the rugged shoreline and a small cobble beach as your reward at the end.

Across Route 102A from the Wonderland trailhead is the 420-acre Big Heath, considered one of Maine's "critical areas." Because of its sensitive peatland—wet and squishy and fragile underfoot (not to mention its battalions of mosquitoes)—avoid it. (You'll be skirting its edges, though, if you walk the Hio Trail from the back of Seawall Campground; see *Park Camping,* below.)

Ship Harbor Nature Trail
• Distance: 1.3 miles round-trip
• Rating: Easy, but some uneven ground
• Trailhead: The parking area (with restrooms) for Ship Harbor is less than half a mile west of the Wonderland Parking Area. The trail is on the south side of Route 102A. As with

Wonderland, you can be dropped off by an Island Explorer bus and/or flag one down after your hike.

The Ship Harbor Nature Trail isn't quite as easy as Wonderland—roots can snag you along the way, and rocks can be slippery if it has rained or the tide has receded—but it's even more educational as a family hike. At the Thompson Island Visitor Center, the Hulls Cove Visitor Center, or at Seawall Campground, pick up a copy of the park's 12-page *Ship Harbor Nature Trail* booklet and use it along the way.

Legend has it that the harbor earned its name during the Revolutionary War, when an American privateer, seeking refuge, became stranded here.

If the tide has gone out, follow the trail along the shore first (counterclockwise) so the kids can check out what's been left in the tide pools. If the tide is high, perhaps you'll want to follow the booklet's suggested (clockwise) route. Or you can do a "figure-eight" route. In any case, you won't get lost.

Option: Since Wonderland and Ship Harbor are so close together, consider doing both trails in a morning or afternoon. Carry a picnic and enjoy it on the shore.

Flying Mountain Trail

- Distance: 1.5 miles round-trip
- Rating: Moderately easy
- Trailhead: The trail begins at the end of Fernald Point Road, .8 mile east of Route 102 (at the northern edge of Southwest Harbor). If you're driving from the Bar Harbor area, slow down after passing Echo Lake and take the next left. Drive to the end of the road, park in the Valley Cove lot, and begin at the carved signpost. Fernald Point was the site of the early 17th-century St. Sauveur mission settlement established by French Jesuits. The Island Explorer bus headed to or from Southwest Harbor can drop you off and/or pick you up at the corner of Route 102 and Fernald Point Road; from there, walk down the road to the trailhead.

At 284 feet, Flying Mountain has the lowest of Acadia's 26 summits, so theoretically it shouldn't have one of the best views—but it does. With minimum effort (some minor scrambling up and over, but level at the end), you're surveying the mouth of Somes Sound, including Northeast and Southwest Harbors and Greening Island between them. It hardly gets better than this (well, it does, but this is pretty spectacular).

From the trailhead, the rise through the trees is a bit steep, with some stepped ledges, but it's quick (why rush, though?). At the summit, relax and take photos, then descend toward Valley Cove. You'll encounter roots and rocks, and your knees may complain a bit, but again, it's really not strenuous and it doesn't last long. At the bottom, bear left onto the woods road and return to the parking area.

You can hike the Valley Cove Trail as an extension of the Flying Mountain Trail, but it may be closed April–mid-August, as peregrine falcons have been nesting there in recent years.

Beech Mountain Trail

- Distance: 1.3 miles round-trip
- Rating: Moderate
- Trailhead: From Route 102 in Somesville,

take the Pretty Marsh Road westward to Beech Hill Road. Turn left and continue to the end, climbing gradually to the parking area for Beech Cliff and Beech Mountain.

Several hiking routes merge and converge in the Beech Mountain area. Some begin from a trailhead on the southern side of Beech and can be more strenuous than this one. This hike starts from the northern side. None of the Beech Mountain hikes are particularly convenient to the Island Explorer bus system.

A short distance from the beginning of the Beech Mountain Trail, you'll reach a fork—the Beech Mountain loop. Bear right to do the loop counterclockwise—the rewarding vistas over Long Pond come sooner, and it's less steep this way.

At the summit (839 feet) stands the park's only fire tower, now disused. During unseasonably hot summers, when the ranger-posted fire-danger level is high, volunteers come up to keep an eye on things, but small charter planes do most of the fire patrols these days. Besides having great views of Long Pond, from here you can see as far as Blue Hill to the north-

summit rocks, Acadia Mountain

GEORGE DEWOLFE, COURTESY FRIENDS OF ACADIA

west and the Cranberry Isles to the south. A knob near the summit is a prime viewing spot for the migration of hawks (and other raptors) in September.

From the summit, continue your counterclockwise route or backtrack the way you came, heading down to the trail junction and back to the parking area.

Option: If you're particularly fascinated by mosses and lichens (and have brought insect repellent), consider a three-mile round-trip to Beech Mountain that begins with a lovely walk-in-the-woods starting at the same trailhead. Instead of taking the Beech Mountain Trail, follow the Valley Trail on fairly level ground for just under a mile. Then bear right onto the Beech Mountain South Ridge Trail and start climbing stone steps (lots of them) toward the summit. Descend from the summit via the Beech Mountain loop route, going clockwise (left) to take advantage of the Long Pond vistas.

Acadia Mountain Trail

- Distance: 2.5 miles round-trip
- Rating: Difficult
- Trailhead: From Somesville (west of Bar Harbor), take Route 102 southward for just over three miles, alongside Echo Lake, until you see

the signposted Acadia Mountain parking lot. Cross the road to the trailhead. (The Island Explorer's route from Bar Harbor to Southwest Harbor goes right along Route 102; request a stop to start your hike and flag down the bus when you've finished the hike.)

Climb the steps and continue to the junction with the St. Sauveur Mountain Trail. (If you're up for a much longer hike, do an Acadia and St. Sauveur loop, for a 3.8–4-mile round-trip.) Continue left on the Acadia Mountain Trail, where it's briefly deceptively flat and lovely. After you cross a fire road (your eventual return route), begin the rocky, ledgy ascent, following cairns.

It's less than a mile to the open summit—with fantastic views up and down Somes Sound. (Actually, there's a sort of double summit, with the second one being only slightly lower than the 641-foot maximum height.) In summer, you'll find wild blueberries. The descent toward the Sound is longer and quite steep—take it slowly. At the bottom, when you reach the spur to Man o' War Brook, detour briefly to follow the brook to Somes Sound. Allegedly, Revolutionary War vessels stocked up on water here during their exploits along the Maine coast. Return to the trailhead via an easy walk on the mile-long fire road.

Other Recreation

BIKING

Since bikes are *not allowed* on hiking trails in Acadia, the **Park Loop Road** provides the best workout for mountain bikers, but its prime drawback is the volume of car and RV exhaust fumes you'll be inhaling if you decide to take this route in the middle of the day at the height of summer. So don't. (Park-wide ozone alerts are not common, but they do occur in Acadia; see *Environmental Issues* in the *Introduction* to this book.) Nor are the Park Loop's shoulders as wide as they might be to comfortably accommodate a great many bikes. Besides, on most of the one-way section of the Park Loop, over-

flow auto parking is allowed in the right lane. Dodging cars ain't fun. The 27-mile route is indeed spectacular, so if you want to bike it, plan your pedaling for early in the day (around 7 A.M. in summer), later in the day (around "happy hour," when everyone else has packed it in and headed for bars and/or restaurants), or during "shoulder" months (June, September, even October).

The better alternative is to bring, borrow, or rent a bike and take advantage of the spectacular **Carriage-Road System**—57 miles of crushed-rock roadways with nary a car in sight (bikes are allowed on only 45 of the 57 miles; 12 miles are on private land; be alert for signs).

MOUNT DESERT ISLAND

Rental-bike information appears in the *Mount Desert Island Communities* chapter. Also see *Guided Tours* earlier in this chapter for information about VBT's Acadia bicycle tours.

At every junction in the carriage-road system stands a tall wooden post with a number and directional signs. Use these numbers, together with the park's free carriage-road map, to navigate the network. Also very helpful are a couple of portable books—*A Pocket Guide to the Carriage Roads of Acadia National Park,* by Diana Abrell, and *A Pocket Guide to Biking on Mount Desert Island,* by Audrey Minutolo.

Periodically, carriage roads and their bridges undergo necessary repair, and since such work is possible only in decent weather, *you may encounter closures.* When you obtain the carriage-road map at the Hulls Visitor Center, ask a ranger to indicate on the map any sections that may be under repair and/or closed.

Some sections of the carriage roads are fine for wheelchairs, particularly near Eagle Lake and Bubble Pond.

Note: Since these are multiuse roadways, **bicyclists** in particular should remember and adhere to the rules:

• Bikes yield to everyone (pedestrians, horses, wheelchairs, strollers); pedestrians yield to horses. Horses tend to become skittish around bikes, so be particularly cautious when you're pedaling near them. Better still, pull off to the right, stop, and let them pass.

• Wear a helmet.

• Keep to the right and signal clearly when passing on the left.

• Do NOT speed; speeders are a danger to walkers, horses, children, the disabled, and sometimes themselves.

• Pets must be leashed.

As with the park's hiking trails, it would take a whole book just to focus on all the options on the carriage roads. While the carriage roads make wonderful walking paths, they are the best places in the park for bikes. So most of the route suggestions that follow are geared to cyclists.

Note: It cannot be said often enough: *There is no off-road biking in Acadia, and bikes are not allowed on the hiking trails.*

At the end of the following section, note that there is one recommended carriage-road loop for walking—on private land where bikes are not allowed.

Some Carriage-Road Routes

The **Eagle Lake** and **Witch Hole Pond** loops are probably the most popular in the park—because they're not difficult (thus good for families) and they're close to Bar Harbor, where so many visitors stay. Thus, if you decide to do either of these in the middle of summer, *get an early start.* If you're planning to rent bikes, rent them the night before, so you can be on your way right after breakfast.

If you're doing this anytime between late June and Columbus Day, be sure to check the schedule for the Island Explorer bus and use it to get to and from your starting points. (Each bus can carry two bikes.)

For the **Eagle Lake loop,** the Northeast Harbor (Brown Mountain) bus makes a stop at the head of Eagle Lake on Route 233, or you can pedal or drive from downtown Bar Harbor via Mount Desert Street. At the end of the street, cross over to Route 233 (Eagle Lake Rd.) and follow it to the beginning of this route. (Park in the Eagle Lake Parking Area, across Rte. 233 from the beginning of the carriage road.)

To reach the **Witch Hole Pond loop** from downtown Bar Harbor, take West Street to its end, cross Route 3, then continue on West Street Extension. Take a right on Duck Brook Road and continue from there to the carriage road (starting at numbered signpost 5). *Or* drive to the Hulls Cove Visitor Center, park there, and bike (or walk your bike) up the steep trail to the first carriage-road intersection, number 1. From there, continue to 2 and then veer right to make the circuit via junctions (signposts) 4 and 5 and then to 3, making a loop back to 1. From there, it's pretty much downhill to your car.

Each of those rides is about six miles. If you'd prefer to double your biking mileage, park at the Eagle Lake Parking Area and do both loops from there.

To ride the **Jordan Pond/Bubble Pond loop,** take the Island Explorer bus with your bike to the

© KATHLEEN M. BRANDES

MOUNT DESERT ISLAND

Jordan Pond Parking Area or drive (via the Park Loop Road) to the same area (use the Jordan Pond area, not the Jordan Pond House area). Pedal back along the Park Loop Road (follow bike rules and stay with the traffic; it's two-way here) to the handsome stone Jordan Pond Gate Lodge. Now you have two choices—a clockwise route or a counterclockwise one.

The counterclockwise route allows you a downhill coast along Jordan Pond near the end of your 8.5-mile circuit. Enter the carriage road next to the gatehouse and continue to signpost (junction) 17. Head north, passing Bubble Pond along its west shore—practically in the water—to signpost 7. Bear left around the bottom of Eagle Lake, to signpost 8, continue to 10, then turn south, skirting Jordan Pond, to signpost 14. Continue south to 15 and 16, exiting onto the Park Loop Road across from where you entered.

After these warm-up rides, you'll have a good sense of this amazing network. And now how about a hike (really a walk) on private carriage roads, where you won't be dodging bikes. (Bikes are banned from the 12 miles of private Green Rock Company carriage roads; you're free to walk there, however.)

The 3.4-mile **Little Long Pond loop**—part of the 12 miles of carriage roads on private land (but open to the public)—is easy, a "walk-in-the-woods" kind of experience. (If you do this late in the day, use insect repellent.) It's officially Long Pond, but it's known as Little Long Pond to distinguish it from the far larger Long Pond on the west side of the island. From Bar Harbor, take the Island Explorer Jordan Pond bus and get off at Seal Harbor Beach, then walk west a very short distance to Little Long Pond and enter the carriage roads there. Or drive from Bar Harbor either on the Park Loop Road (the two-way section) or on Route 3, via Otter Creek and park in a small lot on the north side of Route 3 at the bottom of Little Long Pond. Head north, on the east shore of the pond, passing signpost 35 and continuing to signpost 28. Bear left toward signpost 24 (and the lovely Cobblestone Bridge), then start heading west and south, meandering to signpost 32. Turn south (left) to signpost 33, where you'll bear left toward 34 and back to Route 3. (You can also do the loop in a clockwise direction, but counterclockwise gets you near the pond right at the start.) If you're using the bus, flag it down—or walk back to the Seal Harbor Beach stop.

SWIMMING

Acadia has a limited number of swimming areas, with the upshot that they and their parking lots are mighty crowded on hot days. Go early in the day or take your chances.

Don't assume you can swim in any freshwater pond or lake you encounter in the park or even elsewhere on the island. Six island locations—Upper and Lower Hadlock Ponds, Bubble and Jordan Ponds, Eagle Lake, and the southern half of Long Pond—are drinking-water reservoirs where swimming and windsurfing are banned (but boating is allowed). Don't let your dog swim in these ponds, either. Five of the six are within the park; Long Pond borders the park.

Also see Penobscot and Sargent Mountains, above, under *Hiking*; Sargent Pond is a lovely spot to cool off midhike.

Sand Beach

Located slightly below the Park Loop Road, Sand Beach is the park's (and the island's) biggest sandy beach. Lifeguards are on duty during the summer, and even then, the biggest threat can be hypothermia. The salt water is terminally glacial—in mid-July, it still might not reach 60° F; by September, it's usually warmer, though the air will be cooler. Even though kids seem not to notice, they can become chilled quickly; keep an eye on their condition. The best solution is to walk to the far end of the beach, where a warmer, shallow stream meets the ocean. Also, if you arrive here on the incoming tide, after the sun has warmed up the cove's bottom, the water temperature is marginally higher. On a hot August day, arrive early; the parking lot fills up. Bring a picnic. There are changing rooms and restrooms. Dogs are *not* allowed on Sand Beach. *Hint:* After hiking nearby Great Head on a hot day, go for a swim at Sand Beach—you'll be surprisingly grateful for the chilly water.

> *The salt water is terminally glacial—in mid-July, it still might not reach 60° F; by September, it's usually warmer. After hiking nearby Great Head on a hot day, go for a swim at Sand Beach—you'll be surprisingly grateful for the chilly water.*

Echo Lake

The park's most popular freshwater swimming site, staffed with a lifeguard and inevitably crowded on hot days, is **Echo Lake,** south of Somesville on Route 102 and well signposted. Pets are not allowed on the beach.

Other Swimming Spots

A less-crowded, small saltwater beach, not in the park, is at the head of the harbor in chic Seal Harbor, a few miles east of Northeast Harbor.

If you have a canoe, kayak, or rowboat, you can reach swimming holes in **Seal Cove, Round,** and **Somes Ponds** (all on the western side of Mount Desert). Round and Seal Cove Ponds have shorelines bordering the park. The eastern shore of **Hodgdon Pond** (also on the western side of the island) is accessible by car (via Hodgdon Road and Long Pond Fire Road).

The northern end of **Long Pond** has a small beach near the boat-launching area along Route 102, between Somesville and Pretty Marsh.

Another popular swimming hole is **Lake Wood,** at the northern end of Mount Desert. It has a small beach and auto access. To get to Lake Wood from Route 3, head west on Crooked Road to unpaved Park Road. Turn left and continue to the parking area, which will be crowded on a hot day, so arrive early.

ROCK CLIMBING

Acadia has a number of splendid sites prized by climbers: the sea cliffs at Otter Cliffs and Great Head; South Bubble Mountain; Canada Cliff (on the island's western side); and the South Wall and the Central Slabs on Champlain Mountain. The climbing season usually runs May–October. Occasionally, it can be extended at either end, but you'd have to be on or near the island to be able to catch the decent weather before it deteriorates. (Heck, that can happen even in summer.)

If you haven't tried climbing, *never* do it yourself, without instruction. Best advice is to contact one of Bar Harbor's two climbing operations. From mid-May to October, **Acadia Mountain Guides Climbing School** (198 Main St., P.O. Box 937, Bar Harbor 04609, 207/288-8186 or 888/ 232-9559, off-season P.O. Box 121, Orono 04473, 207/866-7562, www.acadiamountainguides .com) offers all levels of instruction and guided climbs for individuals and families in Acadia as well as in Camden, Clifton, and Baxter State Park. **Atlantic Climbing School (ACS)** (24 Cottage St., 2nd floor, P.O. Box 514, Bar Harbor 04609, 207/288-2521) provides basic half-day courses (3.5 and 4.5 hours), including a "family climbing experience," all by reservation (minimum age is eight). You'll learn just enough to introduce you to the sport and do an initial basic climb—with guides and in line with park rules. ACS also offers a series of courses for intermediate climbers.

All gear is provided by both firms. Costs vary widely, depending on climbing site, number of climbers, and session length.

If you're an experienced climber, Jeff Butterfield, ACS's founder, has written the "must-have" book on the subject: *Acadia: A Climber's Guide,* which covers all the best-known routes as well as some lesser-known crags. Routes are described and rated (with maps and symbols), and there's all kinds of other essential information. For instance, the book recommends that South Bubble climbers be sure they're wearing helmets for protection from rocks dropped ("by yahoos," as he puts it) from hiking trails overhead. At $25 for a 160-page book, it's expensive—but it may save your life. How valuable is that? (It's even entertaining just reading the route names: Selfless Bastard, Homosexual Armadillo, Fear of Flying, Arms Race, Pickled Amnesiac, and dozens more.)

Some park regulations you need to know for Acadia climbing:

• Don't leave your dog tied up or on the loose while you're climbing.

• The park's bridges are off-limits for climbing or bouldering.

• From April to mid-August, while peregrine falcons are nesting, the Central Slabs area on The Precipice is almost always closed.

• Sign in at the registration box at climbing sites—registration is required at Otter Cliffs, the South Wall, and Canada Cliff.

If you've forgotten any climbing gear or need replacements, the best source is on the ground floor next to ACS: **Cadillac Mountain Sports** (26 Cottage St., Bar Harbor 04609, 207/288-4532, www.cadillacsports.com).

WINTER SPORTS

As mentioned earlier, these miles of car-free carriage roads are fantastic for cross-country skiing and snowshoeing. The only problem is that even though Acadia gets about five feet of snow during an average winter, it's not like a ski resort, where there's a base and more snow keeps piling on top of it. Here, it might snow one day and

cross-country skiing, Eagle Lake carriage road

GEORGE DEWOLFE, COURTESY FRIENDS OF ACADIA

MOUNT DESERT ISLAND

rain or thaw the next. But now and then, a bumper crop of snow creates a winter wonderland for days and even weeks. Acadia's proximity to the ocean and its Gulf Stream current means that you take your chances with snow. January and February can be good bets . . . but then again, you never know.

Cross-country skis and snowshoes are available for rent from **Cadillac Mountain Sports** (26 Cottage St., Bar Harbor 04609, 207/288-4532, www.cadillacsports.com), which is open all year. Snowmobiles are allowed on only two miles of the carriage roads, as well as on the road to the Cadillac summit.

For carriage-road information and other visitor information about Acadia during the winter, when the Hulls Cove Visitor Center is closed, contact Park Headquarters (Eagle Lake Rd., Rte. 233, P.O. Box 177, Bar Harbor 04609, 207/288-3338, www.nps.gov/acad/), which is open all year. In winter, it's open 8 A.M.–4:30 P.M. daily except national holidays; in summer, it's closed on weekends.

The park publishes a very handy *Winter Activities Guide,* a foldout map/brochure that explains what you can and cannot do, where you can and cannot go—including snowmobile routes and the two sections of the Park Loop Road that are open to cars.

The park's **Blackwoods Campground** (Rte. 3, Otter Creek, five miles south of Bar Harbor) is open year-round for any hardy souls who are up for the experience. Water comes from a hand pump, and there's a pit toilet. Reservations are not required November–April, and winter camping is free.

Park Camping

Mount Desert Island has at least a dozen private (commercial) campgrounds, but there are only two—**Blackwoods and Seawall**—within park boundaries on the island. (A third park campground is on Isle au Haut.)

Blackwoods and Seawall have *no* hookups. Both have seasonal restrooms (no showers) and dumping stations. Dishwashing stations have recently been added at Seawall and will soon be added at Blackwoods. Less than half a mile from Blackwoods, and even closer to Seawall, are coin-operated hot showers and small markets for buying incidental supplies.

Maximum capacity at each site is six persons and one large tent (or two small ones).

Both campgrounds are wooded—with no sea views but not far from the water. In June, be prepared for blackflies; in July and August, bring insect repellent for mosquitoes.

Environmental note: Firewood collection is no longer allowed within Seawall's grounds. Rather than scrounge for what little duff remains around the campgrounds in order to build a campfire, stop on your way to Acadia and pick up a stash of firewood. All along Route 3 in Trenton, and along Route 3 on Mount Desert (near the clusters of commercial campgrounds), you'll see signs for firewood for sale (usually around $2, sometimes less). Bring your own to Blackwoods and Seawall and do your part to preserve the status quo.

Also from the environmental viewpoint, the propane-powered Island Explorer buses serve both Blackwoods and Seawall between late June and Columbus Day. Leave your vehicle at your campsite and do your park and island exploring by bus.

Quiet time in both campgrounds is from 10 P.M.–6 A.M.

Both campgrounds also have **amphitheaters,** where park rangers present free, hour-long evening programs (various starting times) during the summer on a variety of natural- and cultural-history topics. Noncampers are also welcome at these events, and there's wheelchair access. Some of the programs have included "Forces of Nature," "Avian Mysteries," "Acadia's Treasures," "The French in Acadia," and "All Things Furry." Even sing-alongs are sometimes on the schedule. Blackwoods has programs several nights a week; Seawall programs tend to be on weekend evenings.

BLACKWOODS CAMPGROUND

With more than 300 campsites, **Blackwoods Campground,** just off Route 3, five miles south of Bar Harbor, is open all year. Because of its location on the east side of the island, it's also the more popular of the two campgrounds. Reservations are required only June 15–September 15. Call 800/365-2267; have your credit card handy. Or register online at http://reservations.nps.gov. Cost is $20 per site per night. Camping is free December–March, and no reservations are necessary; winter facilities include pit toilets, fire rings, and a hand-operated water pump. Off-season, when the bathrooms are still open, there is a minimal camping fee.

If you're staying at Blackwoods, consider adding the **Cadillac South Ridge Trail** to your hiking list. You can access the trail at the entrance to the campground and do a 7.5-mile round-trip. The hike is moderate, with a couple of quite easy stretches (the last part is the steepest). Of course, you can drive to the Cadillac summit and get the same fabulous 360-degree views, but this hike makes you feel you earned it.

SEAWALL CAMPGROUND

Reservations are not accepted at **Seawall Campground,** on Route 102A in the Seawall district, four miles south of Southwest Harbor—it's first come, first served. But in midsummer, you'll need to arrive as early as 8:30 A.M. (when the ranger station opens) to secure one of the 200 or so sites. Seawall is open Memorial Day weekend through September. Cost is $20 per night for drive-up sites and $14 per night for walk-in sites.

RV length at Seawall is limited to 35 feet, with the width limited to an awning extended no more than 12 feet. Generators are no longer allowed in the campground.

While you're at Seawall, take the opportunity to hike or bike on the **Hio Trail,** an old Acadia fire road that begins at the back of the campground (behind Loop C) and goes over to Route 102. It's an easy four-mile round-trip. The path is mostly wooded, passing near the Big Heath, so if you take the trail late in the day, be sure to use insect repellent.

MOUNT DESERT ISLAND

Mount Desert Island Communities

Perhaps no national park has as symbiotic a relationship with its "feeder towns" as Acadia National Park. Is it a chicken-and-egg situation? Not really. Whereas other national parks have served as magnets for the creation of clusters of new towns, the towns that surround Acadia are long-termers—island communities that made do and eked out a living from fishing and boatbuilding long before the first 19th-century "rusticators" unloaded their families and steamer trunks—and long before the first chunk of pristine island real estate was donated to the nation.

Mount Desert Island's official towns (tax-collecting entities with all the bureaucracy that ensues) are **Bar Harbor, Mount Desert, Southwest Harbor,** and **Tremont.** Within each of these are villages—some with post offices and zip codes, some without. Bar Harbor, for instance, includes the villages of Hulls Cove, Salisbury Cove, Town Hill, and Eden (all in the northern sector of the island), and part of the village of Otter Creek.

The town of Mount Desert can be the most confusing, since it includes the villages of Seal Harbor, Hall Quarry, Pretty Marsh, Beech Hill, Somesville, Northeast Harbor, and part of Otter Creek.

Be sure to drive or bike (or, between late June and Columbus Day, take the Island Explorer bus) around the smaller villages, especially Somesville, Bass Harbor, and Bernard. Views are fabulous, the pace is slow, and you'll feel you've stumbled upon "the real Maine."

Bar Harbor, on Frenchman Bay

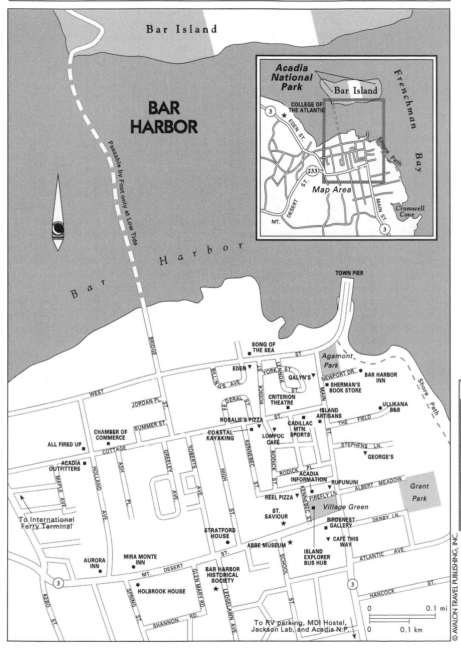

Bar Island

BAR HARBOR

Passable by Foot only at Low Tide

Bar Harbor

TOWN PIER

Map inset:
Acadia National Park
Bar Island
COLLEGE OF THE ATLANTIC
EDEN ST.
Frenchman Bay
Shore Path
233
Map Area
DESERT
MT.
ST.
MAIN ST.
Cromwell Cove
3

SONG OF THE SEA
BRIDGE
Agamont Park
EDEN
GALYN'S
NEWPORT DR.
BAR HARBOR INN
Shore Path
WEST
JORDAN PL.
BILLING'S AVE.
YORK
KNOX ST.
ST.
FEDERAL ST.
CRITERION THEATRE
RODICK
SHERMAN'S BOOK STORE
ROSALIE'S PIZZA
ISLAND ARTISANS
ULLIKANA B&B
CHAMBER OF COMMERCE
SUMMER ST.
COASTAL KAYAKING
CADILLAC MTN. SPORTS
THE FIELD
ALL FIRED UP
COTTAGE
GREELEY ST.
ROBERTS AVE.
KENNEBEC
LOMPOC CAFE
RODICK
STEPHENS LN.
GEORGE'S
ACADIA OUTFITTERS
ASH
HOLLAND AVE.
PL.
HIGH ST.
ACADIA INFORMATION
RUPUNUNI
ALBERT MEADOW
Grant Park
MAPLE AVE.
REEL PIZZA
KENNEBEC ST.
FIREFLY LN.
To International Ferry Terminal
ST. SAVIOUR
Village Green
BIRDSNEST GALLERY
DERBY LN.
STRATFORD HOUSE
ABBE MUSEUM
CAFE THIS WAY
AURORA INN
MIRA MONTE INN
MT. DESERT
GLEN MARY RD.
ISLAND EXPLORER BUS HUB
ATLANTIC AVE.
SCHOOL ST.
3
HANCOCK ST.
KEBO ST.
SPRING ST.
HOLBROOK HOUSE
BAR HARBOR HISTORICAL SOCIETY
LEDGELAWN AVE.
SHANNON RD.

To RV parking, MDI Hostel, Jackson Lab, and Acadia N.P.

0   0.1 mi
0   0.1 km

COMMUNITIES

© AVALON TRAVEL PUBLISHING, INC.

Bar Harbor and Vicinity

In 1996, Bar Harbor celebrated the bicentennial of its founding (as the town of Eden). In the late 19th century and well into the 20th, the town grew to become one of the East Coast's fanciest summer watering holes.

In those days, ferries and steam yachts arrived from points south, large and small resort hotels sprang up, and exclusive mansions (quaintly dubbed "cottages") were the venues of parties thrown by summer-resident Drexels, DuPonts, Vanderbilts, and prominent academics, journalists, and lawyers. The "rusticators" came for the season, with huge entourages of servants, children, pets, and horses. The area's renown was such that by the 1890s, even the staffs of the British, Austrian, and Ottoman embassies retreated here from summers in Washington, D.C.

The establishment of the national park in 1919, and the arrival of the automobile changed the character of Bar Harbor and Mount Desert Island; two world wars and the Great Depression took an additional toll in myriad ways; but the coup de grâce for Bar Harbor's era of elegance came with the Great Fire of 1947. Whole books have been written about the October inferno; a fascinating scrapbook and photos at the Bar Harbor Historical Society dramatically relate the gripping details of the story. Even though some of the elegant cottages have survived, the fire altered life here forever.

Arrive in Bar Harbor in mid-July these days, and you'll find it tough to believe that the year-round population is only 4,820. Bar Harbor is liveliest (in both positive and negative senses) in July and August, but the season keeps stretching. Many clued-in travelers try to take advantage of September's prime weather, relative quiet, and spectacular foliage, although even September and October activity has stepped up. Cruise ships have "discovered" Bar Harbor in recent years, most opting for September and October visits. You won't be competing with the passengers for beds, but about 80 percent of them make a perfunctory visit to Acadia, usually by chartered bus. (The cruise visits, incidentally—or not so incidentally—add about $10 million annually to

Cottage Street, Bar Harbor

the island's coffers.) In the dead of winter, the town is close to moribund, kept alive by devoted year-rounders, including students and faculty at the College of the Atlantic (a unique four-year liberal-arts college geared to environmental studies) and the 1,200 or so staff members at the internationally recognized Jackson Laboratory for Mammalian Research.

If you're traveling with children, Bar Harbor can be a very convenient base of operations for exploring Acadia National Park and the rest of the island. In the smallish downtown area, kids can walk around, play in the parks, hang out at the waterfront, buy ice cream, and hit the movies. It's also a source for sporting-gear rentals and the starting point for boat, bus, kayaking, and walking tours. Staying downtown can be a real plus, but the high cost of even ordinary lodging can be a minus—especially for families. Bar Harbor Chamber of Commerce staffers are particularly adept at rounding up rooms, but don't abuse their helpfulness; contact them well ahead if you're planning a peak-season holiday.

SIGHTS

Acadia National Park comes right up to the edge of town, but the Bar Harbor area has plenty of attractions of its own.

Jackson Laboratory for Mammalian Research

World renowned in genetic research, the Jackson Laboratory (600 Main St., Rte. 3, 207/288-6000, www.jax.org) has some 1,200 employees and breeds special mice used to study cancer, diabetes, muscular dystrophy, and other diseases—with considerable success. More than two million mice are shipped from JAX (as it's called locally, or just "the lab") to more than 12,000 research labs worldwide, generating annual revenues of about $48 million. From June through September (except the middle week of August), a lively audiovisual program explains the lab's impressive work, and one of the staff scientists describes his or her work. The free, hour-long "summer visitor program," only on Wednesday, begins at 3 P.M. in the lab's auditorium and ends with ques-

tions from the audience. To check on the topic, or for other information about the Wednesday program, call 207/288-6051. The lab is 1.5 miles south of downtown Bar Harbor.

St. Saviour's Episcopal Church

St. Saviour's Episcopal Church (41 Mount Desert St., Bar Harbor 04609, 207/288-4215, open daily 7 A.M. to dusk), very close to the center of Bar Harbor, boasts Maine's largest collection of Tiffany stained-glass windows. Ten originals are here; an 11th was stolen in 1988 and replaced by a locally made window. Of the 32 non-Tiffany windows, the most intriguing is a memorial to Clarence Little, founder of the Jackson Laboratory and a descendant of Paul Revere. Images in his window include the laboratory, the DNA double-helix, and mice. Volunteers conduct free tours of the Victorian-era church (completed in 1878) at 11 A.M. and 3 P.M. Monday–Saturday and at 3 P.M. Sunday in July and August. Off-season, call to arrange a tour. If you're intrigued by old cemeteries, spend time wandering the 18th-century "village burying ground" next to the church.

Abbe Museum

Across the street from St. Saviour's is the stunning new (built in 2001) Abbe Museum (26 Mount Desert St., Bar Harbor 04609, 207/288-3519, www.abbemuseum.org), a superb place to introduce children (and adults) to prehistoric and historic Native American tools, crafts, and other cultural artifacts. A special feature is the "Circle of the Four Directions," a dramatic space graphically demonstrating the role of the circle in Native American traditions. A $5.8 million capital campaign allowed the museum to create this handsome, 17,000-square-foot space to display and house more than 50,000 objects spanning nearly 12,000 years. Museum-sponsored events include craft workshops, hands-on children's programs, archaeological field schools, and the **Native American Festival** (held at the College of the Atlantic on a Saturday in early July). The museum's gift shop has a small but select stock of Indian basketry and other handwork, as well as books, videos, and CDs. Open Memorial Day weekend to mid-October: 9 A.M.–5 P.M. Mon.–Wed. and 9 A.M.–9 P.M. Thurs.–Sun.; 10 A.M.–5 P.M. Thurs.–Sun. in spring and fall; closed Jan.). Admission is $4.50 adults, $2 children 6–15. (Also be sure to see the original **Abbe Museum,** two miles away at Sieur de Monts Spring in Acadia National Park. Founded in 1928, it is open daily between Memorial Day and mid-October.)

Bar Harbor Oceanarium

At the northern edge of Mount Desert Island, 8.5 miles northwest of downtown Bar Harbor, is the Bar Harbor Oceanarium (Rte. 3, Bar Harbor 04609, 207/288-5005), one of the island's two related aquariums. As with its sister site (in Southwest Harbor), this low-tech, high-interest operation awes the kids— with a tank full of live harbor seals, a marsh walk to check out tidal creatures and vegetation, and a lobsterman and other staffers who answer all their questions and explain lobstering life and lore. At the aquarium's adjacent lobster hatchery, visitors can view thousands of tiny lobster hatchlings. The Oceanarium and the hatchery building are open 9 A.M.–5 P.M. Monday–Saturday, mid-May to late October. Oceanarium tickets are $9.95 adults, $7.95 children 4–12. This gets rather pricey for a family, but discount combination tickets, covering the Bar Harbor and Southwest Harbor sites, are available for $13 adults, $9.95 for kids.

George B. Dorr Natural History Museum

On the College of the Atlantic (COA) campus in a handsome renovated building, the Natural History Museum (105 Eden St., Rte. 3, Bar Harbor 04609, 207/288-5395 or 288-5015, www .coamuseum.org) showcases regional birds and mammals in realistic dioramas made by COA students. The biggest attraction for children is the please-touch philosophy, allowing kids to

The Bar Harbor Oceanarium is a low-tech, high-interest operation that awes the kids—with a tank full of live harbor seals, a marsh walk to check out tidal creatures and vegetation, and a lobsterman and other staffers who explain lobstering life and lore.

feel fur, skulls, and even whale baleen. Tickets are $3.50 adults, $2.50 seniors, $1.50 teenagers, and $1 children (3–12). The museum is open 10 A.M.–5 P.M. Monday–Saturday, mid-June to Labor Day. During the school year, it's usually open 1–4 P.M. Friday, Saturday, and Sunday but it's wise to double-check, as school holidays affect the off-season schedule. (It's closed, for instance, late November to mid-January, as well as the last two weeks in March.) In summer, a daily interpretive program (usually 11 A.M.) focuses on the museum collection; a Wednesday lecture series (7:30 P.M.) runs throughout July and August. The museum also sponsors an excellent and very popular **Family Nature Camp**— six one-week programs—between late June and mid-August; well-in-advance registration is essential (800/597-9500 or www.coa.edu/summer). Families are housed and fed on the campus ($625 per adult, $250 per child 5–17 covers everything). The museum gift shop has a particularly good collection of books and gifts for budding naturalists. The college and its museum are a half mile northwest of downtown Bar Harbor.

About 2.5 miles south of Bar Harbor, at Sieur de Monts Spring, near where Route 3 meets the Park Loop Road, is the summer-only site (late May–mid-October) of the **Abbe Museum.** This was the original locale for the museum, before the downtown Bar Harbor building opened. Everything about this privately funded museum is tasteful, including the park setting, a handsome National Historic Register building, and displays from a 50,000-item collection. Admission is $2 adults, $1 children 6–12.

While you're at Sieur de Monts Spring, take the time to visit the Acadia National Park **Nature Center** (open weekends in early May, then 9 A.M.–5 P.M. daily until mid-October) and the pretty little **Spring House,** and to wander the paths in the **Wild Gardens of Acadia,** a .75-acre microcosm of more than 400 plant species native to Mount Desert Island. Twelve separate display areas, carefully labeled and maintained by the Bar Harbor Garden Club, represent native plant habitats; pick up the map/brochure that explains each.

Historical Walking Tours

How are bikes and kayaks related to a walking tour? Good question. The answer's at **Acadia Bike and Canoe** (48 Cottage St., Bar Harbor 04609, 207/288-9605), headquarters for "A Step Back in Time," a one-hour walking tour of downtown Bar Harbor. The costumed guide (he or she, depending on the schedule) leads you up one street and down the other, all the while staying in Victorian character and sharing the alleged secrets of the rich and famous (and often outrageous) of the 19th century. Sounds kitschy, but it's most entertaining, primarily for adults. The tours occur several times daily, mid-June through September. Reservations aren't required, but they're wise, especially in July and August. Cost is $12 per person. (Tickets are also available at Acadia Outfitters, 106 Cottage Street.)

Bar Harbor Historical Society

The Bar Harbor Historical Society (33 Ledgelawn Ave., Bar Harbor 04609, 207/288-0000, free admission), in its own National Register building, has fascinating displays, stereopticon images, and a scrapbook about the massive 1947 fire that devastated Mount Desert Island. The photographs alone are worth the visit. Also here are antique maps, Victorian-era hotel registers, and much other local memorabilia. The museum is open late June to mid-October, Monday–Saturday 1–4 P.M. In winter, it's open by appointment.

PARKS AND PRESERVES

Shore Path

Bar Harbor's Shore Path, a well-trodden, granite-edged byway built around 1880, is an intown oasis. Along the craggy shoreline are granite-and-wood benches, town-owned **Grant Park** (great for picnics), birch trees, and several handsome mansions that escaped the 1947 fire. Offshore are the four Porcupine Islands. The path is open

6:30 A.M.–dusk, and leashed pets are allowed. Plan on about 30 minutes for the one-mile loop, beginning next to the Town Pier and the Bar Harbor Inn and returning via Wayman Lane, near the Bar Harbor Hospital. There's also access to the path next to the Balance Rock Inn.

Bar Island

Check the *Mount Desert Islander,* the *Bar Harbor Times,* or the Bar Harbor Chamber of Commerce for the times of low tide, then walk across the gravel bar (wear hiking boots or rubberized shoes) to wooded Bar Island (formerly Rodick's Island) from the foot of Bridge Street in downtown Bar Harbor. Archaeologists have confirmed that Native Americans enjoyed this turf in the distant past. (Part of the island now belongs to Acadia National Park.) You'll have the most time to explore the island during new-moon or full-moon low tides, but plan on no more than three hours—about 90 minutes before and 90 minutes after low tide. *Be sure* to wear a watch so you don't get trapped by the tide (for up to 10 hours). The foot of Bridge Street is also an excellent kayak-launching site.

Indian Point/Blagden Preserve

In the far northern corner of the island (still within the Bar Harbor town limits) is a lovely preserve owned by The Nature Conservancy. From the junction of Routes 3 and 102/198, continue 1.8 miles to Indian Point Road and turn right. Go 1.7 miles to a fork and turn right. Watch for the preserve entrance on the right, marked by a Nature Conservancy oak leaf.

Five trails wind through forested, 110-acre Indian Point/Blagden Preserve, a rectangular parcel with island, hill, and bay vistas. Seal-watching and birding are popular—harbor seals on offshore rocks and woodpeckers (plus 130 other species) in blowdown areas. To spot the seals, plan your hike around the time of low tide, when they'll be sprawled on the rocks close to shore. Wear rubberized shoes or boots. Bring binoculars or use the telescope installed here for the purpose. To keep from disturbing the seals, watch quietly and avoid jerky movements. Park near the preserve entrance and follow the Big Woods

COMMUNITIES

Trail, running the length of the preserve. A second parking area is farther in, but then you'll miss walking through much of the preserve. When you reach the second parking area, just past an old field, bear left along the Shore Trail to see the seals. Register at the caretakers' house (just beyond the first parking lot, where you can pick up bird and flora checklists), and respect private property on either side of the preserve. Open dawn–6 P.M. daily, all year.

RECREATION

Acadia National Park of course steals the limelight for most of Mount Desert Island's recreation, but Bar Harbor has its own pursuits—plus several outfitters for anyone headed to Acadia. (See the *Acadia on Mount Desert Island* chapter for info on rock-climbing guides in Bar Harbor.)

Bike Rentals

With all the great biking options, including 45 miles of carriage roads (12 miles of which are off-limits to bicycles) and some of the best roadside bike routes in Maine, you'll want to bring a bike or rent one here. It's worth calling ahead to reserve it before you arrive. Two rental firms based in downtown Bar Harbor also handle repairs. **Acadia Bike & Canoe** (48 Cottage St., Bar Harbor 04609, 207/288-9605 or 800/526-8615, www.acadiabike.com) rents adult mountain bikes for $16/day if you reserve ahead with a credit card (walk-ins are $19/day). Helmet, lock, and map are included. The shop opens daily at 8 A.M. in spring, summer, and fall.

Down the street, at the corner of Route 3, the **Bar Harbor Bicycle Shop** (141 Cottage St., Bar Harbor 04609, 207/288-3886, www .barharborbike.com) has earned a reputation for well-maintained bikes, renting for $17/day (tandems are $32). Price includes a helmet, map, and lock. Hours in summer are daily 8 A.M.–8 P.M., 9 A.M.–5:30 P.M. Tuesday–Saturday other months. On Sunday morning (usually 9 or 10 A.M.), the shop organizes a free group ride. The shop stays open March through Christmas.

If you're headed to Southwest Harbor, perhaps for a day trip to Swans Island, see the information on Southwest Cycle in the *Southwest Harbor* section farther on in this chapter.

Golf

Duffers first teed off in 1888 at **Kebo Valley Golf Club** (100 Eagle Lake Rd., Rte. 233, Bar Harbor 04609, 207/288-5000, www .kebovalleyclub.com), Maine's oldest club and the eighth-oldest in the nation. The 17th hole became legendary when it took President William Howard Taft 27 tries to sink the ball in 1911. Kebo is very popular, with a gorgeous setting, an attractive clubhouse, and decent food service, so tee times are essential; greens fees are the highest on the island ($63 weekdays and weekends). Open daily, May–October, the 18-hole course is a mile west of downtown Bar Harbor.

GETTING AFLOAT

Bar Harbor has so many opportunities for getting out on the water that you really should do it at least once while you're here.

Whale-Watching Excursions

Whale-watching boats go as much as 20 miles offshore, so no matter what the weather in Bar Harbor, dress warmly and take more clothing than you think you'll need—even gloves, if you're especially sensitive to cold. Motion-sensitive children and adults should plan in advance for appropriate medication, such as pills or patches.

Humpback, finback, and minke whales are prime viewing targets for the **Bar Harbor Whale Watch Company** (1 West St., Bar Harbor 04609, 207/288-2386 or 800/942-5374, www.whalesrus.com), sailing from the dock in front of Harbor Place, in downtown Bar Harbor, between early June and mid-October. Its 112-foot, 200-passenger catamaran *Friendship V* is speedy and tends to remain more stable than other boats—a big advantage when (not if) you meet offshore swells. An onboard snack bar has sandwiches and cold drinks, and breakfast on the earliest trip. In case you forget yours, the shop also sells cameras and film and rents binoculars. The schedule varies each month; between July and Labor Day, there are three daily sail-

Bar Harbor Inn Pier, starting point for boating excursions

ings: 8:30 A.M. (3.5-hour puffin- and whale-watching trip) and 1 and 4:30 P.M. (three hours each). Tickets are $43 adults, $25 children 6–14, $8 children five and under.

Undersea Exploring

Fortunately, you don't have to go diving in these frigid waters to see what lurks below; others will do it for you. After the kids have touched the slimy sea cucumbers and sea stars at the Bar Harbor Oceanarium, they'll be primed for **Diver Ed Tours** (27 Main St., Bar Harbor 04609, 207/288-3483, www.divered.com). Former Bar Harbor harbormaster (and College of the Atlantic alumnus) Ed Monat heads the crew aboard the 46-passenger *Seal,* which departs from the Bar Harbor Inn Pier and goes a mile or two offshore. Then a professional diver (often it's Ed) goes overboard with a video camera. You and the kids stay on deck, all warm and dry, and watch the action on a TV screen. There's communication back and forth between diver and deck, so the kids can ask questions as the diver picks up urchins, sea stars, crabs, lobsters, and other sealife. When the diver surfaces, he or she brings a bag of touchable specimens—another

chance to pet some slimy creatures (which go back into the water after show-and-tell). Great concept. Watch the kids' expressions—this is a big hit. The season runs from Memorial Day weekend to Columbus Day, but the schedule varies. Mid-June–August, Monday–Saturday, the two-hour trips depart at 9:30 A.M. and 1:30 and 5:30 P.M. Cost is $30 adults, $25 seniors, $20 children under 12, free for kids under five. Some Diver Ed cruises are part of the Acadia Park Ranger program, and a park naturalist will be on board. Check the park's *Beaver Log* newspaper for the schedule and reservation information.

Sailing

Captain Steve Pagels, under the umbrella of **Downeast Windjammer Cruises** (207/288-4585 or 288-2373, P.O. Box 28, Cherryfield 04622, www.downeastwindjammer.com), offers two-hour daysails on the 151-foot steel-hulled *Margaret Todd,* a gorgeous four-masted schooner with tanbark sails launched in 1998. Between mid-May and mid-October, the sailing season varies. In July and August (weather permitting), there are usually three daily sailings, departing from the Bar Harbor Inn Pier, just east of the

COMMUNITIES

Town Pier in downtown Bar Harbor. Buy tickets ($29.50 adults, $27.50 seniors, $19.50 children under 12) at the pier, or at 27 Main Street, or online with a credit card. The sunset cruise (6:30 P.M.) often includes live music; bring a picnic supper. Captain Pagels also owns the **Bar Harbor Ferry,** which offers service between Bar Harbor and Winter Harbor, as well as the **Cranberry Cove Ferry,** providing service to the Cranberry Isles.

Sea Kayaking

Sea kayaking is wildly popular along the Maine coast, and Bar Harbor has become a major kayaking destination. No experience is necessary to join tours operated by any of the firms in Bar Harbor. Half-day ($45 pp), full-day ($69 pp; bring your own lunch), and multiday sea-kayak tours are on the schedule organized by **Coastal Kayaking Tours** (48 Cottage St., P.O. Box 405, Bar Harbor 04609, 207/288-9605 or 800/526-8615, www.acadiafun.com). The best option for beginners is the 2.5-hour harbor tour, usually beginning at 9 A.M. ($36 pp). By prearrangement, special half-day family tours, usually departing at 1:30 P.M., can handle kids eight and over ($47 pp). A 2.5-hour sunset cruise begins around 5 P.M. (depending on season), at $36 pp, and a three-day inn-to-inn tour, scheduled about once a month, is $599 pp. Other kayak trips are offered mid-May through September. All trips are weather-dependent, and reservations are essential.

Three other firms in Bar Harbor do sea-kayak tours and rentals. New tour operators spring up often; opt for experience. Other companies operate elsewhere on the island; see the *Southwest Harbor and Tremont* section, later in this chapter. Also see *Guided Tours* in the *Acadia on Mount Desert Island* chapter.

Lobstering Cruises

When you're ready to learn The Truth about lobsters, sign up for a cruise aboard Captain John Nicolai's *Lulu,* a traditional Maine lobsterboat. Operating daily from May through September, *Lulu* departs from the Harborside Hotel and Marina Pier (formerly the Golden Anchor Inn

Pier—and still referred to that way by locals) in Bar Harbor (55 West St., 207/963-2341 or 866/235-2341, www.lululobsterboat.com). Between mid-June and mid-August, there are five daily trips (1.75 hours each). Captain Nicolai provides an entertaining commentary on anything and everything, but especially about lobsters and lobstering. He hauls a lobster trap and explains intimate details of the hapless critter. (Lobstering is banned on Sunday June through August; the cruises still operate, but there's no hauling that day. You'll spend more time checking out harbor-seal ledges.) Reservations are required (phone 7–8 A.M.); 12 passengers max (minimum is two adult passengers). Cost is $25 adults, $22 seniors and military, $15 children under 12. No credit cards. Free parking in the hotel lot.

SHOPPING

Bar Harbor's boutiques—running the gamut from attractive to kitschy—are indisputably visitor-oriented; many shut down for the winter, even removing or covering their signs and blanketing the windows. Fortunately, the island has enough of a year-round community to support the cluster of loyal shopkeepers determined to stay open all year, but shop-till-you-droppers will be happiest here between Memorial Day weekend and Columbus Day, and particularly in July and August. (Remember, too, that Bar Harbor isn't Mount Desert's only shopping area.)

Galleries and Crafts

Birdsnest Gallery (12 Mount Desert St., Bar Harbor 04609, 207/288-4054, www .birdsnestgallery.com), has a well-earned reputation for a fine selection of paintings, sculpture, and prints. Prices match the quality. Open 10 A.M.–10 P.M. daily in summer, shorter hours other months, mid-May to mid-October.

Downtown Bar Harbor's best craft gallery is **Island Artisans** (99 Main St., P.O. Box 793, Bar Harbor 04609, 207/288-4214, www.islandartisans .com). More than 50 Maine artists are represented here, and the quality is outstanding. Don't miss it. You'll find basketwork, handmade paper, wood carvings, blown glass, jewelry, weaving, metalwork, ceramics, and more. Open daily, May through October, then Friday and Saturday in November and December. (Island Artisans has a summertime branch at 119 Main St. in Northeast Harbor.)

Souvenirs, Gifts, and Books

Souvenir shops are *everywhere* on Mount Desert Island, so why single out the Acadia shops? If you need to pick up Maine-made mementos for Aunt Alice and Uncle Pete, if the kids need trinkets for pals back home, the Acadia Corporation has several shops in downtown Bar Harbor that can cover it all. Price range is broad, quality is fairly high, and clerks are especially friendly at **The Acadia Shop** (85 Main St., Bar Harbor, 207/288-5600). It's open 8 A.M.–11 P.M. daily in midsummer, 9 A.M.–5 P.M. off-season. At 45 Main St., another branch, **Acadia Outdoors,** 207/288-2422, features sportswear and outdoor accessories.

Toys, cards, and newspapers blend in with the new-book inventory at **Sherman's Book Store** (56 Main St., Bar Harbor 04609, 207/288-3161, www.shermans.com). Even the fusty clutter is user-friendly. Sherman's is just the place to pick up maps and trail guides for fine days and puzzles for foggy days. Open 9 A.M.–5:30 P.M. daily (to 10:30 P.M. in summer), all year.

Musical Instruments

OK, most Acadia vacationers don't expect to shop for musical instruments—but everyone with an affinity for folkloric music gravitates toward **Song of the Sea** (47 West St., Bar Harbor 04609, 207/288-5653, fax 207/288-8136, www.songsea.com), a unique, jam-packed harborfront shop where you can buy guitars, banjos, harmonicas, and tin whistles—as well as such esoterica as hammered dulcimers, doumbeks, didgeridoos, psalteries, and Chilean rainsticks. Ed and Anne Damm are extremely knowledgeable and helpful, even to the point of playing instruments over the phone for call-in orders. Open all year, but hours vary by season (summer: 10 A.M.–8 P.M. Monday–Saturday and noon–6 P.M. Sunday).

Farmers' Market

Between mid-May and late October, the **Eden Farmers' Market** operates out of the YMCA parking lot off Lower Main Street in Bar Harbor 10 A.M.–1 P.M. each Sunday. Vendor specialties include excellent locally made goat cheese, preserves, and prepared Asian goodies.

ENTERTAINMENT

At the height of the summer season, there's plenty of live entertainment—from pub music to park concerts to chamber music to impromptu performances. For rainy days, two cinemas and a unique pottery studio can help while away the time.

Above Rupununi's restaurant, **Carmen Verandah** (119 Main St., Bar Harbor 04609, 207/288-2766, www.carmenverandah.com) is the weekend place to see and be seen. Everything gets rolling about 9:30 P.M.—blues, rock, salsa, bluegrass, funk, zydeco, ska, reggae, you name it—and there's lots of square footage for dancing. Some shows require tickets. Other nights, there's a DJ; karaoke is usually Monday night. Darts and pool round out the picture. Open daily, April to November.

Cinemas

In 2001, new owners assumed the reins of the beautifully refurbished National Historic Landmark **Criterion Theatre** (35 Cottage St., Bar Harbor 04609, 207/288-3441 (films) or 288-5829 (concerts), www.criteriontheatre.com), built in 1932. Now, in addition to screening films, the Criterion puts on concerts, plays, and other special events. You'll soak up the nostalgia in this Art Deco classic with nearly 900 seats (including an elegant floating balcony). Beer, wine, and creative appetizers and sandwiches are available (competing with Reel Pizza, below), and the theater is open all year. Two screenings nightly in summer (usually 7 and 9:30); Saturday and Sunday matinees at 2 P.M.

Combine pizza with your picture show at **Reel Pizza Cinerama** (33 Kennebec Pl., P.O. Box 625, Bar Harbor 04609, 207/288-3811 (films), 288-3828 (food)). Two showings nightly

© KATHLEEN M. BRANDES

the Criterion Theatre, an Art Deco classic

on each of the two screens. All tickets are $5. Doors open at 4:30 P.M.; get there early for the best seats.

Kids' Stuff

Definitely worthy of the Entertainment category is **All Fired Up!** (101 Cottage St., Bar Harbor 04609, 207/288-3130), the perfect answer to "What do we do in the rain?" Solution: Paint your own pottery. You'll often see three generations sharing a booth as they work away at their projects in this bright, airy space. Here's the drill: Select a mug or bowl or whatever from one of the 500 or so white-bisque pottery pieces ($2 and up). Figure out a design (check out "the inspiration center"), choose your colors, and work away. If you opt for a glaze instead of paint, so you can dine off your masterpiece, you'll need to leave it for a few days so it can be kiln-fired (and shipped to your home if you prefer). Studio time (including all the supplies) is $10 per adult, $7 per child. Owner Nina Zeldin inspires even the artistically challenged, and it's all great fun. Open all year. Summer hours (late June to Labor Day) are 9 A.M.–9 P.M. daily.

ACCOMMODATIONS

If you're not planning to camp in one of Acadia National Park's two campgrounds (there are no other lodgings, and there's no backcountry camping), you'll need to search elsewhere on the island for a place to sleep. Bar Harbor alone has thousands of beds in hotels, motels, inns, B&Bs, cottages, and two hostels—and the rest of the island adds to that total, with a dozen private campgrounds thrown into the mix. Nonetheless, lodgings can be scarce at the height of summer (particularly the first two weeks in August), a stretch that just happens to coincide with an outrageously high spike in room rates (sorta like gasoline hikes that "just happen" to occur just before long holiday weekends). Off-season, there's plenty of choice, even after the seasonal places shut down, and rates are always lower, often dramatically so. (The Bar Harbor Chamber of Commerce and the Thompson Island Visitor Center will give you a list of lodgings open year-round, and both offices are helpful for finding beds even at peak times.)

MOUNT DESERT ISLAND FESTIVALS AND EVENTS

This list only skims the surface of the busy schedule in Bar Harbor; check with the Thompson Island Visitor Center or the Bar Harbor Chamber of Commerce for up-to-date listings of other happenings. Also check the weekly *Mount Desert Islander* and *Bar Harbor Times* newspapers.

The **Fourth of July** is always a big deal in Bar Harbor, celebrated with a blueberry-pancake breakfast (6 A.M.), a parade (10 A.M.), a seafood festival (11 A.M. on), a band concert, and fireworks. (Independence Day celebrations in the island's smaller villages evoke a bygone era.)

The Abbe Museum, the College of the Atlantic, and the Maine Indian Basketmakers Alliance sponsor the annual **Native American Festival and Maine Indian Basketmakers' Market**, 10 A.M.–4 P.M., the first Saturday in July, featuring baskets, beadwork, and other handcrafts for sale. There's also Indian drumming and dancing. The festival and market have become hugely popular, so expect to see a crowd. Free admission; held at College of the Atlantic, 105 Eden St. (Rte. 3), Bar Harbor.

The **Arcady Music Festival**, which celebrated its 20th anniversary in 2000, presents evening concerts late July through August at various locations on and off the island. Bar Harbor concerts are Thursday at 8 P.M., at Holy Redeemer Church, 21 Ledgelawn Avenue. The array of music is broad, from ragtime to classical. For information call 207/288-2141 or 288-3151, or visit www.arcady.org.

The **Bar Harbor Music Festival,** a summer tradition since 1967, emphasizes up-and-coming musical talent in a series of classical, jazz, and pop concerts at various island locations early July to early August. (Friday, Saturday, and Sunday are the usual nights, but sometimes concerts are held other evenings. Check locally.) Reservations are wise: 207/288-5744 in July and August, 212/222-1026 off-season.

In even-numbered years, the **Mount Desert Garden Club Tour** presents a rare chance to visit some of Maine's most spectacular private gardens the second or third Saturday in July (confirm the date with the Bar Harbor Chamber of Commerce).

For more music, the **Bar Harbor Town Band** performs free concerts Monday and Thursday evening (8 P.M.) on the Village Green, Main and Mount Desert Streets, Bar Harbor, July to mid-August.

The **Directions Craft Show** fills an August weekend with extraordinary displays and sales of crafts by members of the Maine Crafts Guild. You'll find the show at Mount Desert Island High School, a few miles west of downtown Bar Harbor, on Route 233, Eagle Lake Road. Hours are Friday 5–9 P.M., Saturday and Sunday 10 A.M.–5 P.M. Information: www.mainecraftsguild.com.

Hotels and Motels

One of the town's best-known, most-visible, and best-situated hotels is the **Bar Harbor Inn** (Newport Drive, P.O. Box 7, Bar Harbor 04609, 207/288-3351 or 800/248-3351, www.barharborinn.com), a sprawling complex on eight acres overlooking the harbor and Bar Island. The 153 rooms and suites vary considerably in style, from traditional inn to motel, in three different buildings; rates are $185–355 d late June through August, $75–319 d other months (lowest rates are in April). Continental breakfast is included, and special packages are available—an advantage for families. The kids also will appreciate the heated outdoor pool. Rooms in the Oceanfront Lodge are good family choices, with reasonable rates and terrific views. The Main Inn rooms have seen the most recent upgrades. No pets. Service is particularly attentive. Open late March through Thanksgiving. Other Bar Harbor lodgings under the same management/ownership (www.bar-harbor-hotels.com) are the upscale **Bluenose Inn** and the less expensive, family-oriented **Acadia Inn**, both on Route 3 at the edge of town (on the free Island Explorer bus route), as well as the huge new (2003) **Bar Harbor Grand Hotel**, a four-story neo-Victorian (modeled on Bar Harbor's 19th-century Rodick House) looming over Lower Main Street.

Formerly a budget option, but edging upward in rates, the **Aurora Inn** (51 Holland Ave., Bar Harbor 04609, 207/288-3771 or 800/841-8925, www.aurorainn.com) is a clean, no-frills motel from which you can walk everywhere. Nine smallish ground-floor rooms ($109–149 d June to mid-October, $59–99 off-season) have private baths, phones, fridges, a/c, and cable TV. Children under 18 stay free (but there's not much room for a cot). No pets. Pool privileges at the Quality Inn (under the same ownership), just up the street. Open all year.

Inns and B&Bs

Even the address has charm at **Ullikana Bed & Breakfast** (16 The Field, Bar Harbor 04609, 207/288-9552, www.ullikana.com), an 1885 Victorian Tudor manse close to Bar Harbor's Shore Path. Named Ullikana by its builder, Alpheus Hardy, Bar Harbor's first "cottager," the house has been tastefully updated by owners Hélène Harton and Roy Kasindorf. (French-speaking visitors appreciate Hélène's background as head of the UN International School's French department—and *everyone* appreciates her skills in the kitchen.) Everything blends perfectly here, even their modern-art collection. (Local artist Melita Westerlund's outdoor sculptures add whimsy to the lawns.) Ten comfortable rooms on three floors, all with private baths and some with water views and balconies, are $155–285 d in midsummer, slightly lower in spring and fall. The 1872 Yellow House, across the way, with six more rooms ($235 d), has its own charming character. An amazing breakfast is served on the water-view patio. If you need hiking advice, Roy and Hélène even share secrets of their favorite Acadia trails (they manage to get out for a hike every day). No smoking, no pets; children over 12 are welcome. Reserve well ahead for this very popular B&B. Open May through October.

Cookies *du jour* are a specialty at **Holbrook House** (74 Mount Desert St., Bar Harbor 04609, 207/288-4970, www.holbrookhouse.com), thanks to English-born Lesley DiVirgilio—who's also a midwife and avid quiltmaker. She and husband Phil have brought casual comfort to Holbrook House, making this a welcoming oasis on an often-busy street. Ten first- and second-floor rooms have queen beds, a ceiling fan or a/c, private baths, and bright flowery prints ($130–170

d from late June to mid-October; $90–115 other months). Behind the house are two fully equipped diminutive cottages (dubbed Fern and Pine), ideal for families ($225–235 a night for four). Breakfast is a full-scale affair, served on a homey glassed-in porch that doubles as a gathering place. (Guests also gravitate to the library and the fireplaced parlor.) Holbrook House, built in 1876 and a "great fire" survivor, is open May through November.

Energetic Marian Burns, a former math/science teacher and former president of the Maine Innkeepers Association, is the reason everything runs smoothly at **Mira Monte Inn** (69 Mount Desert St., Bar Harbor 04609, 207/288-4263 or 800/553-5109, fax 207/288-3115, www.miramonte.com), close (but not too close) to downtown. Born and raised here, and an avid gardener (save time for strolling her "secret gardens"), Marian's a terrific resource for island exploring. Ask about her experiences as a college student during the 1947 Bar Harbor fire. The 13 Victorian-style rooms have a/c, cable TV, phones, and other welcome touches ($165–230 d late June to late August; $95–220 other months); two efficiency suites in a separate building are ideal for families. Early and late in the season, special packages are available. Extensive buffet breakfast. No pets, no smoking. Open mid-April through October (the two suites are open all year).

Just down the street from Mira Monte, **Stratford House Inn** (45 Mount Desert St., Bar Harbor 04609, 207/288-5189, fax 207/288-4184, www.stratfordinn.com) is a turn-of-the-20th-century Tudor-style home conveniently close to downtown. Leave the car and walk to shops and restaurants, or pedal to the Acadia carriage roads. This handsome "cottage," built by a Boston publisher, boasts brass beds, a music room, and a library. Hospitable innkeeper Barbara Moulton provides a continental breakfast in the elegant dining room. Ten second- and third-floor rooms (eight have private baths) are $85–175 mid-June to mid-September (two-night minimum). Instead of a lower rate off-season, you'll get three nights for the price of two. No smoking, no pets; children welcome. Open mid-May to mid-October.

Staying away from downtown Bar Harbor, in the northern end of the island, means informality, less hubbub than in Bar Harbor, and relatively lower prices. **The Cove Farm Inn Bed & Breakfast** (Crooked Rd., Bar Harbor 04609, 207/288-5355 or 800/291-0952, www.covefarm.com), run by the Keene family, is a great place to bring the kids and let down your hair. It's not for introverts. Everyone mixes in. You'll find a guest refrigerator and a guest vegetable patch, and you can even use the kitchen to pack picnics and fix supper. The five-acre farm has resident roosters, ducks, and geese. Jerry Keene, an island expert, loves sharing his comprehensive local knowledge. No smoking, no pets. Eleven basic rooms (some private baths, some shared) go for $50–125 d May through October, $35–70 other months, including a full breakfast. (If you're bringing the family, it's $15 per extra person.) The Keenes also have housekeeping cottages available by the week in summer. Open all year. Cove Farm is a quarter mile west of Route 3, near Hulls Cove and the Acadia National Park Visitor Center.

Hostels

The only Maine hostel affiliated with Hostelling International (HI)—once there were six—the **Mount Desert Island Youth Hostel** (321 Main St., P.O. Box 32, Bar Harbor 04609, 207/288-5587, www.hiayh.org/ushostel/nengreg/barhar) has a new location since the summer of 2003. Formerly housed seasonally in a church parish hall, the new hostel has its own building not far from the downtown area (across from Havana Restaurant) and close to Acadia access. Two dorm-style rooms (one male, one female) have 13 beds each—$21 for HI members and students, $25 for nonmembers and nonstudents (lower rates available after mid-September). There are kitchen and dining facilities and *six* showers (far better than the two in the former location). You'll need your own sleeping bag. No smoking, no liquor; 11 P.M. curfew. Open June through October. No credit cards. Reservations (best by mail) are essential, as this is a popular location.

Not officially a hostel, but with a hostel-style atmosphere, only for women, the **MDI YWCA**

(36 Mount Desert St., Bar Harbor 04609, 207/288-5008) has second- and third-floor single and double rooms, as well as a seven-bed solarium (dorm). Located in a historic downtown building next to the library and across from the Island Explorer bus hub, the "Y" lodging has bathrooms on each floor, as well as a laundry room (coin-operated machines), a TV room, and shared kitchen facilities. Free parking, no pets. Zero tolerance for smoking, alcohol, drugs (you'll need to sign an agreement). For July and early August reservations, call way ahead, as the Y is popular with the island's young summer workers. Singles are $37.45, doubles are $32.10 pp, the solarium beds are $26.75 each (rates include tax). No credit cards. Open all year.

Campgrounds

Mount Desert Island's private campgrounds are located at the northern end of the island, down the center, and in the southwest corner. Most are also on the routes of the free Island Explorer bus service, making it easy and economic—and preferable—to leave your car (or RV) at your campsite and avoid parking panic (between late June and Columbus Day). The Thompson Island and Hulls Cove Visitor Centers have a listing of private campgrounds.

At the top of the island, not far from the Thompson Island info center, are two well-sited **campgrounds,** both large, well maintained, and on an Island Explorer bus route. Next to the causeway, and 10 miles northwest of Bar Harbor, **Bar Harbor KOA** (136 County Rd., Bar Harbor 04609, 207/288-3520 or 888/562-5605, fax 207/288-2840, www.koa.com) occupies 32 acres with 200 open and wooded tent and RV sites. (Yes, it's a national chain, but KOA keeps its standards high.) Waterfront views are terrific. Facilities include coin showers and laundry, playground, beach, game areas, and a small shop. Kayak, canoe, and bike rentals are available. Pets are allowed. Rates are $21–41 d, late June to Labor Day, $18–32 other months. Open mid-May to mid-October.

Mt. Desert Narrows Camping Resort (1219 Rte. 3, Bar Harbor 04609, 207/288-4782, www.narrowscamping.com), 1.5 miles from the

COMMUNITIES

top of the island, has fantastic views over Thomas Bay and the Narrows. The 40-acre campground has 239 wooded and open tent and RV sites, heated pool, convenience store, canoe rentals, playground, coin laundry, and live entertainment mid-June to Labor Day. Pets are allowed. Tent sites are $25–50 d (two adults, two kids under 18; two-night minimum) mid-June to Labor Day, lower early and late in the season. If your budget allows, request one of the $50 oceanfront tent sites. RV sites are higher ($38–65 in high season), and there are fees for hookups and visitors. Open May to late October.

Seasonal Rentals

Contact **Lynam Real Estate** (227 Main St., P.O. Box C, Bar Harbor 04609, 207/288-3334, fax 288-3550, www.lynams.com) or **Maine Island Properties** (P.O. Box 1025, Mount Desert 04660, 207/244-4308, fax 207/244-0588, www.maineislandproperties.com) for listings of houses/cottages available by the week or month. In July and August, rates run anywhere from $700–6,000 a week. Both agencies handle rentals in all parts of Mount Desert. (If you decide to stay, they also have residential listings.)

FOOD

You won't go hungry in Bar Harbor. The summer tourism trade, College of the Atlantic students, and Jackson Laboratory staffers sustain the pizzerias, vegetarian bistros, brewpubs, and a handful of creative restaurants. (So far, the only chain fast-foodery with a foothold is Subway.) Of course, almost every restaurant has some variant of lobster—from the basic boiled or steamed to the *haut gourmet*. And even if you're using Bar Harbor as a base of operations for Acadia, don't overlook restaurants elsewhere on the island.

Breakfast

If you're camping, or staying at a motel with nothing appealing on the freebie shelf, downtown Bar Harbor has a couple of great eye-openers.

After you've tried the smoked-salmon Eggs Benedict ($8.95) at **2 cats** (130 Cottage St.,

Bar Harbor 04609, 107/288-2808, www .2catsbarharbor.com), you'll find it tough to think about lunch or dinner. Or try the Mediterranean Breakfast ($7.95), or the raspberry almond pancakes that taste like French toast ($5.75). But if fitness guilt rules your life, 2 cats has fresh fruit bowls, homemade granola, Tofu Scramble ($6.95), low-fat smoothies, and giant glasses of freshly squozen O.J. This informal place has Equal Exchange coffee and one of the cheeriest attitudes in town. Open 7–11 A.M. Monday–Saturday, 8 A.M. –1 P.M. Sunday. (2 cats also has a couple of rooms for rent upstairs, *with* breakfast.)

Down a little alleyway across from the Village Green, in a funky building with higgledy-piggledy decor (well, maroon paint, a wall lined with books, and a refrigerator door loaded with poetry magnets), is a not-very-well-kept secret— **Café This Way** (14 Mount Desert St., Bar Harbor 04609, 207/288-4483, www.cafethisway .com). Launched by a trio of enthusiastic partners, the café has been a hit since it opened in 1997. The breakfast menu is a genuine wake-up call; try the Green Eggs and Sam omelet ($5.95). The café also serves dinner; entrées— East-West Duck or cashew-crusted chicken— are in the $16–23 range, but a couple of the appetizers ($6–10) would be ample for dinner. The wine list is very selective and desserts are outstanding. In summer and fall, Café This Way is open 7–11 A.M. Monday–Saturday, 8 A.M.– 1 P.M. Sunday, and 6–9 P.M. daily for dinner. In winter and spring, alas, it's open only for breakfast (8 A.M.–2 P.M. Wednesday–Sunday).

Pizza

An unscientific but reliable local survey gives the best-pizza ribbon to **Rosalie's Pizza & Italian Restaurant** (46 Cottage St., Bar Harbor 04609, 207/288-5666), where the Wurlitzer jukebox churns out tunes from the 1950s. This family-owned standard gets high marks for consistency with its homemade pizza (in four sizes or by the slice), calzones, and subs—lots of vegetarian options. The sub dubbed Rosalie's Nightmare delivers what it promises. Beer and wine are available. Rosalie's is open daily from 11 A.M., all year.

Combine a pizza with a first-run or art flick at **Reel Pizza Cinerama** (33 Kennebec Pl., Bar Harbor 04609, 207/288-3811 (films), 288-3828 (food)), across from the Village Green, where you order your pizza, grab an easy chair, and watch for your number to come up on the Bingo board. Beer and wine are available, and the doors open at 4:30 P.M. Pizzas ($12–19.25) have cinematic names—Zorba the Greek, The Godfather, Manchurian Candidate. Then there's Mussel Beach Party—broccoli, tomatoes, goat cheese, and smoked mussels. You get the idea. (You don't even have to stay for the flick!) Reel Pizza has occasional Saturday matinees; closed Monday in winter. Be sure to arrive early; the best chairs go quickly.

Efficient, friendly, cafeteria-style service makes **EPI Sub and Pizza Shop** (8 Cottage St., Bar Harbor 04609, 207/288-5853) an excellent choice for picnics or a quick break from sightseeing. The dozen-plus sub-sandwich choices at EPI's (short for epicurean) are bargains (try the Cadillac). If the weather closes in, there are always the pinball machines in the back room. No credit cards. Open 10 A.M.–8 P.M. daily, early February–December (to 9 P.M. July and August). Closed Sunday in November, December, and from February to mid-May.

Box Lunches

If you're heading out for a day in the park, several places in Bar Harbor provide box-lunch service. The best strategy is to place your order the day before and pick it up first thing in the morning, but two of the bakeries open early, so you can dash in, order a lunch, and make a quick getaway. **Cottage Street Bakery & Deli** (59 Cottage St., Bar Harbor 04609, 207/288-3010) opens at 6:30 A.M. Monday–Saturday, and 7 A.M. Sunday. A box lunch (with free insulated bag) is $7.25. Credit cards are accepted. **Morning Glory Bakery** (39 Rodick St., Bar Harbor 04609, 207/288-3041) opens at 7 A.M. Monday–Saturday; closed Sunday. Box lunch is $6.50.

If you happen to be on Route 102 in the Town Hill area around lunchtime, plan to pick up picnic fare at **Mother's Kitchen** (Rte. 102, Town Hill, Bar Harbor 04609, 207/288-4403). The plain,

minuscule building next to Salsbury Hardware is deceiving—it's been operating since 1995 and turns out 20 different sandwiches, as well as deli salads, scones, breakfast sandwiches, great cookies, and pies. They'll even pack up box lunches. Calling ahead would save time, but the whimsically named sandwich combos are tough to describe over the phone. (How about Charlie Noble—homemade chicken salad with walnuts and tarragon, cranberry sauce, and lettuce on onion walnut dill bread—for $5.50?) If you're desperately hungry, there are a few picnic tables outside, but you can find better picnic settings elsewhere. Mother's Kitchen is open 8 A.M.–2 P.M. Monday–Saturday, mid-April through October.

Brewpubs and Microbreweries

Bar Harbor's longest-lived brewpub is the **Lompoc Café** (36 Rodick St., Bar Harbor 04609, 207/288-9392), serving creative lunches and dinners daily 11:30 A.M.–9 P.M., late April to mid-December. How about a lobster-and-avocado quesadilla or crab-shrimp-and-artichoke gratin? Lompoc's hummus has been famous since the café opened in 1989. After 9 P.M., there's just beer and thin-crust pizza until about 1 A.M. The congenial café has a beer garden, a bocce court, and free live entertainment (blues, bluegrass, and jazz) weekends during the summer. (Thursday is open mic night, starting at 9 P.M.)

Lompoc's signature Bar Harbor Real Ale, plus five or six others, is brewed by the **Atlantic Brewing Company** (15 Knox Rd., Town Hill—in the upper section of the island—Bar Harbor 04609, 207/288-2337 or 800/475-5417, www.AtlanticBrewing.com), which produces about 30 barrels of beer a day. Free brewery tours, including tasting, are given daily at 2, 3, and 4 P.M., Memorial Day to Columbus Day. In summer, the brewery also operates a tavern/café serving sandwiches, burgers, deli plates—and of course beer—11:30 A.M.–5 P.M. daily.

Bar Harbor Brewing Company & Soda Works (135 Otter Creek Dr., Rte. 3, Bar Harbor 04609, 207/288-4592, www.BarHarborBrewing.com), begun in 1990 by Tod and Suzi Foster as a mom-and-pop operation, remains a small, friendly, hands-on enterprise producing five kinds of beer and ale in a basement microbrewery. Start off at the log-cabin tasting room/gift shop, where kids can sample Old Fashioned Bar Harbor Root Beer. Free 20-minute tours are given at 3:30 and 4:30 P.M. Monday–Friday, late June through August. During September, tours are Tuesday and Thursday, 3:30 and 4:30 P.M. The brewery is 4.5 miles south of downtown Bar Harbor.

Family Restaurants

Once a Victorian boarding house and later a 1920s speakeasy, **Galyn's Galley** (17 Main St., Bar Harbor 04609, 207/288-9706) has been a popular eatery since 1986. Lots of plants, modern decor, reliable service, a great downtown location (opposite Agamont Park, close to the Town Pier), and several indoor and outdoor dining areas contribute to the loyal clientele. The cuisine is consistently good if not outstandingly creative (dinner entrées $10–22). Dinner reservations are advisable in midsummer. Open for lunch (11:30 A.M.–2 P.M.) and dinner (4–10 P.M. in July and August) daily, except major national holidays; closed in the dead of winter.

About two blocks from Galyn's, **Rupununi** (119 Main St., Bar Harbor 04609, 207/288-2886, www.rupununi.com) gets its name from a river in Guyana—the inspiration of owner Mike Boland, a College of the Atlantic grad. Billed as "an American bar and grill," Rupununi draws a lively, fun crowd for great burgers (even ostrich burgers); veggie, seafood, and meat dinner entrées ($7–25); a few Caribbean and Mediterranean touches; and about two dozen beers on draft. The daily "poacher's special" usually means buffalo or venison. On Sunday, jazz is part of the mix. Open daily 11 A.M.–1 A.M. (food stops at midnight). Upstairs is **Carmen Verandah.** Also part of the ever-expanding Rupununi empire are **Joe's Smoke Shop** (an upscale cigar bar in a former gallery next door) and Havana Restaurant.

Blue-corn crab cakes and A-plus margaritas are specialties at **Miguel's Mexican Restaurant** (51 Rodick St., Bar Harbor 04609, 207/288-5117), home of "The Picasso of Picante" and the island's best Tex-Mex food. Entrées are $8–16. In midsummer, try for the patio. Expect to wait;

this is a popular spot. Open daily for dinner 5–10 P.M., April through October; closed Mondays after Labor Day.

Fine Dining

One of Bar Harbor's fine longtime reliables, **George's** (7 Stephens Ln., Bar Harbor 04609, 207/288-4505, www.georgesbarharbor.com), has upheld its reputation despite a change in ownership. It occupies three attractively laid-out rooms in a restored home tucked away on a downtown side street. Appetizers ($10 and $12) are seafood- and Mediterranean-oriented. All entrées are $25; fixed-price three-course menus are $37 and $40. Mighty hard to resist the lobster strudel. Reservations are essential in July and August. There's terrace dining when weather permits. The restaurant is behind the First National Bank, where there's free evening parking. Open daily 5:30–10 P.M. daily, June through October.

Vaguely Cubanesque cuisine is the hottest new entry on Bar Harbor's restaurant scene. With its mango-colored walls and white tablecloths, and a quiet jazz duo providing the background, **Havana** (318 Main St., Bar Harbor 04609, 207/288-CUBA (2822), www.havanamaine.com) is a year-round winner. Billing its premises as a "no-cellphone zone" and its cuisine as "innovative American with a Latin flair," the café ends up with its own kind of fusion—grilled Chilean swordfish, pasta with Bahian coconut sauce, Jamaican jerk lamb, tuna with Asian mushroom salsa. Entrée range is $16–35; for $5.50, you get a glass of *mojito,* the Cuban national drink. Save room for the chocolate truffle torte or the pumpkin cheesecake with a bourbon glaze. Reservations are essential for weekends and advisable for summer weeknights. Havana is open 5:30–10 P.M. daily, May through October, Wednesday–Saturday the rest of the year.

Even nonvegetarians love the vegetarian and vegan cuisine at **Eden** (78 West St., Bar Harbor 04609, 207/288-4422). Opened in 2003, it was a hit from the start, thanks to a serene, simple setting (two dozen seats, plus a tiny bar) and an emphasis on organically grown everything. South and East Asian specialties include a grilled tofu bento box and tempeh wontons—all beautifully presented. For lunch, opt for a frittata, quesadilla, or the vegan chef's salad. Dinner entrées are $15–17; lunch selections average $7. Open 11:30 A.M.–2:30 P.M. and 6–9:30 P.M. Monday–Saturday, April to November.

The view's the thing at the Bar Harbor Inn's **Reading Room Restaurant** (Newport Drive, Bar Harbor 04609, 207/288-3351, www.barharborinn.com); request a window seat. Once the stuffy Bar Harbor Reading Room, a gentlemen's club, the dining room still has a sweeping curve of windows overlooking Bar Island and Frenchman Bay. Dinner entrées, emphasizing meat and seafood, are commendably creative ($19–30), the wine list is good, desserts are so-so. Soft music plays in the background. Despite the elegant setting, dress is informal, and there's a children's menu. The Sunday brunch buffet (11:30 A.M.–2:30 P.M.) is extremely popular ($22 adults, $11 children); in good weather, it's also served on the terrace. Reservations are essential. Breakfast (mid-April through October) is 7–10:30 A.M., lunch (on the terrace, weather permitting) begins at 11:30 A.M., dinner is 5:30–9:30 P.M.

Five miles south of Bar Harbor, in the village of Otter Creek (which itself is in the town of Mount Desert) is the inauspicious-looking **Burning Tree** (71 Otter Creek Dr., Rte. 3, Otter Creek 04665, 207/288-9331), which is anything but nondescript inside. Chef/owners Allison Martin and Elmer Beal, Jr., have created one of Mount Desert Island's best restaurants. Bright and airy, with about 16 tables in three areas, it serves a casually chic crowd. Reservations are essential in summer. Specialties are imaginative seafood entrées—such as curry pecan flounder, cioppino, crab cakes—and vegetarian dishes made from organic produce. Scallop kebabs have *lots* of scallops, the specialty crab cakes are 90 percent crabmeat, and edible flowers garnish the entrées ($16–22). The homemade breads and desserts are delicious. At the height of summer, the kitchen sometimes runs out of popular entrées. Solution: plan to eat early; it's worth it. The Burning Tree is open for dinner, Wednesday–Monday 5–10 P.M., late June to early October (plus Tuesday in August).

Ice Cream

Only a masochist could bypass **Ben and Bill's Chocolate Emporium** (66 Main St., Bar Harbor 04609, 207/288-3281 or 800/806-3281), a long-running taste-treat-cum-experience in downtown Bar Harbor. The homemade candies and more than 50 ice cream flavors (including a dubious lobster flavor, $35 a bucket to go) are nothing short of outrageous; the whole place smells like the inside of a chocolate truffle. The shop, a cousin of three Massachusetts ice cream parlors, is open March–December: 9 A.M.–10 P.M. daily in spring and fall, 9 A.M.–midnight in summer.

INFORMATION AND SERVICES

The **Bar Harbor Chamber of Commerce** (93 Cottage St., P.O. Box 158, Bar Harbor 04609, 207/288-5103 or 888/540-9990, fax 207/288-2565, www.barharborinfo.com) has an especially helpful staff accustomed to a steady stream of summer walk-ins seeking beds, restaurants, activities, and more. The main office—on the lower level at the right side of the Bar Harbor municpal building—is open daily 8 A.M.–5 P.M. in summer, 8 A.M.–4:30 P.M. weekdays off-season. From Memorial Day to Columbus Day, a "branch" chamber office is located at Harbor Place, 1 West St., next to the Town Pier. (Plenty of Bar Harbor information is also available at the Thompson Island Information Center, just after you cross the bridge from Trenton toward Mount Desert Island.) Bar Harbor's annual visitor information booklet usually is off the presses in January—a big help in making early plans for a summer vacation.

Once you're on Mount Desert, if you manage to bestir yourself early enough to catch sunrise on the Cadillac summit (you won't be alone—it's a popular activity), stop in at the Chamber of Commerce office and request an official membership card for the **Cadillac Mountain Sunrise Club** (they'll take your word for it).

Jesup Memorial Library (34 Mount Desert St., Bar Harbor 04609, 207/288-4245) is open all year: 10 A.M.–5 P.M. Tuesday–Saturday (to 7 P.M. Wednesday).

COMMUNITIES

Newspapers

The newest newspaper on the island scene has already shown its journalistic muscle. The *Mount Desert Islander* (www.mountdesertislander.com) began publication in 2001 under the respected leadership of the former *Bar Harbor Times* editor. Four times each summer, the *Islander* also co-publishes (with the *Ellsworth American*) a very helpful tabloid-format supplement, *Out & About in Downeast Maine,* which goes well beyond fluffy travel info. You'll find history, trail advice, dining and lodging listings, event info, maps, ferry info, and more (the online version of *Out & About* is at www.acadiavisitor.com). *The Bar Harbor Times* (www.barharbortimes.com), founded in 1914, is published each Thursday, with extensive calendar listings.

Public Restrooms

Downtown Bar Harbor has public restrooms in the Harbor Place complex at the Town Pier, in the municipal building (fire/police station) across from the Village Green, and on the School Street side of the athletic field, where there is RV parking. Restrooms are also at the Mount Desert Island Hospital and the International Ferry Terminal.

Photo Services

At the bottom of the Village Green, **First Exposure** (156 Main St., P.O. Box 6, Bar Harbor 04609, 207/288-5868) provides one-hour photo service and sells film and a range of digital cameras. Open 9 A.M.–9 P.M. daily, May through October, shorter hours off-season.

Internet Access

The onetime Opera House Restaurant has transformed itself into **The Opera House Internet Café** (27 Cottage St., Bar Harbor 04609, 207/288-3509). Check your email, download photos, print messages or pix. Hours vary considerably, so wander by or call to check the schedule.

Northeast and Seal Harbors

Ever since the late 19th century, the upper crust from the City of Brotherly Love has been summering in and around Northeast Harbor. Sure, they also show up in other parts of Maine, but it's hard not to notice the preponderance of Pennsylvania license plates surrounding Northeast Harbor's elegant "cottages" from mid-July to mid-August. (In the last decade or so, the Pennsylvania plates have been joined by growing numbers from Washington, D.C., New York, and Texas.)

Actually, even though Northeast Harbor is a well-known name with special cachet, it isn't even an official township; it's a zip-coded village within the town of Mount Desert, which collects the breathtaking property taxes and doles out the municipal services.

The attractive boutiques and eateries in Northeast Harbor's small downtown area cater to a casually posh clientele, while the well-protected harbor attracts a tony crowd of yachties. For their convenience, a palm-sized annual directory, *The Redbook,* discreetly lists owners' summer residences and winter addresses—but no phone numbers. The directory also includes listings for the village of Seal Harbor—an even more exclusive village a few miles east of Northeast Harbor where Princess of Perfection Martha Stewart bought Edsel Ford's palatial estate in 1997, much to the chagrin of long-timers.

Except for two spectacular public gardens and two specialized museums, not much here is geared to budget-sensitive visitors—but there's no charge for admiring the spectacular scenery.

SIGHTS

Somes Sound

As you head toward Northeast Harbor on Route 198 from the northern end of Mount Desert Island, you'll begin seeing cliff-lined Somes Sound on your right. This glacier-sculpted fjord juts five miles into the interior of Mount Desert Island from its mouth, between Northeast and

Brown Mountain carriage-road gate, near Northeast Harbor

Southwest Harbors. Watch for the right-hand turn for Sargent Drive (no RVs allowed), and follow the lovely, granite-lined route along the east side of the sound. Halfway along, a marker explains the geology of this natural fjord, the only one on the eastern seaboard. There aren't many pullouts en route, and traffic can be fairly thick in midsummer, but don't miss it. An ideal way to appreciate Somes Sound is from the water—sign up for an excursion out of Northeast or Southwest Harbor.

Asticou and Thuya Gardens

If you have the slightest interest in gardens (even if you don't, for that matter), allow time for Northeast Harbor's two marvelous public gardens. Information about both is available from the local chamber of commerce. If gardens are extra-high on your priority list, inquire locally about visiting the private Rockefeller garden, accessible on a very limited basis.

One of Maine's best spring showcases is the **Asticou Azalea Garden,** a 2.3-acre pocket where about 70 varieties of azaleas, rhododendrons, and laurels—many from the classic Reef Point garden of famed landscape designer Beatrix Far-

rand—burst into bloom. When Charles K. Savage, beloved former innkeeper of the Asticou Inn, learned the Reef Point garden was being undone in 1956, he went into high gear to find funding and managed to rescue the azaleas and provide them with the gorgeous setting they have today, across the road and around the corner from the inn. Oriental serenity is the key—with a Japanese sand garden, stone lanterns, granite outcrops, pink-gravel paths, and a tranquil pond. Try to visit early in the season, early in the morning, to savor the effect. The garden is on Route 198, at the northern edge of Northeast Harbor, immediately north of the junction with Peabody Drive (Rte. 3). Watch for a tiny sign on the left (if you're coming from the north), marking access to the parking area. Asticou is open daily, sunrise to sunset, between May and November, and blossoming occurs here from May through August, but prime time for azaleas is roughly mid-May to mid-June. A small pillar box suggests a $1 donation, and another box contains an attractively designed garden guide ($2). Pets are not allowed in the garden.

Behind a carved wooden gate on a forested hillside not far from Asticou lies an enchanted

COMMUNITIES

© KATHLEEN M. BRANDES

garden also designed by Charles K. Savage, and inspired by Beatrix Farrand. Special features of **Thuya Garden** are perennial borders, sculpted shrubbery, and Asian touches. On a misty summer day, when few visitors appear, the colors are brilliant. Adjacent to the garden is Thuya Lodge (207/276-5130), former summer cottage of Joseph Curtis, donor of this awesome municipal park. The lodge, with an extensive botanical library and quiet rooms for reading, is open 10 A.M. to 4:30 P.M. daily, late June to Labor Day. The garden is open 7 A.M.–7 P.M., July through September. A collection box next to the front gate requests a donation. To reach Thuya, continue on Route 3 beyond Asticou Garden and the Asticou Inn, and watch for the Asticou Terraces parking area (no RVs, two-hour limit) on the right. Park there, cross the road, and climb the Asticou Terraces Trail (.4 mile) to the garden. Or drive .2 mile beyond the Route 3 parking area, watching for a Thuya Drive sign on the left. Go .5 mile up the road to the small parking area.

After you've visited Thuya Garden, open the back gate, where you'll see a sign for the **Eliot Mountain Trail**, a 1.4-mile moderately difficult round-trip (lots of exposed roots). Near the summit, Northeast Harbor spreads out before you. If you're here in August, sample the wild blueberries. Much of the Eliot Mountain Trail is on private land, so stay on the path and be respectful of private property.

Petite Plaisance

On Northeast Harbor's quiet South Shore Road, Petite Plaisance is a special-interest museum commemorating noted Belgian-born author and college professor Marguerite Yourcenar (pen name of Marguerite de Crayencour), first woman elected to the prestigious Académie Française. From the early 1950s to 1987, Petite Plaisance was her home, and it's hard to believe she's no longer here; her intriguing possessions and presence fill the two-story house—of particular interest to Yourcenar devotees. Free, hour-long tours of the first floor are given in French or English, depending on visitors' preferences. (French-speaking visitors often make pilgrimages here.) The house is open for tours daily, June 15–August 31. No children under 12. Call 207/276-3940 at least a day ahead, 9 A.M.–4 P.M., for an appointment and directions, or write: Petite Plaisance Trust, P.O. Box 403, Northeast Harbor 04662. Yourcenar admirers should request directions to Brookside Cemetery in Somesville, seven miles away, where she is buried.

Great Harbor Maritime Museum

Nautical buffs and kids of all ages will thrill to the model ships, small boats, historic naval equipment (including a 1908 gasoline engine six feet long and four feet tall), and exhibits on the maritime history of the Mount Desert Island area in the small, eclectic Great Harbor Maritime Museum (125 Main St., P.O. Box 145, Northeast Harbor 04662, 207/276-5262), housed in the handsome old village fire station and municipal building. ("Great Harbor" refers to the Somes Sound area—Northeast, Southwest, and Seal Harbors, as well as the Cranberry Isles.) Yachting, coastal trade, and fishing receive special emphasis. What else is here? Antique photos and tools, furniture and clothing—even a working player piano. Special programs and exhibits are held during the summer. The museum allegedly is open 10 A.M.–5 P.M. Tuesday–Saturday, late June to Labor Day, plus weekends in September and October, but the museum's schedule tends to be erratic; call ahead if you want to be sure. Requested donation is $3.

GETTING AFLOAT

Northeast Harbor is the starting point for a couple of boat services (including the mailboat) headed for the **Cranberry Isles.** (Other boats depart from Southwest Harbor; see below.) The vessels leave from the commercial floats at the end of the concrete Municipal Pier on Sea Street.

Captain Rob Liebow's 75-foot *Sea Princess* (Box 545, Mount Desert 04660, 207/276-5352, www.barharborcruises.com) carries visitors as well as an Acadia National Park naturalist on a morning trip (just under three hours) around the mouth of Somes Sound and out to Little Cranberry Island (Islesford) for a 50-minute stopover. The boat leaves Northeast Harbor daily at 9:45 A.M., mid-May to mid-October. Cost is $18 adults, $17 seniors, $12 children under 12, free for children under three. An afternoon trip, departing at 1 P.M. on the same route, spends less time on Islesford but also visits Southwest Harbor. Tickets are the same price as for the morning trip. The *Sea Princess* also does a scenic 1.5-hour Somes Sound cruise, departing daily at 3:45 P.M., late June to early September. Cost is $15 adults, $14 seniors, $10 children under 12. (A retired Acadia naturalist accompanies the two afternoon trips.) The same months, a three-hour sunset/dinner cruise departs at 5:30 P.M. for the Islesford Dock Restaurant on Little Cranberry (Islesford). Cost is $15 adults, $14 seniors, $10 children (not including dinner). Reservations are advisable for all trips, although even that provides no guarantee, since the cruises require a rather hefty 15-passenger minimum. Arrive about 15 minutes before departure to purchase tickets at the booth next to the harbormaster's office, at the head of the Municipal Pier.

See the *Cranberry Isles* section of this chapter for information on the regular ferry/mailboat service between Northeast Harbor and the Cranberries. (These ferries are slightly less expensive, but there's no narration.)

SHOPPING
Gifts, Clothing, and Jewelry
Three upscale shops here are worth a visit and maybe even a major splurge.

Early and late in the season, the summer crowd shops at **The Kimball Shop & Boutique** (Main St., Northeast Harbor 04662, 207/276-3300) to stock up on wedding and Christmas gifts. It's all very tasteful. It's open 9:30 A.M.–5 P.M. Monday–Saturday in June; 9 A.M.–6 P.M. Monday–Saturday and Sunday noon–5 P.M. July and August.

At **Local Color** (147 Main St., Northeast Harbor 04662, 207/276-5544 or 888/582-2250), you'll find—just for a start—stunning silk and chenille sweaters and jackets and exquisite jewelry. Owner Jayn Thomas has impeccable taste. Quality is high, and so are prices. The shop is open 10 A.M.–6 P.M. Monday–Saturday, 10 A.M.–4 P.M. Sunday, Memorial Day weekend through September.

You'll enter another world at **Shaw Contemporary Jewelry** (100 Main St., P.O. Box 608, Northeast Harbor 04662, 207/276-5000 or 877/276-5001, fax 207/276-0716, shawjewelry.com). Besides the spectacular silver and gold beachstone jewelry created by Rhode Island School of Design alumnus Sam Shaw, the work of other jewelers is displayed exquisitely. Plus there are sculptures, Asian art, and rotating art exhibits. It all leads back toward a lovely, light-filled garden. Prices are in the stratosphere, but appropriately so. The gallery is open all year, with a varying schedule depending on the season.

Antiquarian Books
A small but select inventory of preowned books lines the walls at the **Wikhegan Books Book Room** (117 Main St., Northeast Harbor; P.O. Box 370, Mount Desert 04660, 207/276-5079 or 244-7060). Specialties include nautical books,

Native American lore, women, poetry, and antiques. Open 10 A.M.–5 P.M. Monday–Saturday between June and October, the rest of the year by appointment.

Gourmet Provisions

Consider it an adventure to visit the **Pine Tree Market** (121 Main St., Northeast Harbor 04662, 207/276-3335, fax 207/276-0542), where you'll find unusual condiments, a huge wine selection, a resident butcher, fresh fish, deli, and homemade breads and pastries. A landmark here since 1921, the market is open 7 A.M.–7 P.M. Monday–Saturday, 8 A.M.–6 P.M. Sunday; free delivery to your yacht.

Farmers' Market

From late June through August, the **Northeast Harbor Farmers' Market** is set up 9 A.M.–noon each Thursday, on Huntington Road, across from the Kimball Terrace Inn. Look for cheeses, cider, maple syrup, breads and cookies, berries, and vegetables.

ACCOMMODATIONS

Unless you're celebrating a landmark occasion, Northeast Harbor's lodgings may be a little too pricey, but if money's no object and a haute ambience appeals, spring for the **Asticou Inn** (Rte. 3, P.O. Box 337, Northeast Harbor 04662, 207/276-3344 or 800/258-3373, fax 207/276-3373, www.asticou.com). Built in 1883 and refurbished periodically, the classic harbor-view inn has 31 second-, third-, and fourth-floor rooms and suites in the main building, plus 16 rooms and suites in several more modern cottages. Facilities include clay tennis courts, outdoor pool, and access to the Northeast Harbor Golf Club. The elegant, mural-lined dining room, open to the public for Sunday brunch (11:30 A.M.–2:30 P.M.) and dinner (6–10 P.M.) by reservation, has fabulous views of the harbor. Jackets and ties are advised for dinner. Lunch is also open to the public, served 11:30 A.M.–5 P.M.; reservations aren't needed, but you may have to wait on a gorgeous July or August day. The inn is open

mid-May to late October. July and August rates are $302–362 d, two-night minimum. (Two meals are included with the price of accommodation; a European Plan, which includes a continental breakfast buffet, is also available: $225–285.) Early and late in the season, rates are B&B. Try to plan a late-May or early-June visit—you're almost on top of the Asticou Azalea Garden, Thuya Garden is a short walk away, and the rates are lowest ($130–180 d). The Asticou is a popular wedding venue, so if you're looking for a quiet weekend, check the inn's wedding schedule before you book a room.

Acadia National Park's **Blackwoods Campground** is in Otter Creek, roughly between the villages of Otter Creek and Seal Harbor; see the *Acadia on Mount Desert Island* chapter for detailed information.

FOOD

Lobster in the Rough

This isn't exactly a rustic, dine-on-the-dock sort of place—the usual definition of "lobster in the rough"—but it's low-key, wildly popular, and a great place to get lobster and more.

Crab cakes ($15.95) and crab sandwiches are *the best* at the **Docksider** (14 Sea St., Northeast Harbor 04662, 207/276-3965), a family-friendly, unassuming, hole-in-the-wall place inevitably jammed with devoted locals and summer folk. Just up the hill from the chamber office (and slightly down the hill from Main Street), the Docksider has an outside deck, plus a couple of veteran (since forever) waitresses, no view, and a reputation far and wide. At $21.95, the shore dinner (clam chowder, steamed clams, boiled lobster, salad) is one of the best bargains in the state. Wine and beer only. The Docksider changed hands in 2002, but is still under local management, and you'd never know the difference. If you're smitten, buy one of the T-shirts, featuring an upright lobster announcing "Frankly, I don't give a clam." Open for lunch and dinner 11 A.M.–9 P.M. in summer (early bird specials and a 10 percent discount 4:30–6 P.M.). (Also open for breakfast in July and August.) Closed during the off-season.

Fine Dining

At the height of summer, the waiting line extends out the door and down the sidewalk from the popular **151 Main Street** (unsurprisingly at 151 Main St., Northeast Harbor 04662, 207/276-9898), so arrive early to beat the rush or be prepared to join the line (no reservations accepted). The menu includes meatloaf, but wild mushroom gravy elevates it to a taste treat. And it's upward from there . . . to catfish roulade (stuffed with a crab cake), Thai curry shrimps, and a choice list of "small plates" that are easy on the budget ($3–10). Entrées run $14–20. Tasty thin-crust pizzas are $8–10, and pasta dishes are $8–16. Locally grown organic produce appears in many dishes. The ambience is casual, not especially elegant, with booths and tables (and a small bar waiting area). But the food is the thing here—chef/owner Emily Pascal has a sophisticated touch in the kitchen. 151 Main is open Tuesday–Sunday starting at 5 P.M.

Also see the *Accommodations* section, above, for info on the **Asticou Inn's** dining room. See *Food*, in the *Bar Harbor and Vicinity* section (above) for info on the excellent **Burning Tree** restaurant, on Route 3 in Otter Creek. (Otter Creek is a schizo-

phrenic village that belongs partly to the town of Bar Harbor and partly to the town of Mount Desert. Go figure. The Burning Tree draws customers from all over the island, but since it's especially popular with Bar Harbor residents and visitors, it's described in that section.)

INFORMATION AND SERVICES

The harborfront Chamber Information Bureau of the **Mount Desert Chamber of Commerce** (Sea St., P.O. Box 675, Mount Desert 04660, 207/276-5040) is open 9:30 A.M.–4:30 P.M. daily mid-June to mid-October (8 A.M.–6 P.M. at the height of summer). The chamber covers the villages of Somesville, Northeast Harbor, Seal Harbor, Otter Creek, Pretty Marsh, Hall Quarry, and Beech Hill. The extremely cordial staff can provide information on Northeast Harbor's gardens, museums, and trails, in addition to food and lodging. They even organize rental cars and rental tennis rackets (reserve court time here, too). Coin-operated hot showers, designed primarily but not exclusively for the boating crowd, are available here round the clock (after office hours, pick up the key at the harbormaster's office just down the hill next to the Municipal Dock). You can even rent towels and a hair dryer. Free coffee and tea. (The harbormaster's office also has restrooms.)

Southwest Harbor and Tremont

The quirky nature of the island's four town boundaries creates complications in trying to categorize various island segments. Driving from the east side of Somes Sound (Northeast Harbor, in the town of Mount Desert) around to Southwest Harbor on the west side, you'll pass through the precious (really!) hamlet of Somesville and then skirt the village of Hall Quarry (both in the town of Mount Desert . . .). So before getting to Southwest, we'll start this section at the head of the sound—with a bookstore, a summer theater, a couple of campgrounds, and a canoeing/kayaking spot.

SOMESVILLE AND HALL QUARRY

The Somesville Historic District, with its distinctive arched white footbridge, is especially appealing, but traffic gets very congested here along Route 102, so rather than just rubbernecking, plan to stop and look around. (Parking isn't easy, so you may need to walk a bit when you find a space.)

While you're here, don't miss the two-story **Port in a Storm Bookstore** (Main St., Rte. 102, Somesville, Mount Desert 04660, 207/244-4114 or 800/694-4114, fax 207/244-7998, www.portinastormbookstore.com). One of Maine's

COMMUNITIES

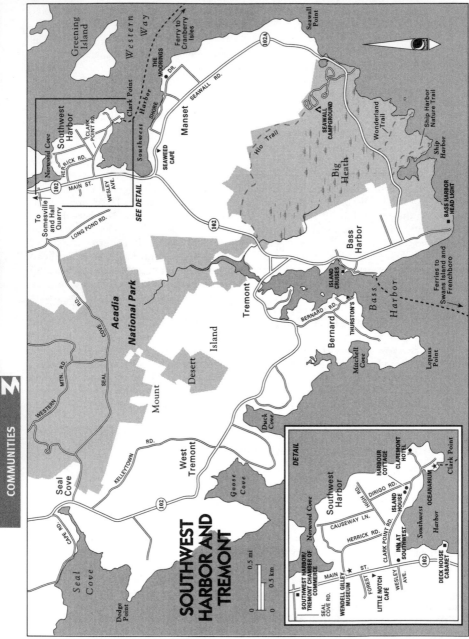

SOUTHWEST HARBOR AND TREMONT

COMMUNITIES

© AVALON TRAVEL PUBLISHING, INC.

the centerpiece of the Somesville Historic District

best independent bookstores, it's totally seductive, guaranteed to lighten your wallet. High ceilings, comfortable chairs, whimsical floor sculptures, open space, and Somes Cove views all contribute to the ambience. Inventory is not huge, but it's well selected—especially nature and children's books—and the staff is very knowledgeable. Especially in summer, noted authors often appear to lecture or sign their books. The shop is open all year 9:30 A.M.–6 P.M. Monday–Saturday, and 1–5 P.M. Sunday.

Somesville is also home to the **Acadia Repertory Theatre** (Rte. 102, Somesville, P.O. Box 106, Mount Desert 04660, 207/244-7260 or 888/362-7480, www.acadiarep.com), which has been providing first-rate professional thespian summer stock on the stage of Somesville's antique Masonic Hall since the 1970s. Classic plays by Wilde, Goldsmith, even Molière, have been staples, as has the annual Agatha Christie mystery. Performances in the 144-seat hall run late June to late August, Tuesday–Sunday at 8:15 P.M. Special children's plays are performed at 10:30 A.M. Wednesday and Saturday in July and August. Adult tickets are $20, seniors and students $15, children $10. (No

credit cards; pay at the box office before the performance.)

On the eastern edge of Somesville, .5 mile from the junction of Routes 198 and 102, the **Mount Desert Campground** (516 Sound Dr., Rte. 198, Somesville, Mount Desert 04660, 207/244-3710, www.mountdesertcampground .com) is especially centrally located for visiting Bar Harbor, Acadia, and the whole western side of Mount Desert Island. The family-owned campground has 148 wooded tent and tent-trailer sites, about 45 on the water. Reservations are essential in midsummer—one-week minimum for waterfront sites, three days for off-water sites in July and August. (Campers book a year ahead for waterfront sites here.) This deservedly popular and low-key campground gets high marks for maintenance, noise control, and convenient tent platforms. From late June through Labor Day, rates are $28–39 d ($33 for a tent platform, $39 for the waterfront sites). Other times, rates are $25–32. No pets from July through Labor Day weekend. No trailers over 20 feet. Kayak rentals are available. Open mid-June to mid-September.

If staying at a quiet, no-frills campground in an outstanding setting appeals, head for Hall Quarry, a few miles south of Somesville. **Somes Sound View Campground** (86 Hall Quarry Rd., Mount Desert 04660, 207/244-3890, www .acadiainfo.com/ssview), among the smallest campgrounds on the island (60 tent and RV sites; max RV length 28 feet), emphasizes tenting and has less of the hyperactivity found at the island's other private campgrounds. Canoe rentals are available, and you can swim in the sound (from a rocky beach). Leashed pets are allowed (vaccinations must be up to date). Sites are $18–25 (two adults, two children); no credit cards. Open Memorial Day to Columbus Day.

Just west of Somesville (take the Pretty Marsh Rd.), and across the road from Long Pond, the largest lake on Mount Desert Island, **National Park Canoe & Kayak Rental** (145 Pretty Marsh Rd., Rte. 102, Mount Desert 04660, 207/244-5854 or 877/378-6907, www.acadia.net/canoe) makes canoeing and kayaking a snap. Just rent the boat, carry it across the road to Pond's End, and launch it. Be sure to pack a picnic. Morning (8:30 A.M.–12:30 P.M.) or afternoon (1–6 P.M.) rate for a canoe or solo kayak is $22, full-day rate is $32. A tandem is $40 for the day, $25 for a half-day. A do-it-yourself sunset canoe or kayak trip (from 5 P.M. on) is $15 pp. Reservations are advisable, and essential in July and August. Open mid-May to mid-October.

If you've brought your own canoe (or kayak), launch it here at Pond's End and head off. It's four miles to the southern end of Long Pond. If the wind kicks up, skirt the shore; if it *really* kicks up from the north, don't paddle too far down the lake, as you'll have a devil of a time getting back.

You can **swim** at Pond's End, and in the upper half of Long Pond, but swimming is banned in the lower half, as it's a drinking-water source. Almost the entire west side of Long Pond is Aca-

dia National Park property, so plan to picnic and swim along there; tuck into the sheltered area west of Southern Neck, a crooked finger of land that points northward from the western shore. Stay clear of private property on the east side of the lake.

SOUTHWEST HARBOR

Southwest Harbor considers itself the hub of Mount Desert Island's "quiet side." In summer, its tiny downtown district is probably the busiest spot on the whole western side of the island (west of Somes Sound), but that's not saying a great deal. "Southwest" has the feel of a settled community, a year-round flavor that Bar Harbor sometimes lacks. And it competes with the best in the scenery department. The Southwest Harbor area serves as a very convenient base for exploring Acadia National Park, as well as the island's less-crowded villages and offshore Swans Island, Frenchboro, and the Cranberry Isles.

> *Southwest Harbor considers itself the hub of Mount Desert Island's "quiet side." It has the feel of a settled community, a year-round flavor that Bar Harbor sometimes lacks, and serves as a very convenient base for exploring Acadia, as well as offshore Swans Island, Frenchboro, and the Cranberry Isles.*

Villages within the town of Southwest Harbor are **Seawall** and **Manset.**

A broad swath of Acadia National Park cuts right through the center of this side of the island, and many of its hiking trails are far less congested than elsewhere in the park. A recently cleared "connector trail" from Southwest Harbor has made access to park trails even easier.

Acadia National Park's **Seawall Campground,** as well as the **Wonderland** and **Ship Harbor Trails,** lie within the town limits of Southwest Harbor. See the *Acadia on Mount Desert Island* chapter for details.

Sights
In the center of Southwest Harbor, the **Wendell Gilley Museum** (41 Herrick Rd., corner of Rte. 102, P.O. Box 254, Southwest Harbor 04679, 207/244-7555, www.acadia.net/gilley)

was established in 1981 to display the life's work of local woodcarver Wendell Gilley (1904–83). The modern, energy-efficient museum houses more than 200 of his astonishingly realistic bird specimens. Don't miss it. Special summer exhibits feature other wildlife artists. Many days, a local artisan gives woodcarving demonstrations, and the gift shop carries an ornithological potpourri—books to binoculars to carving tools. Kids over eight appreciate this more than younger ones. Wheelchair access. Tickets are $3.50 adults, $1 children 5–12, free for children under five. Open 10 A.M.–4 P.M., Tuesday–Sunday June–October (to 5 P.M. in July and August), 10 A.M.–4 P.M. Friday–Sunday in May, November, and December.

Touching a sea cucumber or a sea star may not be every adult's idea of fun, but kids sure enjoy the hands-on experience at the **Southwest Harbor Oceanarium** (Clark Point Rd., Southwest Harbor 04679, 207/244-7330), sister site to the Bar Harbor Oceanarium. A knowledgeable naturalist introduces creatures from a watery touch tank during a tour of the Oceanarium. Two dozen exhibit tanks line the walls of this intriguing, low-tech museum next to the Coast Guard station. It's open 9 A.M.–5 P.M. Monday–Saturday, mid-May to late October. Oceanarium tickets are $6.95 adults, $4.95 children 4–12; combination tickets, covering this and the Oceanarium in Bar Harbor, are $13 adults, $9.95 children.

On the westernmost side of the island, but easily accessible from Southwest Harbor, a nondescript blue building camouflages **The Seal Cove Auto Museum** (Pretty Marsh Rd., Rte. 102, Seal Cove 04674, 207/244-9242), a fantastic collection of more than 100 antique autos and several dozen antique motorcycles—many from the turn of the 20th century. It's easy for kids of any age to spend an hour here, reminiscing and/or fantasizing. Tickets are $5 adults, $2 children under 12. Open 10 A.M.–5 P.M. daily, June 1–September 15. From Southwest Harbor, take Route 102 north to the Seal Cove Road (partly unpaved), then follow it west to the other side of Route 102 (it makes a giant loop) and go north about 1.5 miles to the museum.

Recreation

Acadia National Park, of course, is the recreational focus throughout Mount Desert Island; in the Southwest Harbor area, the main nonpark recreational activities are bike- and boat-related.

At the Southwest Harbor/Tremont Chamber of Commerce office, or at any of the area's stores, lodgings, and restaurants, pick up a free copy of the *Trail Map/Hiking Guide,* a handy foldout map showing more than 20 Acadia National Park hikes on the western side of Mount Desert Island. Trail descriptions include distance, time required, and skill levels (easy to strenuous). In 2001, thanks to a group effort spearheaded by Friends of Acadia, the half-mile-long Western Mountain Connector was opened a few miles north of downtown Southwest Harbor to provide easier access to several Acadia trails on this side of the island.

A veteran business with a first-rate reputation, **Southwest Cycle** (Main St., Southwest Harbor 04679, 207/244-5856 or 800/649-5856) rents bikes by the day and week and is open all year. From June to September, hours are 8:30 A.M.–5:30 P.M. Monday–Saturday, and 10 A.M.–4 P.M. Sunday; it's open 9 A.M.–5 P.M. Monday–Saturday October–May. (See *Islands near Mount Desert* for planning biking day trips to Swans Island or the Cranberry Isles.) The staff at Southwest Cycle will fix you up with maps and lots of good advice for three loops (10–30 miles) on the western side of Mount Desert. The shop also rents every imaginable accessory, from baby seats to jogging strollers.

Getting Afloat

Southwest Harbor is the home of one of the nation's premier boatbuilders, **The Hinckley Company** (130 Shore Rd., Manset, P.O. Box 699, Southwest Harbor 04679, 207/244-5531, fax 207/244-9833, www.hinckleyyachts.com), a name with stellar repute since the 1930s. There are no tours of the Hinckley complex, but most yachtsmen can't resist the urge to look in at the yard. Plus you can stop in at the **Hinckley Shipstore** (207/244-7100 or 800/446-2553) and pick up books, charts, and all sorts of Hinckley-logo gear. The shop is open all year,

COMMUNITIES

7:30 A.M.–5 P.M. Monday–Friday, 8 A.M.–4 P.M. Saturday and 8 A.M.–1 P.M. Sunday.

On the outskirts of Southwest Harbor's downtown, close to the chamber of commerce, is **Maine State Sea Kayak Guide Service** (254 Main St., Southwest Harbor 04679, 207/244-9500, www.mainestatekayak.com). Staffed with experienced, environmentally sensitive kayakers (several are Registered Maine Guides), the company offers four-hour trips, with a choice of half a dozen routes (depending on tide and current conditions), for $46 pp. Maximum group is six tandems; minimum age is 12. All gear is provided, and neophytes are welcome. The season is mid-May to mid-October.

Gifts and Antiquarian Books

In the middle of Southwest Harbor's small shopping area is the **Sand Castle Ocean and Nature Store** (360 Main St., P.O. Box 162, Southwest Harbor 04679, 207/244-4118), a delightful shop with a huge range of handcrafted items, most with a marine theme. Representing the work of dozens of artisans, the shop has wind chimes, jewelry, ceramics, ship models, and lots of other surprises. Open all year—daily in summer, shorter hours off-season.

Luddites, here's your destination. Nicols Fox, author of *Against the Machine: The Hidden Luddite Tradition in Literature, Art and Individual Lives,* touches a chord in all of us who weren't brought up lashed to a laptop. Her **Rue Cottage Books** (360 Main St., P.O. Box 1128, Southwest Harbor 04679), besides containing a collection of anti-tech titles, has an eclectic mix of other specialties—mythology, environment (she's an avid Green), '60s radicals, natural history, Native Americans, and "irresistible old books." If your budget is pinched, she also has a stash of "cheap thrills"—$2 mysteries. Rue Cottage Books is open all year: May to Labor Day, 10 A.M.–5 P.M. daily; off-season, 10 A.M.–4 P.M. Thursday–Saturday.

Entertainment

It's not too far to drive from Southwest Harbor to Bar Harbor for dinner and evening entertainment, but consider staying in Southwest for a dinner theater that even draws customers in the reverse direction. After more than two decades in Bass Harbor, **The Deck House Restaurant and Cabaret Theater** moved in 1997 to a higher-profile location at the Great Harbor Marina (Route 102, 11 Apple Lane, P.O. Box 1506, Southwest Harbor 04679, 207/244-5044, www.thedeckhouse.com). Try to arrive for dinner by 6:30 P.M. to enjoy the spectacular harbor view, have a drink, and order your meal (entrées are $21.95; appetizers and salads are à la carte; children's portions are available). The cathedral-ceilinged dining room holds 140, and the table is yours for the evening (reservations are essential in midsummer). At 8:15 P.M. or so, the young wait-staff, chameleonlike, unveils its other talents—singing, dancing, even storytelling and puppetry. After hearing the dozen-plus numbers, you won't be surprised to learn that many Deck House employees have moved on to Broadway and beyond. Cover charge (for the entertainment) is $7 pp—a bargain. The Deck House is open mid-June to mid-September.

Accommodations

As the Asticou Inn is to Northeast Harbor, the Claremont is to Southwest Harbor. Several pleasant B&Bs add to the mix. Acadia National Park's **Seawall Campground** is also in this part of the island.

When you're ready to splurge, **The Claremont** (P.O. Box 137, Southwest Harbor 04679, 207/244-5036 or 800/244-5036, fax 207/244-3512, www.theclaremonthotel.com) may well be your choice, but you'll have to plan a year ahead to land a room in July or August. The most popular time is the first full week in August, during the annual Claremont Croquet Classic. This wooden grande dame, dominating a six-acre hilltop overlooking Somes Sound, caters to honeymooners, yuppies, and gentrified folk. Service is impeccable; enjoy it.

Guests have access to croquet courts, a clay tennis court, bikes, rowboats, and a library.

The Claremont Dining Room, with a view from every table, is open to the public for breakfast and dinner (jackets and ties requested for dinner). Dining-room reservations are wise in midsummer. Entrée range is $19–23 (not particularly imaginative, but the view's the thing). In July and August, informal lunches (noon–2 P.M.) and cocktails (5:30–9 P.M.) are served in the shorefront boathouse, also open to the public.

Dating from 1884, the main building has 24 rooms (with bath and phones), most of them recently refurbished. Other accommodations are in two other buildings (six-room Phillips House and one-suite Clark House) and 14 housekeeping cottages, with daily rates that range from $170 to $250 in the high season (three-day minimum in cottages). The Rowse House, which sleeps seven and is available only by the week, goes for $3,200 (a week) in summer. Main-building and Phillips House rooms are $220–240 d, two meals included, mid-July through August, plus a hefty 17 percent service and lodging tax. (Rooms without water views can be rented in high season at a B&B rate, $170 d.) Rates are lower in shoulder seasons. Buffet breakfast is included. No pets, no smoking, and, surprisingly, no credit cards. Children are welcome. The hotel and dining room are open mid-June to mid-October; cottages are open late May to late October.

On the outskirts of downtown Southwest Harbor is **The Heron House** (1 Fernald Point Rd., Southwest Harbor 04679, 207/244-0221, www.acadias-heronhouse.com), Sue and Bob Bonkowski's Victorian B&B at the corner of Route 102. Antique St. Bernard prints are a dominant theme, and a live St. Bernard greets you at the door. Three second-floor rooms ($110–125 d mid-June to mid-October; $90–100 May to mid-June; $75 the rest of the year) have a/c and private baths. It's all relaxed and informal; guests can use the refrigerator or grill dinner outside. A former wildlife rehabber and dedicated hiker, Sue has countless suggestions for area hiking. Her hearty breakfasts include edible flowers and unusual herbs. No pets, no smoking, no credit cards. Open all year.

In downtown Southwest Harbor, at the Victorian **Inn at Southwest** (371 Main St., Rte. 102, Box 593, Southwest Harbor 04679, 207/244-3835, www.innatsouthwest.com), guests gather for games, reading, conversation, and afternoon tea in a huge living room with fireplace

and comfortable couches. Built in 1884 as the Freeman Cottage, the elegant building has 13 dormers and a wraparound veranda. Seven second- and third-floor guest rooms—named for Maine lighthouses and full of character—are fitted out with floral prints, ceiling fans, down comforters, and lots more. All have private baths (some are detached). Rates are $110–185 d mid-June to mid-October, $75–135 other months; two-night minimum on holiday weekends. Breakfast is a feast, with such treats as cheesecake crepes and eggs Florentine. No pets, no smoking. Open May through October.

On a quiet side street close to the water in Southwest Harbor is Ann and Charlie Bradford's **Island House** (121 Clark Point Rd., P.O. Box 1006, Southwest Harbor 04679, 207/244-5180, www.islandhousebb.com), filled with exotic paintings and furniture from Ann's youth in Singapore, Malaysia, and India. The hospitality and breakfasts are memorable here. Four appealing rooms named after Maine trees have private baths ($105 d, July through October, $75–95 other months; surcharge for a one-night stay in July and August; three-night specials in winter and spring). The bright, airy Birch Room boasts a skylight. A separate carriage-house apartment, fully equipped, is $130 for two, $155 for four, including breakfast (10 percent discount for staying a week). No smoking, no pets. Open all year. From June through September, the Bradfords also rent **Wood-Sea,** a comfortable two-bedroom summer cottage, for $650–850 a week (depending on the month; July is highest). It's near Bass Harbor Head Light, about five miles from Southwest Harbor.

Next door to Island House, but set well back from Clark Point Road, is **Harbour Cottage** (9 Dirigo Rd., P.O. Box 258, Southwest Harbour 04679, 207/244-5738 or 888/843-3022, www .harbourcottageinn.com), appealingly revamped in 2002, when Javier Montesinos and Don Jalbert took over. Built in 1870, it was the "annex" for Island House, housing the increasing numbers of rusticators who patronized this part of the island. The common rooms are elegant yet cozy; the seven guest rooms ($95–150 d) are done in understated "cottage" style—with whirlpools, steam showers, phones, and data ports. Most have harbor views. Two suites (one is on two levels) are $125–175 for two. A box lunch is available for a small charge, but it's tough to think of lunch after the full breakfast. Guests have free use of bicycles. Open most of the year (call ahead in the dead of winter).

Across the street from Island House and Harbour Cottage is the **Lindenwood Inn** (118 Clark Point Rd., Box 1328, Southwest Harbor 04679, 207/244-5335 or 800/307-5335, www.lindenwoodinn.com), where the lindenblossom fragrance can be intoxicating if you're here in summer. The main house's nine second- and third-floor rooms (private baths) have been imaginatively decorated with artifacts from everywhere. The heated pool is especially welcome after hiking Acadia's trails. Rates in the main building are $105–185 d mid-June to mid-October, $95–155 d other months. Separate housekeeping suites and cottages are $195–275 in high season, $165–225 other months. No pets; smoking only on decks and porches. Open all year.

Around the corner, so to speak, in Manset, hard by the Hinckley Yacht complex, is **The Moorings** (Shore Rd., P.O. Box 744, Manset, Southwest Harbor 04679, 800/596-5523 or 207/244-5523 or 244-3210, www.mooringsinn .com), another lodging that has rooms in several categories—and the comfortable air of an old-fashioned B&B. Chalk that up to the King family's longtime (since the early 1960s) ownership. They've been doing this long enough to get it right. On top of that, the view is unmatched—right on the harbor, looking toward the mouth of Somes Sound. A fantastic place for yachtspotting (Hinckleys galore). Take your pick—10 rooms in the main inn building ($65–110 d), three motel-style rooms with waterfront decks ($105 d), a triplex cottage ($105–135 d), and three separate cottages with decks ($150). The main house is a particularly good choice for solo guests. Continental breakfast is included, and off-season rates (mid-September through June) are even lower. A canoe and a kayak are available for guests, so you can paddle around the harbor. No smoking. Open all year.

Besides several agencies (in Southwest as well as elsewhere on the island) that handle weekly and monthly rentals, the Southwest Harbor/ Tremont Chamber of Commerce keeps a helpful listing of privately owned homes/cottages available for rent. The chamber's annual summer guide usually contains a couple of pages of ads with photos.

Food

You'll find lobster in the rough at **The Captain's Galley at Beal's Lobster Pier** (Clark Point Rd., Southwest Harbor 04679, 207/244-7178 or 244-3202, www.bealslobster.com). It's off Route 102, next to the Coast Guard Station and the Southwest Harbor Oceanarium. This is the real thing—basically dining (well, eating) on the dock—run by the third generation of Beals. A convenient lunch spot if you're taking the kids to the Oceanarium—Beal's sells about 2,500 lobster rolls each summer. Open 9 A.M.–8 P.M. in summer, 9 A.M.–5 P.M. after Labor Day. (Early morning hours are not for breakfast—they allow customers to order lobster shipped nationwide.)

Some of the island's most creative sandwiches and pizza toppings emerge from Arthur and Kate Jacobs's **Little Notch Café** (340 Main St., P.O. Box 1295, Southwest Harbor 04679, 207/244-3357), next to the library in Southwest Harbor's downtown. How about a broccoli, sausage, and black-olive pizza? Or a prosciutto sandwich with asiago and roasted peppers? All this plus Little Notch Bakery's famed breads, sinful desserts, a couple of pasta choices, and homemade soups, stews, and chowders make the café a winner. Open all year: 11 A.M.–8:30 P.M. Monday–Saturday, mid-May to mid-October; open 11 A.M.–7 P.M. Monday–Saturday mid-October to mid-May.

The gorp is the greatest at **Burdocks Natural Foods** (Main St., Rte. 102, P.O. Box 176, Southwest Harbor 04679, 207/244-0108), so stock up here with pound-size packets of interesting trail mixes. No credit cards. Open all year, 9 A.M.–5 P.M. Monday–Friday and 9:30 A.M.–1 P.M. Saturday, plus 10 A.M.–5 P.M. Sunday in summer.

THE LOBSTER EXPERIENCE

N o visit to Acadia National Park and the surrounding region can be considered complete without the "real Maine" experience of a "lobsta dinnah" at a lobster wharf/pound/shack. Keep an eye on the weather, pick a sunny day, and head out.

If you're in the area before Memorial Day or after Labor Day, the options are not as great—many such enterprises have a short season, although more and more at least are staying open through September.

There's nowhere to eat lobster within Acadia National Park (unless you're camping and cook it yourself over a campfire), but Mount Desert Island and the surrounding region provide plenty of opportunities. Almost every restaurant, café, bistro, or whatever serves lobster in some form or other. But as you drive, bus, bike, or walk around, watch for the genuine article—the "real" lobster wharf. You want to eat outdoors, at a wooden picnic table, with a knockout view of boats and the sea. (Incidentally, if you're camping, most lobster wharves will boil lobsters for you for free or a small fee. They'll wrap them in newspaper so they stay warm until you get back to your campsite. Best advice is to order them like pizza: Call ahead and order so they'll be ready when you show up for them.)

At whatever place you choose, the drill is much the same, and the "dinners" are served anytime from 11 A.M. or noon onward (some places close as early as 7 P.M.). First of all, dress very casually so you can manhandle the lobster without messing up decent clothes. If you want beer or wine, call ahead and ask if the place serves it; you may need to bring your own, since many such operations don't have beer/wine licenses, much less liquor licenses. In the evening, carry some insect repellent, in case mosquitoes crash the party. (Many places light citronella candles or dispense Skin-So-Soft to keep the bugs at bay; Mosquito Magnets may soon be doing the job.)

A basic one-pound lobster and go-withs (coleslaw or potato salad, potato chips, and butter for dipping) should run $15–20, based on the seasonal lobster price. Unfortunately, some places use margarine, which might do less damage to your cholesterol level, but it doesn't do any favors for

lobster. Depending on your hunger level—or the length of time since your last lobster—you may want to indulge in a shore dinner (lobster, steamed clams, potato chips, and maybe coleslaw or corn), for which you might have to part with $20 or $25, again depending on the lobster market price. Don't skip dessert; many lobster pounds are known for their homemade pies.

It's not unusual to see lobster-wharf devotees carting picnic baskets with hors d'oeuvres, salads, and baguettes. I've even seen candles and champagne and cloth napkins and bibs. Creativity abounds, but don't stray too far from the main attraction—the crustaceans.

Typically, you'll need to survey a chalkboard or whiteboard menu and step up to a window to order. You'll either give the person your name or get a number. A few places have staff to take your order or deliver your meal (and help you figure out how to eat it), but usually you'll head back to the window when your name or number is called. Don your plastic lobster bib and begin the attack. If you're a neophyte, watch a pro at a nearby table. Some lobster wharves have "how-to" info on printed paper placemats. If you're really concerned (you needn't be), contact the Maine Lobster Promotion Council, 382 Harlow St., Bangor 04401, www.mainelobsterpromo.com. The council produces a brochure with detailed instructions. Don't worry about doing it "wrong"; you'll eventually get what you came for, and it'll be an experience to remember.

Here (in alphabetical order) are five great places to experience lobster between the Schoodic Peninsula and Deer Isle. Each is described in more detail in the regional chapters.

Bernard (Mount Desert Island): Thurston's Lobster Pound, 207/244-7600

Hancock (between Mount Desert and Schoodic): Tidal Falls Lobster Pound, 207/422-6457

Little Deer Isle: Eaton's Lobster Pool, 207/348-2383

Southwest Harbor (Mount Desert Island): Beal's Lobster Pier, 207/244-3202

Trenton (on the access road to Mount Desert Island): Trenton Bridge Lobster Pound, 207/667-2977

Over in Manset, the **Seaweed Café** (146 Seawall Rd., Rte. 102A, Southwest Harbor 04679, 207/244-0572) used to be a secret and, not surprisingly, no longer is. Don't miss it. Reservations are essential at this attractive little place, tucked away on the "back side" of Southwest Harbor. Chef/owner Bill Morrison, a veteran of Aspen and the personal-chef business, uses organic and natural ingredients and fresh local seafood in his "provincial seacoast cuisine," which includes an inventive array of sushi choices ($6–14 for a 10-piece full roll). Entrée range is $18–24; noodle dishes are $13–17. Or try the perfect East-West combo—lobster futo maki sushi, a full roll containing the meat of a 1.5-pound lobster and wasabi béarnaise. (Chicken and duck entrées are also available.) The café is open Tuesday–Saturday 5:30–9 P.M. in summer, weekends during the winter. (Hint: They also do takeout if you're camping at Seawall and feel like treating yourself for dinner.)

Also in Manset, with a spectacular harbor view and hilarious decor (even a lava lamp behind the bar), **Restaurant XYZ** (Shore Rd., Manset, Southwest Harbor 04679, 207/244-5221) specializes in unusual entrées ($16 each) from Xalapa, Yucatán, and Zacatecas (hence, XYZ). Most popular dish? *Cochinitas*—citrus-marinated pork rubbed with *achiote* paste. The margaritas are classic—requiring, allegedly, 1,100 pounds of fresh limes each year. For dessert, try the exquisite XYZ pie. Stroll the Shore Road after dinner. A small adjacent gallery features art and folk crafts by artists from Maine and Mexico. Open for dinner daily in July and August (reserve ahead), Thursday–Saturday in shoulder seasons. XYZ is across from the Manset Town Dock.

Information and Services

At the corner of Route 102 and Seal Cove Road, in the Southwest Harbor Shoppes minimall, the **Southwest Harbor/Tremont Chamber of Commerce** (204 Main St., Rte. 102, P.O. Box 1143, Southwest Harbor 04679, 207/244-9264 or 800/423-9264, fax 207/244-4185, www.acadiachamber.com) is open on an erratic schedule, but you can usually find someone here weekdays in summer. The Thompson Island

Information Center (at the head of Mount Desert Island) has longer and more predictable hours.

Right in the middle of downtown, and recently renovated to double its size, the **Southwest Harbor Public Library** (338 Main St., Southwest Harbor 04679, 207/244-7065, www.swharbor.lib.me.us) is open 9 A.M.–5 P.M. Monday–Friday (to 8 P.M. Wednesday), and 9 A.M.–noon Saturday.

In downtown Southwest Harbor, **public restrooms** are at the southern end of the parking lot behind Carroll's Drug Store (Main Street). Across Main Street, Harbor House also has a restroom, as does the Swans Island ferry terminal in Bass Harbor.

TREMONT: BASS HARBOR AND BERNARD

The town of Tremont is less familiar than its two villages of Bernard and Bass Harbor. The latter has a much higher profile, mostly thanks to **Bass Harbor Head Light** and ferry services to offshore islands. **Tremont** occupies the southwesternmost corner of Mount Desert Island. It's about as far as you can get from Bar Harbor, but the free Island Explorer bus service comes through here on a regular basis during its summer/fall season.

Antiques

Stop in at **E. L. Higgins** (Bernard Rd., P.O. Box 69, Bernard 04612, 207/244-3983, www.antiquewicker.com) for the state's best collection of antique wicker furniture (about 400 pieces at any given time). Three generations work in the shop, housed in two onetime classrooms of an 1890s schoolhouse. Open 10 A.M.–5 P.M., usually daily mid-April through October, but since this is a bit out of the way, call ahead to be sure.

Food

It's really tough to top the experience at **Thurston's Lobster Pound** (Steamboat Wharf Rd., Bernard 04612, 207/244-7600), the best lobster-alfresco deal on the island. Family-oriented Thurston's also has chowders, sandwiches, and terrific desserts. The screened dining room practically sits in the water. Beer and wine available. Open Memorial Day weekend to Columbus Day: 11 A.M.–8 P.M. daily early and late in the season, to 8:30 P.M. in July and August.

If you have a penchant for puns—or can tune them out—head for the family-run **Seafood Ketch Restaurant** (McMullin Ave., Bass Harbor 04653, 207/244-7463). The corny humor begins with "Please no fishing from dining room windows or the deck," and "What foods these morsels be," and goes up or down from there (depending on your perspective). But there's

nothing corny about their seafood roll, an interesting change from the usual lobster or crab roll. There are a few "landlubber delights," but mostly the menu has fresh seafood dishes—including the baked lobster-seafood casserole (a recipe requested by *Gourmet)*. Entrée range is $9–19. This is a prime family spot (with a kids' menu) where the best tables are on the flagstone patio overlooking Bass Harbor. Follow signs for the Swans Island ferry terminal. The Seafood Ketch is open 11 A.M.–9 p.m. daily, late May through October.

Islands near Mount Desert

The most popular **island day-trip destinations** from Mount Desert Island are the Cranberry Isles and Swans Island, but Frenchboro has begun seeing a steadier stream of visitors.

Most commercial and mailboats for the Cranberries depart from Northeast Harbor, although one line originates in Southwest Harbor (all carry bikes but no cars); state car ferries for Swans Island depart from Bass Harbor, south of Southwest Harbor and part of the town of Tremont.

The Maine State Ferry Service also operates the ferry to Long Island (referred to as Frenchboro, the name of the village on the island) from Bass Harbor, but the schedule requires careful planning for day trips.

CRANBERRY ISLES

The Cranberry Isles, south of Northeast and Seal Harbors, comprise **Great Cranberry, Little Cranberry (called Islesford), Sutton, Baker, and Bear Islands.** Islesford and Baker include property belonging to Acadia National Park. Bring a bike and explore the narrow, mostly level roads on the two largest islands (Great Cranberry and Islesford), but *remember to respect private property.* Unless you've asked (and received) permission, *do not* cut across private land to reach the shore.

The Cranberry name has been attributed to 18th-century loyalist governor Francis Bernard, who received these islands (along with all of

Mount Desert) as a king's grant in 1762. Cranberry bogs (now long gone, but there's still a large marsh on the eastern side of the island) on the two largest islands evidently caught his attention. Permanent European settlers were here in the 1760s, and there was even steamboat service by the 1820s.

Lobstering and other marine businesses are the commercial mainstays, boosted in summer by the various visitor-related pursuits. Artists and writers come for a week, a month, or longer; day-trippers spend time on Great Cranberry and Islesford. According to the 2000 census, the Cranberries have 128 year-rounders (primarily on Great Cranberry and Islesford).

Largest of the islands is **Great Cranberry,** where you'll find the **Cranberry General Store** near the dock (207/244-5336), for picnic fixings, and the **Whale's Rib Gift Shop,** about midway along the main road (207/244-5153).

The second-largest island is **Little Cranberry,** locally known as Islesford. (Get a feel for the place by visiting www.islesford.com.) You'll arrive at the newly refurbished Town Dock, one of three adjacent docks (the others are the Fishermen's Wharf and the Islesford Dock). Just east of the Islesford Dock is the handsome brick **Islesford Historical Museum,** operated by the National Park Service (207/288-3338) since 1948. The original collection was established by Harvard/MIT/Haverford professor William Otis Sawtelle (1874–1939), a Bangor native who summered here on the island

© KATHLEEN M. BRANDES

Islesford Historical Museum, part of Acadia National Park (the Blue Duck is at right)

and singlemindedly assembled local memorabilia and even built this brick building to hold it all. The exhibits focus on local history, much of it maritime, so displays include ship models, a full-size dory, household goods, fishing gear, and other memorabilia. The museum is open 9 A.M.–noon and 12:30–3:30 P.M. Monday–Saturday, and 10:45 A.M.–noon and 12:30–4:30 P.M. Sunday, mid-June through September. Free admission, but donations are welcomed. (Across the museum lawn is the **The Blue Duck,** the museum's original site—now dedicated to the island's only public restrooms.)

On the wharf nearest the museum is **The Islesford Dock** (207/244-7494), hanging over the water and serving lunch and dinner 11 A.M.–3 P.M. and 5–9 P.M. Tuesday–Sunday, late June through Labor Day. Sunday brunch is 10 A.M.–2 P.M. Prices are moderate, food is home-cooked and creative, and views across to Acadia's mountains are incredible. If the weather's good, eat on the small deck. Reservations are wise in midsummer. Water taxis are available for returning to Northeast Harbor after dinner. Back along on the same dock is **Islesford Pottery** (Box 309, Islesford 04646, 207/244-9108), Marian

Baker's summertime ceramic studio. A teacher at Maine College of Art in Portland, Marian makes particularly appealing functional pieces, and she carries the work of a couple of other potters. She also sells a handy map of the island ($1, with profits given to charity). Street/road signs are scarce on the island, but the map at least provides orientation. The shop is open daily 10 A.M.–4 P.M., June to Labor Day.

Marian's preteen son, Dan Wriggins—garbed in button-down shirt and tie—has launched himself into the tour-guide business, acquainting visitors with Islesford's specialness in his **Little Cranberry Island Historical Walking Tour.** Tours depart from his mother's shop at 11 A.M. and 1 P.M. on Wednesday, Friday, and Saturday, in July and August only. Cost for a 20-minute tour is $2; an hour-long tour is $6. No credit cards. To find him, call the shop a day ahead, or, as he puts it, "Talk to the potter on the Islesford dock."

Islesford's imaginative postmaster, Joy Sprague, brought the island a bit of postal fame by initiating Maine's busiest stamps-by-mail operation. Many of the other year-round islands' postmasters have now followed suit, aided by the Rockland-based Island Institute, which publishes an order form and address list in each issue of *The Working Waterfront*, its monthly tabloid newspaper. The goal is to save a dozen island post offices from extinction; so far, so good.

Working Waterfront readers feel a real kinship to the Cranberries, thanks to each issue's "Cranberry Report," written by umpteenth-generation island historian Ted Spurling, Jr. (On the island, look for a copy of his charming booklet, *The Town of Cranberry Isles*.)

The post office occupies one corner inside **The Islesford Market** (Main St., 207/244-7667), three short blocks up from the Town Dock. Suzie ("Soos") Krasnow holds forth here—giving advice, baking pizza, marketing her attractive silkscreened notecards, and doing whatever else needs to be done. The market is open Monday–Saturday, mid-June to Labor Day.

Islesford Artists (Mosswood Rd.) is a small but excellent gallery specializing in local artists' depictions of local sites (lots of landscapes/seascapes, naturally). Run by Danny and Katy Fernald, the gallery is open daily, 10 A.M.–5 P.M. in July and August; weekdays 10 A.M.–4 P.M. or by appointment the rest of the season; closed in winter. It's several blocks from the harbor, but there's a sign (and Marian Baker's map will get you there). Or just ask—the islanders are always helpful.

Staying overnight is also an option on Islesford. Frances Bartlett owns the **Braided Rugs Inn** (Main St., P.O. Box 15, Islesford 04646, 207/244-5943) across from the Islesford Market. It's a comfortable, homey place that fits right in with the relaxed pace of the island. Three second-floor rooms (shared bath) go for $70 d, including a full breakfast. Open all year.

Getting There

Decades-old, family-run **Beal & Bunker** (P.O. Box 33, Cranberry Isles 04625, 207/244-3575) provides year-round mailboat/passenger service to the Cranberries from Northeast Harbor. The ferries don't carry cars, but you can take a bike. Or just plan to explore on foot. The summer season, with more frequent trips, runs late June through Labor Day. The first boat departs North-

east Harbor's Municipal Pier at 7:30 A.M. Monday–Saturday; first Sunday boat is 10 A.M. The last boat for Northeast Harbor leaves Islesford at 6:30 P.M. and leaves (Great) Cranberry at 6:45 P.M. The boats do a bit of to-ing and fro-ing on the three-island route (including Sutton in summer), so be patient as they make the circuit. It's a people-watching treat. If you just did a round-trip and stayed aboard, the loop would take about 1.5 hours. Round-trip tickets (covering the whole loop, including intraisland if you want to visit both Great Cranberry and Islesford) are $12 adults, $6 kids under 12 (free for kids under three). Bicycles are $3 round-trip. The off-season schedule operates early May through mid-June and early September through late October; the winter schedule runs late October through April. In winter, the boat company advises phoning ahead on what Mainers quaintly call "weather days."

The **Cranberry Cove Ferry,** purchased by Captain Steve Pagels in 2002, operates a summertime service to the Cranberries, mid-May to mid-October, aboard the 47-passenger *Island Queen*. Pagels also owns the *Margaret Todd* in Bar Harbor and the *Bar Harbor Ferry,* connecting Bar Harbor and Winter Harbor. Contact: 207/244-4882 or 460-1981 (cell), www .downeastwindjammer.com/cranberry. The ferry route begins at the Upper Town Dock (Clark Point Rd.) in Southwest Harbor, with stops in Manset and Great Cranberry before reaching Islesford an hour later. (Stops at Sutton can be arranged.) In summer (mid-June to mid-September), there are six daily round-trips. The first departure from Southwest Harbor is 7 A.M.; last departure from Islesford is 6 P.M. Round-trip fares are $16 adults, less for children. Off-season, call to check the schedule (207/546-2927).

The **MDI Water Taxi,** Captain Wes Shaw's converted lobsterboat, makes frequent on-demand trips to the Cranberries. Call 207/244-7312.

Captain John Dwelley (207/244-5724) also operates a water-taxi service to the Cranberries. His six-passenger *Delight* makes the run from Northeast, Southwest, or Seal Harbor for $40 a trip in the daytime, $45 between 5 and 8 P.M., and

FRENCHBORO, LONG ISLAND

Since Maine has more Long Islands than anyone cares to count, most of them have other labels for easy distinction. Here's a case in point—a Long Island known universally just as Frenchboro, the name of its harbor village. With a year-round population hovering at 38, Frenchboro has had ferry service only since 1960. Since then, the island has acquired phone service, electricity, and satellite TV, but don't expect to notice much of that when you get there. It's a very quiet place where islanders live as islanders always have—making a living from the sea and proud of it. In 1999, when more than half the island (914 acres, including 5.5 miles of shorefront) went up for sale by a private owner, an incredible fund-raising effort collected nearly $3 million, allowing purchase of the land in January 2000 by the Maine Coast Heritage Trust. Some of the funding has been put toward restoration of the village's church and one-room schoolhouse; islanders and visitors will still have full access to all the acreage; and interested developers will have to look elsewhere.

Frenchboro is the subject of *Hauling by Hand*, a fascinating, well-researched "biography" published in 1999 by eighth-generation islander Dean Lunt, now a journalist in Portland. (See *Suggested Reading*.) His website (www.islandportpress.com/frenchboro) has helpful info for visiting the island.

A good way to get a sense of the place is to take the 3.5-hour lunch cruise run by Eric and Kim Strauss of **Island Cruises** (Little Island Marine, Shore Rd., Bass Harbor 04653, 207/244-5785, www.acadiainfo.com/iscruise). The 41-passenger *R. L. Gott* departs at 11 A.M. daily during the summer. The trip allows enough time for a picnic (or lunch at the summertime deli on the dock) and a short village stroll on Frenchboro, then a return through the sprinkling of islands along the 8.3-mile route. Round-trip cost is $20 adults, $10 children 4–11. Be sure to reserve, and if the weather looks iffy, call ahead to confirm. Most of the trip is in sheltered water, but rough seas can put the kibosh on it. Island Cruises also does a two-hour afternoon nature cruise among the islands. You'll find the Island Cruises dock by following signs to the Swans Island Ferry and turning right at the sign shortly before the state ferry dock.

© SHERRY STREETER

Frenchboro Harbor

For an even longer day-trip to Frenchboro, plan to take the *R. L. Gott* during her weekly run for the Maine State Ferry Service. Each Friday from early April to late October, the *Gott* departs Bass Harbor at 8 A.M., arriving in Frenchboro at 9 A.M. The return trip to Bass Harbor is at 6 P.M., allowing nine hours on the island. Round-trip cost is $5.25 adults, $2.25 children (children under five are free). Take a picnic with you, or stop at Lunt's Dockside Deli (207/334-2922), open only in July and August. The island has a network of maintained trails through the woods and along the shore, easy and not-so-easy; some can be squishy and some are along bouldery beachfront. In the center of the island is a beaver pond. (You'll get a sketchy map on the boat, but you can also get one at the Historical Society.) The **Frenchboro Historical Society**, just up from the dock, has interesting old tools, other local artifacts, and a small gift shop. It's open Memorial Day to Labor Day, noon–5 P.M.

The Maine State Ferry Service uses the ferry *Captain Henry Lee* (same one used on the Swans Island route) for service to Frenchboro on Wednesday, Thursday, and Sunday, but the service is only over-and-back (50 minutes each way)—no chance to explore the island.

Extra ferries operate for the island's annual **lobster festival**, usually the second Saturday in August, when islanders and hundreds of visitors gather in the village for lobster galore, games, and more. (For info, call the Lunt & Lunt Lobster Company, 207/334-2922.)

$50 between 8 and 11 P.M. or between 6 and 8 A.M. Inquire about trips to Baker Island.

SWANS ISLAND

Six miles off Mount Desert Island lies scenic, 6,000-acre Swans Island (pop. 327), named after Colonel James Swan, who bought it and two dozen other islands as an investment in 1786. As with the Cranberries, fishing—especially lobstering—is the year-round way of life here; summer sees the arrival of artists, writers, and other seasonal visitors.

With plenty of relatively level terrain (but narrow roads), and a not-impossible amount of real estate to cover, Swans is ideal for a bicycling day trip. The island has no campsites, no public restrooms, a tiny motel, and a tiny B&B. Visitors who want to spend more than a day tend to rent cottages by the week.

If you can be flexible, wait for a clear day, then pack a picnic and catch the first ferry (7:30 A.M.) from Bass Harbor. At the ferry office in Bass Harbor, request a Swans Island map (and take advantage of the restroom). Keep an eye on your watch so you don't miss the last ferry (4:30 P.M.) back to Bass Harbor.

The ferry arrives in the northeast corner of the island. Head off down the main road toward Burnt Coat Harbor. (The island has three villages—Atlantic, Minturn, and Swans Island.) Pedal around to the west side of the harbor and down the peninsula to **Hockamock Head Light** (officially, Burnt Coat Harbor Light). From the ferry landing, Hockamock Head is about five miles, but it's not difficult terrain.

The distinctive square lighthouse, built in 1872 and now automated, sits on a rocky promontory overlooking Burnt Coat Harbor, Harbor Island, lobsterboat traffic, and crashing surf. The keeper's house is unoccupied; the grounds are great for picnics.

If it's hot, ask for directions to one of two prime island swimming spots: **Fine Sand Beach** (salt water) or **Quarry Pond** (fresh water). Fine Sand Beach is on the west side of Toothacher Cove; you'll have to navigate a short stretch of unpaved road to get there, but it's worth the trouble.

Be prepared for chilly water, however. Quarry Pond is in Minturn, on the opposite side of Burnt Coat Harbor from the lighthouse.

On the east side of the island is the weaving barn of the **Atlantic Blanket Company** (Swans Island 04685, 207/526-4492, fax 207/526-4174, www.atlanticblanket.com), where John and Carolyn Grace produce exquisite hand-dyed and handwoven blankets from local white, black, brown, and gray wool. A summer-weight crib blanket runs $375; a winter-weight indigo and white single-bed blanket is $675; quality is flawless. The barn, overlooking the sheep pastures, is open all year, Monday–Saturday 2–5 P.M., other times by appointment. The Graces also do mail order (with a credit card), or you can order online.

A Swans Island summer highlight is the **Sweet Chariot Music Festival**, a three-night midweek extravaganza in early August. Windjammers arrive from Camden and Rockland, enthusiasts show up on their private boats, and the island's Oddfellows Hall is standing-room-only for three evenings of folk singing, storytelling, and impromptu hijinks. In midafternoon of the first two days (about 3:30 P.M.), musicians go from boat to boat in Burnt Coat Harbor, entertaining with sea chanteys. Along the route from harbor to concert, enterprising local kids peddle lemonade, homemade brownies, and kitschy craft items. It's all very festive, but definitely a "boat thing," not very convenient for anyone without waterborne transport.

If you want to stay over, don't expect to find a bed on the island during the festival unless you know someone. Other months (mid-May through October), there's **The Harbor Watch Motel** (111 Minturn Rd., Swans Island 04685, 207/526-4563 or 800/532-7928, www.swansisland.com). The motel's four rooms (two with kitchen facilities) go for $65–80. Bike rentals are $20 a day and all-day kayak rentals are $35.

Getting There

Swans Island is a six-mile, 40-minute trip on the state car ferry *Captain Henry Lee*. Between mid-April and late October, the ferry makes five or six round-trips a day, the first from Bass

COMMUNITIES

134 Mount Desert Island Communities

Harbor at 7:30 A.M. (Sunday 9 A.M.) and the last from Swans Island at 4:30 P.M. Other months, the first and last runs are the same, but there are only four or five trips. For more information, contact **Maine State Ferry Service** (P.O. Box 114, Bass Harbor 04653, 207/244-3254; 303 Atlantic Rd., Swans Island 04685, 207/526-4273; daily recorded info: 800/491-4883, www.state.me.us/mdot/opt/ferry/ferry). Round-trip fares are $10.50 adults, $4.50 children 5–11 (children under 5 are free). Bikes are $10 round-trip per adult, $5 per child. A round-trip ticket for vehicle and driver is $30 May through October. Reservations are accepted only for vehicles. If you've made a vehicle reservation, be sure to be in line at least 15 minutes before departure or you'll risk forfeiting your space.

To reach the Bass Harbor ferry terminal on Mount Desert Island, follow the distinctive blue signs, marked Swans Island Ferry, along Routes 102 and 102A.

Southwest Cycle (Main St., Southwest Harbor 04679, 207/244-5856 or 800/649-5856) rents bikes by the day and week and is open all year. Hours are 8:30 A.M.–5:30 P.M. Monday–Saturday and 10 A.M.–4 P.M. Sunday, June–September; Monday–Saturday 9 A.M.–5 P.M., October–May. It also has ferry schedules and Swans Island maps.(For the early-morning ferry, you'll need to pick up bikes the day before; be sure to reserve them if you're doing this in July or August.)

Schoodic Peninsula

Slightly more than 2,000 of Acadia National Park's acres are on the mainland Schoodic Peninsula—the rest are all on islands (including Mount Desert). World-class scenery and the relative lack of congestion, even at the height of summer, make Schoodic a special Acadia destination.

The Schoodic Peninsula is just one of several "fingers" of land that point oceanward as part of **Eastern Hancock County.** Sneak around to the eastern side of Frenchman Bay to see this region from a whole new perspective. One hour from Acadia National Park's Visitor Center, you'll find Acadia's mountains silhouetted against the sunset, the surf slamming onto Schoodic Point, the peace of a calmer lifestyle.

As with so much of Acadia's acreage on Mount Desert Island, the Schoodic section became part of the park largely due to the deft diplomacy and perseverance of George B. Dorr. No obstacle ever seemed too daunting to Dorr. In 1928, when the owners objected to donating their land to a national park tagged with the Lafayette name (geopolitics being involved at the time), Dorr even managed to obtain congressional approval for the 1929 name change to Acadia National Park—and Schoodic was part of the deal.

While most visitors still arrive by car or RV, a new option opened up in the summer of 2003. The propane-powered **Island Explorer** bus service expanded to include a route in this area between late June and Labor Day. At this writing, the jury is still out on the success of this route, so when you arrive, check to confirm that it's still running.

© KATHLEEN M. BRANDES

Acadia's mountains from Sorrento Harbor

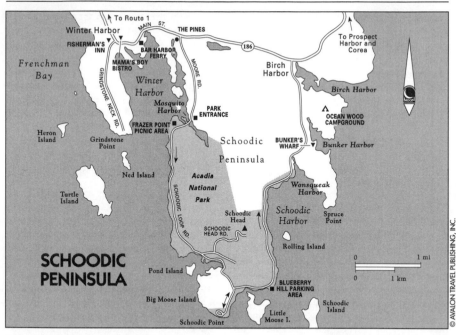

SCHOODIC
PENINSULA

© AVALON TRAVEL PUBLISHING, INC.

Exploring Schoodic and Eastern Hancock County

Rather than just show up on the Schoodic Peninsula, follow the Schoodic Loop Road, and dash back to Mount Desert or elsewhere, plan to spend a couple of days exploring Eastern Hancock County.

There's no official visitor center in this area, so you'll want to stop at the main Acadia Visitor Center on Mount Desert Island, or download Schoodic information before you come.

Twenty-nine miles of the road through the area that includes Schoodic have been designated as the **Schoodic National Scenic Byway.** The route stretches from Sullivan on Route 1 to Gouldsboro and then southward on Route 186 and around the Schoodic Peninsula.

The biggest attractions in this area are the spectacular vignettes and vistas—of offshore lighthouses, distant mountains, close-in islands, and unchanged villages. Check out each small and large finger of land: Lamoine, Hancock Point, Sorrento, and Winter Harbor's Grindstone Neck. Circle the Gouldsboro Peninsula, including Prospect Harbor, and detour to Corea. If you still have enough time, head inland and follow Route 182, a designated Scenic Highway, from Hancock and on to Cherryfield. Accomplish all this and you'll have a fine sense of place. (Make sure to stock up on film, and remember that a wide-angle lens or a panoramic camera is a major asset in this area.)

WINTER HARBOR

Winter Harbor (pop. 988) is known best as the gateway to Schoodic. It shares the area with an old-money, low-profile, Philadelphia-linked summer colony on exclusive Grindstone Neck. Only a few clues hint at the colony's presence, strung along the western side of the harbor. Winter Harbor's summer highlight is the annual Lobster Festival, second Saturday in August. The gala daylong event includes a parade,

abandoned granite quarry, Sullivan

live entertainment, games, and more crustaceans than you could ever consume.

GOULDSBORO

Gouldsboro (pop. 1,941)—including the not-to-be-missed villages of Birch Harbor, Corea, and Prospect Harbor—earned its own minor fame from Louise Dickinson Rich's 1958 book *The Peninsula,* a tribute to her summers on Corea's Cranberry Point, "a place that has stood still in time." Since 1958, change has crept into Corea, but not so's you'd notice. It's still the same quintessential lobster-fishing community, perfect for photo ops.

GETTING THERE

By Car

We'll head for the Schoodic section of Acadia before exploring the rest of the area. To reach the park boundary from Bar Harbor, take Route 3 northward to the head of Mount Desert Island, then across Mount Desert Narrows to Trenton. The usual route is to continue to a congested intersection at the edge of Ellsworth, where you'll pick up Route 1 North (turn right). Stay on Route 1 about 16 miles (through Hancock and Sullivan) until you reach Gouldsboro. From Route 1 in Gouldsboro, the park entrance is eight miles. Take Route 186 south to Winter Harbor. Continue through town, heading east, then turn right onto Moore Road and continue to the park-entrance sign, just before the stone-lined causeway over Mosquito Harbor.

If you're coming from Trenton—the funnel to and from Mount Desert—you can avoid some of the traffic congestion by ducking east via Route 204 toward Lamoine and its state park and then back up to Route 1 via the Mud Creek Road.

By Passenger Ferry

The **Bar Harbor Ferry** (207/288-2984, www.barharborferry.com), owned by Captain Steve Pagels (who also operates the four-masted schooner *Margaret Todd* and ferry service to the Cranberry Isles), runs his Bar-Harbor-to-Winter-Harbor ferry throughout the year (reduced service off-season). You can board the ferry with a bike in Bar Harbor (at the Bar Harbor Inn Pier), disembark in Winter Harbor (at Winter Harbor Marine, on Sargent St.), pedal the short distance to Schoodic, then bike the Schoodic Loop Road, and return later to Bar Harbor on the ferry (last boat is 5 P.M.).

Since the ferry's summer schedule is coordinated with the Island Explorer bus's new summertime Schoodic route, you can board the ferry in Bar Harbor, pick up the bus at the dock in Winter Harbor, and be shuttled along the Schoodic Loop. Stop where you like for a picnic, then board a later bus. Take the last bus back to the ferry and return to Bar Harbor. A super car-free excursion!

There's no charge for the bus; the round-trip ferry ticket is $24 adults, $15 children, $5 bikes. (If that seems steep, consider the savings on gas and wear and tear on your car.)

SCHOODIC PENINSULA

Sights

Except for a few hiking trails, the major sights of Acadia's Schoodic section lie along the six-mile one-way road that meanders counterclockwise around the tip of the Schoodic Peninsula. You'll discover official and unofficial picnic areas, the hiking trailheads, offshore lighthouses, and turnouts with scenic vistas.

SCHOODIC POINT

The highlight of this part of the park is Schoodic Point, with vistas that seemingly go all the way to Spain. The point is at the end of a two-way spur off the Schoodic Loop Road. Although crowds gather at the height of summer, especially when the surf is raging, the two-tiered parking lot, amazingly, seldom fills up. (There are restrooms here, too.) Check local newspapers for the time of high tide and try to arrive here then; the word *awesome* is overused, but it sure describes Schoodic Point's surf performance on the rugged pink granite. The setting sun makes it even more brilliant. This area is open only from 6 A.M. to 10 P.M.

Caution: If you've brought children, keep them well back from the water; a rogue wave can sweep them off the rocks all too easily. It *has* happened. Picnics are great here (make sure you bring a litter bag), and so are the tide pools at mid- to low tide. Birding is spectacular during spring and fall migrations.

And on the subject of birds, you'll see a sign here: "Do not feed gulls or other wildlife." Heed it. Even if you *don't* feed the gulls, they can threaten your lunch if you're having a picnic here. They'll swoop down shamelessly and snatch it away before you even realize they've spotted you. From extensive practice with unsuspecting visitors, they're adept at thievery.

DRIVING TOUR

As with the park territory on Mount Desert Island, the park's acreage on the Schoodic Peninsula

Schoodic Point

LIGHTHOUSES

The best known of this region's coastal beacons is **Bass Harbor Head Light,** part of Acadia National Park. Perched high on a promontory overlooking the entrance to Bass Harbor, it flashes a distinctive red beacon (automated since 1974). To visit the light, take Route 102 to the bottom (southern end) of Mount Desert Island, then take Route 102A and watch for signs. The setting is spectacular and the grounds are accessible during the daytime. (The house is government property, occupied by the Southwest Harbor Coast Guard commander.) Be sure to descend the stairs toward the shore and view the 26-foot tower upward from there.

Roughly from north to south (strictly speaking, though, it's east to west), here are the other still-operating lighthouses in the Acadia Region. All are automated; most are accessible only by boat. None of the light towers are accessible to the public. Three lights in this area—Winter Harbor, Blue Hill, and Pumpkin Island—are no longer used as navigational beacons, although their towers still stand.

Clearly visible (on a clear day, that is) from Acadia's Park Loop Road, **Egg Rock Light** was built in 1875 on bleak, barren Egg Rock, protecting the entrance to Frenchman Bay. The squat, square keeper's house, topped by a square light tower, resembles no other Maine lighthouse. The light, now under the aegis of the Petit Manan National Wildlife Refuge, was automated in 1976.

The Cranberry Isles mailboat out of Northeast Harbor passes dramatically sited **Bear Island Light** on its daily rounds. Located on Acadia National Park land at the entrance to Northeast Harbor, the light tower and its keeper's house are privately leased in exchange for upkeep. (There's no public access to the island.) The automated light has been a privately maintained navigational aid since 1989. The present tower was built in 1889.

Baker Island Light, built in 1828 (during John Quincy Adams's presidency) and rebuilt in 1855, is accessible only by boat, and then via a boardwalk. The brick tower rises 43 feet. Most of the 123-acre island, one of the five Cranberry Isles, is part of Acadia National Park. Charles W. Eliot, president of Harvard (1869–1909) and one of the prime movers behind the establishment of the park, shone

Bear Island Light, a landmark en route to the Cranberry Isles

© KATHLEEN M. BRANDES

a small spotlight on Baker Island when he published a sympathetic short memoir of a 19th-century Baker Island farmer and fisherman. Entitled *John Gilley, One of the Forgotten Millions,* and reprinted in 1989 by Bar Harbor's Acadia Press, it's a must- read—a poignant story of a hardscrabble pioneering life.

Eleven miles out to sea from Bar Harbor, **Great Duck Island Light** stands on a 12-acre parcel owned by the College of the Atlantic (Bar Harbor). It serves as a year-round site (the solar-powered Alice Eno Biological Station) for the college's ecology researchers. The rest of the island is owned by the Nature Conservancy, which has estimated that Great Duck sustains about 20 percent of the state's nesting seabirds. In 2002, some 1,000 pairs of herring gulls nested here; others include Leach's storm petrels, black-backed gulls, and black guillemots. The 42-foot granite-and-brick light tower, built in 1890, was automated in 1986. The light is visible only from private boats, and there's no island access.

The College of the Atlantic also conducts research on the minuscule, barren, remote island surrounding **Mount Desert Rock Light,** built in 1847. The college's Allied Whale program, based in the keeper's house (the Edward Mc Blair Marine Research Station), monitors the movements of finback and humpback whales. The tower rises 68 feet; the automated light is solar-powered. Mount Desert Rock is also an automated NOAA weather

(continued on next page)

SCHOODIC PENINSULA

LIGHTHOUSES (cont'd)

station, cited daily in marine weather reports. There's no public access to the island, but whale-watching boats out of Bar Harbor frequently head this way.

Built in 1872, **Burnt Coat Harbor (or Hockamock Head) Light,** with a distinctive square white tower, protects the entrance to Burnt Coat Harbor on Swans Island, accessible via the Maine State Ferry Service from Bass Harbor on Mount Desert Island. The town-owned light is about five miles from the ferry landing, so a bike comes in handy. Bring a picnic and enjoy it on the lighthouse grounds, with a fabulous view.

Isle au Haut Light, also known as Robinson Point Light, serves as a "night light" for guests at The Keeper's House, a unique B&B on Isle au Haut. Connected by a wooden walkway to The Keeper's House, the brick light tower (built in 1907) overlooks the Isle au Haut Thorofare. Access

to the island is only by ferry or private boat. The tower itself (not open to the public) is owned by the town of Isle au Haut; The Keeper's House is privately owned.

Looking rather lonely without a keeper's house, **Mark Island Light,** also known as Deer Island Thorofare Light, was built in 1857 (the light-keeper's house burned in 1959). All that remain are the 25-foot square tower and a tiny attached shed. Deer Isle's Island Heritage Trust owns the island, which is accessible only by boat—but *not* during seabird nesting season (typically, April through August).

Another light station without a keeper's house (it was intentionally burned in 1963) is **Eagle Island Light,** in East Penobscot Bay, west of the Deer Isle village of Sunset. Built in 1858, it has a 30-foot granite tower. Plans are in the works to deactivate the light. Access is only by boat.

---

has its own driving route. Also named the Park Loop Road, it's best referred to as the Schoodic Loop, to distinguish between the two.

There's no camping in this section of the park, but private camping and other lodging options are available in the area. There are no restaurants or other food sources in the park, but you won't need to go far. While you're driving, if you see a viewpoint you like (with room to pull off), stop; it's a long way around to return.

Just after the causeway, the first park landmark is **Frazer Point Picnic Area,** with lovely vistas, picnic tables, and convenient outhouses. Other spots are fine for picnics, but this is the only official one. If you've brought bikes, leave your car here and do a counterclockwise 12.2-mile loop through the park and back to your car via Birch Harbor and Route 186. It's a fine day trip.

From the picnic area, the **Schoodic Loop Road** becomes one-way. Unlike the Park Loop Road on Mount Desert, no parking is allowed in the right lane. There are periodic pullouts, but not many cars can squeeze in. Despite the fact that this is far from the busiest section of Acadia, it can still be frustrating in the summer months to

be unable to find a space. Best advice, therefore: Stay in the area and do this loop early in the morning or later in the afternoon, perhaps in May or June. (The late-September and early-October foliage is gorgeous, but traffic *does* increase then.)

From this side of Frenchman Bay, the vistas of Mount Desert's summits are gorgeous, behind islands sprinkled here and there.

Go about 2.5 miles from the picnic area and watch for a narrow, unpaved road on the left, across from an "open" beach vista. It winds for a mile up to a tiny parking circle, from which you can follow the trail (signposted "Schoodic trails") to the open ledges on 440-foot Schoodic Head (see *Biking and Hiking;* don't confuse this with Schoodic Mountain, which is well north of here). From the circle, there's already a glimpse of the view, but it gets much better.

Continue on the Schoodic Loop Road, past the site of a former top-secret U.S. Navy communications base (projected to become the Schoodic Education and Research Center, an Acadia facility), and hang a right onto the short (.2 mile) two-way spur to **Schoodic Point.**

along the Schoodic Loop Road

From Schoodic Point, return to the Loop Road and go about a mile to the **Blueberry Hill** parking area, a moorlike setting where the low growth allows almost 180-degree views of the bay and islands. Across the road is the trailhead for the 180-foot-high **Anvil** headland.

From Blueberry Hill, continue another two miles to the park exit, just before Birch Harbor.

Recreation

If you've brought a bike over, try to pedal the Schoodic Loop Road early or late in the day—especially if you're doing a family outing, when everyone tends to cluster together. It's a lovely bike route, but the shoulders on this peninsula are soft and sandy, not great for bikes—so you'll see Share the Road with Bicycles signs along the way. Keep to the right and use the road, not the shoulders.

For **hiking,** there are a few trails in this area—all eventually converging on Schoodic Head. Go about 2.5 miles past the picnic area to the unmarked, unpaved road on your left. For exercise, hike up the mile-long road, although you'll need to keep an eye out for cars, as it's narrow and winding. At the top, on the far side of the parking loop, look for the trailhead signpost and continue on to **Schoodic Head.**

Or you can continue on the Schoodic Loop Road, to the Blueberry Hill parking area, cross the road, and follow the easy **Alder Trail** into the woods—about a mile in and back. Be sure to use insect repellent here, for the marshy areas. (The Alder Trail can be extended to include Schoodic Head and the Anvil Trail, but it's a more difficult hike.)

A short distance beyond Blueberry Hill is a pulloff where you can leave your car while you hike the **Anvil Trail,** almost two miles roundtrip and moderately difficult. (The trailhead is across the road.) You'll still end up on Schoodic Head, again with head-swiveling views.

More than 14,000 acres have been preserved for public access in a huge mountain-and-lake area north and east of Sullivan, the **Donnell Pond Public Reserved Land.** Developers had

SCHOODIC PENINSULA

their eyes on this gorgeous real estate in the 1980s, but preservationists fortunately rallied to the cause. Outright purchase of 7,316 of the acres, in the Spring River Lake area, came through the foresighted Land for Maine's Future program. Route 182, an official Scenic Highway, cuts right through the Donnell Pond preserve.

Major water bodies here are **Donnell Pond** (big enough by most gauges to be called a lake), **Tunk Lake,** and **Spring River Lake;** all are accessible for boats (even, alas, powerboats). Tunk Lake has a few campsites in its southwestern corner. The eastern and southern shores of Donnell Pond have primitive, first-come, first-served sites (no charge), which are snapped up quickly on midsummer weekends. Schoodic Beach, the prime swimming area, is in the southeastern corner of Donnell Pond.

By boat, trailheads at Schoodic Beach and Black Beach provide access to **Caribou, Black,** and **Schoodic Mountains,** with connector trails. None are easy but it's great hiking—and there's an abandoned radio tower on 1,069-foot Schoodic. The Caribou–Black Mountain Loop, clockwise, is about a seven-mile round-trip from the Black Beach boat-access trailhead.

To reach the boat-launching area for Donnell Pond from Route 1 in Sullivan, take Route 200 north to Route 182. Turn right and go about 1.5 miles to a right turn just before Swan Brook. Turn and go not quite two miles to the put-in; the road is poor in spots but adequate for a regular vehicle. The Narrows, where you'll put in, is lined with summer cottages ("camps" in the Maine vernacular); keep paddling eastward to the more open part of the lake.

To reach the vehicle-access trailhead for Schoodic Mountain from Route 1 in East Sullivan, turn off at Route 183 (Lake Road) and drive just over four miles northeastward. Cross the Maine Central Railroad tracks and turn left onto an unpaved road (marked as a Jeep track on the

> *More than 14,000 acres have been preserved for public access in a huge mountain-and-lake area north and east of Sullivan, the Donnell Pond Public Reserved Land. Developers had their eyes on this gorgeous real estate in the 1980s, but preservationists fortunately rallied to the cause.*

USGS map), signposted for the Donnell Pond Unit. Continue to the parking area and trailhead. Follow the Schoodic Mountain Loop clockwise, heading westward first. The hike is moderate to strenuous, about five miles round-trip, with some rather steep areas. To make a day of it, pack a picnic and take a swimsuit (and don't forget a camera and binoculars for the summit views). On a brilliantly clear day, you'll see Baxter State Park's Katahdin, the peaks of Acadia National Park, and the ocean beyond. For such rewards, this is a popular hike, so don't expect to be alone, especially on fall weekends, when the foliage colors are spectacular.

Still within the preserve boundaries, but farther east, you can put in a canoe at the northern end of Long Pond and paddle southward into adjoining Round Pond. In early August, Round Mountain, rising a few hundred feet from Long Pond's eastern shore, is a great spot for gathering blueberries and huckleberries. The put-in for Long Pond is on the south side of Route 182 (park well off the road), about two miles east of Tunk Lake.

GOLF

Play a nine-hole round at the **Grindstone Neck Golf Course** (Grindstone Avenue, Winter Harbor 04693, 207/963-7760) just for the dynamite scenery and for a glimpse of this exclusive, late-19th-century summer enclave. Established in 1895, the public course attracts a tony crowd; 150-yard markers are cute little birdhouses. Tee times usually aren't needed, but it's best to call ahead to make sure. The course is open early June through September.

KAYAKING AND BIKING

Master Maine Guide Danny Mitchell operates **Mooselook Guide Service** (761 So. Gouldsboro Rd., Rte. 186, Gouldsboro 04607, 207/963-7720, www.mooselookguideservice .com), with three-hour kayak tours departing at 9 A.M. and 5:30 P.M. Cost is $40 pp. Mooselook also rents kayaks ($30 a day for a single, $40 for a tandem), canoes ($25 a day), and mountain bikes ($15 a day). A car rack is $1 extra. Kayak tours are weather-dependent.

Entertainment

The **Pierre Monteux School for Conductors and Orchestra Musicians** (Rte. 1, P.O. Box 469, Hancock 04640, 207/422-3931, www.monteuxschool.org), a prestigious summer program founded in 1943, presents two well-attended concert series starting in late June and running through July. Known also as the Domaine School, it has achieved international renown for training dozens of national and international classical musicians. Among its alumni are Erich Kunzel, Sir Neville Marriner, Lorin Maazel, and David Zinman. Five Wednesday concerts (7:30 P.M.) feature chamber music; six Sunday concerts (5 P.M.) feature symphonies. Concerts are held in the School Hall on Route 1. Tickets for Sunday are $12 adults, $5 students; tickets for Wednesday are $5. Arrive at least half an hour early, as there are no reserved seats.

The nearest cinemas are in Ellsworth and Bar Harbor, as are lots of other entertainment possibilities.

SHOPPING

Zero in on Eastern Hancock County to shop for everyone on your list who appreciates unusual crafts and gifts. Hancock, Sullivan, and Gouldsboro are loaded with great gallery-shops.

Art and Crafts Galleries

Bet you can't keep from smiling at the whimsical animal sculptures of talented sculptor/painter Philip Barter. His work is the cornerstone of the eclectic, two-room **Barter Family Gallery** (Shore Road, Box 102, Sullivan 04664, 207/422-3190), on a back road in Sullivan. But there's more: Barter's wife and seven children have put their considerable skills to work producing braided rugs, jewelry, and other craft items sold here at

moderate prices. No credit cards. The gallery, 2.5 miles northwest of Route 1, is signposted soon after you cross the bridge over the river from Hancock. It's open all year; the family home is attached. Summer hours are 10 A.M.–5 P.M. Tuesday–Saturday.

Artist Paul Breeden, best known for the remarkable illustrations, calligraphy, and maps he's done for *National Geographic,* Time-Life Books, and other national and international publications, displays and sells his paintings at the **Spring Woods Gallery** (40A Willowbrook Ln., Route 200, Sullivan 04664, 207/422-3007, www.willowbrookgarden.com). Also filling the handsome modern gallery space are paintings by Ann Breeden, metal sculptures and silk scarves by the talented Breeden offspring, and Pueblo artifacts from the American Southwest. The beautifully landscaped gallery, .2 mile north of Route 1, is open 9 A.M.–5 P.M. Monday–Saturday, May–October.

Gifts and More Crafts

Lunaform (Cedar Lane, P.O. Box 189, West Sullivan 04664, 207/422-0923, www .lunaform.com) is in a class by itself. First there's the setting—gorgeous landscaped grounds surrounding an abandoned granite quarry. Then there's the realization that many of the wonderfully aesthetic garden ornaments created here look like hand-turned *pottery;* they are in fact hand-turned, but made of steel-reinforced concrete. Buy an urn or pot or fountain and dazzle your friends, and even your enemies. It takes a bit of zigging and zagging to get here. After you cross the bridge into Sullivan, go left onto Hog Bay Road, then take the next right (Track Road). After .5 mile, go left into Cedar Lane. Lunaform is open 9 A.M.–5 P.M. Monday–Friday.

Blue-and-white Japanese-style motifs predominate at **Gull Rock Pottery** (325 Eastside Rd., Hancock 04640, 207/422-3990), Torj and Kurt Wray's studio and shop 1.5 miles south of Route 1 (the driveway is another half mile). They'll also do special orders of their wheel-thrown, hand-painted, dishwasher-safe pottery. No credit cards. The shop is open 9 A.M.–5 P.M. Monday–Saturday all year.

Overlooking Hog Bay, 3.6 miles north of Route 1, Charles and Susanne Grosjean have been the key players at **Hog Bay Pottery** (245 Hog Bay Rd., Route 200, Franklin 04634, 207/565-2282) since 1974. Inside the casual, laid-back showroom are Charlie's functional, nature-themed pottery and Susanne's stunning handwoven rugs. They produce a mail-order catalog and often fill custom orders. The shop, next to their house, is open daily, May–October; call ahead other months.

Chickadee Creek Stillroom (Rte. 186, P.O. Box 220, West Gouldsboro 04607, 207/963-7283 or 800/969-4372, www.chickadeecreek.com) is a toy store for herb fanciers. Jeanie and Fred Cook seem to have thought of everything—potpourri, teas, wreaths, fresh herbs for cooking. The barn/shop, 1.7 miles south of Route 1, is open 10 A.M.–4 P.M. Tuesday–Sunday, May–mid-October, variable hours other months. Request a copy of the mail-order catalog.

Visiting the **U.S. Bells Foundry and Store** (56 West Bay Rd., Rte. 186, Prospect Harbor 04669, tel./fax 207/963-7184, www.usbells.com) is a treat for the ears, as browsers try out the many varieties of cast-bronze bells made in the adjacent foundry by Richard Fisher. If you're lucky, he may have time to explain the process—particularly intriguing for children, and a distraction from their instinctive urge to test every bell in the shop. Foundry hours are 8 A.M.–4 P.M. Monday–Thursday. The store also carries a tasteful selection of Shaker items, pottery, jewelry, and Cindy Fisher's handmade

quilts. It's open 9 A.M.–5 P.M. Monday–Friday and 9 A.M.–2 P.M. Saturday, all year. U.S. Bells is .25 mile up the hill from Prospect Harbor's post office.

Just up the road (toward Route 1) from U.S. Bells, Cindy and Bill Thayer's enthusiasm is contagious as they explain their prolific 133-acre organic farm—home to hairy Scotch Highland cattle, turkeys, sheep, pigs, chickens, and border collies. At **Darthia Farm** (51 Darthia Farm Rd., Rte. 186, Gouldsboro 04607, 207/963-7771 or 963-2770, or 800/285-6234), kids love feeding the pigs and riding on the hay wagon; parents can check out Hattie's Shed for Cindy's outstanding ikat weavings and work by half a dozen other craftspeople. Farm tours and horse-drawn wagon rides occur each Tuesday and Thursday at 2 P.M. in July and August. The farmstand—stocked with organic veggies, pesto, jams, and vinegars—is open 8 A.M.–6 P.M. Monday–Friday, 8 A.M.–noon Saturday, June–September. If you can't visit Hattie's Shed, request a mail-order catalog. The farm is 1.7 miles south of Route 1.

Bartlett's Winery

German and Italian presses, Portuguese corks, and Maine fruit all go into the creation of Bob and Kathe Bartlett's award-winning dinner and dessert wines: apple, pear, blueberry, raspberry, blackberry, strawberry, and loganberry. Founded in 1982, **Bartlett Maine Estate Winery** (Chicken Mill Pond Road, R.R. 1, Box 598, Gouldsboro 04607, 207/546-2408, fax 207/546-2554) produces more than 25,000 gallons annually in a handsome wood-and-stone building designed by the Bartletts. They don't give tours, but you're welcome to sample the wines, and you can buy single bottles and gift packages. Bartlett's, a half mile south of Route 1 in Gouldsboro, is open 10 A.M.–5 P.M. Monday–Saturday from Memorial Day weekend to Columbus Day, or by appointment off-season.

Practicalities

ACCOMMODATIONS

There are no lodgings in the Schoodic section of the park, but within less than a half hour of the Schoodic parkland, you'll have your choice of an impressive range of places to sleep—from an elegant French-style country inn with a fantastic restaurant to a rustic campground with lovely wilderness sites.

Inns

Buffered from the highway by a tall hedge, **Le Domaine** (Route 1, HC 77, Box 496, Hancock 04640, 207/422-3395 or 800/554-8498 outside Maine, fax 207/422-2316, www.ledomaine .com) has gained a five-star reputation for its restaurant, founded by the mother of present owner/chef Nicole Purslow in 1946—long before fine dining had cachet here. But that's only part of the story. Above the restaurant is a charming, five-room, country-French inn, newly updated in the spring of 2000. The 80-acre inn property, nine miles east of Ellsworth, is virtual Provence, an oasis transplanted magically to Maine. On the garden-view balconies, or on the lawn out back, you're oblivious to the traffic whizzing by. Better yet, follow the lovely wooded trail to a quiet pond. Three guest rooms ($285 d, $200 B&B) and two suites ($370 d, $285 B&B) all are named after locales in Provence. Two meals are included with the price of accommodation; continental breakfast, usually including croissants, can be served in your room or in the dining room. No smoking indoors. Alert the inn if you'll be arriving after 5:30 P.M., when the staff has to focus on dinner. The ultra-French restaurant, with a 5,000-bottle wine cellar and lovely Provençal decor, is open to the public 6–9 P.M. Tuesday–Sunday. Reservations are essential, especially in July and August. The tab may dent

Within less than a half hour of the Schoodic parkland, you'll have your choice of an impressive range of places to sleep—from an elegant French-style country inn with a fantastic restaurant to a rustic campground with lovely wilderness sites.

your budget (entrées $23–30), but stack that up against plane fare to France. Le Domaine's season is early June through November.

Follow Hancock Point Road 4.8 miles south of Route 1 to the three-story, gray-blue **Crocker House Country Inn** (Hancock Point Rd., Hancock 04640, 207/422-6806, fax 207/422-3105, www.maineguide.com/downeast/crocker), Rich Malaby's antidote to Bar Harbor's summer traffic. Built as a summer hotel in 1884, the inn underwent rehabbing a century later, and it continues to be updated, but it retains a decidedly old-fashioned air. Eleven rooms (private baths) are $90–130 d mid-June to mid-October; $75–90 d other months. Breakfast is included. Guests can relax in the common room or reserve spa time in the carriage house. Nearby are clay tennis courts, quiet walking routes past Hancock Point's elegant seaside "cottages," and a unique octagonal public library. The inn will pack picnic lunches (extra charge) for day trips to Campobello Island, Acadia, or Lamoine State Park. If you're arriving by boat, request a mooring. Two attractive dining rooms are open to the public for dinner (daily 5:30–9 P.M.; entrées $19–25) and Sunday brunch (11 A.M.–2 P.M. July to Labor Day weekend); reservations are essential. The inn is open daily, mid-April to Columbus Day, then Thursday–Sunday through New Year's Eve.

B&Bs

About 12 miles east of Ellsworth is the **Island View Inn** (12 Miramar Ave., Rte. 1, Sullivan 04664, 207/422-3031), its name the height of understatement. Out front are the peaks of Mount Desert, a remarkable panorama. Four of the seven rooms (all private baths) capture the view from this updated turn-of-the-20th-century summer home run by Evelyn Joost and

© KATHLEEN M. BRANDES

Corea Harbor's lobsterboat fleet

her daughter Sarah. Rooms are $95–125 d July to mid-September, $85–110 d other times. The Island View has a private beach, but the water is terminally chilly. Guests have free use of a canoe, a paddleboat, and a dinghy. No smoking; children over six and pets are welcome. Open Memorial Day weekend to Columbus Day.

Sorrento is such a low-key place that lots of people don't realize it exists—much less that it has a B&B. **Bass Cove Farm Bed & Breakfast** (312 Eastside Rd., Rte. 185, Sorrento 04677, tel./fax 207/422-3564, www.basscovefarm.com) was opened in 1992 by spinner/weaver/gardener/editor Mary Ann Solet and her husband, Michael Tansey, a group-home supervisor whose résumé also includes the Harry S. Truman Manure Pitchoff Championship at the annual Common Ground Country Fair. Mary Ann can rattle off dozens of ideas for exploring the area, particularly in the craft department, and she raids her extensive vegetable garden daily to produce a hearty, healthful breakfast. Two first-floor rooms (one with private bath; $55 and $80 d) and a second-floor suite ($90 d, plus $10 for kitchen use) have quilt-covered beds and other

homey touches. (Rates are $45–80 other months.) No smoking, no pets; well-behaved children are welcome. The B&B is open all year, but be sure to call ahead off-season.

Aptly named, **The Sunset House Bed & Breakfast** (54 Clinic Rd., Rte. 186, West Gouldsboro 04607, 207/963-7156 or 800/233-7156, www.sunsethousebnb.com) overlooks the setting sun off to the west and water from more than one direction. Most of the seven rooms (four with private baths) in Carl and Kathy Johnson's charming three-story Victorian home have water views. Jones Pond, Gouldsboro's swimming hole, borders the property; bring a canoe and launch it here—but not before launching into award-winning chef Carl's generous breakfast. Kathy's homemade goat cheese is often on the menu. Rates are $79 d with shared bath, $99 d with private bath May–October; two-night minimum on weekends July through October. No smoking, no pets. Open all year; lower rates off-season. In winter, you can go ice-skating and cross-country skiing. Sunset House is .25 mile south of Route 1, in the village of West Gouldsboro. The Johnsons also own The Fisherman's Inn in Winter Harbor.

Overlooking the Gouldsboro Peninsula's only sandy saltwater beach, **Oceanside Meadows Inn** (Route 195, Corea Road, P.O. Box 90, Prospect Harbor 04669, 207/963-5557, fax 207/963-5928, www.oceaninn.com) is a jewel of a place on 200 acres with fabulous perennial and organic gardens, wildlife habitat, and nature trails. The elegant 1860s Captain's House has seven attractive rooms and the 1820 Shaw farmhouse next door has another seven; all have private baths ($128–198 d July to mid-October, $98–188 d other months). Each room has a copy of Louise Dickinson Rich's *The Peninsula*—a thoughtful touch. Breakfast is an impressive multicourse event, staged by the energetic husband-and-wife team of Sonja Sundaram and Ben Walter, who seem to have thought of everything—hot drinks are available all day, and there is a guest fridge, beach toys, even popcorn for the fireplace. Well-behaved children are welcome; no smoking. Pets are allowed on a very limited basis. Open May through October. As if all that weren't enough, Sonja and Ben have totally restored the 1820 timber-frame barn out back—creating the **Oceanside Meadows Innstitute for the Arts and Sciences.** Local art hangs on the walls, and from mid-June to late September, the 125-seat barn has a full schedule of classical concerts and lectures on natural history, Native American traditions, and more. Some are free, some require tickets; all require reservations. Most programs are Thursday nights at 7:30 P.M. Oceanside Meadows is six miles off Route 1.

Even more of a detour, and definitely worthwhile, is Bob Travers and Barry Canner's **Black Duck Inn on Corea Harbor** (Crowley Island Road, P.O. Box 39, Corea 04624, 207/963-2689, fax 207/963-7495, www.blackduck.com), literally the end of the line on the Gouldsboro Peninsula. Set on 12 acres in this timeless fishing village, the B&B has four handsomely decorated rooms (private and shared baths) for $105–165 d (the latter for the small suite). Across the way are two little seasonal cottages, one rented by the day ($130, three-night minimum) and one by the week. The inn and Corea are geared to wanderers, readers, and anyone seeking serenity (who isn't?). Rocky outcrops dot the property and a

nature trail meanders to a mill pond; in early August, the blueberries are ready. For when the fog socks in, the large parlor has comfortable chairs and loads of books. No pets, no smoking. Open April to December.

Something of a categorical anomaly, **The Bluff House Inn** (Bluff House Rd., Rte. 186, P.O. Box 249, Gouldsboro 04607, 207/963-7805, www.bluffinn.com) is part motel, part hotel, part B&B—a seemingly successful mix in a contemporary building overlooking Frenchman Bay on the west side of the Gouldsboro Peninsula. Verandas wrap around the first and second floors, so bring binoculars for osprey and bald eagle sightings. The eight second-floor rooms (private baths; $69–105 d June through October, less off-season) are decorated in "country" fashion, with quilts on the very comfortable beds. (In hot weather, request a corner room.) Breakfast is generous continental, including excellent baked goodies. In summer, walk the steep path to the shore; in winter, you can cross-country ski on the owner's 400 acres across the road. No smoking, no pets. Open all year.

Motel with Cottages

The Pines (17 Main St., Rte. 186, Winter Harbor 04693, 207/963-2296, www.ayuh.net) occupies a prime spot (corner of Main St. and Moore Rd.) as close as you can get to the beginning of the Schoodic Loop Road. The combo of motel, log cabins, and cottages means you have some choice—but Marshall and Almeda Rust have made this a popular place, so book early. Nothing fancy here, but everything is clean and comfortable—in, yes, a pine-wooded setting. Cottages are $55 a night, log cabins are $70. Children are welcome. Open all year.

Campgrounds

On a wooded finger of land projecting eastward from the Schoodic Peninsula, **Ocean Wood Campground** (East Schoodic Rd., P.O. Box 111, Birch Harbor 04613, 207/963-7194) gets kudos for eco-sensitivity, noise control, and 16 fantastic wilderness sites, most on the ocean. Don't expect frills; nature provides the entertainment. The 70 campsites (20 with hookups) are $15–29.

Pets (leashed) and guests are allowed at regular sites, but not at the wilderness ones. No credit cards; free hot showers. Open early May to late October, the campground is a terrific base for exploring the Schoodic section of Acadia National Park. (Note, however, that the campground is at the *end* of the one-way Schoodic Loop Road. No problem hiking back into the park area the wrong way, but if you're driving or biking, you'll need to go around, about five miles, via Route 186, to do the loop.)

If Ocean Wood is full, consider booking a site at 55-acre **Lamoine State Park** (23 State Park Rd., Rte. 184, Lamoine 04605, 207/667-4778), which is along the shortcut route from Mount Desert Island to Schoodic. In July and August, when every campsite on Mount Desert Island is booked solid, those in the know go to the wooded, no-frills campground at Lamoine. Park facilities include a pebble beach and picnic area with a spectacular view, a boat-launch ramp, and a children's play area. Day-use admission is $3 adults, $1 children 5–11. Camping (61 sites) is $20 per site per night for nonresidents ($15 for Maine residents), plus a $2-per-night fee for reservations; no hookups; two-night minimum, 14-night maximum. (Camping season is mid-May to mid-September. From January 2, reserve online at www.state.me.us/doc/parks/reservations/ using a credit card, or call 207/287-3824 weekdays.) Leashed pets are allowed, but not on the beach, and cleanup is required. The park is open daily, mid-May to mid-October, and popular in winter for cross-country skiing and snowshoeing.

Seasonal Rentals

Set back from the highway 12 miles east of Ellsworth, **Sullivan Harbor Farm** (Rte. 1, P.O. Box 96, Sullivan 04664, 207/422-3735 or 800/422-4014, www.sullivanharborfarm.com) is a beautifully sited property with spectacular sea and mountain views. (The word "farm" is a bit misleading—it's a long way from agriculture.) Across the road from a quiet cove, the driveway curves through two giant outcrops higher than a car—great lookout points for watching the passing scene. Three whimsically named cottages are available by the week

($850–1,450, with three-night stays possible after Labor Day). The two-bedroom Cupcake cottage and three-bedroom Guzzle have phones and cable TV; one-bedroom Milo does not (bring a cell phone and you're all set, or use the phone in the main house). All are comfortably and attractively outfitted (views of Frenchman Bay from Guzzle and Cupcake). Ask owners Joel Frantzman and Leslie Harlow to steer you toward their favorite ponds and hiking trails—they'll even lend you a canoe or kayak. Or just hang out in the peaceful backyard or visit their spotless **Sullivan Harbor Smokehouse** and ship your pals some fantastic cold-smoked salmon (they also do hot-smoked salmon, not to mention fabulous salmon pâté). Sullivan Harbor's product has become the salmon *du jour* for some of the biggest-name restaurants and high-end provisioners in New England and beyond. Leslie's whimsical metal sculptures elevate the concept of "lawn art," and she accepts commissions under the name of Heezy How's Sculptures.

Next to their Black Duck Inn, Barry Canner and Bob Travers operate **Black Duck Properties** (Crowley Island Road, P.O. Box 39, Corea 04624, 207/963-2689 or 877/963-2689, fax 207/963-7495, www.blackduck.com), handling both home sales and seasonal rentals. Corea is the primary focus, with harborfront cottages a specialty, but they can suggest suitable spots in Winter Harbor, Gouldsboro, and Prospect Harbor. Most of the rentals forbid smoking. Weekly rental range is $600–1,500, with $800 being a fairly typical rate.

FOOD

There's no food in the park's Schoodic section, so if you're planning a picnic, you'll need to stock up along the way—in Winter Harbor or Prospect Harbor if you haven't done so earlier.

Country Stores

By definition, old-fashioned country stores are eclectic sources of local color, last-minute items, and plenty of answers to your questions. Some good examples are right in this area.

Lots of people stop at **Dunbar's Store** (Rte. 1, Sullivan 04664, 207/422-6844) just to admire the view—although in recent years it's become harder and harder to see above the trees. Then they go inside the old-fashioned market and almost always manage to make a purchase—maybe compensation of sorts for the scenery. Some even offer to buy the place. More of a grocery store and a gossip center than a fast-food source, Dunbar's is open 8 A.M.–9 P.M. Monday–Saturday and 9 A.M.–6 P.M. Sunday, all year.

Farther east on Route 1, in a new building that replaced a half-century-old country store, **Young's Market** (Rte. 1, Gouldsboro 04607, 207/963-7774) also has a fabulous view—along with pizza, gasoline, ATM, fishing gear and bait, auto parts, and more. It's open 5 A.M.–9 P.M. daily, all year.

Ice cream from the traditional soda fountain is the specialty at **Gerrish's Store** (352 Main St., Winter Harbor 04693, 207/963-5575), officially the J. M. Gerrish Store. The only hitch is that it's seasonal, open May to December. And it's become a bit yuppified, so penny candy and postcards coexist with gourmet goodies and designer coffee. But no matter; it's fun. Open 8 A.M.– 5 P.M. daily.

In "downtown" Prospect Harbor is the best picnic solution in the area. The **Downeast Deli** (Rtes. 186 and 195, Prospect Harbor 04669, 207/963-2700) will fix you right up with a footlong hoagie for $5.50–7.25. There are a dozen other sandwich choices (even PB&J), plus hot hoagies, hot dogs, reubens, and pizza. Service is swift. The deli is open 5 A.M.–9 P.M. Monday–Thursday, 5 A.M.–10 P.M. Friday and Saturday, and 7 A.M.–8 P.M. Sunday.

Family Restaurants

Don't be put off by the lobster "sculpture" outside **Ruth & Wimpy's Kitchen** (Rte. 1, R.R. 1, Box 405, Hancock 04640, 207/422-3723); you'll probably see a crowd as well. This family-fare standby serves hefty dinner sandwiches ($4–7), seafood and steak ($7–15), and exotic cocktails, as well as lobster dinners, pizza, and a sense of humor. Bring the kids. Five miles east of Ellsworth, close to the Hancock Point turnoff,

Ruth & Wimpy's is open all year except January for lunch and dinner.

Get your dose of local color at **Chase's Restaurant** (193 Main St., Winter Harbor 04693, 207/963-7171), the best place for grub and gossip in Winter Harbor. This seasoned booth-and-counter operation turns out first-rate fish chowder, fries, and onion rings. No credit cards. It's open all year for breakfast, lunch, and dinner.

Fine Dining

Besides the restaurants listed below, consider the elegant dining rooms at **Le Domaine** and **The Crocker House,** described under *Accommodations.*

The Fisherman's Inn (7 Newman St., Rte. 186, Winter Harbor 04693, 207/963-5585, www.fishermansinnrestaurant.com), established in 1947, has had a roller-coaster history, with good phases and bad ones. Now it's in a decidedly "up" phase, under the ownership of Kathy Johnson and her award-winning chef/husband, Carl. The only remaining tradition seems to be the "gourmet cheese spread" served to every table—but you'll also have a sample of salmon pâté from Carl's latest venture, Grindstone Neck of Maine (excellent smoked seafood, www.grindstoneneck.com). As is probably obvious, seafood is the specialty here, and it's all carefully prepared. Carl's won several awards for his New England clam chowder ($4.95). Asian influences are evident, too. Entrée range is $15–22 (the gigantic Fisherman's Mixed Grill is $27). The ambience is decidedly casual, with wooden booth seating. Open for dinner (4:30–9 P.M.) daily, Memorial Day to mid-October, and for lunch (11:30 A.M.–2:30 P.M.) in midsummer.

Directly across the street from the Fisherman's Inn, and looking rather like a Portland restaurant parachuted into this coastal village, stands **Mama's Boy Bistro** (10 Main St., Rte. 186, Winter Harbor 04693, 207/963-2365, www.mamasboybistro.com). Begun as a small-scale bakery, then a bakery-café, it's now a full-scale brunch-and-dinner place, in a multi-peaked building with a huge open cooking area, a light woody feel, and the waitstaff garbed in big-city black-and-white duds. Tables under the roofline overlook the harbor; mezzanine tables overlook the cooking area. A lovely Japanese garden greets you at the entrance. Co-owner Lucas St. Clair earned his chef's stripes at Cordon Bleu's London school (and some survival skills from the National Outdoor Leadership School) before launching the bistro with co-owner Jennifer Amara. (The name started out as something of a joke. Mama, a dedicated environmental activist who founded the Burt's Bees empire, helped her son establish his enterprise on a sound financial footing. The bistro, fortunately, is no joke.) Entrées are $16–25; everything is à la carte, so the bill adds up. (Try the peekytoe crab-cakes appetizer, $10.) Open daily, Memorial Day to Labor Day, for dinner (5–9:30 P.M.) and Sunday brunch (10 A.M.–2 p.m.); open Wednesday through Sunday from Labor Day to Columbus Day, and weekends until New Year's Day.

Less pretentious than the bistro, but more sophisticated than its name sounds, is family-owned **Bunker's Wharf** (260 East Schoodic Dr., Birch Harbor 04613, 207/963-2244), a mile from the end of the Schoodic Loop Road (and a stop on the Island Explorer bus route). In good weather, try for a table on the patio, where you're practically in the harbor. Well, even inside you're almost in the water—two dining rooms overlook a small working wharf. It's one of those places that "feels like Maine," yet your dinner comes with herb focaccia and olive oil, and entrées ($15–23) have such untypical Maine sauces as thyme *velouté* and lime *beurre blanc*. And a steamed lobster dinner comes with carrots, green beans, and cornbread pudding ($21.95). Soup-and-salad lunches run $4–11, the latter for lobster stew. Open noon to 10 P.M. daily for lunch and dinner, late May into December. (A massive stone fireplace takes the chill off bad-weather days.)

Lobster in the Rough

Thank the Ellsworth-based Frenchman Bay Conservancy for buying the four-acre **Tidal Falls Preserve** (off Eastside Rd., Hancock), overlooking Frenchman Bay's only reversing falls (roiling water when the tide turns), and opening it to public access. When a half-century-old lobster pound went on the market a few years ago, the conservancy hastened into action, raised more than half a million dollars, and purchased the property. Today, a dozen picnic tables on the lawn overlook the falls, and seals often haul out on nearby ledges. It's an idyllic spot. In summer, **Tidal Falls Lobster** (207/422-6457) leases the site, featuring lobsters (at the going rate), lobster rolls, steamed mussels, and even steak ($16.95) and hot dogs ($2.50), as well as a few appetizers and side dishes (garlic bread is $2.50). A small building provides shelter for diners in poor weather. The preserve is open year-round, sunrise to sunset; the lobster pound is open noon–9 P.M. Thursday–Sunday and 5–9 P.M. Monday–Wednesday, late June through Labor Day. From Route 1 in Hancock, watch for Eastside Rd. (on the right if you're going north). Turn and continue to the signposted left for the preserve (the last .1 mile is unpaved).

INFORMATION AND SERVICES

Information about Acadia National Park on the Schoodic Peninsula is available on Mount Desert Island at the park's **Hulls Cove Visitor Center** and at the **Thompson Island Visitor Center,** at the head of the island.

To plan ahead, see the Acadia website (www.nps.gov/acad/), where you can download a Schoodic map. To see the Island Explorer bus schedule for Schoodic as well as all of Mount Desert Island, log on to www.exploreacadia.com. The Bar Harbor Ferry schedule is at www .barharborferry.com.

For advance information about Eastern Hancock County, contact the **Schoodic Peninsula Chamber of Commerce** (P.O. Box 381, Winter Harbor 04693, 207/963-7658, www .acadia-schoodic.org) and request its handy map and brochure, revised annually. The nearest convenient **information center** is run by the Ellsworth Area Chamber of Commerce (P.O. Box 267, Ellsworth 04605, 207/667-5584, www

.ellsworthchamber.org), on the Route 1/3 commercial strip, close to where the highway forks toward Mount Desert Island and Eastern Hancock County. It's open daily in July and August; Monday–Saturday from mid-June to mid-September; and weekdays 9 A.M.–4:30 P.M. the rest of the year.

Emergencies

For any emergency in this area, whether in the Schoodic section of Acadia or in other parts of Eastern Hancock County, **dial 911.** The nearest hospital is **Maine Coast Memorial Hospital** in Ellsworth.

Blue Hill Peninsula

As the crow flies, it's a short hop between Acadia National Park on Mount Desert Island and the park acreage on Isle au Haut. By boat, it's a brief cruise, but you'll need your own yacht or kayak. Overland, however, you'll exit Mount Desert Island, cut through Ellsworth, and then traverse the Blue Hill Peninsula. Near the tip of the peninsula, you'll cross the soaring bridge onto Little Deer Isle and then continue to Deer Isle to reach Stonington, from where the ferry departs for Isle au Haut. You'll cover about 55 miles, plus the boat trip (45 minutes) across the bay to Isle au Haut. The distance doesn't sound like much, but the winding two-lane roads make for a slow albeit lovely meander. If you're driving directly from Bar Harbor to Stonington, allow at least two hours.

So don't rush it. Allow enough time to explore Blue Hill and Castine (and surrounding towns), then continue to Little Deer Isle and Deer Isle. Spend a night or two, poke into the many shops and galleries, hike Blue Hill Mountain or wander Castine's streets, try the restaurants, and go biking or kayaking.

Blue Hill shorefront

The **Blue Hill Peninsula,** more than once dubbed "The Fertile Crescent" (although hardly reminiscent of the Mesopotamian version), is unique. Few other Maine locales harbor such a high concentration of artisans, musicians, and hyperactive retirees juxtaposed with top-flight wooden boat builders, lobstermen, and umpteenth-generation Mainers. Perhaps surprisingly, the mix seems to work.

The peninsula—part of the **East Penobscot Bay Region**—comprises several towns and villages with markedly distinctive personalities: **Blue Hill, Surry, Brooklin, Brooksville, Sedgwick,** and **Castine.**

Blue Hill

Twelve miles south of Route 1 is the hub of the peninsula, Blue Hill (pop. 2,390), exuding charm from its handsome old homes to its waterfront setting to the shops, restaurants, and galleries that boost its appeal.

Eons back, Native American summer folk gave the name *Awanadjo* ("small, misty mountain") to the minimountain that looms over the town and draws the eye for miles around. The first permanent settlers arrived after the French and Indian War, in the late 18th century, and established mills and shipyards. More than 100 ships were built here between Blue Hill's incorporation in 1789, and 1882—bringing prosperity to the entire peninsula.

Critical to the town's early expansion was its first clergyman, Jonathan Fisher, a remarkable fellow who—with perhaps a touch of hyperbole—has even been likened to Leonardo da Vinci. In 1803, Fisher founded Blue Hill Academy (predecessor of today's George Stevens Academy), then built his home (now a museum), and eventually left an immense legacy of inventions, paintings, engravings, and poetry.

Throughout the 19th century and into the 20th, Blue Hill's granite industry boomed, reaching its peak in the 1880s. Scratch the Brooklyn Bridge and the New York Stock Exchange, and you'll find granite from Blue Hill's quarries. Around 1879, the discovery of gold and silver brought a flurry of interest, but little came of it. Copper was also found here, but quantities of it, too, were limited.

At the height of industrial prosperity, tourism took hold, attracting steamboat-borne summer boarders. Many succumbed to the scenery, bought land, and built waterfront summer homes. Thank these summer folk and their offspring for the fact that music has long been a big deal in Blue Hill. The Kneisel Hall Chamber Music School, established in 1902, continues to rank high among the nation's summer music colonies. (New York City's Blue Hill Troupe, devoted to Gilbert and Sullivan operettas, was named for the longtime summer home of the troupe's founders.)

SIGHTS

A few of Blue Hill's elegant houses have been converted to museums, inns, restaurants, even some offices and shops, so you can see them from the inside out. To appreciate the private residences, you'll want to walk, bike, or drive around town.

Parson Fisher House

The 1814 Parson Fisher House, named for the brilliant Renaissance man who arrived in Blue Hill in 1794, immerses visitors in period furnishings and Jonathan Fisher lore. And Fisher's feats are breathtaking: a Harvard-educated preacher who also managed to be an accomplished painter, poet, mathematician, naturalist, linguist, inventor, cabinetmaker, farmer, architect, and printmaker. In his spare time, whenever that was, he fathered nine children. Fisher also pitched in to help build this yellow house on Tenney Hill (44 Mines Rd., Rte. 15/176, P.O. Box 527, Blue Hill 04614, 207/374-2459, www.jonathanfisherhouse.org), which served as the Congregational Church parsonage. Now it contains intriguing items created by Fisher, memorabilia that volunteer tour

guides delight in explaining. Don't miss it. Open 2–5 P.M. Monday–Saturday July–mid-September. Admission is $5.

Holt House

In downtown Blue Hill, a few steps off Main Street, stands the Holt House (Water St., Blue Hill 04614, 207/326-8250), home of the Blue Hill Historical Society. Built in 1815, the Federal-style building contains restored stenciling, period decor, and masses of memorabilia contributed by local residents. Open 1–4 P.M. Tuesday and Friday, July and August.

Bagaduce Music Lending Library

At the foot of Greene's Hill in Blue Hill is one of Maine's more unusual institutions, a library where you can borrow by mail or in person from a collection of more than 175,000 scores and sheet music. Somehow this seems entirely appropriate for a community that's a magnet for music lovers. Annual membership is $10 ($5 for students); the library publishes six catalogs of its holdings; borrowing fees range from $1 to $2.50 per piece—and you can keep it for up to two months. The Bagaduce Music Lending Library (3 Music Library Ln., Rte. 172, P.O. Box 829, Blue

"Jonathan Fisher" plays host at the Parson Fisher House

Hill 04614, 207/374-5454, www.bagaducemusic .org) is open 10 A.M.–3 P.M. Tuesday, Wednesday, and Friday all year, or by appointment.

The Old Cemetery

Walk or drive up Union Street (Route 177), past George Stevens Academy, and wander The Old Cemetery, established in 1794. If gnarled trees and ancient headstones intrigue you, you'll be pleased—there aren't many good-sized Maine cemeteries older than this one.

PARKS AND RECREATION

Blue Hill Mountain

"Mountain" seems a fancy label for a 943-footer, yet Blue Hill stands alone, visible even from Maine's Midcoast Region. The surrounding land and its mile-long Osgood Trail are owned by the

Blue Hill Heritage Trust (P.O. Box 222, Blue Hill 04614, 207/374-5118). Pick up a brochure/map from the chamber of commerce office. On a clear day, head for the summit and take in the wraparound view. Climb the fire-tower steps (but not the communication tower) for even more of the view. In mid-June, the lupines along the way are breathtaking; in August, the wild blueberries are ripe for the picking; in fall, the colors are spectacular—with reddened blueberry barrens added to the variegated foliage. Go early in the day; it's a popular easy-to-moderate hike, 1.5–2 hours round-trip. A short loop on the open lower slopes takes only half an hour. Take Route 15 (Pleasant Street) to Mountain Road. Turn right and go .8 mile to the trailhead (on the left) and the small parking area (on the right). You can also walk (uphill) the mile from the village. The trail can be squishy, especially in the wooded sections, so you'll want rubberized or waterproof shoes or boots.

Scenic Routes

Parker Point Road (turn off Route 15 at the Blue Hill Library) takes you from Blue Hill to Blue Hill Falls the back way, with vistas en route toward Acadia National Park. For other great views, drive the length of **Newbury Neck,** in nearby Surry, or head west on Route 15/176 toward Sedgwick, Brooksville, and beyond.

Golf and Tennis

The golf course at the Blue Hill Country Club is private; see the next chapter for info on Deer Isle's nine-hole Island Country Club, where there are also public tennis courts.

Biking

Most of Maine's side roads are not especially bike-friendly, so be especially cautious, alert to traffic, and wary of soft (as in sandy) shoulders and paving dropoffs. If you're arriving in Blue Hill via Ellsworth, rentals are available at the **Bar Harbor Bicycle Shop** (193 Main St., Ellsworth 04605, 207/667-6886, www.barharborbike .com). Full-day rental for a medium-tech bike is $17. In Blue Hill, contact Anna Snow for mountain bikes at **Rocky Coast Outfitters**

© KATHLEEN M. BRANDES

morning mist over Blue Hill Peninsula

(Grindleville Rd., P.O. Box 351, Blue Hill 04614, 207/374-8866). Both firms also handle kayak rentals.

Kids' Stuff

A great way to raise kids' environmental consciousness is to enroll them in summer activities sponsored by the **MERI Center for Marine Studies** (55 Main Street, P.O. Box 1652, Blue Hill 04614, 207/374-2135, www.meriresearch.org). During July and August, MERI (Marine Environmental Research Institute), a nonprofit marine-ecology organization, schedules daylong island trips, "ecocruises," and beach walks, plus a variety of naturalist-led morning and afternoon programs geared to specific age groups. (Fees run $20–35 a person; cruises depart from Brooklin, south of Blue Hill.) Special family activities occur two or three days a week, and there are evening lectures. The MERI Center, which has a touch tank, a marine lending library, and exhibit space, is open all year, Monday through Saturday.

At the end of Water Street, just beyond the hospital, **Blue Hill Town Park** has picnic tables, a very creative playground (including little houses), and a terrific view. Pick up picnic fixings at The Vinery or Pain de Famille or the Blue Hill Co-op and bring it all here. A playground is also next to the **Blue Hill Consolidated School** (off High Street).

Getting Afloat

A favorite spot for experienced kayakers and canoeists is **Blue Hill Falls,** which churns with white water when the tide turns. Check for times of high and low tide. Roadside parking is illegal there, but the law is too often ignored. The Route 175 bridge is narrow, and cars often stop suddenly as they come over the hill, so be particularly cautious here.

For guided kayak tours, see *Getting Afloat* in the *Deer Isle* section of the following chapter.

Unless you own a boat or know a member of the Kollegewidgwok Yacht Club in East Blue Hill (207/374-5581), there's no sailing out of Blue Hill. If you're trailing a boat, use the public boat launch down on the harbor. *Kollegewidgwok,* incidentally, is a Penobscot Indian word meaning "blue hill on shining green water."

ENTERTAINMENT AND EVENTS

Variety and serendipity are the keys here. Check local calendar listings and tune in to radio station **WERU** (89.9 and 102.9 FM, www.weru.org), the area's own community radio; there might be announcements of concerts by local resident pianist Paul Sullivan or the Bagaduce Chorale, or maybe a contra dance or a tropical treat from Carl Chase's Atlantic Clarion Steel Band or Flash-in-the-Pans Community Band. In 2003, *Esquire* named WERU one of the nation's top 12 radio stations. WERU's *Salt Air* program guide appears quarterly, or you can check its website. In 1997, after nearly 10 years in a converted henhouse in East Blue Hill, the station moved its headquarters to Route 1 in East Orland. WERU's summer highlight is the annual **Full Circle Summer Fair,** usually held the second weekend in August (Sat. evening and 9 A.M.–5 P.M. Sun.) at the Blue Hill Fairgrounds (Rte. 172, on the outskirts of downtown Blue Hill). Eclectic music (of course), politically correct (and delicious) food, great crafts, and lots more—including talks on social justice and the environment. A unique event, often with big-name speakers and performers (admission $8).

Music lovers will enjoy the **Kneisel Hall Chamber Music Festival.** Since the early 20th century, chamber-music students have been spending summers perfecting their skills and demonstrating their prowess at the Kneisel Hall Chamber Music School (Pleasant St., Route 15, P.O. Box 648, Blue Hill 04614, 207/374-2203, www.kneisel.org). Faculty concerts run Friday evening (8:15 P.M.) and Sunday afternoon (4 P.M.), late June to mid-August. The concert schedule is published in the spring, and reserved-seating tickets ($26 inside, $19 on the veranda outside; nonrefundable) can be ordered by phone. There is also unreserved tent seating ($10) for the Friday evening and Sunday afternoon concerts. An even less expensive option is a $30 pass that provides an unreserved ticket for FanFare events: eight young artist concerts (four in July and four in August, at 2 and 7:30 P.M.), open rehearsals on Friday

(9 A.M.) for faculty concerts, and half a dozen evening master classes (8 P.M.). Kneisel Hall is about a half mile from the center of town.

Chamber music continues in winter thanks to the volunteer efforts of the **Blue Hill Concert Association.** Five or six concerts are performed between January and March at the Congregational Church, a handsome, traditional New England spired edifice on Main Street. For the schedule, contact the Blue Hill Concert Association, P.O. Box 140, Blue Hill 04614.

In late July or early August, the **Academy Antiques Show** draws a huge crowd to the George Stevens Academy on Union Street in Blue Hill. Formerly held in Ellsworth, this three-day event has been going since 1937 and is awaited all year. Admission is $7 and lunch and tea are available. Doors open at 10 A.M. each day. (For the exact date, check the website (www.maineantiquedigest .com) of the *Maine Antique Digest,* a nationally renowned monthly publication that includes a show and auction calendar in each issue.

Held at the Blue Hill Fairgrounds (Rte. 172, Blue Hill, 207/374-3701) during the extended Labor Day weekend (first weekend in September), **Blue Hill Fair** is one of the state's best agricultural fairs. Besides the food booths (good-for-you fare competes with fried dough), a carnival, fireworks, sheepdog trials, and live musical entertainment, you can check out the blue-ribbon winners for finest quilt, beefiest bull, or largest squash. (No pets are allowed.)

SHOPPING
Antiques and Art Galleries

If folk art is your interest, stop in at **Anne Wells Antiques** (Rte. 172, Blue Hill 04614, 207/374-2093), where painted furniture and hooked rugs are specialties. Open 10 A.M.–5 P.M. weekdays, May to mid-October. Off-season, call for an appointment.

Blue Hill Antiques (8 Water St., Blue Hill 04614, 207/374-2199 or 207/326-4973, fax 326-9772)—specializing in 18th- and 19th-century French and American furniture—attracts a high-end clientele (Martha Stewart has been spotted here). Open 10 A.M.–5 P.M. Monday–Saturday, otherwise by appointment.

The same patrons seek out Brad Emerson's **Emerson Antiques** (Water St., Blue Hill 04614, 207/374-5140), concentrating on early Americana, such as hooked rugs and ship models. Open 10 A.M.–5 P.M. Monday–Saturday, mid-May to mid-October, otherwise by appointment.

Across from the Blue Hill Fairgrounds stands the new home of **Belcher's Antiques** (232 Ellsworth Rd., Rte. 172, Blue Hill 04614, 207/374-3751, www.belchersantiques.com), formerly headquartered in Deer Isle. Twig furniture is a specialty, along with a broad range of eclectic collectibles, including great old signs. Open daily in summer; call ahead off season.

The **Liros Gallery** (14 Parker Point Rd., P.O. Box 946, Blue Hill 04614, 207/374-5370 or 800/287-5370, www.lirosgallery.com) has been dealing in Russian icons since the mid-1960s. Prices are high, but the icons are fascinating. The gallery also carries Currier & Ives prints, antique maps, and 19th-century British and American paintings. Open all year: 9 A.M.–5 P.M. Monday–Friday, 10 A.M.–5 P.M. Saturday. In July and August, Serge Liros is also open Sundays (noon–5 P.M.)

Count on seeing outstanding contemporary art during the monthly summer shows at the **Leighton Gallery** (24 Parker Point Rd., Blue Hill 04614, 207/374-5001, www.leightongallery.com). Owner Judith Leighton has earned a reputation as one of Maine's best art connoisseurs/dealers. Don't miss the sculpture garden out back. Open 10:30 A.M.–5 P.M., Monday–Saturday and noon–5 P.M. Sunday, mid-May–mid-October.

If bronze sculpture appeals, check out the **Jud Hartmann Gallery** (Main St. at Rte. 15, P.O. Box 753, Blue Hill 04614, 207/374-9917 or 207/359-2544, www.judhartmanngallery.com). It carries Hartmann's figures—many of Native Americans—and paintings by Maine and non-Maine artists. The spacious, well-lighted gallery space is open 10 A.M.–5 P.M. Monday–Saturday, mid-June to mid-September.

Describing the wildly whimsical figures created by **Laura Balombini** (Mattson Rd., P.O. Box 733, Blue Hill 04614, 207/374-5142, www.lbalombini.com) is tough. Her materials are wire and polymer clay—combined magically. The shapes are great, the colors are brilliant—each piece is a "wanna-have." Sign up for one of her two-day workshops ($150) and learn to make your own magic. Her studio is open by appointment throughout the year; call ahead for directions (she's on the outskirts of town).

Books

Blue Hill's literate population manages to support two full-service, year-round, independent bookstores. Best selection is at **Blue Hill Books** (2 Pleasant St., Rte. 15, Blue Hill 04614, 207/374-5632, www.bluehillbooks.com), thanks to knowledgeable owners Nick Sichterman and Mariah Hughs. Open 9:30 A.M.–5:30 P.M. Monday–Saturday all year; also Sunday in July and August. The store organizes an "authors series" during the summer. Around the corner, **North Light Books** (Main St., Blue Hill 04614, 207/374-5422), carrying a healthy inventory of Maine and children's books, is open all year.

Crafts, Gifts, and More

Blue Hill has two noted, year-round pottery workshops, both turning out wheel-thrown ware with distinctive lead-free glazes—not surprising, since one workshop evolved from the other. First came **Rowantrees Pottery** (Union St., Rte. 177, P.O. Box 802, Blue Hill 04614, 207/374-5535, www.rowantreespottery.com), then **Rackliffe Pottery** (132 Ellsworth Rd., Rte. 172, Box 393, Blue Hill 04614, 207/374-2297 or 888/631-3321, www.acadiainfo.com/rackliffepot). Rowantrees is open 8:30 A.M.–5 P.M. Monday–Saturday June–September. Winter hours are 8:30 A.M.–3:30 P.M. weekdays. Rackliffe is open 8 A.M.–4 P.M. Monday–Saturday, plus noon–4 P.M. Sunday in July and August.

On Tenney Hill, about two miles from downtown, is a "don't miss." **Mark Bell Pottery** (Rte. 15, Blue Hill 04614, 207/374-5881), in a tiny building signaled only by a small roadside sign, is the home of exquisite, award-winning porcelain by the eponymous potter. The delicacy of each vase, bowl, or whatever, is astonishing, and the glazes are gorgeous. Open daily all year (he and his family live on the premises).

On Main Street in Blue Hill, **North Country Textiles** (Levy House, 207/374-2715, www.northcountrytextiles.com) and **Handworks Gallery** (Levy House, P.O. Box 918, 207/374-5613) are craft galleries featuring high-quality work by Maine artisans. Hard-to-resist and reasonably priced baby blankets, jackets, and placemats are specialties of the veteran North Country enterprise. North Country is open all year: 10 A.M.–5 P.M. Monday–Saturday in summer, Thursday–Saturday in winter. Handworks is open 10 A.M.–5 P.M. daily, May–December.

Across Main Street from Handworks (owned by his wife, Marcia), Peter Stremlau has opened **New Cargoes** (49 Main St., P.O. Box 1105, Blue Hill 04614, 207/374-3733, fax 374-5599), following somewhat in the Pier One/Crate & Barrel tradition. Furniture, linens, notecards, candles, and on and on. The shop name is apt—new things arrive on a regular basis. Bet you can't walk out of here empty-handed. Open all year—daily in summer, three days a week in the depth of winter.

Just up the street from New Cargoes is **The Clown** (5 Main St., Blue Hill 04614, 207/374-3838, www.the-clown.com), an impressive blend of European antiques, wine, art, and gourmet condiments—most with an Italian accent. Starting with a shop in Stonington, owners Kyle Wolfe and Martin Kolk expanded to Portland and now to Blue Hill—plus they schedule weeklong wine, art, language, and food workshops at Tramonti, their farm in Tuscany ($2,500 plus airfare). The Blue Hill shop is open all year, 9:30 A.M.–5:30 P.M. Tuesday–Saturday (plus Sunday, 1–5 P.M. in July and August).

Blue Hill Wine Shop (Main St., P.O. Box 71, Blue Hill 04614, 207/374-2161), tucked into a converted horse barn, carries a huge selection of wines, plus teas, coffees, and blended tobaccos and unusual pipes for diehard, upscale smokers. Monthly wine tastings (2–5 P.M.,

last Saturday of the month) are always an adventure. Open 10 A.M.–5:30 P.M. Monday–Saturday all year.

And then a little farther afield . . . The Himalayas meet Blue Hill at Jeff Kaley's **Asian World Imports** (Pleasant St., Rte. 15, P.O. Box 1234, Blue Hill 04614, tel./fax 207/374-2284, www.asianworldimports.com). A Nepal Peace Corps veteran, Kaley seeks out eco-sensitive suppliers using fair-trade practices, bringing back custom-made Nepalese, Tibetan, Indian, Thai, and Vietnamese clothing, jewelry, and artifacts, as well as organic Himalayan tea. The shop is *loaded* with treasures. Open 10 A.M.–6 P.M. Monday–Saturday late May to early September, other months by chance or appointment. Jeff "gives back" by supporting schools and construction projects in Nepal; he also leads small-group cultural tours in Nepal and Tibet; contact him for details.

Local gardeners, farmers, and craftspeople peddle their wares at the Blue Hill Farmers' Market. It's a particularly enduring market, well worth a visit.

Farmers' Market and Natural Foods

Local gardeners, farmers, and craftspeople peddle their wares at the Blue Hill Farmers' Market, set up 9–11:30 A.M. Saturday. It's a particularly enduring market, well worth a visit. Demonstrations by guest chefs are often on the agenda. The major season is Memorial Day weekend to Labor Day weekend, at the Blue Hill Fairgrounds (Rte. 172, just north of downtown). During September, the market is held (same hours) in the Liberty School parking lot (South St., Rte. 172, at the opposite end of town).

Also see the *Blue Hill Food Co-op and Café*, later in this chapter.

ACCOMMODATIONS

Don't visit Blue Hill for cheap sleeps or eats; visit for the handful of select inns, B&Bs, restaurants, and shops. Remember, though, that rooms are scarce in July and August, as well as on summer and fall holiday weekends (Memorial Day, Labor Day, Columbus Day). Reserve well ahead or show up during quieter times.

The nearest **campgrounds** are in East Orland and Ellsworth, not far away.

Inns and B&Bs

On a quiet side street close to town, **The Blue Hill Inn** (Union St., Rte. 177, P.O. Box 403, Blue Hill 04614, 207/374-2844 or 800/826-7415, fax 207/374-2829, www.bluehillinn.com) has been welcoming guests since 1840. If you're trying to imagine a classic country inn, this would be it. Hosts Mary and Don Hartley do everything right. Stay here if you enjoy antiques, warm hospitality, and classic New England inns. Nine rooms and two suites, all with private baths, boast real chandeliers, four-posters, down comforters, fancy linens, working fireplaces, braided and Oriental rugs. The third-floor garret suite is ideal for families with well-behaved children; a first-floor room is wheelchair-accessible. Rear rooms overlook the extensive cutting garden, with chairs and a hammock. The library, dominated by a Persian chandelier, has masses of local information on an old country-store counter. Nonalcoholic refreshments are available all day; superb hors d'oeuvres are served 6–7 P.M. in two elegant parlors or the garden. Doubles are $138–185, depending on the season. A suite in the elegant adjacent Cape House—the ground floor of a tiny dwelling—is $220–255, depending on season (off-season, it's available for $165 a day). Twice a year (usually May and October), the inn puts on gala wine-dinner weekends; the multicourse gourmet dinners are outstanding. At other times, there are excellent restaurants nearby. The innkeepers will arrange for Kneisel Hall tickets, kayak rentals, cruises, massages, and more. Two-day minimum on summer weekends; no TV, no smoking, no pets; children over 10 are welcome. Open mid-May through October.

Two miles north of town, at the **Blue Hill Farm Country Inn** (Rte. 15, P.O. Box 437, Blue Hill 04614, 207/374-5126, www .bluehillfarminn.com), a huge refurbished barn serves as the gathering spot for guests. If the weather is lousy, you can plop down in front of the oversize woodstove and start in on cribbage or other games. Antique sleigh-runner banisters lead to the barn's seven second-floor rooms—all with private baths, skylights, hooked rugs, and quilts ($99 d, June through October; $85 the rest of the year). Breakfast is generous continental. During the summer, visiting jazz or classical musicians sometimes entertain in the barn, but it all eases off early. A wing of the farmhouse has seven more rooms with shared baths and more quilts ($85 d, June through October; $75 the rest of the year; a cozy single is $75, lower off-season). On the inn's 48 acres are well-cleared nature trails, an 18th-century cellar hole, and a duck pond. Limited accommodations for kids under 12. No TV, no smoking, no pets. Open all year.

There's something about a lighthouse, even an unofficial one. Plan ahead and you can book the Lighthouse Suite, in the base of the round tower at **First Light Bed & Breakfast** (821 East Blue Hill Rd., Blue Hill 04614, 207/374-5879, www.firstlightbandb.com). Innkeeper Beverly Bartlett, a retired nursing professor, has three lighthouse-themed rooms in her B&B: the suite (private bath) plus two others (shared bath) that can be combined as a suite. The light tower, built by an eccentric previous owner, is the perfect place for sealwatching, birding, or just plain soaking up the wraparound view. Rooms are $105–175 d (two-night minimum), with an amazing breakfast—how can anyone resist blueberry-stuffed French toast? No pets (two long-haired dachshunds play the roles of assistant innkeepers), no smoking, no credit cards. Open all year. From downtown Blue Hill, take Route 176 toward East Blue Hill. When you reach a cove spanned by a bridge, First Light will be ahead of you, on your right—can't miss it.

Motel

Blue Hill's only motel is the **Heritage Motor Inn** (60 Ellsworth Rd., Rte. 172, P.O. Box 453, Blue Hill 04614, 207/374-5646, www .bhheritagemotorinn.com), a clean, no-frills, 22-room year-round place on Greene's Hill. Rooms have cable TV, a/c, coffeemakers, and great views of Blue Hill Bay. Doubles are $95–98 in July and August, $62–83 other months. No pets, no smoking. Open all year. (The motel also rents townhouses by the week—$1,150 in July and August.)

Seasonal Rentals

Weekly (or longer-term) rentals can pay off if you have a large family or are planning a group vacation. The Blue Hill Peninsula has lots of rental cottages, camps, and houses, but the trick is to plan ahead. This is a popular area in summer, and many renters sign up for the following year before they leave town. For information, contact **Peninsula Property Rentals** (Main St., P.O. Box 611, Blue Hill 04614, 207/374-2428, fax 374-5496, www.peninsulapropertyrentals.com).

FOOD

Lunch and More

Picnic fare is available at **Merrill & Hinckley** (Union St., Blue Hill 04614, 207/374-2821), a quirky, 150-year-old, family-owned grocery/general/country store. Open 7 A.M.–9 P.M. Monday–Saturday, 8 A.M.–9 P.M. Sunday. M&H also carries liquor and wine.

Want great pizza? Go directly to **Ovenworks** (Water St., Blue Hill 04614, 207/374-5775). Try a large (18-inch) "Nadia"—olives, roasted garlic, prosciutto, onions, and fresh tomatoes—for $17. Ovenworks also has small (16-inch) pizzas, "killer calzones," hot and cold subs, and vegetarian sandwiches. Pizza slices are available at lunchtime, and coffee and pastries in the morning. (Or, if you're craving solitude, start your day with Italian scrambled eggs with *garlic bread,* $5.75.) Open 9 A.M.–9 P.M. Tuesday–Saturday all year.

The **Blue Hill Food Co-Op and Café** (Greene's Hill, Rte. 172, P.O. Box 1133, Blue Hill 04614, 207/374-2165; café 207/374-8999) sells organic produce and grains, cheeses, organic coffee, and more. Breads are terrific here. Sandwiches, salads, and soups—many with ethnic over- and undertones—are available in the café. The staff will pack it all up for a picnic, too. Hours are 8 A.M.–7 P.M. Monday–Friday, 8 A.M.–6 P.M. Saturday, and 10 A.M.–5 P.M. Sunday. The market is open to the public; co-op members receive a discount.

On the other side of the village, **Pain de Famille** (Main St., Blue Hill 04614, 207/374-3839), has earned an outstanding reputation for its unusual selection of breads. Not as organized for picnics as the co-op, but you can pick up Greek pockets or readymade sandwiches and designer juices. Obviously, bread is the thing (fantastic focaccia). Open 7 A.M.–6 P.M. Monday–Thursday, 7 A.M.–7 P.M. Friday, and 9 A.M.–1 P.M. Saturday and Sunday.

Fine Dining

Save your money and dine at **Arborvine** (Main St., Blue Hill 04614, 207/374-2119, www.arborvine.com), but don't plan to show up in summer without a reservation. Chef/owner John Hikade and his wife, Beth, finally have their own restaurant, after various locales (and a catering business) in the area. A conscientiously renovated two-century-old Cape-style house has four dining areas, each with a different feel and understated decor. Entrées are in the $18–24 range, and there's always at least one for vegetarians. The freshest of seafood and local produce are hallmarks here, with everything artistically presented. The wine list is smallish but select. Open for dinner all year: 5:30–9 P.M. Tuesday–Sunday in summer, Friday–Sunday in winter.

Attached to Arborvine at the rear of the house is **The Vinery** (207/374-2441), a bright, modern wine bar that also serves light lunches noon–2 P.M. Wednesday–Saturday. In good weather, aim for one of the tables in the lovely garden—no water view, but a great setting.

INFORMATION AND SERVICES

After years with no information center, Blue Hill finally has one—conveniently sited in the center of town: **The Blue Hill Peninsula Chamber of Commerce** (28 Water St., P.O. Box 520, Blue Hill 04614, 207/374-3242, www.bluehillpeninsula.org).

The **Blue Hill Public Library** (Main St., 207/374-5515), is open 10 A.M.–6 P.M. Tuesday, Wednesday, and Friday, 10 A.M.–8 P.M. Thursday, 10 A.M.–2 P.M. Saturday.

Newspapers

Useful local publications are Blue Hill's *Weekly Packet* and the *Ellsworth American,* both published every Thursday. The *Packet* carries extensive events listings and lots of local ads. The *Bangor Daily News* covers local news for this area but also carries state, national, and international stories.

Emergencies

For **fire and police** emergencies, call 911. To contact the **Peninsula Ambulance Corps,** call 911. The respected **Blue Hill Memorial Hospital** (57 Water St., Blue Hill 04614, 207/374-2836, www.bhmh.org) has 24-hour emergency-room service.

Public Restrooms

Blue Hill has no public restrooms, and restaurant owners aren't particularly happy about noncustomers asking to use theirs. Public buildings that have restrooms are the Blue Hill Town Hall (Main Street), Blue Hill Public Library (Main Street), and Blue Hill Memorial Hospital (Water Street).

Photo Services

Photo-developing service is available at the grocery/general store **Merrill & Hinckley** (Union St., Blue Hill 04614, 207/374-2821); it's open 7 A.M.–9 P.M. Monday–Saturday, 8 A.M.–9 P.M. Sunday. One-hour photo service is available about a mile up the Route 15 hill from downtown at **Rite-Aid** (17 So. Main St., Trade Winds Marketplace, Blue Hill 04614, 207/374-3565). The store is open 8 A.M.–9 P.M. daily.

Laundromat

The **Blue Hill Laundry** (Main St., Blue Hill, 207/374-2777) is open 7 A.M.–9 P.M. daily in summer and 7 A.M.–6 P.M. the rest of the year.

Brooklin, Brooksville, and Sedgwick

Nestled near the bottom of the Blue Hill Peninsula, between Blue Hill and Deer Isle and along the watery thoroughfare known as Eggemoggin Reach, this often-missed area offers superb hiking, kayaking, and sailing, plus historic homes and unique shops, studios, lodgings, and personalities.

Best-known town is **Brooklin** (pop. 841), thanks to two magazines: *The New Yorker* and *WoodenBoat.* Wordsmiths extraordinaire E. B. and Katharine White "dropped out" to Brooklin in the 1930s and forever afterward dispatched their splendid material for *The New Yorker* from here (and the beloved children's story *Charlotte's Web* was created here). The Whites' former home, a handsome colonial not open to the public, is on Route 175 in North Brooklin, 6.5 miles from the Blue Hill Falls bridge.

In 1977, *WoodenBoat* magazine moved its headquarters to Brooklin, where its 60-acre shoreside estate attracts builders and sailors and dreamers from all over the globe.

Nearby **Brooksville** (pop. 911) drew the late Helen and Scott Nearing, whose *Living the Good Life* made them role models for back-to-the-landers. Their compound now verges on "must-see" status for devotees. Buck's Harbor, a section of Brooksville, was the setting for *One Morning in Maine,* one of the late Robert McCloskey's beloved children's books. (Until his death in 2003, McCloskey lived on Scott Island, off Little Deer Isle.)

Oldest of the three towns is **Sedgwick** (pop. 1,102, incorporated in 1789), which once included all of Brooklin and part of Brooksville. Now wedged *between* Brooklin and Brooksville, it includes the hamlet of Sargentville, the Caterpillar Hill scenic overlook, and a well-preserved complex of historic buildings.

The influx of pilgrims continues in this peninsula—many of them artist wannabes bent on capturing the spirit that has proved so enticing to creative types.

BLUE HILL PENINSULA

© KATHLEEN M. BRANDES

Buck's Harbor

SIGHTS

On Naskeag Point Road, 1.2 miles from "downtown" Brooklin (Route 175), a small sign marks the turn to the world headquarters of the *WoodenBoat* empire. (Also based here are *Professional Boatbuilder* and *Hope* magazines.) Buy magazines and books and logo-stamped gear in the store (open 9 A.M.–5:30 P.M. weekdays), stroll the grounds, or sign up for one of the dozens of one- and two-week spring, summer, and fall courses in seamanship, navigation, boatbuilding, sailmaking, marine carving, and more. Special courses are geared to kids, women, pros, and all-thumbs neophytes; the camaraderie is legendary, and so is the cuisine. School visiting hours are 8 A.M.–5 P.M. Monday–Saturday June–October. For more information, contact the WoodenBoat School (Naskeag Point Road, P.O. Box 78, Brooklin 04616, 207/359-4651, fax 359-8920, www.woodenboat.com).

Now used as the museum/headquarters of the Sedgwick-Brooklin Historical Society, the 1795 **Reverend Daniel Merrill House** (Rte. 172, P.O. Box 171, Sedgwick 04676, 207/359-4447) was the parsonage for Sedgwick's first permanent minister. Inside the house are period furnishings, old photos, toys, and tools; a few steps away are a restored 1874 schoolhouse, an 1821 cattle pound (for corralling wandering bovines), and a hearse barn. The complex, a mile north of the junction with Route 175, is open Sunday 2–4 P.M. in July and August, or by appointment. Admission is free but donations are welcomed. Pick up a brochure during open hours and guide yourself around the buildings and grounds. The **Sedgwick Historic District,** crowning Town House Hill, comprises the Merrill House and its outbuildings plus the imposing 1794 Town House and the 23-acre Rural Cemetery (oldest headstone dates from 1798) across Route 172.

Forest Farm, home of the late Helen and Scott Nearing, is now the site of **The Good Life Center** (372 Harborside Rd., Box 11, Harborside 04642, 207/326-8211, www.goodlife.org). Advocates of simple living and authors of 10 books on the subject, the Nearings created a trust to perpetuate their farm and philosophy. Resident stewards lead tours Thursday–Tuesday 1–5 P.M. in July and August (Thursday–Wednesday the rest of the year, but be sure to call ahead off-season before showing

boathouse and dock, *WoodenBoat* headquarters, Brooklin

up). Copies of Nearing books are available for sale. From late June to mid-September, Monday-night programs (7 P.M.) at the farm feature presentations by gardeners, philosophers, authors, activists, and other guest speakers. Suggested donation for a tour or a Monday lecture is $5. Occasional work parties, workshops, and conferences are also on the center's schedule. For additional information, contact the Trust for Public Land, 33 Union St., Boston, MA 02108, 617/367-6200. The farm is on an unpaved road on Orr's Cove in Harborside, not the easiest place to find. Call for directions or check the website. If you're hiking in Holbrook Island Sanctuary, relatively close to the farm, ask there for directions.

PARKS, PRESERVES, AND RECREATION

In the early 1970s, foresighted benefactor Anita Harris donated to the state 1,230 acres in Brooksville that would become a state park— **Holbrook Island Sanctuary** (Box 280, Brooksville 04617, 207/326-4012). From Route 176, between West Brooksville and South Brooksville, head west on Cape Rosier Road, fol-

lowing brown-and-white signs for the sanctuary. Go first to the headquarters, about 2.5 miles in, and pick up a trail map and bird checklist from the box next to the door. Park across the dirt road (next to the outhouse). The easy Backshore Trail (about 30 minutes) starts here, or go back a mile and climb the steepish trail to **Backwoods Mountain** for the best vistas. Also in the park are shore-front picnic tables and grills, four old cemeteries, a beaver flowage, and super birding during spring and fall migrations. Leashed pets are allowed; no bikes on the trails; no camping. Admission is free. Officially open May 15–October 15, but the access road and parking areas are plowed for cross-country skiers.

Or you can take a picnic to the **Bagaduce Ferry Landing,** in West Brooksville off Route 176, where there are picnic tables and cross-river vistas toward Castine.

A small, relatively little-known beach is Brooklin's **Pooduck Beach.** From the Brooklin General Store (Route 175), take Naskeag Point Road about half a mile, watching for the Pooduck Road sign on the right. Drive to the end. You can also launch a sea kayak into Eggemoggin Reach here.

E. B. WHITE: SOME WRITER

Every child since the mid-1940s has heard of E. B. White—author of the memorable *Stuart Little, Charlotte's Web,* and *Trumpet of the Swan*—and every college kid for decades has been reminded to consult his *Elements of Style,* but how many realize that White and his wife Katharine were living not in the Big City but in the hamlet of North Brooklin, Maine? It was Brooklin that inspired Charlotte and Wilbur and Stuart, and it was Brooklin where the Whites lived very full creative lives.

Abandoning their desks at *The New Yorker* in 1938, Elwyn Brooks White and Katharine S. White bought an idyllic saltwater farm on the Blue Hill Peninsula and moved here with their young son Joel, who became a noted naval architect and yachtbuilder in Brooklin before his untimely death in 1997. Andy (as E. B. had been dubbed since his college days at Cornell) produced 20 books, countless essays and letters to editors, and hundreds (maybe thousands?) of "newsbreaks"—those wry clipping-and-commentary items sprinkled through each issue of *The New Yorker.* Katharine continued wielding her pencil as the magazine's standout children's-book editor, donating many of her review copies to Brooklin's Friend Memorial Library, one of her favorite "causes." (The library also has two original Garth Williams drawings from *Stuart Little,* courtesy of E. B., and a lovely garden dedicated to the Whites.) Katharine's book, *Onward and Upward in the Garden,* a collection of her *New Yorker* gardening pieces, was published in 1979, two years after her death.

E. B. White's writing studio

© SHERRY STREETER

Later in life, E. B. sagely addressed the young readers of his three award-winning children's books: "Are my stories true, you ask? No, they are imaginary tales, containing fantastic characters and events. In real life, a family doesn't have a child who looks like a mouse; in real life, a spider doesn't spin words in her web. In real life, a swan doesn't blow a trumpet. But real life is only one kind of life—there is also the life of the imagination. And although my stories are imaginary, I like to think that there is some truth in them, too—truth about the way people and animals feel and think and act."

E. B. White died on October 1, 1985, at the age of 86. He and Katharine and Joel left large footprints on this earth, but perhaps nowhere more so than in Brooklin.

For both **golf** and **tennis,** the best and closest choice is the Island Country Club, on Deer Isle.

Biking

Roads here are particularly narrow and winding, with poor shoulders, so be especially attentive; mountain bikes are a wise idea. (If you're driving, share the road with bicycles!) Bring your own bike if you can; rentals are available in Blue Hill, Deer Isle, and Ellsworth. If you're up to a 40-plus-mile circuit of low-to-moderate difficulty, start in Blue Hill (check with the town hall or the hospital about parking) and go counterclockwise, following Routes 15, 176, and 175 through West and South Brooksville (Buck's Harbor), Brooksville, Sargentville, Sedgwick, Brooklin, and back to Blue Hill. (The same circuit makes a good day trip by car from Blue Hill.) See below for food and lodging possibilities en route. Carry a water bottle and arm yourself with a picnic lunch from one of the local general stores.

Scenic Routes

No one seems to know how **Caterpillar Hill**

Brooklin

got its name, but its reputation comes from a panoramic vista of water, hills, and blueberry barrens—with a couple of convenient picnic tables where you can stop for lunch, photos, or a ringside view of sunset and fall foliage. The signposted rest area is on Route 175/15, between Brooksville and Sargentville, next to a small gift shop. Watch out for the blind curve when you pull off the road. Between Sargentville and Sedgwick, Route 175 offers nonstop views of Eggemoggin Reach, with shore access to the Benjamin River just before you reach Sedgwick village. The 40-mile cycling circuit described above includes both Caterpillar Hill (the only really tough section) and the Sedgwick area.

Two other scenic routes, via car or bike, are **Naskeag Point** in Brooklin, and **Cape Rosier,** westernmost arm of the town of Brooksville. Naskeag Point Road begins off Route 175 in "downtown" Brooklin, heads down the peninsula for 3.7 miles past the entrance to WoodenBoat Publications, past Amen Farm (home of the late author Roy Barrette), to a small shingle beach (limited parking) on Eggemoggin Reach, where you'll find picnic tables, a boat launch, a sea-

sonal toilet, and a marker commemorating the 1778 Battle of Naskeag, when British sailors came ashore from the sloop *Gage,* burned several buildings, and were run off by a ragtag band of local settlers.

Cape Rosier's roads are poorly marked, perhaps deliberately, so consult your DeLorme *Maine Atlas and Gazetteer* (see *Suggested Reading*). The Cape Rosier loop takes in Holbrook Island Sanctuary, Goose Falls, the hamlet of Harborside, and plenty of water and island views.

GETTING AFLOAT

Native Trails (Miller Rd., P.O. Box 240, Waldoboro 04572, 207/832-5255), headed by Mike Krepner, is working to re-create the ancient Minnewokun Canoe Trail, a 25-mile circuit of the southeast corner of the Blue Hill Peninsula—including the Bagaduce River and Eggemoggin Reach—used by Native Americans to tap the fisheries of the Bagaduce Estuary. The name allegedly means "many-angled route," and that it is. The 15-mile section between Castine and Walker Pond is already a popular (mostly flatwater) paddling route.

© KATHLEEN M. BRANDES

Contact Native Trails for a map and an update on the project's status. (Mike is also the founder of the Igas Island Company, which manufactures—exclusively with solar power—first-rate, durable backpacks and other travel gear. My 10-year-old Igas Island daypack has seen the world and still looks none the worse for wear.)

See the *Castine* section of this chapter, as well as the *Deer Isle and Isle au Haut* chapter, for information on sea kayaking.

ENTERTAINMENT AND EVENTS

Nightlife is mostly catch-as-catch-can in this area (it's not why most people are here). Head for Blue Hill if you feel the urge for live music—or Bar Harbor if you want even more choices. But if you're a fan of steel-band music, arrange to be in downtown South Brooksville, Buck's Harbor, when Carl Chase's **Flash-in-the-Pans Community Steel Band** takes over the street outside the Buck's Harbor Market every other Monday night (7:30–9 P.M.), mid-June to early September. The musicians aren't professionals, but you'd never know it. Local papers carry the summer schedule (call 207/374-5247) for the two-dozen-member band, which performs in various area locales and deserves its devoted following.

Wooden boats are big attractions hereabouts, so when a huge fleet sails in for the **Eggemoggin Reach Regatta** (usually the first Saturday in August, but the schedule can change), crowds gather. Don't miss the parade of wooden boats. The best locale for watching the regatta itself is on or near the bridge to Deer Isle, or near the Eggemoggin Landing grounds on Little Deer Isle. For details, contact *WoodenBoat* (P.O. Box 78, Brooklin 04616, 207/359-4651, www.woodenboat.com).

The nearest **cinemas** are the Grand Auditorium in Ellsworth and the Criterion Theatre and Reel Pizza Cinerama in Bar Harbor. Films sometimes appear on the schedule at the Stonington Opera House, and the Alamo Theatre in Bucksport (about 20 miles to the west, via Rte. 1) also draws customers from this area.

SHOPPING

Antiques

When you feel the urge for a slate sink, a clawfoot tub, brass fixtures, hand-hewn beams, or a Palladian window, **Architectural Antiquities** (Harborside 04642, 207/326-4938, www.archantiquities), on Cape Rosier, is just the ticket—a restorer's delight. Prices are reasonable for what you get, and they'll ship your purchases. No credit cards. Open all year by appointment; ask for directions when you call. Painted country furniture, decoys, and unusual nautical items are specialties at Peg and Olney Grindall's **Old Cove Antiques** (Rte. 15, Reach Rd., Sargentville 04673, 207/359-2031 or 207/359-8585). The weathered-gray shop, across from the Eggemoggin Country Store, is open 10 A.M.–5 P.M. daily, late May to Labor Day, other times by appointment.

Antiquarian Books

Whimsical signs—Unattended Children Will Be Sold as Slaves; Jackets Please, Gentlemen—adorn the walls of **Wayward Books** (Rte. 15, RFD 26B, P.O. Box 79, Sargentville 04673, 207/359-2397, fax 359-5507), a bright, open shop camouflaged by an unassuming gray exterior just north of the suspension bridge to Little Deer Isle. Owned by Sybil Pike, a former staffer at the Library of Congress, Wayward has 15,000 or so "medium-rare" titles in such creative categories as "civil liberties" and "books on books." Open 10 A.M.–5 P.M. Tuesday–Friday and noon–5 P.M. Saturday, mid-May through December.

Gifts and Crafts (and Wine)

On Route 175 (Reach Road) in Sedgwick, watch for a small sign for **Mermaid Woolens** (Sedgwick 04676, 207/359-2747), source of Elizabeth (Betsy) Coakley's wildly colorful handknits—vests, socks, and sweaters. They're pricey but worth every nickel. She also does seascape paintings. Clever woman. The shop is open 10 A.M.–5 P.M. Tuesday–Saturday in summer, by appointment in winter.

Three varieties of English-style hard cider are specialties at **The Sow's Ear Winery** (Rte. 176 at Herrick Road, Brooksville 04617, 207/326-

© KATHLEEN M. BRANDES

windjammer schooner *Victory Chimes*, anchored in Buck's Harbor

4649), a minuscule operation in a funky, gray-shingled building. Winemaker Tom Hoey also produces sulfite-free blueberry, chokecherry, and rhubarb wines; he'll let you sample it all. Ask to see his cellar, where everything happens. No credit cards. Open 10 A.M.–5 P.M. Tuesday–Saturday or by appointment, early May through December; it's not a bad idea to call ahead in any case. The other half of the business, upstairs, is **The Silk Purse,** where weaver Gail Disney creates handwoven rag rugs; she'll also accept commissions. The Silk Purse is open the same months, same days, but 9 A.M.–1 P.M.

Nautical books, T-shirts, gifts, food (including homemade bread), and boat gear line the walls and shelves of the shop at **Buck's Harbor Marine** (on the dock, South Brooksville 04617, 207/326-8839, www.bucksharbor.com). Owned by boating author Jerry Kirschenbaum and his wife, Lois, the marina is open 9 A.M.–5 P.M. daily Memorial Day to Columbus Day (8 A.M.–7 P.M. in August).

ACCOMMODATIONS

Cottage Colonies

The two operations in this category feel much like informal family compounds—where you quickly become an adoptee. Don't even think about dropping in, however; successive generations of hosts have catered to successive generations of visitors, and far-in-advance reservations are essential for July and August. Many guests book for the following year before they leave. We're not talking fancy; some of the cottages are old-shoe rustic, all are of varying sizes and decor. Most of the cottages have cooking facilities; both colonies offer two meals with the price of accommodation in July and August. Both also have hiking trails, playgrounds, rowboats, and East Penobscot Bay on the doorstep.

Jim and Sally Littlefield are the enthusiastic fourth-generation hosts at **Oakland House Seaside Resort** (435 Herrick Rd., Brooksville 04617, 207/359-8521 or 800/359-7352, www .oaklandhouse.com), a sprawling 50-acre complex of 15 wooded and waterfront cottages, as well as Shore Oaks Seaside Inn. Much of this land, now threaded with fabulous hiking trails, was part of the original king's grant to Jim's ancestors (Jim's the eighth generation to live on the land, and his daughter—also Sally—has now become the fifth generation to work here!). Weekly rates for two adults, mid-June to Labor Day: $1,193–2,370, which includes breakfast and dinner; lower rates for children. Thursday is lobster-picnic night on the beach. Biggest bargains are early May to mid-June and September–October, when you can rent a whole cottage, without meals, for $475–1,295 weekly. Special packages are often available in spring and fall. The Lone Pine cottage has an astonishing toaster collection; on the mantel in another is a carved owl bequeathed to the cottage by a guest. Lots of wonderful tradition here! Rowboats are free for guests, and the staff organizes a variety of boat excursions on request. And wait till you see the gorgeous gardens—including perennials, native medicinal plants, and a kitchen garden. Two cottages (Lone Pine and Boathouse) are winterized and available all year; the other cottages are closed in winter. *Hint to procrastinators:* Although cottages normally are rented on a weekly basis, there are "specials" for short-term cottage stays, often including two meals per day, during the season. Oakland House also rents cottages on a short-term, space-available basis if you book within two weeks of arrival time. That way, the Littlefields fill any vacancies (although there aren't many) and guests can enjoy cottage comforts and gourmet dinners without having to commit to a week-long stay. If your schedule is flexible, call to check.

The fourth generation also manages the **Hiram Blake Camp** (220 Weir Cove Rd., Harborside 04642, 207/326-4951), but with a difference: the second and third generations still pitch in and help with gardening, lobstering, maintenance, and kibitzing. Fifteen cottages line the shore of this 100-acre complex. Don't bother bringing reading matter: the dining room has ingenious ceiling niches lined with countless books. Open Memorial Day through September. One-week minimum (beginning Saturday or Sunday) July and August, when cottages go for

$1,225–$2,350 a week (including breakfast, dinner, and linens). Off-season rates (no meals or linens, but cottages have cooking facilities) are $550–750 a week. Best chances for getting a reservation are in June and September. Pets allowed; smoking permitted in cabins.

Inns and B&Bs

A few steps up from the half-mile-long shorefront at the Oakland House Seaside Resort is **Shore Oaks Seaside Inn** (same address, phone, and website as Oakland House), a handsome large stone summer home carefully restored to its Arts and Crafts heritage. Hang out for too long in the common rooms or the veranda rockers and you might never leave; this place is magical. Ten first-, second-, and third-floor rooms (seven with private baths), go for $149–385 d, with two meals included (a bargain considering their five-course gourmet dinners and weekly lobster feast), mid-May to late October; two-night minimum on weekends. No pets, no smoking; children over 14 are welcome. Open May through October.

The Brooklin Inn and **The Lookout** both offer accommodations as well; each is described in the *Food* section.

Seasonal Rentals

For information on one-week or longer cottage rentals, contact **Peninsula Property Rentals** (Main St., Blue Hill 04614, 207/374-2428, www.peninsulapropertyrentals.com).

FOOD
Breakfast, Lunch, and Tea

Competition is stiff for lunchtime seats at the **Morning Moon Café** (in the center of Brooklin, junction of Rte. 175 and Naskeag Point Rd., Brooklin 04616, 207/359-2373), mostly because *WoodenBoat* staffers consider it an annex to their offices. "The Moon" is a friendly hangout for coffee, pizza, and great sandwiches and salads—or order it to go. Open 7 A.M.–2 P.M. and 5–8 P.M. Tuesday–Sunday all year.

In North Brooksville, where Route 175/176 crosses the Bagaduce River, stands the **Bagaduce Lunch**, a popular takeout stand (outdoor tables only) open daily 11 A.M.–8 P.M., early May–mid-September. Check the tide calendar and go when the tide is changing; order a lobster roll, settle in at a picnic table, and watch the reversing falls. The food is so-so, the setting is tops.

English cream tea under the apple trees is the highlight of a visit to the **Blue Poppy Garden** (1000 Reach Road, Rte. 175, Sedgwick 04676, 207/359-2739, fax 359-8597, www.bluepoppygarden .com). But there's more—a two-story post-and-beam barn holds a shop with hard-to-resist garden accessories, Portuguese cachepots, cards, a lending library of unusual garden books, and even imported seeds so you can grow your own blue poppies (they're blooming in June here at the garden). Two miles of nature trails wind through the premises and you can even spend the night in one of the main house's three B&B rooms. Blue Poppy is open May to mid-September; the shop is open 10 A.M.–5:30 P.M. in July and August. Tea served 2:30–5:30 P.M. daily by reservation in July and August.

Country Stores

Across the street from the Morning Moon Café, the **Brooklin General Store** (1 Reach Rd., junction of Rte. 175 and Naskeag Point Rd., Brooklin 04616, 207/359-8817), vintage 1872, carries groceries, beer and wine, newspapers, takeout sandwiches, and local chatter. It's open 5:30 A.M.–7 P.M. Monday–Saturday and 8 A.M.– 5 P.M. Sunday.

On Route 175 in Sedgwick, overlooking the Benjamin River, the **Sedgwick Store** (207/359-6689) has an even more interesting inventory, including a good supply of gourmet goodies. It's open 7 A.M.–6 P.M. Monday–Saturday all year.

Sargentville's center (small as it is) has the well-stocked **Eggemoggin Country Store** (R.R. 1, Box 4710, Sargentville 04673, 207/359-2125), source of everything from meat and muffins to beer, wine, liquor, fresh breads, lobster pizza, spit-grilled chicken—and public restrooms. The warehousey place is open all year, 6 A.M.–9 P.M. Monday–Saturday and 7A.M.–9 P.M. Sunday (7A.M.–8 P.M. off-season).

Box lunches and boat lunches are specialties at the **Buck's Harbor Market** (Rte. 176, South Brooksville 04617, 207/326-8683, fax 326-9577), a low-key, marginally yuppified general store popular with yachties in summer and everyone else the rest of the year. Breakfast, above-average pizza, quiche, exotic condiments, freshly baked focaccia, live lobsters, and round-the-clock fax service. The market is open 7 A.M.–8 P.M. Monday–Saturday, 8 A.M.–8 P.M. Sunday all year. With the café here at the market and summertime steel-band street concerts outside, this can be a busy corner.

Behind the Buck's Harbor Market is the aptly named **Café OutBack** (Rte. 176, South Brooksville 04617, 207/326-8982). The congenial café—including a bar seating an extra 18 and outside tables in good weather—serves dinner 5:30–9 P.M. Wednesday–Monday in summer, with a reduced schedule in winter.

Fine Dining

The attractive restaurant at **Oakland House Seaside Resort** (435 Herrick Rd., Brooksville 04617, 207/359-8521 or 800/359-7352, www .oaklandhouse.com) is open to the public by reservation mid-June through Labor Day for its daily five-course dinners, breakfast buffets, Sunday brunches, and Thursday night shorefront lobster picnics. Entrée range is $17–21.

Owners Gail and Chip Angell at **The Brooklin Inn** (P.O. Box 25, Rte. 175, Brooklin 04616, 207/359-2777, www.brooklininn.com) have seen a steady stream of enthusiastic patrons since they took over here in 2000. Boat nuts to the core, the Angells are certainly in the right place— roughly midway between *WoodenBoat* magazine and the noted Brooklin Boatyard. Dinner entrées are in the $14–24 range, with a major emphasis on organically grown/raised food. The inn's smoke-free Irish pub is open Monday–Saturday—try the Guinness beef stew! The dining room is open for dinner 5:30–9 P.M. Tuesday–Sunday; reservations are advisable. Open all year, but be sure to call ahead off-season, when the dining room is closed Monday and Tuesday. Upstairs are five simple, comfortable rooms sharing two baths ($95 d, including a full breakfast). No pets or smoking.

Also in Brooklin, at the tip of Flye Point, **The Lookout** (Flye Point Road, off Rte. 175, North Brooklin, 207/359-2188, www.acadia.net/lookout), has a knockout view of Herrick Bay. Dinner is served 5:30–8:30 P.M. Tuesday–Sunday in summer, occasionally off-season. Entrée range is $15–25. Depending on demand, the inn puts on summertime lobsterbakes Monday and Thursday at 6 P.M. ($25 pp). Reservations are required.

INFORMATION AND SERVICES

The best source of information about Brooklin, Brooksville, and Sedgwick is the website of the **East Penobscot Bay Association** (www.penobscotbay.com). Request a copy of its handy flyer/map. Once you've landed on Route 172 or 175, pop into one of the small roadside convenience stores and start asking questions. The clerks—often the owners—know it all cold, and these markets always have a fair share of local color. Of course, they won't object if you also buy something while you're there.

Since most visitors in this area start in Blue Hill, see that section for more advice—as well as for information on coping with any **medical emergencies.**

Libraries

The public libraries in this area are small and welcoming, but hours are limited. The award-winning **Friend Memorial Library** (Rte. 175, Brooklin 04616, 207/359-2276) is open 10 A.M.–4 P.M. Tuesday, Friday, and Saturday; until 8 P.M. Wednesday; and until 6 P.M. Thursday in summer; closed Wednesday in winter. The library's lovely Circle of Friends Garden, with benches and brick patio, is dedicated to the memory of longtime Brooklin residents E. B. and Katharine White. Other area libraries are the **Free Public Library** (1 Town House Rd., Rte. 176, Brooksville 04617, 207/326-4560), open 9 A.M.–5 P.M. Monday and Wednesday, 6–8 P.M. Thursday, and 9 A.M.–noon Saturday; and **Sedgwick Village Library** (Main St., Sedgwick 04676, 207/359-2177), open 5–7 P.M. Wednesday, 3–5 P.M. Thursday, and 9 A.M.–noon Saturday.

Castine

Castine (pop. 1,343) is a gem of a place—a serene New England village with a tumultuous past that goes back more than two centuries. Once beset by geopolitical squabbles, saluting the flags of three different nations (France, Britain, and Holland), its only crises now are limited to local political skirmishes. This is an unusual community, a National Historic Register enclave that many people never find. If you're staying in Blue Hill or Deer Isle or even Bar Harbor, it's worth spending a day here. Or bunk here and use Castine as a base for exploring the village and beyond. Either way, you won't regret it.

Originally known as Fort Pentagoet, Castine received its current name courtesy of Jean-Vincent d'Abbadie, Baron de St.-Castin. A young French nobleman manqué who married a Wabanaki princess named Pidiwamiska, d'Abbadie ran the town in the second half of the 17th century and eventually returned to France.

A century later, in 1779, occupying British troops and their reinforcements scared off potential American seaborne attackers (including Colonel Paul Revere), who turned tail up the Penobscot River and ended up scuttling their more than 40-vessel fleet—a humiliation known as the Penobscot Expedition. Although it's all but forgotten in the history books, it's still one of America's worst naval defeats.

During the 19th century, peace and prosperity became the bywords for Castine—with lively commerce in fish and salt—but it all collapsed during the California Gold Rush and the Civil War trade embargo, leaving the town down on its luck.

Today a major presence is Maine Maritime Academy, yet Castine remains the quietest imaginable college town. Students in search of a party school won't find it here; naval engineering is serious business.

What visitors discover is a year-round community with a busy waterfront, an easy-to-conquer layout, a handful of hostelries and shops, wooded trails on the outskirts of town, and an astonishing collection of splendid Georgian and Federalist architecture.

Of the many historical landmarks scattered around town, one of the most intriguing must be the sign on "Wind Mill Hill," at the junction of Route 166 and State Street: "On Hatch's Hill there stands a mill. Old Higgins he doth tend it. And every time he grinds a grist, he has to stop and mend it." In smaller print, just below the rhyme, comes the drama: "Here two British soldiers were shot for desertion." Castine indeed has quite a history.

SIGHTS

To appreciate Castine fully, you need to arm yourself with the Castine Merchants Association's visitors' brochure/map (all businesses and lodgings in town have copies) and follow the numbers on bike or on foot. With no stops, walking the route takes less than an hour, but you'll want to read dozens of historical plaques,

peek into public buildings, shoot some photos, and perhaps even do some shopping.

Museums

Highlights of the walking tour include the late-18th-century **John Perkins House,** moved to Perkins Street from Court Street in 1969 and restored with period furnishings. It's open for guided tours Sunday and Wednesday 2–5 P.M. July and August; admission is $5.

Next door, **The Wilson Museum** (Perkins Street, 207/326-9247, www.wilsonmuseum.org), founded in 1921, contains an intriguingly eclectic two-story collection of prehistoric artifacts, ship models, dioramas, baskets, tools, and minerals assembled over a lifetime by John Howard Wilson, a geologist/anthropologist who first visited Castine in 1891 (and died in 1936). Among the exhibits are Balinese masks, ancient oil lamps, cuneiform tablets, Zulu artifacts, pre-Incan pottery, and assorted local findings. Don't miss this, even though it's a bit musty. (The only comparable Maine institutions are the Nylander Museum, in Caribou, and the L. C. Bates Museum in Hinckley.) Open 2–5 P.M. Tuesday–Sunday, late May through September; free admission.

Dyce's Head Lighthouse, Castine

Open the same days and hours as the Perkins House (but with no admission fee) are the **Blacksmith Shop,** where a smith does demonstrations, and the **Hearse House,** containing Castine's 19th-century winter and summer funeral vehicles. The nonprofit **Castine Scientific Society,** P.O. Box 196, Castine 04421, operates the four-building complex.

At the end of Battle Avenue stands the 19th-century **Dyce's Head Lighthouse,** no longer operating; the keeper's house is owned by the town. Alongside it is a public path (signposted) leading down a wooden staircase to a tiny patch of rocky shoreline on which stands the beacon that has replaced the lighthouse.

Maine Maritime Academy

The state's only merchant-marine college (and one of only seven in the nation) occupies 35 acres in the middle of Castine. Founded in 1941, the academy awards undergraduate and graduate degrees in such areas as marine engineering, ocean studies, and marina management, preparing a student body of about 750 men and women for careers as ship captains, naval architects, and marine engineers. The academy owns a fleet of 60 vessels, including the historic research schooner *Bowdoin,* flagship of arctic explorer Admiral Donald MacMillan, and the 498-foot training vessel TV *State of Maine,* berthed down the hill at the waterfront. In 1996–97, the *State of Maine,* formerly the U.S. Navy hydrographic survey ship *Tanner,* underwent a $12 million conversion for use by the academy. Midshipmen conduct free 30-minute tours of the vessel on weekdays in summer (about mid-July to late August). The schedule is posted at the dock (usually 8 A.M.–4 P.M.), or call 207/326-4311 to check. Weekday tours of the campus can be arranged through the admissions office (Castine 04420, 207/326-2206 or 800/227-8465 outside Maine, www.mainemaritime.edu). Campus highlights include three-story Nutting Memorial Library, in Platz Hall (open daily during the school year, weekdays in summer and during vacations); the Henry A. Scheel Room, a cozy oasis in Leavitt Hall containing memorabilia from late naval architect

Abbott School, home of the Castine Historical Society

Henry Scheel and his wife, Jeanne; and the well-stocked bookstore (Curtis Hall, 207/326-9333), open 8 A.M.–3 P.M. weekdays.

Strolling Through Town

The highest point in town is **Fort George State Park,** site of a 1779 British fortification. Nowadays, little remains except grassy earthworks, but there are interpretive displays and picnic tables.

Main Street, descending toward the water, is a feast for historic-architecture fans. Artist Fitz Hugh Lane and author Mary McCarthy once lived in elegant houses along the elm-lined street (neither building is open to the public). On Court Street between Main and Green stands turn-of-the-20th-century **Emerson Hall,** site of Castine's municipal offices. Since Castine has no official information booth, you may need to duck in here (it's open weekdays) for answers to questions.

Across Court Street, **Witherle Memorial Library,** a handsome early 19th-century building on the site of the 18th-century town jail, looks out on the Town Common. Also facing the Common are the Adams and Abbott Schools, the former still an elementary school. The **Abbott School,** built in 1859, has been carefully restored for use as a museum/headquarters for the **Castine Historical Society** (P.O. Box 238, Castine 04421, 207/326-4118). A big draw at the volunteer-run museum is the 24-foot-long Bicentennial Quilt, assembled for Castine's bicentennial in 1996. The museum is open 10 A.M.–4 P.M. Tuesday–Saturday and noon–4 P.M. Sunday, July through Labor Day. From Memorial Day weekend to July, and Labor Day to Columbus Day, there's a reduced schedule. Admission is free, but donations are welcomed. The historical society, founded in 1966, organizes lectures, exhibits, and special events (some free) in various places around town.

On the outskirts of town, across the narrow neck between Wadsworth Cove and Hatch Cove, stretches a rather overgrown canal (signposted British Canal) scooped out by the occupying British during the War of 1812. Effectively severing land access to the town of Castine and making it an island, the Brits thus raised havoc, collected local revenues for eight months, then departed for Halifax with enough funds to establish Dalhousie College (now Dalhousie University). Wear waterproof boots to walk the canal route; the best time to go is at low tide.

PARKS, PRESERVES, AND RECREATION

Witherle Woods, a 96-acre preserve owned by Maine Coast Heritage Trust and managed by the Conservation Trust of Brooksville, Castine, and Penobscot, is a popular walking and bicycling area with a maze of numbered trails. Adjacent property is privately owned, so carry a trail map and stick to it. Access is via a shaded path signposted Hatch Natural Area, from Battle Avenue, near the Manor Inn. Local lodgings keep a supply of maps, or contact (by phone or mail) the **Conservation Trust of Brooksville, Castine, and Penobscot** (P.O. Box 421, Castine 04421, 207/326-9711). The trust owns 244 acres on the Blue Hill Peninsula and has been a conscientious steward of the natural resources of Castine, Penobscot, and Brooksville since 1977. In summer, its members schedule natural-history walking tours; inquire when you arrive. Also ask locally about the **Henderson Natural Area** and other preserves, some accessible only by boat.

If a waterfront picnic sounds appealing, buy the fixings at Bah's Bakehouse and settle in on the grassy earthworks along the harborfront at **Fort Madison,** site of an 1808 garrison (then Fort Porter) near the corner of Perkins and Madockawando Streets. The views from here are fabulous, and it's accessible all year.

Golf and Tennis
The **Castine Golf Club** (Battle Avenue and Wadsworth Cove Road, Castine 04421, 207/326-8844) dates to 1897, when the first tee required a drive from a 30-step-high mound. Redesigned in 1921 by Willie Park Jr., the nine-hole course is open May 15–October 15. Starting times are seldom required, and greens fees are reasonable. The club also has four clay tennis courts. Call to schedule court time.

Swimming
Backshore Beach, a crescent of sand and gravel on Wadsworth Cove Road (turn off Battle Avenue at the Castine Golf Club), is a favorite saltwater swimming spot, with views across the bay to Stockton Springs. Be forewarned, though, that ocean swimming in this part of Maine is not for the timid. The best time to try it is on the incoming tide, after the sun has had time to heat up the bottom. At mid- to high tide, it's the best place to put in a sea kayak. Park along the road.

If a pool sounds more attractive, you can swim in the **Cary W. Bok indoor pool** at Maine Maritime Academy for $4 a person. Lap-swimming hours are 6:15–7:15 A.M. Monday, Wednesday, and Friday; open swimming is 4:15–6:15 P.M.

weekdays and 2–5 P.M. Sunday. Call 207/326-4311, ext. 457, to confirm.

GETTING AFLOAT

Based at Dennett's Wharf is **Castine Kayak Adventures** (P.O. Box 703, Castine 04421, 207/326-9045, www.castinekayak.com), spearheaded by Registered Maine Guide Karen Francoeur. Known locally as Kayak Karen, she's particularly adept with beginners, delivering wise advice from beginning to end. All skill levels are accommodated. Full-day tours usually occur Wednesday (9 A.M.–3 P.M.); cost is $105 pp, including an island lunch and usually lots of bird and seal sightings. Half-day tours, any day except Wednesday, are 9 A.M.– noon and 1–4 P.M. Cost is $55 pp. Two-hour **sunset tours** are $40 pp; the two-hour **sunrise tour** includes breakfast for $45 pp. Friday nights there are special **phosphorescence tours** under the stars (weather permitting), for $45 pp.

Eaton's Boatyard (Sea Street, P.O. Box 123, Castine 04421, 207/326-8579, fax 326-4727) is a full-service marina renting moorings by the day or week. You can also buy live lobsters May–October or order them shipped anywhere year-round.

SHOPPING
Antiques and Galleries

Tucked into the back of the 1796 Parson Mason House, one of Castine's oldest residences, **Leila Day Antiques and Gallery** (53 Main Street, Castine 04421, 207/326-8786) is a must for anyone in the market for folk art, period furniture, quilts, and unusual contemporary Shard pottery (from Dover-Foxcroft, Maine). Access is via a lovely, flower-lined walkway. The shop, established in 1978, is open 10 A.M.–5 P.M. daily, Memorial Day weekend through September, by appointment the rest of the year.

McGrath-Dunham Gallery (9 Main St., Castine 04421, 207/326-9175, www.mcgrathdunhamgallery.com), a well-lighted, two-story space, shows work by painter/printmaker Greg Dunham and more than 50 other artists. Open 10 A.M.–5 P.M. daily, late May to mid-October.

Books

Driving toward Castine on Route 166, watch on your right for a small sign for **Dolphin Books and Prints** (314 Castine Rd., P.O. Box 225, Castine 04421, 207/326-0888, www.dolphin-book.com), where Leon ("Pete") and Liz Ballou have set up their antiquarian business after a dozen years in Camden and decades in the publishing world. Specialties are botanical prints, first editions, biographies, and maritime books. Open 10 A.M.–5 P.M. Wednesday–Saturday June–September, but call ahead to be sure.

In downtown Castine, a block up from the waterfront, **The Compass Rose Bookstore and Café** (3 Main St., Castine 04421, 207/326-9366 or 800/698-9366, compassrose.booksense.com) carries an ever-expanding selection of new books, cards, games, and prints chosen by owners Ruth Heffron and John Vernelson. The booklovers' atmosphere here is contagious—the epitome of an independent bookshop. In the back of the store is the aptly named **Linger Longer Café**, serving hot and cold drinks (espresso, too) and tasty baked goods. Open all year. Summer hours are 10 A.M.–5 P.M. Monday–Saturday and 9 A.M.–2 P.M. Sunday. Closed Sunday and Monday from mid-October to mid-June.

Clothing and Gifts

Water Witch (Main Street, Castine 04421, 207/326-4884, www.waterwitch-me.com) specializes in Indonesian batik and Liberty fabric, clothing, and accessories. Buy off the rack or choose a fabric and a style and Jean de Raat will have it made up flawlessly within a few days. Don't expect a bargain—a made-to-order dress will cost in the triple digits—but it's a lot less than flying to London or Jakarta.

Just down the street, close to the harbor, **Four Flags** (19 Water St., P.O. Box 232, Castine 04421, 207/326-8526) carries high-quality Maine and nautical gifts, plus an excellent card selection. Open daily 9:30 A.M.–5 P.M., April–December, reduced schedule January–March. A branch store is now open on Main Street in Blue Hill.

ACCOMMODATIONS

Inns

The three-story **Castine Inn** (33 Main Street, P.O. Box 41, Castine 04421, 207/326-4365, fax 326-4570, www.castineinn.com) earns a stellar rating for its stunning semiformal gardens, helpful staff, and mural-lined dining room with award-winning menu. The 19 second- and third-floor rooms and suites are simply furnished, gradually being updated from their 1890s origins, with twin or queen beds, private baths, and good lighting ($90–215 d, with full breakfast, in summer). Two-night minimum July and August. Lots of interesting artwork is everywhere and there's a simpatico air, encouraged by enthusiastic young innkeepers Amy and Tom Gutow. In the small, English-style pub, hikers, bicyclists, and kayakers mingle with less energetic guests. No pets, no smoking. Open May through October.

Just across the street is the three-story **Pentagöet Inn** (26 Main St., P.O. Box 4, Castine 04421, 207/326-8616 or 800/845-1701, www.pentagoet.com), a whimsically eccentric Queen Anne concoction. Innkeepers Jack Burke and Julie Van de Graaf took over the century-old inn in 2000. Decor is Victorian in the 16 rooms, with antique furnishings and lots of pastels. Doubles (all with private baths) are $85–195, including a hearty breakfast (on the deck in good weather). Borrow one of the inn's bikes and explore around town. The inn's dining room is open to guests and the public Monday–Saturday 5:30–8 P.M. Reservations are required. The Pentagöet's Passports Pub is a fascinating gathering spot—decorated with globetrotter treasures and photos from exotic locales. Open May through October. Pets are allowed on a limited basis; no smoking.

Once the summer "cottage" of a New York Yacht Club commodore, **The Manor Inn** (Battle Ave., P.O. Box 873, Castine 04421, 207/326-4861 or 877/626-6746, fax 207/326-0891, www.manor-inn.com) overlooks town and harbor from five mostly wooded acres elevated above Battle Avenue. Though the atmosphere is informal, there are lots of elegant architectural touches. Nancy Watson and Tom Ehrman took over in 1998, upgrading beds, linens, and furniture; more renovations are ahead. The 13 second- and third-floor rooms are an eclectic mix—some with canopied beds and fireplaces, all with private baths. Breakfast is generous continental. Rates are $110–230 d in July and August, $95–165 d other months. Two-night minimum on weekends. Well-behaved kids and pets are allowed ($25 per visit for pets); no smoking except on the porch. A separate guest building has a TV and games, as well as Nancy's yoga studio; guests are welcome to join her classes (8 A.M. Monday, Wednesday, and Friday; $12 fee for drop-ins). The trailhead for Witherle Woods is close by. Open mid-February to mid-December.

The **Castine Harbor Lodge** (147 Perkins St., P.O. Box 215, Castine 04421, 207/326-4335, www.castinemaine.com) is just about as close as you can get to the harbor without being in it. Verandas are everywhere for taking in the view. The imposing Victorian, built in 1893, has 16 rooms (most with private bath) for $85–245 d, including continental breakfast. Pets are $10/day. A separate "honeymoon cottage" goes for $1,250 a week. The other three large inns in town all have pubs, but the lodge has the Bagaduce Oyster Bar, with a smashing view of the harbor. Open all year, but call ahead in the dead of winter.

Castine's least-fancy (and least-expensive) rooms are at the tiny **Village Inn,** set back from Main and Water Streets (P.O. Box 183, Castine 04421, 207/326-9510), where summer rates are $75 d (shared bath) and $95 d (private bath and water view). (Starting in November, rates are $65 and $85 d.) The simple four-room inn is directly above Bah's Bakehouse, but noise doesn't seem to be a huge problem. Open all year.

Seasonal Rentals

Perched in a field along the edge of Hatch's Cove, with terrific views, are the six two-bedroom log cabins of **Castine Cottages** (33 Snapp's

Wy., Rte. 166, P.O. Box 224, Castine 04421, 207/326-8003, www.castinecottages.com), operated by Alan and Diana Snapp. Weekly rates are $600, late June to late September, $430 the rest of the year ($25 per week for each extra person). Off-season, cottages sometimes are available for $75–150 per night. Bring your own sheets and towels (or the Snapps will provide them for $10 pp).

Several Castine realtors have listings for summer cottage rentals; start with **Castine Realty** (5 Main St., P.O. Box 234, Castine 04421, 207/326-9392, fax 326-9518, www .castinerealty.com).

FOOD

Country Store

Castine Variety (1 Main St., Castine 04421, 207/326-8625) technically isn't a country store, since it's smack downtown, close to the waterfront. But it fits the definition of one of those something-of-everything markets, and it even has the original 1920 ice cream counter. Grab some breakfast here (the Fitch family gets going early!), buy a newspaper, pick up a pizza, order a lobster roll, whatever. The store is open 5 A.M.–7 P.M. daily all year (to 10 P.M. in summer).

Lunch and More

On lower Main Street is a tiny sign for **Bah's Bakehouse** (Water Street, Castine 04421, 207/326-9510), a higgledy-piggledy eatery of three rooms and a deck at the end of an alleyway beneath the Village Inn. Its slogan is "creative flour arrangements," and creative they are. Stop here for morning coffee, cold juices, interesting snacks and salads, homemade soups, wine or beer, and the best sandwiches in town ($2.50–7; eat in or take out). Bah's will pack a picnic basket for you or deliver an order dockside. Open 7 A.M.–5 P.M. daily March through December.

Dennett's Wharf (15 Sea Street, next to the Town Dock, P.O. Box 459, 207/326-9045, www.dennettswharf.com) is a colorful barn of a place with outside deck and front-row windjammer-watching seats in summer. The service is particularly cheerful, and kids are welcomed. The best sandwich is grilled crabmeat. The crayoned kids' menu includes the usual suspects, such as mac-'n'-cheese ($4.50), hot dogs ($3.50), and gummy dinosaurs for dessert. Try attaching a dollar bill to the soaring ceiling; countless others have. Dinner entrées are $11–24. Open daily 11 A.M.–midnight, May–Columbus Day. This is the best place in town for live music; some performances require a ticket, but they seldom cost more than $5. The bar serves a four-draft sampler for $3.75. Open daily, May–Columbus Day. The Castine Kayak Adventures operation is based here.

Fine Dining

Three of Castine's large inns—The Castine Inn, the Pentagöet Inn, and the Manor Inn—compete for customers with their elegant dining rooms. The choice can be difficult, but who can complain?

At the **Castine Inn** (33 Main St., Castine 04421, 207/326-4365, www.castineinn.com), chef/co-owner Tom Gutow has won acclaim for his small but select menu, with entrées in the $20–32 range. Seafood is the specialty; try the award-winning crab cakes. Desserts are superlative. Tables are well-spaced, and around the room are wonderful murals of Castine, painted by a previous innkeeper. Appetizers and meals are also available in the pub. The restaurant is open for dinner Wednesday–Monday May to late October, then Thursday–Saturday.

The dining room at **The Manor Inn** (Battle Ave., Castine 04421, 207/326-4861, www .manor-inn.com) overlooks the gardens and lawn. Dinner is served from an extensive menu, including vegetarian choices (entrées $16–29), 5:30–9:30 P.M. Tuesday–Saturday in summer (Tuesday night there's an extensive buffet). Reservations are essential on Tuesdays and weekends. The inn's cozy Pine Cone Pub has a smaller and less pricey menu. Highlight of the season is the July 4 Pig Roast, with plenty of good music, for $20 pp. Be aware that the inn is a favorite venue for wedding receptions, so the dining room often is closed on summer Saturdays. Call ahead or check the website.

INFORMATION AND SERVICES

Castine has no local information office, but all businesses and lodgings in town have copies of the Castine Merchants Association's visitors' brochure/map. For additional information, contact the **Castine Town Office** (Emerson Hall, Court St., Castine 04421, 207/326-4502, www.castine.me.us/). The Town Office is open 11 A.M.–3 P.M. Monday–Friday.

Witherle Memorial Library (Court St., Box 202, Castine 04421, 207/326-4375, www.witherle.lib.me.us/) is open 4–8 P.M. Monday, 11 A.M.–5 P.M. Tuesday–Friday, and 11 A.M.–2 P.M. Saturday. The library holds an especially good book sale the first Saturday in August, at Maine Maritime Academy's Smith Gym. Also accessible to the public is the **Nutting Memorial Library,** in Platz Hall on the Maine Maritime Academy campus. It's open 8 A.M.–4:30 P.M. Monday–Friday during the summer, longer hours during the school year.

Newspapers

The *Castine Patriot* (www.penobscotbaypress.com/castinepatriot/), published every Thursday, has the best local coverage, including calendar listings. Its website has lots of helpful local links. The *Bangor Daily News* carries local, state, and a smidgen of international news. The *Ellsworth American* is published every Thursday. From June through September, the *American* publishes **Out & About in Downeast Maine,** a free monthly vacation supplement in tabloid format.

Emergencies

Castine's police are deputies in the **Hancock County Sheriff's Department,** in Ellsworth (207/667-7575). **Castine Community Health Services** (Court and Dyer Sts., 207/326-4348) has 24-hour emergency service (on a first-responder basis) and X-ray and lab facilities. For police, fire, and ambulance emergencies, dial 911. The nearest acute-care hospital is Blue Hill Memorial Hospital.

Other Services

The Castine **post office** (Main St., between Court and Perkins Sts., Castine 04421, 207/326-8551) reportedly is the nation's oldest continuously used post office, dating from 1815. A hamhanded government attempt to move it several years ago resulted in an unholy outcry. It worked. The building has since been upgraded, expanded to the rear, and left in its prominent downtown location. **Public restrooms** are on the Town Dock, at the foot of Main Street.

Deer Isle and Isle au Haut

To reach Acadia National Park's acreage on Isle au Haut, you'll need to wend your way through Little Deer Isle and Deer Isle, then board the Isle au Haut ferryboat for the 45-minute trip across the Deer Island Thorofare to the island. In summer, you can go directly to the park's Duck Harbor landing; other months, it's a hike through the woods.

Thus, Deer Isle and Isle au Haut are inexorably linked yet distinctly separate and very different. Deer Isle's main town of Stonington is a metropolis compared to Isle au Haut (1,152 souls versus 79). The sidewalks roll up relatively early in Stonington, but there's not much even in the way of pavement on Isle au Haut. Deer Isle has stepped tentatively into the 21st century; Isle au Haut remains pretty much in the 20th— and the early 20th at that. (Let it be said, though, that electricity came to Isle au Haut in 1970; telephone service soon followed.)

© KATHLEEN M. BRANDES

Goose Cove, Deer Isle

ISLE AU HAUT

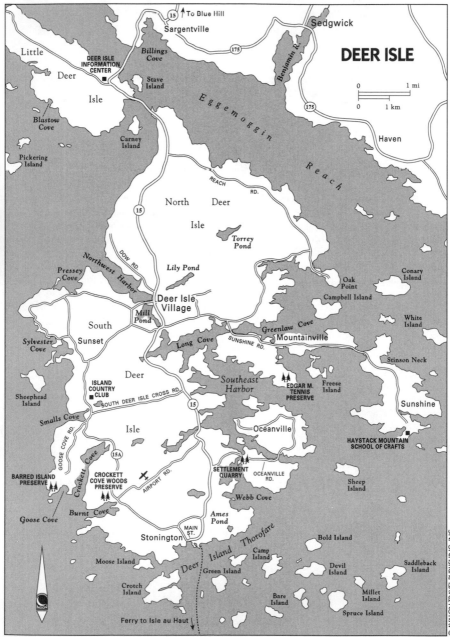

To Blue Hill

Sargentville

Sedgwick

Little

Deer

Isle

DEER ISLE INFORMATION CENTER

Billings Cove

Stave Island

Benjamin R.

DEER ISLE

0   1 mi

0   1 km

Blastow Cove

Carney Island

Pickering Island

Eggemoggin

Haven

REACH RD.

North   Deer

Isle

Torrey Pond

Reach

Northwest Harbor

Pressey Cove

DOW RD.

Lily Pond

Oak Point

Campbell Island

Conary Island

Deer Isle Village

Mill Pond

White Island

Sylvester Cove

South

Sunset

Long Cove

Greenlaw Cove

SUNSHINE RD.

Mountainville

Stinson Neck

Deer

ISLAND COUNTRY CLUB

SOUTH DEER ISLE CROSS RD.

Southeast Harbor

EDGAR M. TENNIS PRESERVE

Freese Island

Sunshine

Sheephead Island

Smalls Cove

Isle

15

Oceanville

HAYSTACK MOUNTAIN SCHOOL OF CRAFTS

GOOSE COVE RD.

15A

Crockett Cove

CROCKETT COVE WOODS PRESERVE

SETTLEMENT QUARRY

OCEANVILLE RD.

Sheep Island

BARRED ISLAND PRESERVE

AIRPORT RD.

Webb Cove

Goose Cove

Burnt Cove

Ames Pond

MAIN ST.

Stonington

Deer Island Thorofare

Bold Island

Saddleback Island

Moose Island

Camp Island

Devil Island

Crotch Island

Green Island

Millet Island

Bare Island

Spruce Island

Ferry to Isle au Haut

MOON

Deer Isle

"Deer Isle is like Avalon," wrote John Steinbeck in *Travels with Charley*, "it must disappear when you are not there." Deer Isle (the name of both the island and its midpoint town) has been romancing authors and artisans for decades, but it's unmistakably real to the quarrymen and fishermen who've been here for centuries. These long-timers are a sturdy lot, as even Steinbeck recognized: "I would hate to try to force them to do anything they didn't want to do."

Early 18th-century maps show no name for the island, but by the late 1800s, nearly 100 families lived here, supporting themselves first by farming, then by fishing. In 1789, when Deer Isle was incorporated, 80 local sailing vessels were scouring the Gulf of Maine in pursuit of mackerel and cod, and Deer Isle men were circling the globe as yachting skippers and merchant seamen. At the same time, in the once-quiet village of Green's Landing (now called Stonington), the shipbuilding and granite industries boomed, spurring development, pros-perity, and the kinds of rough hijinks typical of commercial ports the world over.

Green's Landing became the "big city" for an international crowd of quarrymen carving out the terrain on Deer Isle and nearby Crotch Island, source of high-quality granite for Boston's Museum of Fine Arts, the Smithsonian Institution, a humongous fountain for John D. Rockefeller's New York estate, and less showy projects all along the eastern seaboard. The heyday is long past, but the industry did extend into the 20th century (including a contract for the pink granite at President John F. Kennedy's Arlington National Cemetery gravesite). Today, Crotch Island is the site of Maine's only operating island granite quarry.

Measuring about nine miles north to south (plus another three miles for Little Deer Isle), the island of Deer Isle today has a handful of hamlets (including Sunshine, Sunset, Mountainville, and Oceanville) and two towns—Stonington and Deer Isle—with a population of 3,028. Road access is via Route 15 down the

ISLE AU HAUT

© SHERRY STREETER

Stonington Harbor

length of the Blue Hill Peninsula. A huge suspension bridge, built in 1939 over Eggemoggin Reach, links the Sargentville section of Sedgwick with Little Deer Isle; from there, a sinuous, .4-mile causeway connects to the northern tip of Deer Isle.

Eight miles off Stonington lies 5,800-acre Isle au Haut, about 60 percent of which belongs to Acadia National Park.

SIGHTS

Sightseeing on Deer Isle means exploring back roads, browsing the galleries, walking the trails, hanging out on the docks, and soaking up the ambience.

The 1830 **Salome Sellers House** (Rte. 15A, Sunset Village, no phone), a repository of local memorabilia, is the headquarters of the **Deer Isle–Stonington Historical Society.** Volunteer guides love to provide tidbits about various items; seafarers' logs and ship models are particularly intriguing. Just north of the Island Country Club and across from Eaton's Plumbing, the house is open 1–4 P.M. Wednesday and Friday, early July to mid-September. Admission is free but donations are welcomed.

Close to the Stonington waterfront, the **Deer Isle Granite Museum** (Main St., P.O. Box 469, Stonington 04681, 207/367-6331), was established to commemorate the centennial of the quarrying business hereabouts. The best feature of the small museum is a 15-foot-long working model of Crotch Island, center of the industry, as it appeared at the turn of the 20th century. Flatcars roll, boats glide, and derricks move—it all looks very real. The museum is open 9 A.M.–5 P.M. daily Memorial Day to Labor Day. Admission is free.

Another downtown-Stonington attraction is a Lilliputian complex known hereabouts as the **"Miniature Village."** Some years ago, the late Everett Knowlton created a dozen and a half replicas of local buildings and displayed them on granite blocks in his yard. Since his death,

> *Sightseeing on Deer Isle means exploring back roads, browsing the galleries, walking the trails, hanging out on the docks, and soaking up the ambience.*

they've been restored and put on display each summer in town—along with a donation box to support the upkeep. The village is set up on East Main Street (Route 15), across from the Union Trust bank.

PARKS AND PRESERVES

Foresighted benefactors have managed to set aside precious acreage for respectful public use on Deer Isle. The Nature Conservancy owns two properties, **Crockett Cove Woods Preserve** and **Barred Island Preserve.** For information, inquire at the Chamber of Commerce or contact the Conservancy (14 Maine St., Fort Andross, Brunswick 04011, 207/729-5181). The conscientious steward of other local properties is the **Island Heritage Trust (IHT)** (3 Main St., at Rte. 15, P.O. Box 42, Deer Isle 04627, 207/348-2455). When the office is open (usually 10:30 A.M.–3 P.M. weekdays July and August; 10 A.M.–2 P.M. Tuesday and Thursday off-season), you can pick up note cards, photos, T-shirts, and maps and information on hiking trails and nature preserves. A particularly handy booklet is *Wild Flowering Plants of Deer Isle,* which has flower-identification drawings but also trail maps for three island preserves and info on others. Proceeds of note-card and T-shirt sales benefit the IHT's efforts, including the purchase of 51 acres of the abandoned Settlement Quarry, on Webb Cove (off Oceanville Road) in Stonington.

Settlement Quarry

This is one of the easiest, shortest hikes (a stroll, really) in the area, leading to an impressive vista. From the parking lot on Oceanville Road (just under a mile off Route 15), marked by a carved granite sign, it's about five minutes to the top of the old quarry, where the viewing platform (aka the "throne room") takes in the panorama—all the way to the Camden Hills on a good day. In early August, wild raspberries are an additional enticement. Three short loop trails lead into the

ISLE AU HAUT

© KATHLEEN M. BRANDES

Settlement Quarry, Deer Isle

surrounding woods from here. A map is available in the trailhead box.

Holt Mill Pond and Edgar Tennis Preserves

Inquire locally about these two preserves. The 100-acre Edgar M. Tennis Preserve, in particular, off the Sunshine Road and down unpaved Tennis Road, has very limited parking, so don't try to squeeze in if there isn't room; schedule your visit for another hour or day. When you go, allow at least 90 minutes to enjoy the 3.5 miles of trails. (Pick up a map at the trailhead.) One trail skirts Pickering Cove, with convenient rocky outcrops for a picnic (carry in, carry out, though). The preserve is open sunrise to sunset.

Crockett Cove Woods Preserve

Donated to The Nature Conservancy by benevolent, eco-conscious local artist/architect Emily Muir (who died at the age of 99 in 2003), 98-acre Crockett Cove Woods Preserve is Deer Isle's natural gem—a coastal fog forest laden with lichens and mosses. Four interlinked trails cover the whole preserve, starting with a short nature trail. Pick up the helpful map/brochure at the regis-

tration box. Wear rubberized shoes or boots and respect adjacent private property. The preserve is open daily, sunrise to sunset, all year. Admission is free; no camping. From Deer Isle Village, take Route 15A to Sunset Village. Go 2.5 miles to Whitman Road, then to Fire Lane 88. The local contact phone number is 207/367-2674.

Ames Pond

Ames Pond is neither park nor preserve, but it might as well be. On a back road close to Stonington, it's a mandatory stop in July and August, when the pond wears a blanket of white and pink water lilies. From downtown Stonington, take Indian Point Road east, just under a mile, to the pond. There's no official parking, so if you're shooting photos, pull off the road as far as possible, respecting private property.

RECREATION

The **Deer Isle Walking Trails Group** (R.R. 1, Box 980, Stonington 04681, 207/367-2448) has produced a handy map—*Walking Trails of Deer Isle*—available for $1 at most island lodgings, at the Island Heritage Trust office on Main

THE MAINE ISLAND TRAIL

In the early 1980s, a "trail" of coastal Maine islands was only the germ of an idea. By the end of the millennium, the **Maine Island Trail Association (MITA)** counted some 4,000 members dedicated to conscientious (i.e., low- or no-impact) recreational use of more than 100 public and private islands along 325 miles of Maine coastline between Portland and Machias.

More than a dozen of these islands (each year, new ones are added and others are subtracted) are in the Acadia region—between Isle au Haut and Schoodic Point. In fact, one of the best island clusters along the entire trail is in the waters off Stonington on Deer Isle.

Access to the trail is only by private boat, and the best choice is a sea kayak, to navigate shallow or rock-strewn coves. Sea-kayak rentals are available in Bar Harbor, Southwest Harbor, Blue Hill, and Stonington, and several outfitters offer island tours (See specific locations for details). The best source of information is the Maine Association of Sea Kayaking Guides and Instructors (MASKGI), whose members agree to adhere to the Leave No Trace philosophy.

The trail's publicly owned islands—supervised by the state Bureau of Public Lands—are open to anyone; the private islands are restricted to MITA members, who pay $45 a year for the privilege (and, it's important to add, the responsibility). With the fee comes the *Maine Island Trail Guidebook,* providing directions and information for each of the islands. With membership comes the expectation of care and concern. "Low impact" means different things to different people, so MITA experienced acute growing pains when enthusiasm began leading to "tent sprawl."

To cope with and reverse the overuse, MITA has created an "adopt-an-island program," in which volunteers become stewards for specific islands and keep track of their use and condition. MITA members are urged to pick up trash, use tent platforms where they exist, and continue elsewhere if an island has reached its assigned capacity (stipulated on a shoreline sign and/or in the guidebook).

A superb complement to the *Maine Island Trail Guidebook* is a copy of *Hot Showers!* by Lee Bumsted, a former MITA staff member (See *Suggested Reading*). Recognizing the need for alternating island camping and warm beds (and hot showers), she has almost singlehandedly alleviated island stress and strain. Some of the B&Bs and inns listed in her guide give discounts to MITA members.

Membership information is available from **Maine Island Trail Association** (P.O. Box C, Rockland 04841, 207/596-6456, www.mita.org).

Street in Deer Isle (207/348-2455), or directly from the trails group. The map shows major and secondary roads, scenic biking and walking paths, birding areas, nature preserves, and boat-launching sites.

Biking

As with so many other parts of Maine, the roads on Deer Isle are narrow and winding, with inadequate shoulders for bikes, so be particularly cautious. In general, Deer Isle is fairly level, so we're not talking rigorous. Route 15, the major north-south artery, has the heaviest traffic, so plan to cycle on the less-busy side routes.

Some lodgings provide bicycles for guests, or you can bring your own. Rental bikes are available from Old Quarry Ocean Adventures for $17 a day or $100 a week (April through October). An easy, five-mile round-trip starts at the Chamber of Commerce information booth on Little Deer Isle. Park your car there and head northwest along Eggemoggin Road to the tip of Little Deer Isle. From the turnaround at road's end, there's a splendid view of Pumpkin Island Light and Cape Rosier (Brooksville) in the distance. If you plan this spin for late afternoon, you can backtrack on Eggemoggin Road and detour down Blastow's Cove Road to Eaton's Lobster Pool for dinner and a sunset.

From Deer Isle Village, a seven-mile bike route goes east along the Sunshine Road, through Mountainville, to Sunshine and south to the Haystack Mountain School of Crafts (some parts of the road are narrow and wind-

Pumpkin Island Light, from Little Deer Isle

ing; be cautious). On the way, stop at Nervous Nellie's. If you happen to be staying at the Sunshine Campground, you can do this route in reverse.

Swimming

The island's only major freshwater swimming hole is the **Lily Pond,** northeast of Deer Isle Village. Just north of the Shakespeare School, turn into the Deer Run Apartments complex. Park and take the path to the pond, which has a shallow area for small children.

Golf and Tennis

About two miles south of Deer Isle Village, watch for the large sign (on the left) for the **Island Country Club** (Rte. 15A, Sunset, 207/348-2379), a nine-hole public course that's been here since 1928. Starting times aren't needed, and greens fees are moderate; no credit cards. Open late May to late September. Also at the club are three well-maintained tennis courts. Or just commandeer a rocking chair and watch the action from one of the porches. The club's cheeseburgers and crab rolls are among the island's best bargain lunches.

GETTING AFLOAT

Sea Kayaking

With countless islets and lots of protected coves in the waters around Deer Isle, especially off Stonington, sea kayaking has come up fast in the recreation department.

The biggest kayaking (and everything else recreational) operation is **Old Quarry Ocean Adventures** (R.R. 1, Box 700, Stonington 04681, 207/367-8977, fax 367-0964, www.oldquarry.com), an energetic enterprise that also provides a rather astonishing range of outdoor-adventure choices. Captain Bill Baker's ever-expanding outfit rents canoes, kayaks, gear, sailboats, bikes, moorings, and platform tentsites, and even arranges burials at sea and weddings. All-day guided tours in single kayaks are $95pp; tandems are $150 for two. Half-day tours are $50 and $90, respectively. Rental rates for experienced kayakers are $45 per day for a single, $60 for a tandem. Half-day rates are $30 and $45, respectively. They'll deliver and pick up anywhere on Deer Isle for a fee of $20. If you're bringing your own kayak, you can park your car ($5 a day) and launch from here ($5 per boat for launching).

ISLE AU HAUT

ISLE AU HAUT

© CHARLOTTE CUSHMAN

the *Miss Lizzie*, ready for a cruise

Other options at Old Quarry include lobster-boat tours, even a lobsterbake ($24 a person) if you arrange it in advance. Old Quarry is off the Oceanville Road, less than a mile from Route 15, next to the Settlement Quarry preserve. It's well signposted.

A smaller kayaking outfitter is in the village of Sunset (not surprisingly, located on the western side of the island). **Granite Island Guide Service** (66 Dunham Point Rd., Deer Isle 04627, 207/348-2668, www.graniteislandguide.com) is owned by Professional Maine Guides Dana Douglass and his wife, Anne. June through September, all-day guided trips, including lunch, are $90 adults, $60 children under 13. Half-day trips are $50 adults, $40 children under 12. The half-day trip starts in Stonington Harbor. They also lead canoe trips (maximum eight people) on inland rivers. As an ordained Congregational minister, Dana also leads wilderness spirituality canoe and kayak trips under the aegis of the Bangor Theological Seminary. The season begins in early May.

If you become a member of the **Maine Island Trail Association (MITA)** (Box C, Rockland 04841, 207/596-6456, www.mita.org; $45 a year for individuals, $65 for families), you'll receive a handy manual that steers you to more than a dozen islands in the Deer Isle archipelago where you can camp, hike, and picnic—eco-sensitively, please. MITA members are firmly committed to the low-impact Leave No Trace principles. (The 400-page manual/guidebook covers more than 100 public and private islands, and some mainland sites, on the 325-mile-long Maine Island Trail.) Boat traffic and island activity can be a bit heavy at the height of summer, so to best appreciate the tranquility of this area, try this in September, after the Labor Day holiday. Nights can be cool, but days are likely to be brilliant.

If you're not up for self-propulsion, from mid-June through Labor Day, the *Miss Lizzie* departs at 2 P.M. daily from the Isle au Haut Boat Company dock in Stonington for a one-hour narrated trip among the islands. Cost of the memorable trip is $14 adults, $6 kids under 12. Reservations are advisable, especially in July and August. Parking is available at the pier. The *Miss Lizzie* is also part of the regular mailboat/passenger-ferry service to offshore Isle au Haut—**Isle au Haut Boat Company** (Seabreeze Avenue, P.O. Box 709,

Stonington 04681, 207/367-5193 or 367-6516, fax 367-6503, www.isleauhaut.com).

ENTERTAINMENT AND EVENTS

Stonington's National Historic Register landmark, the 1912 **Opera House,** a onetime vaudeville venue, gained a new lease on life in the summer of 2000 when four New York women renovated the building. They have been providing the community with a full summer calendar (Memorial Day through September) of films, plays, lectures, concerts, and workshops. A three-day jazz festival takes the stage in late July. Organized as Opera House Arts, the group has won over the skeptics and created a new kind of stir in Stonington. Check locally for the schedule (207/367-2788, www.operahousearts.org)—there's always something in the works at the arts center.

From early June to late August, on varying weeknights, evening slide programs, lectures, concerts, and demonstrations start at 8 P.M. at the **Haystack Mountain School of Crafts,** in Sunshine (See *Special Courses* later in this chapter).

Mid-July (usually the third weekend) brings the **Stonington Lobsterboat Races,** very popular competitions held in the harbor, with lots of possible vantage points and accompanying festive activities. Stonington is one of the major locales in the lobsterboat race circuit.

In August—usually the second weekend—the **Round-the-Island Sailboat Race** doesn't offer much for spectators except the sight of a fleet of billowing sails, but there are other related activities in town.

SHOPPING

Antiques
In Deer Isle Village, about midisland, you'll find **Old Deer Isle Parish House Antiques** (Church St., Rte. 15, P.O. Box 445, Deer Isle 04627, 207/348-9964 or 367-2455), a funky shop heavy into vintage clothing, antique kitchen utensils, and other collectibles. Open 11 A.M.–6 P.M. Monday–Friday and 2–6 P.M. Saturday and Sunday mid-June through October.

Anyone on the trail of rare books should also be sure to stop en route to Deer Isle at Wayward Books, in Sargentville, on the Sedgwick side of the Deer Isle bridge.

When you get to the bottom of the island, **The Clown** (Main St., Stonington 04681, 207/367-6348, www.the-clown.com) awaits. The imaginative owners came up with this combination of art, antiques, and . . . food and wine. Look, it works. In fact, it has worked so well that there are year-round branches in Blue Hill and Portland's Old Port district. Part of the key is Tramonti, the owners' farm in Tuscany, source of wines and extra-virgin olive oil. The shop inventory also includes Deruta pottery, unusual furnishings, and other "necessities." Art openings are also wine tastings—a fine idea. Open 10 A.M.–6 P.M. Tuesday–Saturday June through October, plus Sunday and Monday in July and August.

Art and Craft Galleries
Thanks to the presence and influence of **Haystack Mountain School of Crafts,** hypertalented artists and artisans lurk in every corner of the island. Most are tucked away on back roads, and many have studios open to the public, so watch for roadside signs and pick up a free copy (available in shops and galleries statewide) of the Maine Crafts Association's annual *Maine Guide to Crafts and Culture.* The MCA, formerly headquartered here on the island, is now based in Portland (207/780-1807, www.mainecrafts.org).

Name a craft and Mary Nyburg probably has an example in her high-ceilinged barn, the **Blue Heron Gallery** (22 Church St., Rte. 15, Deer Isle 04627, 207/348-2940). Formerly a Haystack board member and still an honorary trustee, she provides a retail outlet for the work of the school's internationally renowned faculty—printmakers, blacksmiths, potters, weavers, papermakers, glassworkers, and more. Prices are reasonable. The gallery is open 10 A.M.–5:30 P.M. Monday–Saturday and 1–5:30 P.M. Sunday, June through September.

The **Deer Isle Artists Association (DIAA)** is headquartered less than a mile northwest of Deer Isle Village (13 Dow Rd., P.O. Box 634, Deer Isle

188 Deer Isle and Isle au Haut

04627, 207/348-2330). The DIAA's co-op gallery features two-week exhibits of paintings, prints, drawings, and photos by local pros. Open daily, 1–5 P.M., mid-June through Labor Day.

One of the island's premier galleries gained a larger home in 1996 when Elena Kubler moved **The Turtle Gallery** (61 N. Deer Isle Rd., Rte. 15, Deer Isle 04627, 207/348-9977, www.turtlegallery.com) to a handsome space formerly known as the Old Centennial House Barn (owned by the late Haystack director Francis Merritt). Group and solo shows of contemporary paintings, prints, and crafts are hung upstairs and down, and there's usually sculpture in the garden. Just north of Deer Isle Village—across from the Shakespeare School, oldest on the island—the gallery is open 10 A.M.–5:30 P.M. Monday–Saturday and 2–6 P.M. Sunday, Memorial Day weekend through September.

In downtown Stonington, **Eastern Bay Gallery** (602 Main St., Stonington 04681, 207/367-6368) occupies a bright, airy space at the far end of the main drag. Look for unique jewelry, functional granite objects, knitted hats, pottery, and lovely handwoven chenille pieces. The gallery is open 9 A.M.–5 P.M. Monday–Saturday Memorial Day to mid-September (also on Sunday during July and August).

In the kind of unlikely setting that is typical of Deer Isle, you'll come across **William Mor Oriental Rugs** (663 Reach Rd., Deer Isle 04627, 207/348-2822, www.williammororientalrugs.com). Bill Mor, a longtime potter, now imports natural-dyed Afghan and Tibetan rugs via the nonprofit Cultural Survival organization—stunning work for a worthy cause. The shop is open daily 10 A.M.–5 P.M., mid-May through October. Reach Road is a mile south of the Route 15 causeway between Little Deer Isle and Deer Isle; the shop is 3.3 miles off Route 15.

Even before you get as far as Bill Mor's shop, stop in at the **Greene-Ziner Gallery** (73 Reach

Rd., Deer Isle 04627, 207/348-2601), where Melissa Greene turns out incredible painted and incised pottery and Eric Ziner works magic in metal sculpture. Your budget may not allow for one of Melissa's pots (in the four-digit range), but I guarantee you'll covet them. The gallery also displays the work of several other local artists. Open Tuesday–Sunday noon to 5 P.M.

On Route 15, about 500 feet south of Reach Road, is the compact home of **George Hardy** (207/348-2885), a self-taught folk carver who's been featured in a solo video and turns out incredibly imaginative carved and painted animals. George is here most days, but call ahead to be sure. Watch for the Hardy Folk Carving sign, bring your wallet (cash only), and carry home an unusual treasure.

Thanks to the presence and influence of Haystack Mountain School of Crafts, hypertalented artists and artisans lurk in every corner of the island. Most are tucked away on back roads, and many have studios open to the public.

Gifts and Books

If you're looking for Maine pottery, weaving, metalwork, pewterware, imported tiles, or walking sticks, go directly to the **Harbor Farm Store** (Rte. 15, P.O. Box 64, Little Deer Isle 04650, 207/348-7755 or 800/342-8003, www.harborfarm.com), one of the state's best gift shops. Based in a mid-19th-century schoolhouse a mile south of the Deer Isle suspension bridge, the shop carries thousands of very unusual, high-quality items, and it's all available by mail as well. Hours are 10 A.M.–5 P.M. Monday–Saturday as well as noon–5 P.M. Sunday June to Christmas; closed Sunday other months.

Deer Isle may be the unlikeliest spot in all of Maine for an African gift shop, but it's here. **Deepest Africa Imports** (22A Dow Rd., Deer Isle 04627, 207/348-6624) is the creation of South African–born Jackie Pelletier, who has stocked her small shop with carvings, baskets, handprinted fabrics, traditional jewelry, and more. Several of her sources are cottage industries supporting women and the disadvantaged, and she donates 10 percent of her profits to the Soweto Township Hospice in South Africa. The shop, .8

mile off Route 15, is open 1–5 P.M. Tuesday through Saturday throughout the summer

Now for a bit of whimsy—no, a *lot* of whimsy. From Route 15 in Deer Isle Village, take the Sunshine Road east 2.9 miles to **Nervous Nellie's Jams and Jellies** (598 Sunshine Road, Deer Isle 04627, 800/777-6845, www.nervousnellies.com). Outstandingly creative condiments are the rule here; sample the hot pepper jelly, blackberry peach conserve, or ginger syrup. The promotional brochures are hilarious. Best time to come is May to early October, 9 A.M.–5 P.M., when the shop operates the ultracasual **Mountainville Café,** serving tea, coffee, and delicious scones—with, of course, Nervous Nellie's products. While you're at it, the surrounding meadow teems with whimsical wood and metal sculptures (all for sale) by Nellie's owner Peter Beerits, who scavenges his "art supplies" from dumps and salvage firms. The condiments are available by mail, but seeing the sculpture extravaganza is half the fun. The shop is open the same hours as the café.

In downtown Stonington, below the Opera House, **Dockside Books & Gifts** (West Main St., P.O. Box 171, Stonington 04681, 207/367-2652) carries just what its name promises, with a specialty in marine and Maine books. The rustic two-room shop is open May to November. Don't miss the view from outside the shop.

Back up the island in Deer Isle Village, you'll find **The Periwinkle** (8 Main St., Deer Isle 04627, 207/348-2256), where Neva Beck carries a fine inventory of Maine books, as well as crafts, notecards, and gifts. The shop is open 9 A.M.–noon and 1–5 P.M. weekdays, and 9 A.M.–noon Saturday, June through September.

P.S. After all this browsing, you just might need a double-dip cone from **Harbor Ice Cream,** across the street from The Periwinkle.

Clothing

Women need to be cautious going into **The Dry Dock** (Main St., P.O. Box 485, Stonington 04681, 207/367-5528)—the merchandise instantly sells itself. Imported women's clothing from Nigerian, Tibetan, and Indian cottage industries, unique jewelry, and unusual notecards are just some of the options in one large room and a

smaller back room. The shop, under the same ownership as the Eastern Bay Gallery, is open daily, 9 A.M.–5 P.M., throughout the summer.

Farmers' Market

Every Friday in May through October,, the Congregational Church parking lot in Deer Isle Village is the locale for the **Deer Isle–Stonington Farmers' Market,** selling smoked meats, fresh herbs and flowers, produce, maple syrup, jams and jellies, and more. Hours are 10 A.M.–noon.

ACCOMMODATIONS

Inns

The most elegant place to sleep on Deer Isle is in one of the 12 antiques-filled rooms at Dan and Michele Brown's **Pilgrim's Inn** (20 Main St., P.O. Box 69, Deer Isle 04627, 207/348-6615 or 888/778-7505, www.pilgrimsinn.com), a beautifully restored colonial building overlooking the peaceful Mill Pond. In summer, doubles with private bath are $195–200 for eight "deluxe" rooms and $130–180 for four smaller, simpler rooms (two of them on the third floor). Three close-by cottages, convenient for families, are $215 and $225. The National Historic Register inn began life in 1793 as a boardinghouse named The Ark; be sure to check out the fascinating guestbook, with names dating to 1901. The inn has sloping lawns, bikes for guests, a gift shop (The Rugosa Rose), and a fine dining room serving dinner to guests and the public. No pets. Open mid-May to mid-October.

Just when you're convinced you're lost, and the paved road has turned to dirt, you arrive at **Goose Cove Lodge** (Goose Cove Rd., P.O. Box 40, Sunset 04683, 207/348-2508 or 800/728-1963 outside Maine, fax 207/348-2624, www.goosecovelodge.com), a 21-acre hillside complex of rustic and modern cottages and cabins and main-lodge rooms and suites—all with private baths, most with fireplaces, and many with stunning views of secluded Goose Cove. Rates vary widely here, and so does the decor; the cost can add up (food and drink gratuities and taxes add 25 percent to the quoted rate). Thirteen cottages and cabins (some requiring triple occupancy, or payment for same) are $225–550 a night in summer, less in spring and fall. Cabins and cottages require a one-week minimum July to Labor Day, and cancellation rules are rigidly enforced. Eight suites and double rooms go for $170–280 in summer, less in spring and fall. The inn organizes nature walks and astronomy talks and provides maps and descriptions of local trails, including The Nature Conservancy's **Barred Island Preserve,** close to the lodge property. Bikes, small kayaks, games, and a library are available for guests. The dining room is also open to the public by reservation for dinner. No pets, no smoking. Children are welcome; the lodge's Kid Camp (free) is a major asset. Kids eat together at 5:30 and play games until 8:30—while their parents have a peaceful dinner. The inn is open mid-May to mid-October (the dining room opens in mid-June). The lodge is 4.5 miles from Route 15, via Deer Isle Village.

B&Bs

In 1995, a longtime downtown-Stonington landmark known as the Captain's Quarters changed hands, became **The Inn on the Harbor** (Main St., P.O. Box 69, Stonington 04681, 207/367-2420 or 800/942-2420, fax 207/367-5165, www.innontheharbor.com), and headed a bit upscale. But not totally; the attractively updated 1880s complex still has an air of unpretentiousness. Most of the 13 rooms and suites (private baths) have fantastic harbor views and private or shared decks where you can keep an eye on lobsterboats, small ferries, windjammers, and pleasure craft. (Binoculars are provided.) An espresso bar is open 11 A.M.–4:30 P.M. Nearby are antiques, gift, and craft shops; guest moorings are available. High-season rates (Memorial Day to Columbus Day) are $110–175 d, including continental breakfast ($60–110 d the rest of the year). No pets; smoking only on decks. Open all year, but call ahead off-season.

In downtown Stonington, just up the hill from the Inn on the Harbor and convenient for walking to everything (even a small sandy beach a mile away), is **Près du Port** (West Main St. and Highland Ave., P.O. Box 319, Stonington 04681,

207/367-5007, www.presduport.com). This bright B&B is ably run by amiable innkeeper Charlotte Casgrain, retired from many summers teaching at a Deer Isle French summer camp and a career as a Greenwich, Connecticut, French teacher. Two rooms have vanity sinks and detached baths, one has a private bath ($110 d, including lodging tax and breakfast). You can even schedule a massage on Tuesday afternoons. Children are welcome, and a toy cupboard provides entertainment for the precomputer kids. No credit cards. Open May 1 through October. When Deer Isle beds are scarce at the height of summer, Charlotte is the best resource for dozens of last-minute overnight rooms in local homes. This location is ideal if you're en route to or returning from Isle au Haut.

Eggemoggin Reach is almost on the doorstep at **The Inn at Ferry Landing** (77 Old Ferry Rd., Deer Isle 04627, 207/348-7760, fax 348-5276, www.ferrylanding.com), overlooking the long-abandoned Sargentville–Deer Isle ferry wharf. The view is wide open from the inn's great room, where guests gather to read, play games, talk, and watch passing windjammers. Professional musician Gerald Wheeler has installed two grand pianos in the room; it's a treat when he plays. His wife, Jean, is the hospitable innkeeper and breakfast maven. Three water-view guest rooms and a suite have private baths ($110–165 d May through October, $100–125 November–April). Two-night minimum July and August. A harpsichord and a great view are big pluses in the suite. The Mooring, an annex that sleeps five, is rented by the week ($1,300, without breakfast). No smoking, no pets; kids are welcome in the annex. The inn is open all year except Thanksgiving and Christmas.

Geared to sea kayakers and the low-key boating set is **Oceanville Seaside Bed & Breakfast** (Oceanville Road, R.R. 1, Box 890, Stonington 04681, 207/367-2226, www.geocities.com/oceanville2002/photos.html), Tim and Kathy Emerson's mid-19th-century Cape-style home. It's tough to find a more idyllic setting for a paddling or sailing rest stop—a secluded, pink-granite-lined cove overlooking ocean and islands. The kitchen and living room in this informal spot have tin ceilings and great views. Nearby are miles of trails. A first-floor room (shared bath) is $80 d; the three-room second-floor suite (private bath), sleeping five, is $90 d ($25 per extra person). Kathy's fabulous breakfasts are included; she'll prepare dinner—extra charge; bring your own liquor (BYOL)—by prior arrangement. No smoking, no credit cards (personal checks are OK), no small children. Pets are allowed on a case-by-case basis (the Emersons' dog Inca is in residence). A mooring is available for guests; kayakers can paddle in and paddle out on any tide. As if all that isn't enough, the Emersons can send you off to spruce-covered Sheep Island, owned by their family, for hiking, birding, and picnicking. The B&B, east of Stonington in the hamlet of Oceanville, is open June through October, by reservation only.

Seasonal Rentals

For house and cottage rentals by the week, month, or season, contact **Sargent's Rentals** (P.O. Box 115, Stonington 04681, 207/367-5156, fax 367-2444) or **Island Vacation Rentals** (P.O. Box 446, Stonington 04681, 207/367-5095). Plan well ahead, as the best properties get snapped up as much as a year in advance.

Campgrounds

Deer Isle has a limited number of campsites, so plan to reserve ahead if you're thinking about camping. Offshore, on Isle au Haut, are a few sought-after lean-tos managed by Acadia National Park and available only by reservation (See the *Isle au Haut* section of this chapter).

Sunshine Campground (1181 Sunshine Rd., Deer Isle 04627, 207/348-2663 or 367-8977, www.sunshinecampground.com), managed by Old Quarry Ocean Adventures, has 22 wooded RV (maximum 40 feet) and tent sites for $22–26 for two (children under five are free). Hookups are available, and facilities include laundry, playground, firewood, and a small store. Leashed pets are allowed. Best of all, you can launch a kayak at Old Quarry's compound and sign up for any of their activities. Open mid-June through Labor Day. From Deer Isle Village, the camp-

ground is on the Sunshine Road, 5.7 miles east of Route 15.

Old Quarry Ocean Adventures (R.R. 1, Box 700, Stonington 04681, 207/367-8977, fax 367-0964, www.oldquarry.com) has its own tent-camping area (no RVs) at its complex near the Settlement Quarry. Ten well-spaced wooded sites with platforms are $24–28 for two ("overflow" sites, without platforms, may be available for $15). Other pluses here include hot showers, camping gear for rent, firewood and lobsters for sale, and a pond for swimming.

FOOD

Stonington is a dry town, so you'll want to plan ahead to buy beer or wine for dinner (except for the Pilgrim's Inn and Goose Cove Lodge, which have liquor licenses). Burnt Cove Market can fix you up with the regular stuff; buy fine wines at The Clown (See *Shopping*).

Family Restaurants

In July or August, don't show up at **Finest Kind Dining** (70 Center District Crossroad, P.O. Box 388, Deer Isle 04627, 207/348-7714) without a dinner reservation. This log-cabin family-run restaurant is no longer a secret. Nothing fancy—just homemade all-American food served conscientiously in a come-as-you-are setting. Pizza, pasta, prime rib, seafood. And save room for dessert. Wheelchair access; liquor license. Open May–October, daily 5–9 P.M. The restaurant, owned by the Perez family, is halfway between Route 15 and Sunset Road (Route 15A). The Perezes also own the adjacent **Round the Island Mini Golf** (same phone, open the same months) and rent canoes, kayaks, and bicycles.

Best pizza on the island? Head for **Burnt Cove Market** (Rte. 15, Stonington, 207/367-2681). Besides pizza, you can get fried chicken and sandwiches, plus beer and wine. The store is open 6 A.M.–8 P.M. Monday–Thursday, 6 A.M.–9 P.M. Friday and Saturday, and 9 A.M.–8 P.M. Sunday all year.

The Fisherman's Friend Restaurant (School St., Rte. 15A, Stonington 04681, 207/367-2442), run for more than a quarter of a century by Jack and Susan Scott, gets high marks for respectable food, generous portions, fresh seafood, and outstanding desserts. If lobster stew is your thing, order it here. And you can't beat the Friday fish fry for $7.50. It's all very casual—pine paneling, booths, and reasonable prices. BYOL. Across from the community center (formerly an elementary school, hence the street name), it's open daily 11 A.M.–8 P.M. (to 9 P.M. in midsummer), April to late October.

Cafés

Creativity defines the menu at **Lily's Café** (Rte. 15, P.O. Box 653, Stonington 04681, 207/367-5936), in a cute house at the corner of the Airport Road just over two miles from downtown. It's all very casual; order at the counter and choose a table—but you may have to wait, as Lily's is a favorite. (Some of the tables have fun windowpane shadowboxes.) Eat here or assemble an *haut gourmet* picnic: veggie and meat sandwiches, Mediterranean salads, cheeses, and homemade soups and breads. BYOL. Upstairs, the Chef's Attic carries an eclectic mix of cottage accessories, and art exhibits brighten the walls in July and August. Lily's is open 7 A.M.–4 P.M. Monday, Tuesday, and Friday; 7 A.M.–8 P.M. Wednesday and Thursday. Alas, it's closed weekends.

In downtown Stonington, the aptly named **Harbor Café** (Main St., Stonington 04681, 207/367-5099), the town's major breakfast destination, attracts a crowd. In summer, it opens daily at 6 A.M., closing at 8 P.M. Monday–Thursday and 9 P.M. Friday, when the seafood fry packs 'em in (seconds are free). It's also open to 9 P.M. Saturday and 3 P.M. Sunday.

Fine Dining

Both restaurants in this category are conveniently linked to lodgings. If you have the time, and your wallet and waistline will stand it, be sure to try them both. (They also both have full liquor licenses.)

At the **Pilgrim's Inn** (20 Main St., P.O. Box 69, Deer Isle Village 04627, 207/348-6615, fax 348-7769, www.pilgrimsinn.com), dinner is a scheduled affair, elegantly casual, in the restored barn. At 6 P.M., delicious hors d'oeuvres are served in the common room; at 7 P.M., the multicourse dinner begins, featuring a choice of about three entrées. Reservations are required; fixed-price tab is $35 (plus tax, tip, wine). This is a grown-up kind of place, so don't bring children unless they qualify as angelic. Open mid-May to mid-October.

Running head-to-head with the Pilgrim's Inn in the culinary department is **Goose Cove Lodge** (Goose Cove Rd., P.O. Box 40, Sunset 04683, 207/348-2508, fax 348-2624, www.goosecovelodge.com), where creative dinners are served to guests and the public, by reservation, in the attractive main lodge restaurant called The Point, Tuesday–Sunday. Entrée range is $12–27. (Shorts are not allowed at dinner.) Entertainment follows dinner three nights a week. Call well ahead for holiday and weekend reservations; Goose Cove may be remote, but it's no secret. Open mid-May to mid-October.

Lobster in the Rough

Eaton's Lobster Pool (Blastow's Cove, Little Deer Isle, 207/348-2383) qualifies in this category because you can order your crustaceans by the pound, but in fact, it's slightly more gussied up than the eat-on-the-dock places. (There are a few tables on the outdoor deck, and some shorefront picnic tables for takeout customers.) You'll find more interesting food and faster service at other island restaurants, but you'd be hard put to find a better view than here on Blastow's Cove. Dramatic sunsets can even subdue the usual din in the rustic dining room. BYOL; no credit cards; smoking only outside. Reservations are advisable, especially on weekends. Open 5–9 P.M. daily, mid-June to mid-September; open Friday–Sunday, mid-May to mid-June and mid-September to early October. Look for signs across from the Chamber of Commerce information booth.

INFORMATION AND SERVICES

The **Deer Isle–Stonington Chamber of Commerce** (P.O. Box 490, Deer Isle 04627, 207/348-6124, www.deerislemaine.com) has a summer information booth on a grassy triangle on Route 15 in Little Deer Isle, .25 mile after crossing the bridge from Sargentville (Sedgwick). Staffed by volunteers, the office has a rather erratic schedule, even during the height of summer: allegedly 10 A.M.–4 P.M. weekdays and 11 A.M.–5 P.M. Sunday.

Across from the Pilgrim's Inn, the **Chase Emerson Memorial Library** (Main St., Deer Isle Village 04627, 207/348-2899) is open 11 A.M.–3 P.M. Wednesday and 9 A.M.–noon Saturday. The **Stonington Public Library** (Main St., Stonington 04681, 207/367-5926) is open 12:30–4:30 P.M. Tuesday and Friday and 10 A.M.–noon Saturday.

Emergencies

The **Island Medical Center** (Airport Rd., South Deer Isle, 207/367-2311), a division of Blue Hill Memorial Hospital, handles minor medical problems. The nearest round-the-clock emergency room is at **Blue Hill Memorial Hospital** (Water St., Blue Hill 04614, 207/374-2836, www.bhmh .org). Throughout Deer Isle, to contact **the police and fire departments** or to summon an **ambulance,** call 911.

Newspapers

Island Ad-Vantages (207/367-2200, www .penobscotbaypress/islandadvantages.com), published every Thursday, includes the *Compass* supplement, listing area events and activities. Regular features include "The Fisheries Log" (going rates for seafood, including lobsters and crabmeat). The same publisher also owns Blue Hill's *Weekly Packet.*

The Ellsworth American (63 Main St., Ellsworth 04605, 207/667-2576, www

.ellsworthamerican.com), published every Thursday, produces a monthly summer tabloid supplement, *Out & About in Downeast Maine,* with feature articles, maps, ads, and calendar listings that include Deer Isle. The supplement is available free at shops, lodgings, and restaurants throughout the area.

Public Restrooms

Public restrooms are located at the Stonington Town Hall on Main St. (open 8 A.M.–4 P.M. Monday–Friday), and at the Chase Emerson Library in Deer Isle Village.

SPECIAL COURSES

Internationally famed artisans—sculptors and papermakers, weavers and jewelers, potters and printmakers—become the faculty each summer for the unique **Haystack Mountain School of Crafts** (Sunshine Rd., P.O. Box 518, Deer Isle 04627, 207/348-2306, fax 348-2307, www.haystack-mtn.org). Chartered in 1950, the school has weekday classes and round-the-clock studio access for the adult students, from beginners to advanced professionals. Portfolio review is required for advanced courses. Two or three evenings a week (8 P.M.) between late June and early August, faculty and visiting artists present slide/lecture programs open to the public in the Gateway Building, close to the entrance to the campus. An hour-long Wednesday (1 P.M.) tour of the architecturally and scenically dramatic 40-acre shorefront campus usually includes visits to some of the studios. None of the work is for sale. Haystack is seven miles east of Deer Isle Village.

Isle au Haut

Looking rather like a teardrop released from the southern tip of Deer Isle, Isle au Haut has only relatively recently appeared on most travelers' radar screens. Somewhat responsible for elevating the island's profile have been a unique lighthouse-based inn (established in 1986) and the publication of *The Lobster Chronicles*, by Isle au Haut–based author Linda Greenlaw, the female fishing-boat skipper featured in *The Perfect Storm*.

But Isle au Haut will never be overcrowded and overrun—amenities are minimal, and access is primarily controlled by the mailboat/passenger ferry linking it to Stonington on Deer Isle.

About 79 souls call 5,800-acre Isle au Haut home year-round, most of them eking out a living from the sea. Each summer, the population temporarily swells with day-trippers, campers, and cottagers—then settles back in fall to the measured pace of life on an island six miles offshore.

Samuel de Champlain, threading his way through this archipelago in 1605 and noting the island's prominent central ridge, came up with the name of *Isle au Haut* ("High Island"). Appropriately, the island's tallest peak (543 feet) is now named **Mount Champlain**. Incorporated in 1868, Isle au Haut became, courtesy of political horse-trading, part of Knox County, whose shire town (Rockland) is nearly four hours away by boat and car.

About 60 percent (most of the southern half) of six-mile-long Isle au Haut belongs to **Acadia National Park,** thanks to wealthy summer visitors who began arriving in the 1880s. It was their heirs who, in the 1940s, donated valuable acreage to the federal government. Today, this offshore division of the national park has a well-managed 18-mile network of trails, a few lean-tos at the park's Duck Harbor Campground, several miles of unpaved road, and summertime passenger-ferry service to the park entrance at the campground.

In the island's northern half are the private residences of fisherfolk and summer folk, what passes for a village (a general store and post office), a five-mile paved road (seven miles of unpaved roads), and the only lodgings. The only vehicles on the island are owned by residents.

If spending the night on Isle au Haut sounds appealing (it is), you'll need to plan well ahead; because of the scarce lodgings, and the campground's handful of lean-tos, it's no place for spur-of-the-moment sleepovers. (Even spontaneous day trips aren't always possible in July and August, when the ferry tends to be heavily booked and the Park Service imposes a limit on visitors to its part of the island.)

A weather note: Fog is no stranger to Isle au Haut (or, for that matter, many other Maine islands and coastal areas), so keep in mind that even though it almost never halts boat service, it can affect what you see. Fog shouldn't faze hikers or walkers, but it certainly affects photographers. Then again, moody fog shots have their own special appeal. There's nothing you can do about fog, so make the best of it.

GETTING THERE

Unless you have your own vessel, the only access to Isle au Haut's town landing is via the private mailboat/passenger ferry owned by the **Isle au Haut Boat Company** (Seabreeze Avenue, P.O. Box 709, Stonington 04681, 207/367-5193, fax 207/367-6503, www.isleauhaut.com), which generally operates four daily trips, Monday–Saturday, and one on Sunday, between mid-June and Labor Day. Other months, there are two or three trips Monday–Saturday. The best advice is to request a copy of the current schedule, covering dates, variables, fares, and surcharges.

April to mid-October round-trips are $32 adults, $16 kids under 12 (two bags each). Other charges (round-trip prices): bikes ($16), kayaks/canoes (assessed by length, $30 minimum), pets ($8), credit card usage ($2 pp). Winter rates are half-price. Weather seldom affects the schedule, but be aware that ultraheavy seas could cancel a trip.

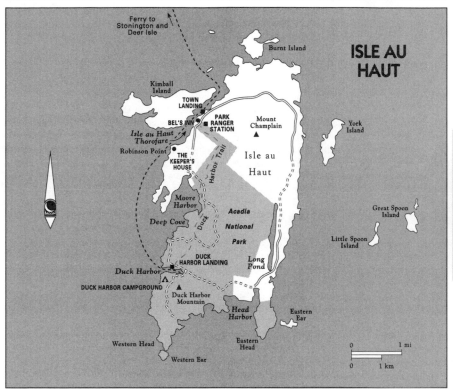

© AVALON TRAVEL PUBLISHING, INC.

From mid-June to Labor Day, Monday–Saturday, there is twice-daily (10 A.M. and 4:30 P.M.) ferry service from Stonington to **Duck Harbor,** at the edge of Acadia National Park's campground. For a day trip, this Duck Harbor schedule allows you seven hours on the island. No boats or bikes are allowed on this route, and no dogs are allowed in the campground. A park ranger boards the boat at the Isle au Haut town landing and goes along to Duck Harbor to answer questions and distribute maps. Before mid-June and after Labor Day, and on Sundays during the peak season, you'll be offloaded at the Isle au Haut town landing, about five miles from Duck Harbor. The six-mile boat passage from Stonington to the Isle au Haut town landing takes 45 minutes; the trip to Duck Harbor tacks on 15 minutes more.

From mid-June through August, on Sundays and holidays, there is one round-trip boat from Stonington to Isle au Haut and return. The rest of the year, there is no Sunday service.

Ferries depart from the Isle au Haut Boat Company Dock, Seabreeze Avenue, off East Main Street in downtown Stonington, at the southern tip of Deer Isle. Outdoor parking ($9 a day) is available close to the ferry landing. Arrive at least an hour early to get all this settled so you don't miss the boat. Better yet, spend the night in Deer Isle or Blue Hill before heading to Isle au Haut. (See the *Blue Hill Peninsula* chapter.)

RECREATION

Mention Acadia National Park and most people think of Bar Harbor and Mount Desert Island, where nearly three million visitors arrive each year. The Isle au Haut section of the park sees maybe 5,000 visitors a year—partly because only 50 people a day (not counting campers) are allowed to land here. But the remoteness of the island and the scarcity of beds and campsites also contribute to the low count.

Near the town landing, where the year-round mailboat docks, is the **Park Ranger Station** (207/335-5551), where you can pick up trail maps and park information—and use the island's only public facilities. (Do yourself a favor, though: Plan ahead by downloading Isle au Haut maps and information from the Acadia National Park website, www.nps.gov/acad/.)

Hiking

Hiking on Acadia National Park trails is the major recreation on Isle au Haut, and even in the densest fog, you'll see valiant hikers going for it. A loop road circles the whole island; an unpaved section goes through the park, connecting with the paved nonpark section. Walking on that is easy. Beyond the road, none of the park's 18 miles of trails could be labeled "easy"; the footing is rocky, rooty, and often squishy. But the trails *are* well marked, and the views—of

islets, distant hills, and ocean—make the effort worthwhile.

The most-used park trail is the four-mile (one way) **Duck Harbor Trail,** connecting the town landing with Duck Harbor. Figure about two hours each way. (You can either use this trail or follow the island road—mostly unpaved in this stretch—to get to the campground when the summer ferry ends its Duck Harbor runs.) Even though the summit is only 314 feet, the toughest trail is **Duck Harbor Mountain,** about 1.2 miles (one way) that'll take you three to four hours round-trip if you return the way you came. (Rather than return via the trail's steep, bouldery sections, cut off at the Goat Trail and return to the trailhead that way.) For terrific shoreline scenery, take the **Western Head** and **Cliff Trails,** at the island's southwestern corner. If the tide is out (and *only* if it's out), you can walk across the tidal flats to the quaintly named Western Ear for views back toward the island. Western Ear is private, so don't linger. The **Goat Trail** adds another four miles (round-trip) of moderate hiking east of the Cliff Trail; views are fabulous and birding is good, but if you're only here for a

© CHARLOTTE CUSHMAN

Isle au Haut vista

day, you'll need to decide whether there's time to catch the return mailboat.

Other Island Recreation

Biking is limited to the 12 or so miles of paved and unpaved roads. If you're staying at The Keeper's House or Bel's Inn, you can borrow a bike, which is handy around the "village" and for going swimming in Long Pond. Mountain bikes are not allowed on the park's hiking trails, and rangers try to discourage park visitors from bringing them to the island. Remember that the mailboat carries bikes *only* to the town landing, not to Duck Harbor.

For superb **freshwater swimming,** head for Long Pond, a skinny, 1.5-mile-long swimming hole running north-south on the east side of the island, abutting national park land. You can bike over there, clockwise along the road, almost five miles, from the town landing. Or bum a ride from an island resident. If you're here only for the day, though, there's not enough time to do this *and* get in a long hike. Opt for the hiking—or do a short hike and then go for a swim (shallowest part is at the southern tip).

CAMPING

The only camping on Isle au Haut is at the Acadia National Park campground. So you'll need to get your bid in early to reserve one of the five six-person lean-tos at **Duck Harbor Campground,** open May 15–October 15. Before April 1, contact the park for a reservation request form: Acadia National Park, P.O. Box 177, Bar Harbor 04609, 207/288-3338, www.nps.gov/acad. Any time after April 1 *(not before, or they'll send it back to you)*, return the completed form, along with a check for $25, covering camping for up to six people for a maximum of five nights between May 15 and June 15; three nights between June 15 and September 15; and five nights again between September 15 and October 15. Mark the envelope: "Attn: Isle au Haut Reservations." Competition can be stiff at the height of summer, so list alternate dates for that period. The park refunds the check if there's no space; otherwise, you'll receive a "special-use permit" *(DO NOT forget to bring it along).* There's no additional camping fee.

ISLE AU HAUT

© CHARLOTTE CUSHMAN

lean-to at Duck Harbor Campground, Acadia National Park

Unless you don't mind backpacking about four miles to reach the campground, try to plan your visit between mid-June and Labor Day, when the mailboat from Stonington makes a stop in Duck Harbor. It's wise to call the Isle au Haut Boat Company or check its website for the current ferry schedule before choosing dates for a lean-to reservation.

Trash policy is carry-in/carry-out, so pack a trash bag or two with your gear. Also bring a container for carting water from the campground pump, since it's .3 mile from the lean-tos. It's a longish walk to the general store for food—when you could be off hiking the island's trails—so bring enough to cover your stay. Pets are not allowed in the campground.

The three-sided lean-tos are big enough (8 feet by 12 feet, 8 feet high) to hold a small (two-person) tent, so bring one along if you prefer being fully enclosed. Alternatively, a tarp will do the trick. (Also bring mosquito repellent—some years, the critters show up here en masse.)

The best part about staying overnight on Isle au Haut is that you'll have so much more than a day-tripper's seven hours to enjoy this idyllic island.

ACCOMMODATIONS

The most exotic and priciest overnight option is **The Keeper's House** (P.O. Box 26, Isle au Haut 04645, 207/469-1174, www.keepershouse .com), Maine's only light-station inn. Attached to Robinson's Point Light (automated) and within night sight of three other lighthouses, the five-room inn gets booked up months ahead. Judi Burke, daughter of a Cape Cod lightkeeper, bought the 1907 National Historic Register building with her husband, Jeff, in 1986. As avid recyclers and environmentalists, they're happy to explain the inn's "off-the-grid" systems. They also take guests out in their 1950s motor launch, powered by bio-diesel. The top-floor Garret Room has the only private bath. The three other

rooms in the main building share two baths. The best view is from The Keeper's Room, overlooking the light tower and Isle au Haut Thorofare. Detached from the main house is the rustic Oil House, with a solar shower and private outhouse. Guests relax outdoors or gather in the small living room. The Oil House is $300 d; the main-house rooms are $325–375, covering three meals, including candlelight dinners; no red meat is served. BYOL (beer or wine) and pack lightly. A two-night minimum July through Labor Day (as well as all weekends) escalates the tab. Single-speed bikes are available free for guests. If you're going hiking or biking, the Burkes will pack you a box lunch (lunch isn't served at the inn). No electricity, no phones, no smoking, no credit cards, no pets, no stress. Nirvana. (Read all about it in Jeff's 1997 book, *Island Lighthouse Inn*.) The inn is open mid-May through October.

A simpler and slightly less pricey lodging option is **Bel's Inn** (Isle au Haut 04645, 207/335-2201), run by hospitable Belvia MacDonald in her home—conveniently located next to the town landing, with an unbeatable view. Bel has two cozy second-floor rooms (shared bath) for $250 d (double bed) and $265 (king bed), including three meals. Lunch is picnic fare, which she'll pack up for hikers. BYOL for dinner. She has accumulated a stash of bikes, so you can help yourself and pedal around the island. No credit cards, no minimum stay, no smoking, no pets. Open June to November.

FOOD

Isle au Haut is pretty much a BYO place—and that means BYO food. There is no restaurant. Unless you're staying at The Keeper's House or Bel's Inn, the only source of food is the **Isle au Haut General Store,** not far from the town landing. Thanks to the store, you won't starve, but don't expect an extensive inventory. On the other hand, food probably won't be your prime interest here—Isle au Haut is as good as it gets.

Resources

Suggested Reading

History

Brechlin, E. *Bygone Bar Harbor: A Postcard Tour of Mount Desert Island and Acadia National Park*. Camden, ME: Down East Books, 2002. A charming little book with reproductions of 100 historic postcards.

Collier, S. F. *Mount Desert Island and Acadia National Park: An Informal History*, rev. ed. Camden, ME: Down East Books, 1978. An oft-cited source for island and park history.

Dorr, G. *The Story of Acadia National Park*. 3d ed. Bar Harbor: Acadia Publishing, 1997 (reprinted, combining 1942 and 1948 originals). How Acadia began—and the roller-coaster struggles involved—related by George Dorr, "the Father of Acadia."

Helfrich, G. W., and G. O'Neil. *Lost Bar Harbor*. Camden, ME: Down East Books, 1982. Fascinating collection of historic photographs of classic, turn-of-the-century "cottages," most obliterated by Bar Harbor's Great Fire of 1947.

Morison, Adm. S. E. *The Story of Mount Desert Island*. Boston: Little, Brown, 1960. A quirky, entertaining little history—from Native Americans to 20th-century Americans—by the late maritime historian, a longtime Mount Desert summer resident.

Natural History and Nature Guides

Edwardsen, E. *Longstreet Highroad Guide to the Maine Coast*. Atlanta: Longstreet Press, 1999. Attractively presented general guide, with especially helpful natural-history information; more than 50 pages devoted to Mount Desert Island, Isle au Haut, and the Schoodic Peninsula.

Grierson, R. G. *Acadia National Park: Wildlife Watcher's Guide*. Minocqua, WI: NorthWord Press, 1995. You're not likely to see any creature in the park that isn't mentioned in this handy guide.

Kendall, D. L. *Glaciers & Granite: A Guide to Maine's Landscape and Geology*. Unity, ME: North Country Press, 1993. Explains knowledgeably why Maine looks the way it does.

Newlin, William V. P. *Lakes & Ponds of Mt. Desert*. Camden, ME: Down East Books, 1989. Covers more than the title reveals—includes great picnicking, hiking, biking advice, from a longtime summer resident. Out of print, but try used book stores.

Perrin, S. *Acadia's Native Flowers, Fruits, and Wildlife*. Fort Washington, PA: Eastern National, 2001. This handy reference to the park's flora and fauna runs chronologically through three seasons (spring through fall). It's not a complete field guide, but rather a selective collection of photos in a portable square format.

Pierson, E. C., J. E. Pierson, and P. D. Vickery. *A Birder's Guide to Maine*. Camden, ME: Down East Books, 1996. An expanded version of *A Birder's Guide to the Coast of Maine*. A valuable resource for any ornithologist, novice or expert, for exploring Acadia (and the rest of Maine).

Scheid, M. *Discovering Acadia: A Guide for Young Naturalists*. Mount Desert, ME: Acadia Publishing, 1990. A delightful book for children—as well as the adults who accompany them.

Carriage Roads

Abrell, D. *A Pocket Guide to the Carriage Roads of Acadia National Park.* Camden, ME: Down East Books, 1985, 1995. A dozen excellent carriage-road loops (ranging from 1.2 to 11.1 miles) for hiking, biking, or horseback riding—presented in a portable format.

Roberts, A. R. *Mr. Rockefeller's Roads.* Camden, ME: Down East Books, 1990. The fascinating story behind Acadia's scenic carriage roads, written by the granddaughter of John D. Rockefeller, Jr. (who created them).

Lighthouses

Thompson, C. *Maine Lighthouses: A Pictorial Guide.* 3d ed. Mount Desert, ME: CatNap Publications, 2001. What they look like, how to find them (sometimes only by boat), with some historical and contemporary background.

Recreation Guides

General (Multisport)

Evans, Lisa Gollin. *An Outdoor Family Guide to Acadia National Park.* Seattle: The Mountaineers, 1997. An excellent resource for hiking, biking, and paddling with kids in Acadia.

Monkman, J. and M. *Discover Acadia National Park: A Guide to Hiking, Biking, and Paddling.* Boston: Appalachian Mountain Club Books, 2000. Well-planned and well-written guide, in the Appalachian Mountain Club tradition, including foldout AMC map.

Hiking

Gillmore, R. *Great Walks of Acadia National Park & Mount Desert Island.* rev. ed. Goffstown, NH: Great Walks (P.O. Box 410, Goffstown, NH 03045), 1994. Two dozen trails in Acadia—some stretch the limits of their definition of "walks."

Kong, D., and D. Ring. *Hiking Acadia National Park.* Guilford, CT: Globe Pequot/Falcon Guide, 2001. Excellent hiking guide, with useful, accurate descriptions of 94 trails on Mount Desert Island, Isle au Haut, and the Schoodic Peninsula. The authors include a list of their 25 favorites and advocate the Leave No Trace philosophy.

St. Germain, T. A., Jr. *A Walk in the Park: Acadia's Hiking Guide.* 10th ed. Bar Harbor: Parkman Publications, 2000. Arguably the best Acadia hiking guide, in a handy Michelin-style vertical format. Bar Harbor resident St. Germain hikes a thousand miles a year in Acadia, so he's the expert. The book includes plenty of historical tidbits about the trails, the park, and the island. Part of the proceeds go to the Acadia Trails Forever campaign to maintain and rehabilitate the park's trails.

Rock Climbing

Butterfield, J. *Acadia: A Climber's Guide.* The most up-to-date and thorough climbing guide for the park.

Bicycling

Minutolo, A. *A Pocket Guide to Biking on Mount Desert Island.* Camden, ME: Down East Books, 1996. A third-generation islander's expert advice; covers the whole island, not just the park.

Stone, H. *25 Bicycle Tours in Maine: Coastal and Inland Rides from Kittery to Caribou.* 3d ed. Woodstock, VT: Backcountry Publications, 1998. Includes half a dozen Acadia routes.

Kayaking/Canoeing

Brechlin, E. D. *A Pocket Guide to Paddling the Waters of Mount Desert Island.* Camden, ME: Down East Books, 1996. Registered Maine Guide Brechlin recommends 17 places to paddle your kayak or canoe—in salt water as well as freshwater ponds and lakes. This little handbook (64 pages) includes locations for parking and launching areas, as well as route maps.

Bumsted, L. *Hot Showers! Maine Coast Lodgings for Kayakers and Sailors.* 2d ed. Brunswick, ME: Audenreed Press, 2000. Excellent, well-researched resource for anyone paddling or cruising the shoreline and yearning for alternatives to a sleeping bag.

The Maine Island Trail Guidebook. Rockland, ME: Maine Island Trail Association, updated annually. Available only with MITA membership (annual dues $45, www.mita.org), providing access to dozens of islands along the watery trail, including many in the Acadia region between Schoodic Point and Deer Isle.

Miller, D. S. *Kayaking the Maine Coast.* Woodstock, VT: Backcountry Guides, 2000. Thoroughly researched guide by a veteran kayaker; good maps and particularly helpful information. With this book and a copy of *Hot Showers!*, you're all set.

Cruising Guide
Taft, H., J. Taft, and C. Rindlaub. *A Cruising Guide to the Maine Coast.* 4th ed. Peaks Island: Diamond Pass Publishing, 2002. Don't even consider cruising the coast around Acadia without this thoroughly researched volume.

Offshore Islands

General
Conkling, P. W. *Islands in Time: A Natural and Cultural History of the Islands of the Gulf of Maine.* 2d ed. Camden, ME: Down East Books, and Rockland, ME: Island Institute, 1999. A thoughtful overview, including cultural and natural history, by the president of Maine's Island Institute.

Isle au Haut
Greenlaw, L. *The Lobster Chronicles.* New York: Hyperion, 2002. Essays on island life, warts and all, by the talented writer and lobster-

woman who first gained fame as a swordfishing skipper in *The Perfect Storm.*

Pratt, C. *Here on the Island.* New York: Harper & Row, 1974. An appealing, realistic portrait of life on Isle au Haut several decades ago.

Frenchboro (Long Island)
Lunt, D. L. *Hauling by Hand: The Life and Times of a Maine Island.* Frenchboro, ME: Islandport Press, 1999. A sensitive history of Frenchboro (aka Long Island), eight miles offshore, written by an eighth-generation islander, now a journalist.

Cranberry Isles
Eliot, C. W. *John Gilley: One of the Forgotten Millions.* Bar Harbor: Acadia Press, 1989 (reprint of 1904 book). Poignant story of 19th-century life in the Cranberries, as told by the Harvard president who was instrumental in the establishment of Acadia.

Pictorial
Blagden, T., Jr., and C. R. Tyson, Jr. *First Light: Acadia National Park and Maine's Mount Desert Island.* Englewood, CO: Westcliffe Publishers, and Bar Harbor: Friends of Acadia, 2003. A gorgeous, large-format book with spectacular photographs.

Wilmerding, J. *The Artist's Mount Desert: American Painters on the Maine Coast.* Princeton, N.J.: Princeton University Press, 1995. A respected art historian's perspective on Mount Desert's magnetic attraction to such American artists as Thomas Cole, Frederic Church, and Fitz Hugh Lane.

Reference
The Maine Atlas and Gazetteer. Yarmouth, ME: DeLorme, updated annually. You'll be hard put to get lost on the roads in this region or anywhere else in Maine if you're carrying this essential volume; 70 full-page (oversize format) topographical maps with GPS grids.

Internet Resources

Acadia National Park
www.nps.gov/acad/

This comprehensive site provides extensive detailed information about Maine's only national park. Download natural- and cultural-history articles, accessibility charts, list of hiking trails, FAQ, maps of the park and its outlying sections (Isle au Haut and Schoodic Peninsula), and the latest issues of the *Beaver Log,* the park's summer newspaper. Also included is a link for online reservations at Blackwoods Campground, as well as info for making Isle au Haut camping reservations.

Island Explorer Bus System
www.exploreacadia.com

Everything you need to know about using the propane-fueled, fare-free Island Explorer buses (operating late June–Columbus Day on Mount Desert, late June–Labor Day on the Schoodic Peninsula). Included are suggestions for getting to Mount Desert without a car, as well as for exploring the park with the bus.

Friends of Acadia
www.friendsofacadia.org

A very active nonprofit organization that acts as a financial safety net for the park and also organizes frequent volunteer work parties for various maintenance projects in the park. Its newsletters are posted on the website, as is information about where and when you can volunteer.

Bar Harbor Chamber of Commerce
www.BarHarborMaine.com

Access to information about Mount Desert Island's major town. In addition to its helpful website, with lodging links, its annual visitor booklet is published earlier than most, allowing trip planning to begin January.

Southwest Harbor/Tremont Chamber of Commerce
www.acadiachamber.com

Visitor information (including accommodations, restaurants, activities, shops) for the southwest corner of Mount Desert Island. The chamber's visitor booklet is especially informative, and the chamber has a free map of hiking trails on the west side of Mount Desert.

Abbe Museum
www.abbemuseum.org

The website enhances the museum's focus on Native American history, traditions, and contemporary culture. (The year-round museum is in Bar Harbor; the summer-only building is on park land at Sieur de Monts Spring.)

Downeast Windjammers
www.downeastwindjammer.com

More (and less) than what the name sounds like, this site has information on the windjammer schooner *Margaret Todd,* sailing out of Bar Harbor, as well as ferry services to the Schoodic Peninsula (also www.barharborferry.com) and the Cranberry Isles.

Isle au Haut Ferry
www.isleauhaut.com

Schedule and fare information for year-round ferry service from Stonington (on Deer Isle) to Isle au Haut.

Maine State Ferry Service
www.state.me.us/mdot/opt/ferry/ferry.htm

Schedule and fare information for ferries to offshore islands, including Swans and Frenchboro; regular updates for cancellations and changes.

Island Institute
www.islandinstitute.org

The institute serves as a clearinghouse/advocate

for Maine's islands; the website provides links to the major year-round islands.

Maine Island Trail Association
www.mita.org
The mission and activities of MITA, as well as information on becoming a member and receiving the annual guidebook to the island trail.

Deer Isle–Stonington Chamber of Commerce
www.deerislemaine.com
Where to sleep and eat on Deer Isle, en route to Acadia National Park on Isle au Haut.

Schoodic Peninsula Chamber of Commerce
www.acadia-schoodic.org
Where to sleep and eat in Eastern Hancock County near Acadia National Park's Schoodic Peninsula section.

Maine Office of Tourism
www.visitmaine.com
The state's official tourism site, very comprehensive. See links to the Downeast and Acadia Region.

Maine Tourism Association
www.mainetourism.com
This private organization subsidized by the state serves as the tourism information clearinghouse (an odd arrangement, but it seems to work). Links to all categories of tourism information, from activities to lodging to restaurants.

State of Maine
www.maine.gov
Award-winning official website with helpful links to every state government department. Buy a fishing license online, reserve a campsite at Lamoine State Park (near Acadia), or check the fall-foliage conditions via the site's Leaf-Cam. (You can also access foliage info at www.mainefoliage.com, where you can sign up for weekly email foliage reports in September and early October.)

Maine Archives and Museums
www.mainemuseums.org
The Maine Arts and Heritage Tourism Partnership has produced this useful site (a printed guide is also available) with links to dozens of major and minor museums. Opening hours and admission fees are provided, although some fees listed are out of date.

Maine Department of Transportation, Office of Passenger Transportation
www.state.me.us/mdot/biketours
Downloadable PDF maps for Maine bicycle tours. Spearheaded by the efforts of department head John Balicki, this office has advocated relentlessly for off-road bike trails and improved road shouldering.

Public Transit in Maine
www.new-england-public-transit.org/me/
Comprehensive website providing information on buses, trolleys, ferries, and trains. Maine has no well-organized public-transit network, and this shows what a hodgepodge it is, but the links are useful and mostly up to date.

Bay Ferries
www.catferry.com
Schedule and fare information for the passenger-and-car high-speed catamaran ferry operating daily (mid-May–mid-October) between Bar Harbor and Yarmouth, Nova Scotia.

National Weather Service
www.erh.noaa.gov/er/gyx/
Latest weather reports and weather alerts, with links to tide information. (Also try www.weather.com.)

Maine Lobster Promotion Council
www.mainelobsterpromo.com
Links for ordering Maine lobster and organizing your own lobsterbake, plus recipes for preparing lobster in more ways than you ever thought possible.

Index

Gardens, Parks, and Preserves

Lighthouses

Museums and Historic Houses

Ponds and Lakes

Acknowledgments

It takes *so much more* than a village . . . to assemble a book on Acadia National Park. Dozens of people assisted with this project—providing advice and cautions, sharing restaurant and hiking tips, lending photos, and much more—and I'm hugely grateful to everyone who did so.

On Mount Desert Island, thanks go to Acadia staffers Judy Hazen Connery and Charlie Jacobi; former Acadia superintendent Paul Haertel, who not surprisingly has decided to retire on the island; former Acadia writer/editor Kristen Britain, who contributed the Flora and Fauna section of this book; Ken Olson and Marla Major of Friends of Acadia; transportation consultant Tom Crikelair; Virginia Farnsworth of the Bar Harbor Chamber of Commerce; Deborah Dyer of the Bar Harbor Historical Society; Earl Brechlin of the *Mount Desert Islander;* Rosie Seton of College of the Atlantic, Roy Kasindorf and Hélène Harton of Ullikana; and Joan Howard of Petite Plaisance.

Elsewhere in the Acadia region, thanks to Barbara Feller-Roth of Castine, Ellen Devine of Sorrento, Jean Hendrick of Deer Isle, Sally M. Littlefield of Brooksville, Irene Whitney of Surry, and Monique Hashey of the University of Maine.

For endless research help, thanks to Richard E. Winslow III, Pat Messler, Sherry Streeter, Hilary Nangle, and Barbara Feller-Roth.

For helpful advice, appreciation goes to Charlotte Cushman, Sandra Garson, Carolyn May, Jayne Persson, Molly Sholes, and Colleen and Amanda Newcomb.

Thanks to the unflappable team of Charlene Williams and Rose Whitehouse at Nancy Marshall Communications.

Moral support has come from everyone mentioned above, but also from Eileen and Peter Spectre, Joan Grant, Peter Randall, Carole and Woody Emanuel, Ursula and Steve McAllister, and Lurelle Cheverie.

For putting together all the pieces of this puzzle, kudos to the crew at Avalon Travel—including Bill Newlin, Kevin McLain, Naomi Alder Dancis, Amber Pirker, Monica Boyle, Keith Arsenault, Rebecca Browning, Candace English, Justin Marler, and Jacob Goolkasian.

Last but not least, I could never find enough words to thank my long-suffering husband, Michael Drons, who uncomplainingly whipped up dinners, provided funds, ran interference, washed dishes, relayed messages, and did puppy patrol—even as he was launching his own new business.

U.S.~Metric Conversion

1 inch = 2.54 centimeters (cm)
1 foot = .304 meters (m)
1 yard = 0.914 meters
1 mile = 1.6093 kilometers (km)
1 km = .6214 miles
1 fathom = 1.8288 m
1 chain = 20.1168 m
1 furlong = 201.168 m
1 acre = .4047 hectares
1 sq km = 100 hectares
1 sq mile = 2.59 square km
1 ounce = 28.35 grams
1 pound = .4536 kilograms
1 short ton = .90718 metric ton
1 short ton = 2000 pounds
1 long ton = 1.016 metric tons
1 long ton = 2240 pounds
1 metric ton = 1000 kilograms
1 quart = .94635 liters
1 US gallon = 3.7854 liters
1 Imperial gallon = 4.5459 liters
1 nautical mile = 1.852 km

To compute Celsius temperatures, subtract 32 from Fahrenheit and divide by 1.8. To go the other way, multiply Celsius by 1.8 and add 32.

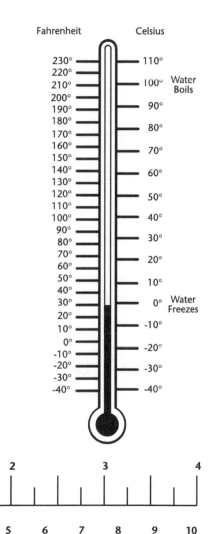

Keeping Current

Although we strive to produce the most up-to-date guidebook humanly possible, change is unavoidable. Between the time this book goes to print and the moment you read it, a handful of the businesses noted in these pages will undoubtedly change prices, move, or even close their doors forever. Other worthy attractions will open for the first time. If you have a favorite gem you'd like to see included in the next edition, or see anything that needs updating, clarification, or correction, please drop us a line. Send your comments via email to atpfeedback@avalonpub.com, or use the address below.

Moon Handbooks Acadia National Park
Avalon Travel Publishing
1400 65th Street, Suite 250
Emeryville, CA 94608, USA
www.moon.com

Editor and Series Manager: Kevin McLain
Copy Editor: Candace English
Graphics Coordinators: Amber Pirker, Justin Marler
Production Coordinator: Jacob Goolkasian
Cover Designer: Kari Gim
Interior Designers: Amber Pirker, Alvaro Villanueva, Kelly Pendragon
Map Editor: Naomi Adler Dancis
Cartographers: Kat Kalamaras, Suzanne Service
Indexer: Kathleen M. Brandes

ISBN: 1-56691-577-5
ISSN: 1546-8062

Printing History
1st Edition—March 2004
5 4 3 2 1

Text © 2004 by Kathleen M. Brandes.
Maps © 2004 by Avalon Travel Publishing, Inc.
All rights reserved.

3-8-04   *14.95*

Avalon Travel Publishing is a division of Avalon Publishing Group, Inc.